Core Text Series

- Written with authority by leading subject experts
- Takes a focussed approach, leading law students straight to the heart of the subject
- Clear, concise, straightforward analysis of the subject and its challenges

Series Editor: Nicola Padfield

Company Law: Alan Dignam and John Lowry

Constitutional and Administrative Law: Neil Parpworth

Criminal Law: Nicola Padfield

Employment Law: Robert Upex, Richard Benny and Stephen Hardy

European Union Law: Margot Horspool and Matthew Humphreys

Evidence: Roderick Munday

Family Law: Mary Welstead and Susan Edwards

Intellectual Property Law: Jennifer Davis

Land Law: Kevin Gray and Susan Francis Gray

Medical Law: Jonathan Herring

The Law of Contract: Janet O'Sullivan and Jonathan Hilliard

The Law of Trusts: James Penner

The Legal System: Kate Malleson, Richard Moules

Tort: Stephen Hedley

For further information about titles in the series,
please visit www.oup.co.uk/series/cts

OXFORD
UNIVERSITY PRESS

CORE TEXT SERIES

Intellectual Property Law

Fourth Edition

JENNIFER DAVIS

Series Editor
NICOLA PADFIELD

OXFORD
UNIVERSITY PRESS

Great Clarendon Street, Oxford, OX2 6DP,
United Kingdom

Oxford University Press is a department of the University of Oxford.
It furthers the University's objective of excellence in research, scholarship,
and education by publishing worldwide. Oxford is a registered trade mark of
Oxford University Press in the UK and in certain other countries

© Oxford University Press 2012

The moral rights of the authors have been asserted

First Edition published 2001
Second Edition published 2003
Third Edition published 2008

Impression: 1

Public sector information reproduced under Open Government Licence v1.0
(http://www.nationalarchives.gov.uk/doc/open-government-licence/
open-government-licence.htm)

Crown Copyright material reproduced with the permission of the
Controller, HMSO (under the terms of the Click Use licence)

British Library Cataloguing in Publication Data
Data available

Library of Congress Cataloging in Publication Data
Library of Congress Control Number: 2012932680

ISBN 978-0-19-958142-9

Printed in Great Britain by
Ashford Colour Press Ltd, Gosport, Hampshire

Preface

Once a subject encountered only occasionally by students, the law of intellectual property is now widely taught. Debates surrounding intellectual property—for example, about gene patenting or copyright on the internet—have found their way into the popular press. A generation raised on the computer and the brand will appreciate the significance of intellectual property and the law which relates to it in modern society. The law of intellectual property has changed as rapidly as the character of the global economy. Information and its surrounding technologies, biotechnology and branding have all become increasingly important in international trade. Intellectual property has come to acquire a central position in the global economy.

The purpose of this book is first to provide a basic understanding of the law of intellectual property. It deals with the six areas of law conventionally understood as falling under its rubric: copyright, confidential information, unregistered and registered trade marks, patents, and industrial designs. To fully understand the nature of the law of intellectual property, it is important to be aware of the wider context in which intellectual property is produced and the law applied. Throughout this book, attention will be paid to this wider context. The chapters which follow recognise the economic and social influences on the development of the law of intellectual property. They also examine some of the ethical questions which are raised when the law is used to protect intellectual capital. Of course, it is hoped that the reader will come away with a better understanding of the legal protection afforded to intellectual property rights. But the book also aims to convey to the reader some of the excitement which naturally arises as the law of intellectual property advances into what are often uncharted territories, whether it be of human creative endeavour, the virtual world of the internet, or of international commerce.

For this fourth edition, I owe a considerable debt of gratitude to Tanya Aplin who was always ready to read and comment on the manuscript.

Jennifer Davis
January 2012

Contents

Table of secondary legislation

Table of international instruments

Table of cases

1 An introduction to intellectual property

SUMMARY

- The definition of intellectual property
- The development of intellectual property law
- The justification for intellectual property rights: the 'Law and Economics' and 'labour' justifications and their critics
- The international dimension to intellectual property rights: WIPO and TRIPS
- Remedies for the infringement of intellectual property rights: damages, an account of profits, delivery up and injunctions
- Pre-trial relief: interim injunctions and search orders

Defining intellectual property

1.1 The subject of this book is intellectual property. The following six chapters each examine a separate area of intellectual property: copyright, confidential information, unregistered trade marks (passing off), registered trade marks, patents and industrial design rights. The first question to ask is: What brings these very diverse areas of the law together under the rubric 'intellectual property'? The World Intellectual Property Organization (WIPO) has offered one suggestion. According to WIPO, intellectual property refers to the 'products of the mind: inventions, literary and artistic works, any symbols, names, images, and designs used in commerce'. In a similar vein, the World Trade Organization (WTO) has offered its own definition: 'Intellectual property rights are rights given to people over the creation of their minds.' It goes on: 'Creators can be given the right to prevent others from using their inventions, designs or other creations. These rights are known as "intellectual property rights".' But even these very general definitions of intellectual property and its associated rights are problematic. They exclude, for instance, the most basic product of the mind–ideas–which are not generally protected as intellectual property. At the other extreme, confidential information is conventionally viewed as a type of intellectual property, even though it is difficult to see how a secret, for instance, a marital secret such as a lesbian affair (*Stephens v Avery* (1988)), constitutes a 'product of the mind', although it may certainly have commercial value.

The abstract nature of intellectual property

1.2 Another way to think about intellectual property is to ask not what it is, but rather what the various kinds of intellectual property, patents, copyright, industrial designs, trade marks and confidential information have in common. One answer has been to point to the abstract or intangible nature of intellectual property. Unlike a piece of land or a car, for example, intellectual property has no material existence. As a consequence, while it would be possible to write a book about a body of land which describes its picturesque and plant-yielding qualities but entirely ignores how it is owned and who has the right to use it, a book on intellectual property law could not take the same approach. Patents and trade marks, for example, cannot be discussed except as a form of property, for they come into being precisely at the point when they are legally recognised (for a discussion, see Drahos, *A Philosophy of Intellectual Property* (1996), ch 2). Although intellectual property may be intangible or abstract, once in existence intellectual property rights have much in common with the rights associated with real property. For the most part, intellectual property rights can be assigned or bequeathed. Those who 'trespass' on another's intellectual property can be held to account. Ownership generally gives an exclusive right to exploit the property or to give others a licence to do so in a variety of ways (Litman, 'The Public Domain' [1990] *Emory Law Journal* 971). It is also the case that, while intellectual property is itself intangible, it will be embodied in real objects. A Coca-Cola sign, a best-selling novel and a new wonder drug may each constitute the physical embodiment of an intellectual property right: a registered trade mark, a copyright and a patent, respectively.

The boundaries of intellectual property

1.3 The analogy with real property breaks down again, however, when the question is raised of how to mark off the boundaries of intellectual property. The area of a piece of land may be measured in metres. But, given its intangible nature, how is one to demarcate the area of protection conferred by an intellectual property right? Can one determine, for instance, the size of the monopoly offered by a patent or the extent of a trade secret? This is a question which will be raised throughout this book in relation to each of the rights discussed. However, a general point may be made at once. Such boundaries may not be identified unless and until they are legally challenged. It is useful to offer an initial example. X manufactures and sells crisps under the registered mark 'McTatties'. Y starts to sell crisps under the mark 'McTatties'. By selling crisps marked 'McTatties', Y will clearly have trespassed upon X's registration and X will have the right to stop him. Having learned his lesson, Y instead sells crackers under the mark 'McTaggies'. X brings infringement proceedings against Y. It will now be up to the court to decide whether the rights in the mark 'McTatties' accorded to X by registration extend to his preventing Y from using a different mark on different goods. In making its decision, the court will take into account a range of factors such as the distinctiveness of X's mark, its reputation, or how both goods are sold (all of which may, themselves, change over time). In the end, the court must make a judgment. It is the result of this judgment which will mark out the boundaries of X's rights in the mark 'McTatties', rather than the mere fact of its presence on the Trade Mark Register (see Chapter 5 on Trade Marks).

The development of intellectual property law

1.4 Each of the diverse intellectual property rights covered by this book has, of course, its own separate history. The first patent for an invention was granted as early as 1565. Registered trade marks were only brought into existence by the Trade Marks Act 1875. The design right was introduced as late as 1988. More recently, the UK has acquired a database right, which, although examined here in the chapter on copyright, is actually governed, in part, by quite different legal rules and procedures. Obviously, each of these areas of intellectual property law has been shaped in response to changing economic and social conditions, and these changes will be mapped in some detail in the relevant chapters. More generally, it has been suggested that the idea that there is a discrete body of law which can be placed under the rubric of 'intellectual property law' and which can encompass such diverse legal areas as patents and copyright, trade marks and industrial design rights emerged in the UK only in the second half of the nineteenth century. Its emergence has been attributed to a shift away from seeing intellectual property rights primarily as rewards for mental labour to instead viewing them as important economic assets. Under the latter view, it is, of course, possible to place copyright, traditionally understood as a reward for individual creativity, side by side with trade marks, which might be viewed more as products of the market than of the mind. Once this view of intellectual property had taken hold, its remit could easily be stretched over time to include, for example, sound recordings, cable programmes or, most recently, electronic databases, whose production may involve no intellectual creativity at all (Sherman and Bently, *The Making of Modern Intellectual Property Law* (1999), Part 4). Indeed, in 2007, the Patent Office, which deals, inter alia, with the registration of trade marks, patents and with industrial designs, changed its operating name to the UK Intellectual Property Office.

The justification for intellectual property rights

1.5 Undoubtedly, most 'new' intellectual production draws from a common stock of knowledge, language and ideas. If intellectual property rights are too widely drawn, then this common stock will be depleted, impoverishing intellectual life and inhibiting intellectual production, whether it be of useful inventions, books, music, films or trade symbols. To protect this common stock, limits have been placed on the protection afforded by intellectual property rights. In principle, for example, it is not possible to own a copyright in an idea, nor to patent a discovery. The law defines a number of circumstances in which it is possible to make use of another's intellectual property–without infringing his or her rights, such as the fair dealing provisions in copyright (see para **2.73** et seq). Furthermore, in contrast to most other property rights, ownership in intellectual property is time limited. At the end of the period of protection, the intellectual creations protected by these rights will return to the common stock, or 'public domain', as it is often termed. Once in the public domain, it may be used by others to produce new intellectual capital. Nonetheless, despite these limitations, there continues to be intense debate as to what belongs in the public domain and, by contrast, what should be available to private ownership. These debates, as they relate to individual intellectual property rights, will be examined in the course of this book. There are, however, two general arguments which are commonly advanced to justify the private ownership of intellectual capital, which are worth an initial examination.

The 'Law and Economics' justification

1.6 The 'Law and Economics' approach to legal studies is generally concerned with the role of the law in the efficient allocation of economic resources. Those who favour this approach have noted a particular problem in relation to the creation of intellectual property. Because of its intangible nature, intellectual property poses what economists refer to as a 'public goods' problem. Intellectual property can be costly and time-consuming to produce, and may require a considerable degree of inventiveness or originality. Yet, once this 'mental' investment has been embodied in a material form, it may be relatively cheap and easy to reproduce. Furthermore, there may be no limit to the extent to which it can be copied, with each copy having as much value as the original. Without intellectual property rights, it is argued, what is to prevent others from taking advantage of (or 'free riding' on) this intellectual capital, without incurring its original costs? As a result, according to this argument, intellectual property rights offer an important incentive for the creation of new intellectual capital. Without them, individuals and companies would be deterred from making the necessary initial investment to produce intellectual capital, and hence the market would be impoverished. Furthermore, in the long term, without the incentive to produce offered by intellectual property rights, there would be other social costs. The public domain would inevitably be depleted, since eventually this intellectual property would be expected to become part of the public domain and to form the basis for future intellectual production (van den Bergh, 'The Role and Social Justification of Copyright: A "Law and Economics" Approach' [1996] *Intellectual Property Quarterly* 17).

1.7   To take an example, a pharmaceuticals company, Thermo Ltd, invests several years and many millions of pounds in developing a chemical compound which can cure the common cold. It sells the compound in tablet form, the physical ingredients of which are inexpensive and easily acquired. To recoup its investment and to turn a profit, Thermo Ltd will want the price of the tablet to reflect not simply the cost of manufacture but also the price of development. A rival pharmaceuticals company analyses the tablet. It can manufacture and sell the tablets far more cheaply than Thermo Ltd, but nonetheless at a huge profit, because it has no need to recoup the costs of the initial investment in the development process. It can, in effect, 'free ride' on Thermo Ltd's creative effort. If, however, Thermo Ltd had patented the invention, it would have been able to prevent its embodiment in any tablets except those manufactured or licensed by itself. The cost of the licence would, in effect, be a charge for the use of the patent over and above the cost of producing the tablets, which may in itself be negligible. The same point can be made about best-selling novels, DVDs or trade-marked sports shoes, where, in all cases, the cost of the materials may be far outweighed by the value of the intellectual property which they embody. Indeed, in the case of music and movies bought or streamed over the internet, there is of course no material cost at all.

Intellectual property and competition

1.8   The application of intellectual property rights may be seen to offer a solution to the public goods problem. Nonetheless, it may also have social and economic costs. The enforcement of intellectual property rights may be viewed as anti-competitive. For instance, in the example cited above, Thermo's patent will of course raise the cost of the drug to consumers by preventing cheaper competitive products going on the market. If Thermo has a monopoly on the drug, it may, if it chooses, raise its price beyond one which the majority of the public is able to pay. Others may be deterred from exploiting similar inventions to the general benefit of the consuming public because of a fear of possible legal action by Thermo, whether or not it would be successful. Indeed, it is fair to say that there is an inherent tension between intellectual property rights and free competition, which has been widely recognised in the prevailing law, and which will be considered in the course of this book (Lemley, 'Ex Ante Versus Ex Post Justifications For Intellectual Property Law' [1994] 71 *University of Chicago Law Review* 129).

The 'labour' justification for intellectual property

1.9 Despite this tension, the 'Law and Economics' approach to intellectual property rights has generally been favoured by advocates of free-market economics. It rests on an underlying assumption that rational individuals will seek to maximise their economic gains and will be disinclined to act if they expect to receive only a marginal economic benefit. Hence, there is the need for intellectual property rights to solve the public goods problem. An alternative and highly influential justification for intellectual property which embodies a more rights-based approach, rests on the ideas of the eighteenth-century philosopher, John Locke. The Lockean approach, derived from his *Second Treatise of Government*, begins from a different premise: that individuals have a right to the fruits of their labour. Put briefly, this approach assumes the existence of an uncultivated 'common', which is characterised by an abundance of goods. Property rights are granted to those whose labour adds value to the goods they take from the commons, provided that, as a result of their labour, the common stock is also increased or, as Locke put it, provided 'enough and as good' is left in the commons for others to enjoy.

1.10 It is easy to see how the Lockean approach might be applied to intellectual property. In the case of intellectual property, the commons would be represented by the public domain. The public domain retains those intellectual goods which either nobody may own or exploit (such as ideas or discoveries, which, if they were extracted, would not leave 'enough and as good') or, conversely, those intellectual goods which are free to be expropriated as intellectual property, provided the necessary labour is expended upon them. In essence, this would mean that the finished 'intellectual product' would leave the public domain once it meets the relevant legal criteria for protection, for instance, as a copyright work or a registered trade mark. Advocates of the Lockean view usually maintain that such expropriation from the public domain will not breach the 'enough and as good' imperative. Instead, over time, intellectual property rights will actually serve to enrich the public domain. Intellectual property rights encourage individuals to place their creations before the public. Once these creations become public, they will themselves engender new ideas and encourage further creativity. Eventually, given the time-limited nature of intellectual property rights, these intellectual goods will return to the public domain (for an account of the Lockean and the alternative Hegelian approach, see Hughes, 'The Philosophy of Intellectual Property' [1988] *Georgetown Law Journal* 287).

1.11 The rights-based approach to intellectual property has long been favoured by continental countries. By contrast, as was suggested above (see para **1.4**), the development of intellectual property rights in the UK has largely reflected more pragmatic considerations, particularly the protection of economic investment. The Law and Economics and the labour justifications for intellectual property rights are, of course, neither mutually exclusive nor contradictory. Indeed, all these approaches have been vulnerable to the same general criticism, which centres on the extent and treatment of the public domain. In particular, it is argued that the present international intellectual property regime fails to recognise that some intellectual capital may be produced and exploited co-operatively, and, as a result, social justice demands that it should be protected against private ownership. For instance, it happens that the chemical compound that constitutes Thermo's cold cure actually occurs naturally in the leaf of a tree which is indigenous to India. The leaf has been used in India for many centuries as a cold cure. Aware of this fact, Thermo has analysed the chemical make-up of the leaf and reconstituted it in its laboratories. Susan visits Chile and overhears a 'folk song' which is widely sung in the villages, although no one is sure of its origins. Susan returns to England, translates and arranges the song, which becomes a best-seller. The argument goes that an intellectual property regime which rewards Thermo and Susan, with a patent or copyright, respectively, but provides no mechanism for rewarding the farmers of India or the villagers of Chile, is unjust. Indeed, for an example of controversy in just this area, the reader is referred to the debate surrounding attempts by a multinational chemical company to patent products derived from the Indian neem tree, long known by local farmers to increase soil fertility.

1.12 While much of this criticism emanates from developing countries, which may be seeking to protect what is often characterised as 'traditional forms' of knowledge, this is not exclusively the case. For example, similar controversy has been provoked in both the UK and the USA over the possibility of conferring a private monopoly over words and symbols which also have a wide popular meaning. A prominent example was the successful attempt by the US Olympic Committee to prevent a San Francisco gay rights group from using the word 'Olympic' in promoting the 'Gay Olympic Games' (*San Francisco Arts and Athletics v United States Olympic Committee* (1987)). Critics of the decision argued that, given its long history and the positive associations which have, over time, been embodied in the word by the public at large, 'Olympic' should be freely available. More recently, in the UK, the Court of Appeal denied the estate of Elvis Presley a registered trade mark for the singer's name in relation to memorabilia. The decision relied in large part on the court's recognition that, given the singer's enormous popularity, the public had now attributed its own meaning to the name 'Elvis', which it should be free to use (*Elvis Presley Trade Marks* (1999); see also para **5.112**).

1.13 Both in terms of domestic law and at the international level, there has been growing pressure to frame intellectual property protection in ways which recognise the co-operative production of knowledge or the common ownership of its raw material. An example is the UN Biodiversity Convention, a product of the 1992 Earth Summit in Rio de Janeiro. Following pressure from developing nations, the Rio Convention sets out as one of its aims to preserve and protect the knowledge, resources and practices of indigenous communities. At art 15(9), it recognises the sovereign rights of states over their natural resources, so that the authority to determine access to genetic resources should rest with national governments and be subject to national legislation. The Rio Convention has not found universal favour, not least because of its potential challenge to patent rights. However, in a parallel development, a number of governments have come to separate agreements with companies seeking to exploit their natural resources for the purposes of research. In perhaps the most publicised example, Iceland, through a company, DeCode Genetics, negotiated a $200m payment from a major biotechnology company for access to that country's gene pool. The company plans to use the Icelanders' highly uniform DNA to develop new drugs and diagnostic tests.

The international dimension to intellectual property rights

1.14 Although many intellectual property rights are territorially based, so that a UK trade mark registration protects that trade mark only in the UK, intellectual property has always had a strong international dimension. As will be seen in the course of this book, European Union law has had a transformative impact on intellectual property rights in the UK. International agreements and the resulting organisations which are concerned with individual intellectual property rights, such as the European Patent Convention and the Community Trade Mark Regulation, will be discussed where appropriate. However, two international organisations–WIPO and WTO–have been concerned with intellectual property more generally, and their role is considered below.

The World Intellectual Property Organization

1.15 The beginnings of WIPO are to be found in two nineteenth-century international treaties relating to intellectual property. The Paris Convention for the Protection of Intellectual Property (1883) covered inventions, trade marks and industrial designs. The Berne Convention for the Protection of Literary and Artistic Works (1886) dealt with copyright in a range of works: literary, artistic and musical. The effect of these conventions was to confer reciprocal protection on signatory countries, so that their nationals were accorded the same intellectual property rights in other Member States as were accorded in their own. Initially, the Paris and Berne conventions were administered by separate offices and then together in Berne. In 1974, WIPO was established as a specialised agency of the UN charged with promoting and administering intellectual property matters on behalf of its members. Today, WIPO administers a range of treaties apart from the Paris and Berne conventions. Among the most notable are the Patent Convention Treaty and the Madrid Agreement relating to trade marks, both of which offer signatories a simplified route to obtaining protection in other countries (see para **5.12**). WIPO also administers a number of classification systems for international property rights, such as the Nice Agreement which classifies goods and services for the purpose of trade mark registration.

1.16 Since its inception, WIPO has provided a forum for its members to discuss issues relating to intellectual property, and a base from which to launch international agreements. As the value of intellectual property grows in relation to world trade, it is inevitable that WIPO will see its importance enhanced. For example, since 1994, WIPO has provided an Arbitration and Mediation Centre for the settlement of disputes relating to intellectual property. The Centre is well placed to deal with the increased opportunities for conflict inherent in the spread of global information systems and e-commerce, such as the rising number of disputes over internet domain names, now a key area of the Centre's work.

WTO and TRIPS

1.17 In 1996, an agreement between WIPO and WTO came into force. The purpose of the agreement was to provide for co-operation between the two bodies in the implementation of the TRIPS agreement. TRIPS (Trade-Related Aspects of Intellectual Property Rights) was the product of WTO's 1988–94 Uruguay Round of trade negotiations. It came into effect in 1995. Its broad purpose is to harmonise the manner in which intellectual property is protected worldwide and to provide a mechanism for settling disputes between WTO members.

1.18 The effect of the TRIPS agreement is to set out the minimum standards to which Member States must adhere in relation to intellectual property rights of all kinds, including copyright, patents, trade marks, industrial designs and trade secrets. It also seeks to ensure that Member States have adequate mechanisms in place to enforce these rights. While in a number of areas the standards of protection specified by TRIPS reflect those contained in earlier intellectual property treaties, such as the Paris and Berne conventions, in others the standard of protection required by TRIPS is more rigorous, and it also covers intellectual property rights such as databases, which may not be covered by earlier treaties.

1.19 For its supporters, TRIPS is viewed as a crucial tool to protect what has come to be one of the most significant areas of world trade and, therefore, a potential source of damaging disputes between nations. A product of free-market ideology, TRIPS ensures that owners of intellectual property rights will have a level playing field, not just at home, but overseas. It aims to minimise the barriers to free trade which might be thrown up when different countries offer different levels of protection to intellectual property. Inevitably, TRIPS has also attracted criticism. In particular, while countries such as the UK and the USA in most respects found little conflict between their own intellectual property regimes and the TRIPS requirements, for many developing countries implementing TRIPS involved major transformations of their domestic law. At one level, the provisions of TRIPS took account of this anomaly. While developed countries were given a year after TRIPS took effect to ensure compliance, the agreement allowed transitional periods of five to ten years for 'developing' and 'least-developed' countries to do the same. A further provision has extended exemptions on pharmaceutical patent protection for least-developed countries until 2016. Nonetheless, it has been argued on behalf of these latter countries that a level playing field in relation to intellectual property rights may not be universally beneficial. For example, many developing countries, as has already been suggested, offer a wealth of resources which might be exploited by pharmaceutical companies in search of new products. These same countries may not, however, have the technical expertise or financial resources to develop these products domestically to the point that they would receive the extensive patent protection which ensures compliance with TRIPS. Instead, such protection may find its way to foreign-based multinationals. TRIPS has also been criticised for failing to recognise that traditional forms of knowledge may need a different type of protection from that offered in prevailing intellectual property regimes. A more immediate problem has been raised by the need of poor countries, particularly in Africa, to have access to drugs for treating AIDS and other endemic diseases. For the most part, such drugs have patent protection and, as a result, their cost has been beyond the ability of such countries to pay. TRIPS permits drugs patents to be overridden in cases of national emergency, allowing countries to make generic drugs, but only for domestic consumption (art 31(f)). However, many of the countries most in need of the drugs did not have the ability to produce them. In August 2003, an agreement was reached which would allow countries producing generic copies of patented products under compulsory licence to export them to countries facing national health emergencies. On the one hand, it can be argued that WTO has provided a useful international forum for such an agreement to be reached. On the other, it has been noted that the agreement is hedged with a number of conditions which may make it difficult to put into practice. To a considerable extent, the debates surrounding TRIPS encapsulate the wider issues concerning the measurement of the public domain. As intellectual property becomes ever more valuable and hence the drive for stronger rights to protect it more intense, it is inevitable that the debate will remain central to how the law of intellectual property develops in the future (Milius, 'Justifying intellectual property in traditional knowledge' [2009] *Intellectual Property Quarterly* 185.).

Remedies for the infringement of intellectual property rights

1.20 In succeeding chapters, this book will examine those issues relating to remedies which are raised by particular intellectual property rights. However, it is possible to make some general points at the outset. The first concerns jurisdiction. Most intellectual property cases are brought in the Chancery Division of the High Court. Patents and registered design cases are heard in the Patents Court. In addition, the Copyright, Designs and Patents Act 1988 established the Patents County Court, which offers a cheaper and more speedy forum for patent, design, trade mark and copyright disputes. Copyright cases may also be brought in the county court. The 'Woolf Reforms' introduced by the 1998 Civil Procedure Rules are generally applicable to intellectual property cases. Following the incorporation of the European Convention on Human Rights (ECHR) into domestic law by the Human Rights Act 1998, it too has come to play an increasingly important role in intellectual property actions. In particular, art 1, Protocol I (the right to property), art 8 (the right to private and family life, home and correspondence) and art 10 (the right to freedom of expression), all have obvious relevance to a number of intellectual property rights. More recently, the EU passed Directive 2004/48 on the enforcement of intellectual property rights. Intended to harmonise the civil procedures and remedies across the EU, the Directive was implemented in the UK by the Intellectual Property (Enforcement, etc) Regulations (SI 2006/1928). According to the Commission, harmonisation will prevent 'pirates and counterfeiters' from taking advantage of differences in enforcement mechanisms in Member States by carrying out their illicit activities where these are currently 'less effective'. The level of protection is high, going beyond that required by TRIPS. All Member States are required to provide, inter alia, injunctions to halt the sale of counterfeit or pirated goods, measures such as the seizure of suspected offenders' bank accounts and powers for judicial authorities to force those selling pirated or counterfeit goods to disclose information about their activities. The Directive has been criticised for being over-broad and potentially threatening to both individual civil liberties and innovation. It has been suggested, for example, that it will enable rights-holders to obtain personal information about private individuals, who are allegedly connected to the infringement of intellectual property rights. These might include private individuals who engage in music-file swapping over the internet. For its part, the Commission maintains that the enhanced sanctions implemented by the Directive will be used only against commercial infringers whose activities might cause 'significant harm' to the rights-holder (for a critical view, see Cornish et al, 'Procedures and Remedies for Enforcing IPRs: the European Commission's Proposed Directive' [2003] *European Intellectual Property Review* 447). In fact, implementing the Directive in the UK did not necessitate any major changes to UK law. Indeed, certain orders such as the search order and the freeze order which were peculiar to the UK, before the passage of the Directive, are now to be provided across the EU. The debate over the Directive illustrates the inherent tensions in the field of intellectual property between rights-holders seeking to maximise the legal protection afforded to their property, and the need for the law to protect individual access to both fair-dealing provisions and the public domain. It is a debate which will figure prominently in the following pages.

Criminal actions

1.21   In certain cases, copyright and trade mark actions may also be brought in criminal courts. The use of the criminal law has been largely aimed at activities such as the pirating of copyright materials, for example, DVDs or CDs, or the use of trade marks on counterfeit goods, which may be extremely lucrative and carried out on a considerable commercial scale. Criminal actions can have a deterrent effect. They give the rights-holder the assistance, where necessary, of state agencies such as the Trading Standards Office to ensure enforcement. They may not be as costly as civil actions. However, criminal actions also carry disadvantages. They can take time to initiate and they will not carry the range of remedies both pre- and post-trial which are available in civil actions (see, for example, the case of *R v Crown Court at Harrow, ex p Unic Centre Sarl* (2000) concerning forfeiture). For some time now, the EU has also been considering a similar directive on criminal measures aimed at ensuring the enforcement of intellectual property rights.

Civil actions

1.22   A common feature of many intellectual property actions is that speed is of the essence. The claimant's aim is generally to stop a threatened or an on-going infringement of his rights by obtaining an injunction against the alleged infringer's future activities. Furthermore, once a claimant obtains an interim (or pre-trial) injunction, the defendant may have little incentive to contest the action further. If, for example, he is using a trade mark on a new product which the claimant alleges he is infringing, he is unlikely to suspend the marketing of the product pending the outcome of a trial. Instead, he will almost certainly seek to cut his losses, choose a new trade mark and reach a settlement. As a result, most intellectual property actions are settled at the pre-trial stage and the usual remedy, where the claimant is successful, is a permanent injunction together with costs. Injunctions are looked at below (see para 1.28 et seq).

1.23 Apart from injunctions, the main remedies in intellectual property cases are: delivery up, damages and an account of profits. For the reasons suggested above, the latter two remedies are comparatively underused in intellectual property actions (see para 1.22). In most intellectual property actions, liability is determined first. Where the claimant chooses to continue, damages are usually determined or an account made at a separate hearing. The third remedy–delivery up of infringing articles–is particularly appropriate where the intellectual property is embodied in a material form, and may accompany the other two.

An account of profits

1.24 A claimant must choose between damages or an account of profits. In order to assist in making the election, a claimant is entitled to the disclosure of relevant information by the defendants, such as financial records (*Island Records Ltd v Tring International plc* (1995)). It is relatively unusual for a claimant to opt for an account of profits, not least because the process of reckoning may be complex and the outcome uncertain. Furthermore, in copyright cases, where a claimant opts for an account of profits, he cannot then seek exemplary damages under s 97(2) of the Copyright, Designs and Patents Act 1988 (*Redrow Homes Ltd v Betts Bros plc* (1998) HL).

1.25 An account of profits considers the profit made by the infringer rather than the harm suffered by the claimant (*Celanese v BP* (1999)). According to Laddie J in *Celanese*, the purpose of an account of profits is not to 'punish' the defendant but to ensure that he does not unjustly enrich himself at the claimant's expense. The defendant is treated as if he has 'conducted his business and made profits on behalf of the plaintiff'. An account of profits raises the same issue of causation as is raised in assessing damages (see para 1.26). The question to be asked is whether the infringer's profits were a result of his infringement of the claimant's rights (*Imperial Oil v Lubrizol* (1996)). There is strong authority that a defendant cannot lessen his liability by arguing that he might have made the same profit by following a non-infringing course. Nor can a claimant argue that the defendant should have made higher profits than he did (*Celanese*). There has been debate as to whether profits should be assessed incrementally (by looking at the difference between actual profits and those which would have been made without infringement) or, alternatively, whether they should be apportioned, that is, paid only from that part of the defendant's business which is infringing. In *Celanese*, which concerned patent infringement, Laddie J preferred apportionment. Here, the invention at issue, although useful, was 'small' and contributed less than 20 per cent of the profits of the plants in which it was used. The result was that the defendant was ordered to pay a sum less than it had already admitted as being appropriate based on an incremental approach. An account of profits has generally been viewed as an equitable remedy. However, following the House of Lords decision in *A-G v Blake* (2001), it is now accepted law that an account of profits is available for breach of contract in exceptional cases, where the normal remedies–damages, specific performance and injunction–are inadequate (*Experience Hendrix LLC v PPX Enterprises Inc* (2003)). The principle would be that, whether or not the claimant would have been better off if the wrong had not been committed, the wrongdoer ought not to gain an advantage for free and should make some reasonable recompense. Assessment of the latter would pay regard to any profit made by the wrongdoer. An example is the *Blake* case itself, which concerned a breach of a covenant by an ex-employee not to reveal confidential information gained in the course of his employment (see para **3.87** for details of *Blake*).

Damages

1.26 Damages in intellectual property actions are assessed following the same principles as other torts (*General Tire and Rubber Co v Firestone Tyre and Rubber Co Ltd* (1975) HL; *Gerber Garment Technology Inc v Lectra Systems Ltd* (1997) CA). The victim should be restored to the same position he would have been in if no wrong had been done. Furthermore, the victim should only recover loss which is caused by the defendant's wrongful act and is a reasonably foreseeable result of it. In the case of damages, then, the court will look to see how the claimant would have profited without the defendant's infringing acts, rather than, as with an account of profits, looking to the infringer's profit. While the imposition of damages is not intended to punish the defendant, nonetheless 'the defendants being wrongdoers', damages should be liberally assessed (*General Tire*, per Lord Wilberforce). The onus is on the claimant to prove the extent of his loss.

Assessing damages

1.27 The two most obvious ways a claimant may profit from his intellectual property are that he may exploit it himself or he may license it to others. In the first case, the claimant will seek to recover damages based on his loss of profit. Quantum can be difficult to assess. For example, in circumstances where the claimant and the defendant are not alone in the market and there are others competing with them, the extent of the claimant's loss attributable to the defendant's activities in particular may not be immediately apparent. The question as to what damages should be attributed to the infringement also arises. In *Gerber Garment Technology Inc v Lectra Systems Ltd* (1997), a patents case, the Court of Appeal held that the claimant's loss need not necessarily be restricted to those activities which constituted infringement of the patent. It could extend to loss of sales on articles which were commonly sold together with the patented goods. By contrast, in the copyright case, *Work Model Enterprises Ltd v Ecosystem Ltd* (1996), the High Court found that the defendant's infringement of the claimant's brochure did not affect the claimant's sales of its products, which were advertised in the brochure. Despite its infringement of the brochure, the defendant competed perfectly lawfully with the claimant when selling its own goods. (See also, *Gary Fearns (t/a Autopaint International) v Anglo-Dutch Paint & Chemical Co Ltd* (2010).) The situation is rather more straightforward where the damage is for loss of a licensing opportunity. Damages will follow the cost of the licence. In the third case, where the claimant neither profits from manufacture nor licenses his product, the court will assess damages based on a reasonable royalty. This, too, can be difficult. According to Lord Shaw in *Watson, Laidlaw & Co Ltd v Pott, Cassels and Williamson* (1914), 'compensation is to be assessed on the basis of inference, conjecture and the like, by the exercise of sound imagination and the practice of the broad axe' (cited in *Blayney (t/a Aardvark Jewelry) v Clogau St David's Gold Mines* (2003), per Sir Andrew Morritt V-C; see also *AEI Rediffusion Music Ltd v Phonographic Performance Ltd (No 2)* (1998) and *General Tire and Rubber Co v Firestone Tyre and Rubber Co Ltd* (1975)). In cases before it, the Copyright Tribunal will look at comparable licences.

Pre-trial relief

Injunctions

1.28 Damages and an account of profits are awarded for past misconduct. By contrast, injunctions address future conduct. They are designed to restrain threatened breaches of the claimant's rights (*Coflexip SA v Stolt Comex Seaway MS Ltd* (1999), per Laddie J). In general, once liability has been established in an intellectual property action, the claimant may expect to be awarded a final injunction. Exceptions may arise where there has been a long delay in bringing the action or the court has taken the view that there is no likelihood of a repetition of the infringing act, but examples are few. There are also particular problems raised in relation to confidential information (see para **3.81**). In the interesting decision in *Coflexip*, Laddie J questioned the appropriateness in intellectual property actions of final injunctions, which are characteristically broadly drawn to restrain all future infringements of the claimant's rights by the defendant. He suggested instead that in certain cases a 'narrow form' of injunction, which restrains the repetition only of the infringing act for which the defendant has been found liable, might be more appropriate. The latter approach has the advantage of certainty for the defendant, particularly in patent actions such as *Coflexip*, where the scope of the protected invention may not always be entirely clear. A broad approach was taken by the High Court in *Microsoft Corpn v Electro-Wide Ltd* (1997). In that case, the court granted an injunction to restrain the defendants from reproducing a substantial part of *any* operating system software in which the claimant had copyright (not just the software they had already infringed), because it took the view that the defendants were interested in copying whatever operating systems software was currently saleable.

Interim injunctions

1.29 An interim injunction prohibits the defendant from carrying out the allegedly infringing act until trial. Although an interim injunction precedes a finding of liability, its effect is frequently to bring the matter to a close. The guidelines for granting an interim injunction were set out by the House of Lords in *American Cyanamid Co v Ethicon Ltd* (1975). Before *American Cyanamid*, the courts had habitually looked to the relative strength of the claimant's case as the main factor in deciding whether to grant an interlocutory (now an interim) injunction. The claimant had to show a (serious) prima facie case before the court would go on to examine the balance of convenience in favour or against granting an injunction. In *American Cyanamid*, a patents case, Lord Diplock held that there was no such rule. Instead, the court need only be sure that there was a serious question to be tried. Once that had been established, the court should go on to look at whether the balance of convenience lay in 'granting or refusing the relief which was sought'. In particular, according to Lord Diplock, the court should look to see whether the claimant would be adequately compensated by damages if he were to succeed at trial and in the meantime the defendant continued its alleged infringement or, conversely, whether, the defendant would be adequately compensated at trial by damages if prevented from doing the allegedly infringing acts until trial. The ability of either party to pay such damages was another important factor. Where these questions were evenly balanced, the court should look at the comparative strength of each case.

1.30 Following *American Cyanamid*, there was some debate as to whether and to what extent courts should continue to assess the strength of the parties' cases in determining whether or not to grant an interim injunction. For instance, in *Series 5 Software Ltd v Philip Clarke* (1996), Laddie J said that it should continue to be one of the four 'major' factors which the court should bear in mind. The others are the extent to which damages are likely to be an adequate remedy and the ability of the other party to pay, the balance of convenience and the maintenance of the status quo. Following the passage of the Human Rights Act 1998, in the particular situation where one party to an action asserts a right of confidence and the other seeks to justify disclosure by reference to free expression, the balance of convenience test is not the correct approach. The claimant will need to show that he is likely to establish at trial that publication should not be allowed in order to obtain an injunction (*Imutran Ltd v Uncaged Campaigns Ltd* (2002)). Furthermore, s 12(3) of the Human Rights Act has been interpreted to mean that the threshold for granting an interim injunction in cases involving a breach of confidence may be higher where freedom of the press is at issue (*Cream Holdings v Banerjee* (2004) HL, see para **3.81**).

1.31   An example of an action where the claimant failed to obtain an interim injunction was the passing-off case, *Dalgety Spillers Foods Ltd v Food Brokers Ltd* (1994). The claimant sold 'Golden Wonder Pot Noodles'. It accused the defendants of passing off their product 'Nissin Cup Noodles' as its own, because of similarities in the packaging. The claimant sought an interim injunction, which was refused on the balance of convenience. In particular, the High Court was impressed by the defendants' argument that if an interim injunction were granted to prevent them from selling their 'Nissin Cup Noodles' in the UK, the commercial uncertainty of waiting for a trial would force them to change their packaging, not just in the UK (as a result of the injunction), but in Europe, where their product was also sold. Having done so, they would be unable to change the packaging back and, as a result, an interim injunction would effectively determine the action.

Other pre-trial relief: Norwich Pharmacal orders, Mareva injunctions, search orders

1.32   A Norwich Pharmacal order places an individual (or business) who becomes involved in another's wrongdoing, whether or not innocently, under a duty to disclose any information which might identify the wrongdoer (*Norwich Pharmacal Co v Customs and Excise Commissioners* [1974] AC 133). In the context of disputes involving intellectual property, the order has been used, for example, by rightsholders seeking to compel ISPs to identify individuals illegally downloading music. In *Productores de Musica de Espana (Promusicae) v Telefonica de Espana SAU* (Case-275/06) (2008), the European Court of Justice held that while it is appropriate to use such orders in intellectual property cases, in doing so courts must ensure that a fair balance with the fundamental rights of the individual concerned is maintained.

1.33   The Mareva injunction (now called a 'freezing injunction') prevents a defendant from disposing of assets on which a claimant may have a claim, both before and after judgment. It is often combined with a search order. Like the Mareva injunction, a search order (formerly an Anton Piller order) is a powerful weapon in the armoury of any claimant, and has been particularly widely used in intellectual property actions. The search order requires the defendant to allow the claimant (or his representatives) to enter his premises to search for, seize or take copies of, as the case may be, relevant goods and/or documentation. The defendant may also be ordered to provide information about allegedly infringing acts. The order is granted at an *ex parte* (without notice) hearing, and is intended to be used where there is a genuine risk that the defendant, if he had notice of the search, might destroy the relevant materials. The claimant cannot enter the defendant's premises without his permission, but the defendant may be in contempt of court if that permission is refused (see, for example, *Taylor Made Gold Co Inc v Rata and Rata* (1996)). The search order thus entails potentially serious inroads into the defendant's rights and, since its introduction in the 1970s, has been hedged with an increasing number of safeguards for the defendant.

1.34 The search order was first developed by the Court of Appeal in *Anton Piller KG v Manufacturing Processes Ltd* (1976), which concerned, inter alia, passing off and confidential information. In his judgment, Ormrod LJ set out the three criteria for granting the order, which still pertain today. The claimant must have a strong prima facie case. There must be clear evidence that the defendants have in their possession incriminating goods or documents and that, if put on notice, there is a genuine risk that they might destroy them. Third, the potential damage to the claimant must be very serious. Following the *Anton Piller* case, the order was adopted enthusiastically by claimants seeking to preserve incriminating evidence in intellectual property actions, which they believed might otherwise be lost. However, it also came in for a strong measure of judicial criticism (*Columbia Picture Industries Inc v Robinson* (1986)). A key area of concern was the difficulty faced by many defendants of obtaining expert and urgent legal advice upon the service of an order, particularly if it occurred outside of business hours. This was a point taken up by the Vice-Chancellor in *Universal Thermosensors Ltd v Hibben* (1992) which concerned confidential information. In *Universal Thermosensors*, the order was served in the early hours of the morning at the defendants' homes and their business addresses. At one house, a woman was alone with her children when the order was served. Following a claim by the defendants for damages relating to the effects of an interim injunction granted with the order, the Vice-Chancellor set down a number of guidelines which must be followed when executing a search order. These have now been incorporated into a standard form of the order set out in a 1996 Practice Direction. Most importantly, the order must be served and its execution overseen by an independent Supervising Solicitor. In addition, the order should be executed during business hours and on a weekday to ensure that the defendant is able to obtain legal advice (see also *Gadget Shop Ltd v Bug.Com Ltd* (2001)).

1.35 Search orders frequently require defendants to provide self-incriminating information. For instance, a defendant may be ordered to disclose the whereabouts of allegedly infringing material or to provide other information about alleged infringements. Following a number of successful legal challenges, including one which went to the House of Lords (*Rank Film Distributors Ltd v Video Information Centre* (1982)), the privilege against self-incrimination in civil proceedings was set aside by s 72 of the Supreme Court Act 1991. However, it continues to apply in criminal proceedings which might be brought as a result of complying with the order.

1.36 In the period since its introduction, the courts have become far more sparing in their willingness to grant search orders. Indeed, compared to its earliest incarnations, the search order can no longer be seen as overwhelmingly favouring the claimant. A challenge to the search order was mounted in the European Court of Human Rights (*Chappell v United Kingdom* (1989)). It was based on the right to privacy guaranteed by art 8. The court rejected the challenge, holding that the order, as it had been developed by the UK courts, did not violate the claimant's rights. Nonetheless, it is submitted that it may still be open to criticism. For example, a defendant served with a search order, especially a private individual living outside a metropolitan area, may find himself unable to obtain the level of expert legal advice which would place him on a level footing with the claimant during the execution of the order.

1.37 The search order is, of course, of purely domestic origin and application. The role of the UK and, indeed, of foreign courts in enforcing intellectual property rights infringed overseas, and granting 'cross-border injunctions' or 'extra-territorial injunctions', is a complex one and beyond the remit of this book. Suffice to say, given the enormously important international aspect of so much intellectual property, it will be an area of increasing importance. It has already been noted that WTO and WIPO are taking a key role in settling international intellectual property disputes. The EU has also passed a number of directives aimed at harmonising the law in relation to enforcement, trade marks, designs and new technology. Each of these directives will be considered later in this book. In 2007, the US, Japan and Switzerland, quickly joined by a number of other countries and trading areas, including the EU, began negotiating the Anti-Counterfeiting Trade Agreement (ACTA) (Leith, 'ACTA: the anti-counterfeiting crack-down' [2011] *Entertainment Law Review* 81). The primary purpose of ACTA is to establish multilateral standards of enforcement for intellectual property rights, much as TRIPS established multilateral standards for their protection. Among the central concerns of ACTA are establishing both strong border controls to combat the import and export of counterfeit goods and ensuring that signatories also have robust civil and criminal penalties for intellectual property right infringement. The interested countries agreed a final draft of ACTA in 2010, which was approved by the EU Parliament in the same year. Clearly, the movement towards harmonising broad swathes of intellectual property law both at the level of the

EU and internationally stems from both a recognition of and a reaction to the extent to which protecting intellectual property may entail crossing national boundaries: a task which, as we will see in the pages that follow, has become massively more complex with the rise of the internet.

SELF-TEST QUESTIONS

1   Is the optimum level of legal protection for intellectual property compatible with the existence of a healthy public domain?

2   To what extent can intellectual property rights be treated as a largely domestic concern?

3   'The courts have finally found the correct balance between the interests of the claimant and the defendant in granting Anton Piller (search) orders and interim injunctions.' Do you agree?

FURTHER READING

Blakeney, M, 'International proposals for the criminal enforcement of intellectual property rights: international concern with counterfeiting and piracy' [2009] *Intellectual Property Quarterly* 1.

Bonadio, E, 'Remedies and sanctions for the infringement of intellectual property rights under EC law' [2008] *European Intellectual Property Review* 320.

Boyle, J, *Shamans, Software & Spleens: Law and the Construction of the Information Society* (Harvard University Press, 1996).

Cornish, W R, Llewellyn, D and Aplin, T, *Intellectual Property* (7th edn, Sweet & Maxwell, 2010).

Huaiwen, H, 'The Development of free trade agreements and international protection of intellectual property rights in the WTO era-new bilateralism and its future' [2010] *International Review of Intellectual Property and Competition Law* 256.

Kuniar, K, 'The Enforcement Directive: Its Effects on UK law' [2006] *European Intellectual Property Review* 92.

Landes, W M and Posner, R A, *The Economic Structure of Intellectual Property* (Belknap Press, 2003).

Lessig, L, *The Future of Ideas: The Fate of the Commons in a Connected World* (Random House, 2001).

Milius, D, 'Justifying intellectual property in traditional knowledge' [2009] *Intellectual Property Quarterly* 185.

Moss, D and Rogers, G, 'Damages for Loss of Profits in Intellectual Property Litigation' [1997] *European Intellectual Property Review* 425.

2 Copyright

SUMMARY

- The origin and development of copyright
- The Copyright, Designs and Patents Act 1988: copyright works, fixation and original-ity, and secondary works
- Authorship, ownership and duration of copyright
- Infringement: the restricted acts, primary infringement, authorisation and secondary infringement
- The permitted acts: fair dealing, criticism and review, reporting current events, and the public interest defence
- Moral rights
- Dealing with copyright
- Civil and criminal remedies
- Copyright and the new technology
- Databases
- Copyright and the international context: exhaustion of rights and competition law

Copyright: its origins and development

2.1 Copyright law in the UK is governed by the Copyright, Designs and Patents Act 1988 (CDPA 1988), as amended by the Copyright and Related Rights Regulations 2003 (SI 2003/2498). The Regulations, which came into force in October 2003, implemented the Information Society Directive (EC) 2001/29 on the harmonisa-tion of certain aspects of copyright and related rights in the information society (ISD). The 1988 Act governs copyright dealings in the UK. There is, however, an important international dimension to UK copyright law. The Berne Convention

1886 set minimum standards of protection internationally among participating countries, such as the UK, by giving authors of works exploited in any participating country other than their own the same rights afforded to nationals of those countries. Further international regulation was achieved through a number of later Acts and conventions, most notably the Rome Convention 1960 (concerned with neighbouring rights: see para **2.28**) and the Act of Paris 1971, which increased the uniformity of protection between participating states and the range of works to be offered protection. At the same time, there has been an ever-growing convergence in copyright protection among members of the EU as the result of a series of directives relating, inter alia, to copyright term, software, databases and digital technology.

The history of copyright protection

2.2 Changes in copyright protection have had a close relationship with developments in reproduction technologies. Early interest in copyright protection in the UK coincided with the introduction of the printing press. At first, copyright law was designed primarily to protect the economic investment of printers and publishers, rather than the creative efforts of authors. However, the first copyright statute, the Statute of Anne 1710, did recognise the author as owner of copyright, and gave a limited term of protection to works of 28 years. Sixty years later, the famous case of *Donaldson v Beckett* (1774), itself a commercial struggle between London and provincial publishers, established that literary copyright was a statutory right, and so of limited term, rather than a common law right and therefore of perpetual duration. It has been suggested that this decision stemmed both from the House of Lords' dislike of monopolies and also from its recognition that publishers rather than authors would be the group most likely to benefit from any enhanced protection. It was not until the nineteenth century that authors came to be seen as central to copyright protection, as romantic ideas of the author as a creative and original genius increasingly took hold. The Copyright Act 1842, for which a number of prominent authors lobbied, increased the term of protection to 42 years from publication, or seven years beyond the death of the author, whichever was the longer. From the late nineteenth century, changes to copyright law reflected the rapid introduction of new technologies of reproduction and a growing impetus for UK law to conform to international standards. This was true of the two major copyright reforms of the twentieth century before the CDPA 1988. The Copyright Act 1911 (CA 1911) further increased the term of protection to the life of the author plus 50 years, and also introduced reforms which brought the UK law into line with the Berne Convention. Furthermore, the CA 1911 also took account of important advances in the technology of music reproduction, introducing protection for the first time to sound recordings. Similarly, the Copyright Act 1956 (CA 1956) allowed the UK to ratify the Brussels Act of the Berne Convention and provided specific protection for films and television recordings, while the CDPA 1988 incorporated, inter alia, changes to international protection under the 1971 Paris Act. The 1988 Act has now been amended to implement the Information Society Directive, which allows for ratification of the WIPO Copyright Treaty and the WIPO Phonograms and Performance Treaty, and which is intended to offer increased protection to digital works.

The justification for copyright

2.3 Since the nineteenth century, it has been usual to justify the existence of copyright protection by arguing that it protects the creative investment of the author. The justification may be a moral one. In this view, the author has a natural right to ownership of the fruits of his own labour, a stance commonly associated with the philosophical writings of John Locke. Or justification may be more practical. So it is suggested that, without such protection, authors will have no economic incentive to create. Perhaps because of its early influences, copyright law in the UK has continued to be more often justified on grounds of commercial utility. By contrast, in Europe, the tradition has been to view copyright in terms of a natural right accruing to the author. A third justification for copyright lies in its perceived social benefit. It is argued that authors will be encouraged to disseminate their works to the public if they are able, through copyright laws, to profit from so doing. Furthermore, the limited term of copyright ensures that at some point these same works will be freely available to enrich both culture generally, and to provide the foundation for future creation. It was for these latter reasons that the framers of the US Constitution included a provision for copyright protection (Davies, *Copyright and the Public Interest* (2002)).

2.4 All of these justifications may be challenged. First, how much do authors actually benefit from copyright protection? It has probably always been true that the entrepreneur who produces and markets the work is most likely to reap the financial rewards of copyright. In many cases, the author will have signed away his copyright as a prerequisite for publication. It is certainly the case that, whereas in the nineteenth century authors were at the forefront of lobbying for increased copyright protection, today that role is more often taken by record companies, film studios and publishers. The inclusion of 'moral rights' in the UK copyright regime stems from a recognition that authors, all too often, are not the beneficiaries of copyright protection. Moral rights attach to authors, whether or not they have alienated the copyright in their works (see para **2.85**). Second, just how important is the 'author'? Recent trends in scholarship have called into question the romantic emphasis on the originality of creative output, and have suggested that much of it is either derivative or shaped by popular culture. From this viewpoint, it is common to emphasise the difficulty in determining where the work of one author ends and the original output of another begins, a necessary prerequisite for finding copyright infringement. Further, it is argued that if copyright protection is drawn too broadly, cultural life will be impoverished because authors will have more limited access to other works on which their own creative output depends. This latter view raises urgent questions about whether the copyright term is too long, how much creative output should remain in what is often termed the 'public domain', and how broad exceptions to copyright protection should be. Finally, does copyright offer appropriate protection for the products of new technologies? Perhaps more so than other types of intellectual property, copyright was the creature of a particular technology: the printing press. Since the eighteenth century, the technical means for reproducing works has constantly evolved, and copyright laws have evolved with them. There is now increasing debate as to whether copyright law with its initial foundation in earth-bound works, most notably books, is really sufficiently flexible to offer protection to categories of work, many of which, produced in cyberspace, have no tangible existence at all.

The Copyright, Designs and Patents Act 1988

2.5 As its title suggests, the CDPA 1988 is concerned with a number of areas of intellectual property law, not exclusively copyright. Parts III and IV of the Act provided a much-needed overhaul of the law governing industrial designs (see Chapter 7). Parts V and VI are concerned with some aspects of patent and trade mark law, including the introduction of Patents County Courts, an important innovation at the time. Part II is concerned entirely with performance rights, which the CDPA 1988 introduced. This chapter is primarily concerned with Part I of the Act, which sets out the substantive law of copyright in the UK, and will include, where appropriate, the changes made to the CDPA 1988 by the Copyright and Related Rights Regulations 2003. In a final section, 'Copyright and the new technology' (para **2.93** et seq), the implementation of the ISD will be examined in more detail. The 1988 Act begins, as one might expect, with a definition of copyright works.

Copyright works (CDPA 1988, s 1)

2.6 The Copyright, Designs and Patents Act 1988 identifies three categories of works in which copyright subsists. They are:

- original literary, dramatic, musical or artistic works;
- sound recordings, films or broadcasts;
- typographical arrangements of published editions.

A 'work' is not defined by the CDPA 1988 except in a circular way. A 'copyright work' means a work of any of those descriptions in which copyright subsists (s 1(2)). In the case of literary, dramatic, musical or artistic works, whether a work is a 'work' for copyright purposes is inseparable from whether it is 'original', since copyright subsists only in original works. Recently, in *Infopaq International v Danske* (2009), the Court of Justice examined the meaning of a 'work' in the context of the reproduction right (art 2 of the ISD). The reproduction right provides authors with the exclusive right to authorise or prohibit the reproduction of the whole or a part of their works. The Court of Justice was asked, inter alia, to determine the scope of protection afforded by art 2. It concluded that to attract copyright protection, a work needs to be original in the sense that is it the author's 'own intellectual creation', a criterion which is already used in a number of EU Member States. This has led some to argue that copyright works can no longer be confined to those categories identified in s 1, CDPA, but might extend to any work which embodies the author's own intellectual creation. Under this criterion, a copyright work might, for example, include a computer interface (*Bezpečnostní softwarová asociace v Ministerstvo kultury* (2010) CJEU) (Derclaye, E, '*Infopaq International A/S v Danske Dagblades Forening* (C-5/08): wonderful or worrisome? The impact of the ECJ ruling in Infopaq on UK copyright law' [2010] *European Intellectual Property Review* 247). Others disagree, suggesting that at best the decision in *Infopaq* harmonises the standard of originality for all works but not the subject matter which might constitute a copyright work. The question of what constitutes originality or the 'author's own intellectual creation', for copyright purposes, is examined below (paras **2.15** and **2.16**).

Literary works (CDPA 1988, s 3(1))

2.7 A 'literary work' means any work, other than a dramatic or musical work, which is written, spoken or sung. It has been held that a literary work should provide some element of either information and instruction, or pleasure in the form of literary enjoyment (*Hollinrake v Truswell* (1894)). But to qualify as a literary work, there is certainly no need for the work to have any intrinsic literary merit, however defined (*University of London Press Ltd v University Tutorial Press Ltd* (1916); see *Infopaq v Danske* (2009) and originality, para **2.16** below). Examination papers have been held to be original literary works. So, too, have a list of foxhounds, a trade catalogue and football coupons. Tables, compilations and computer programs (as well as preparatory design material for a computer program) are specifically defined as literary works, although the Database Directive (EC) 96/9 shortens the length of protection given to certain compilations (see para **2.111**).

De minimis

2.8 For copyright to subsist in a literary work, it must be more than *de minimis*. Single words will not attract copyright protection. The word 'Exxon' was held not to be a literary work by the Court of Appeal (*Exxon Corpn v Exxon Insurance Consultants International Ltd* (1982)). Since 'Exxon' is both original, being an invented word, and conveys information about the source of the goods to which it applies, it is arguable that the 'Exxon' decision was actually taken on public interest grounds. There has been a long-standing judicial reluctance to endow single words with copyright protection, largely because simple words or phrases, as the basic building blocks of language, should be available for public use. Also, if words have commercial value, such as 'Exxon' itself does, they may well be protected as trade marks or by an action in passing off, and dual protection would be undesirable (Cullabine, 'Copyright in Short Phrases and Single Words' [1992] *European Intellectual Property Review* 205). Similarly, the courts have suggested that the taking of a title alone is very unlikely to infringe copyright (*Francis, Day and Hunter Ltd v Twentieth Century Fox Corpn Ltd* (1939)). However, following the decision in *Infopaq v Danske* (2009), it has been argued that copyright might subsist in both newspaper headlines and titles, assuming they are the author's intellectual creation. In *Newspaper Licensing Agency (NLA) v Meltwater* (2010) HC; (2011) CA), the court understood this to mean that they will be protected, not based on their substantiality, but rather on whether they are sufficiently 'original' (see para **2.16**; see also *Shetland Times v Dr Jonathan Wills* (1997)).

Dramatic works (CDPA 1988, s 3(1))

2.9 These include works of dance or mime, in the sense that acting, dancing or mime must be intrinsic to the presentation of the work. Or, put another way, a dramatic work 'must have sufficient unity to be capable of performance'. Dialogue cannot, on its own, constitute a dramatic work and is, instead, protected by literary copyright, although a work without dialogue (that is, a mime) can. The 'dramatic format' of the quiz show, 'Opportunity Knocks', which included gimmicks such as stock phrases and the use of a 'clapometer', was held to lack the necessary 'unity' to constitute a dramatic work (*Greene v Broadcasting Corpn of New Zealand* (1989)).

2.10 The question as to whether a film can constitute a dramatic work was addressed by the Court of Appeal in *Norowzian v Arks Ltd (No 2)* (1999). The claimant, in this case, directed a short film called 'Joy' which consisted of a man dancing to music. The visual impact of the film was the result of the filming and editing techniques employed by the claimant, which had the effect of allowing the actor to perform a routine which would be physically impossible in 'real life'. The first defendant produced an advertisement for Guinness entitled 'Anticipation' which featured similar dancing and props. Indeed, the defendant had been instructed by Guinness to produce a commercial broadly similar to 'Joy'. The claimant alleged copyright infringement. Among the questions for the High Court was whether the film 'Joy' was itself a dramatic work or whether it was a recording of a dramatic work. Rattee J held that, while a film might record a dramatic work, it cannot be a dramatic work per se. Nor was 'Joy' the recording of a dramatic work. A dramatic work must be something which is capable of being physically performed. In particular, a work of dance or mime must be capable of being danced or mimed. In this case, the film, because of the way it was edited, was not a recording of anything that was or could be danced by anyone. Nonetheless, it was argued that 'Joy' was a work of some originality, 'a manifestation of the film maker's art'. The problem accepted by the court was that CDPA 1988 appeared to afford no protection to an original work of art which *was* a film, as long as the film itself was not copied, although it would protect an original work which was recorded *by* a film. The claimant appealed, and the question of whether a film, itself, could be a 'dramatic work' was re-considered by the Court of Appeal. Nourse LJ held that in his judgment a film can be a dramatic work for the purposes of the CDPA 1988. The definition of a dramatic work must be given its ordinary and natural meaning. His own summary was that a dramatic work is a work of action with or without words or music, which is capable of being performed before an audience. A film would often, although not always, be such a work. Furthermore, a film can be both a recording of a dramatic work and itself a dramatic work. Nourse LJ agreed with Rattee J that 'Joy' was not a recording of a dramatic work. 'Joy', being original and a work of action capable of being performed before an audience, was itself a dramatic work. Nourse LJ compared it to a cartoon. Nonetheless, in this case there was no copyright infringement because 'Anticipation' was not a copy of a substantial part of 'Joy'. There were indeed similarities between the filming techniques and editing styles of the two films, but no copyright subsisted in 'mere style and technique'.

Musical works (CDPA 1988, s 3(1))

2.11   These are works consisting of music, exclusive of any words or action intended to be sung, spoken or performed with the music. What is protected as 'music', for copyright purposes, has been widely defined. It may include not only the musical notation of a work, but also other elements which make some contribution to the sound of the music when performed, such as performing indications, tempo and performance practice indicators (*Sawkins v Hyperion Records Ltd* (2005), per Mummery LJ). Song lyrics, like dialogue in a play, attract separate protection as literary works.

Fixation and originality

2.12 For copyright to subsist in a literary, dramatic or musical work it must be original and it must be fixed. To understand both originality and fixation, it is first necessary to consider the dichotomy between ideas and their expression in relation to copyright works. This is a subject which will be discussed at greater length in relation to infringement below (see para **2.53**).

The idea–expression dichotomy

2.13 It is often said that copyright subsists in the expression of an idea and not the idea itself (*Hollinrake v Truswell* (1894)). Like most generalisations, there is some truth in this statement, but the reality is rather more sophisticated. There are numerous judicial decisions where ideas have been held not to have copyright protection. For instance, the idea or 'concept' for the format of 'Opportunity Knocks', taken in isolation, was held not to be the subject of copyright (*Greene v Broadcasting Corpn of New Zealand* (1989)). But, in other cases, both the idea and its expression converged to make them inseparable. An example of this difficulty arises with computer software and copyright. It is, of course, entirely possible to 'express' an original program in a completely different computer code, yet both the original program and the 'copy' may embody the same ideas as to structure or 'look' and 'feel'. A number of decisions have seen the court willing to give some protection to the latter (see para **2.98** et seq).

Fixation

2.14 Copyright does not subsist in a literary, dramatic or musical work unless or until it is recorded, in writing or otherwise (s 3(2)). Writing includes any form of notation or code, whether by hand or otherwise, and regardless of the method by which, or medium in or on which it is recorded (s 178). Writing includes, for example, computer code recorded in software. The methods of recording covered by the CDPA 1988 remain an open category to cope with technological developments. A copyright work comes into existence at the time at which it is recorded. It is immaterial whether the work is recorded with the permission of the author. Where the work is recorded, copyright may subsist both in the recording as well as in the underlying work (s 3(3)). For instance, a sound recording of a speech will be protected as a sound recording, and the speech itself as a literary work. In *Walter v Lane* (1900), a *Times* reporter took down in shorthand and verbatim a speech given by Lord Rosebery. The speech was subsequently published. It was held that the reporter had acquired copyright in his report of the speech by virtue of the skill and judgement he had employed in reporting it. It is submitted that Lord Rosebery would also have acquired a copyright in the speech, as it had now been recorded, or fixed (see also *Express Newspapers plc v News (UK) Ltd* (1990)).

Originality: the UK approach

2.15 Copyright subsists only in *original* literary, dramatic and musical works. 'Original' is not defined in the CDPA 1988. To understand how the UK courts have defined originality in relation to copyright it is useful to return to the general rule that there can be no copyright in an idea without its embodiment in a 'work'. Copyright is not concerned with the originality of the underlying idea. It is the form in which the idea is expressed which must be original. To be protected by copyright, a work must have originated from the author. That is its creation must have entailed the expenditure of the author's own 'labour, skill and judgement' (*University of London Press Ltd v University Tutorial Press Ltd* (1916)). According to the UK courts, it is this 'labour, skill and judgement' which is protected by copyright. The approach to originality in copyright may be contrasted with the novelty requirement of patentability (see para **6.33** et seq). An invention is deemed not to be novel if it is described in an earlier publication, even if the subsequent inventor had no knowledge of and had thus not 'copied' the earlier invention (Gravells, 'Authorship and Originality: The Persistent Influence of *Walter v Lane*' [2007] *Intellectual Property Quarterly* 267).

Originality after *Infopaq*

2.16 The traditional UK approach to originality was however thrown into some doubt by the decision in *Infopaq v Danske* (2009). In *Infopaq*, as we have seen, the Court of Justice concluded that to attract copyright protection, a work needs to be original in the sense that is it the author's 'own intellectual creation' (see para **2.6**). For example, the decision in *Infopaq* involved the reproduction of excerpts from newspaper articles, some as short as eleven words. The Court of Justice looked to see whether the articles had been 'reproduced in part' under Art 2 of the ISD. In order to determine this, the Court of Justice considered the originality of the part of the work that had been reproduced. It held that: 'It is only through the choice, sequence and combination of those words that the author may express his creativity in an original manner and achieve a result which is an intellectual creation.' Its conclusion was that, on this criteria, even a short extract from the articles in question might reflect the author's own intellectual creation.

2.17 A key question raised by *Infopaq* is whether it introduces a more stringent test for originality than the rather mundane 'skill, judgement and labour test' adopted by the UK courts, since it appears to involve an element of creativity. This question was addressed by the Court of Appeal in *Newspaper Licensing Agency Ltd (NLA) v Meltwater Holding BV* (2011). The first claimant NLA, is a licensing body which authorises the use of its members' online publications. Its members are publishers of national newspapers and were also claimants in the proceedings. Meltwater, through its subsidiary Meltwater News, searches media websites for key words (or 'agents') of interest to its clients, public relations firms. It will alert these clients via an email or on its website, Meltwater News. Meltwater News contains a reference to every use of the specified agent within a specified period and sets out: i) a hyperlink to each relevant article; ii) the headline from the article; iii) the opening words of the article after the headline; and iv) an extract from the article showing the context in which the agent appears, by reproducing the agent and some words immediately preceding and following it. The crux of the case was whether Meltwater needed a licence from NLA to provide this service, in the absence of which Meltwater or its clients would be liable for copyright infringement. And the answer to this question in turn resided in whether the newspaper headlines were literary works protected by copyright, independent of the articles to which they attached, and whether the extracts, some as short as eleven words, constituted a substantial part of the articles from which they were taken (for substantiality, see para 2.50). In the High Court, Proudman J had found, inter alia, that newspaper headlines could constitute independent literary works, and Meltwater appealed. Proudman J had noted that headlines were often 'striking and substantial' and that their production might entail considerable skill. As such, she believed that they were independent literary works within the *Infopaq* test. Jackson LJ in the Court of Appeal agreed. And he went on to make clear that the *Infopaq* test did not relate to novelty or merit, but rather to origin, and as such did not disturb the long-standing test for originality, that of 'skill, judgement and labour' which had been established by Peterson J in *University of London Press Ltd. v University Tutorial Press Ltd* (1916) (see also *SAS Institute Inc v World Programming Ltd* (2010)).

Compilations

2.18 Copyright in compilations rewards not the originality of the constituent elements of such compilations, which may be nothing more than a collection of facts, but the skill, effort and judgement which was expended in bringing those elements together in a particular way (*Ladbroke (Football) Ltd v William Hill (Football) Ltd* (1964)). Copyright has been held to subsist in football pools coupons, football fixture lists and television programme schedules (*Football League Ltd v Littlewoods Pools Ltd* (1959) and *Independent Television Publications Ltd v Time Out Ltd* (1984)). The implementation of the Database Directive (EC) 96/9, which introduced the *sui generis* database right, also introduced what is known as the 'art 3 right'. Under art 3 of the Database Directive, copyright will subsist in databases which, by reason of the selection or arrangement of their contents, constitute the author's own intellectual creation. The relationship of art 3 to the protection of compilations under the CDPA 1988 has now been addressed to the Court of Justice by the Court of Appeal in *Football Dataco v Brittens Pools* (2010) (see para **2.115**). This case raised the question of whether a football fixture list is protected as a *sui generis* database, as a copyright work under the CDPA 1988 or whether it attracts copyright under art 3 of the Database Directive. In particular, the Court of Justice has been asked whether, in judging whether a database is an author's own intellectual creation and hence attracts copyright under art 3, the intellectual effort and skill of creating the data, itself, should be excluded; whether 'selection or arrangement' includes adding important significance to a pre-existing item of data (as in fixing the date of a football match); and whether 'author's own intellectual creation' requires more than significant labour and skill from the author, and if so what? In addition, the Court of Justice has been asked whether a database can be protected both under art 3 of the Database Directive and as a copyright work under national copyright law (the *sui generis* database right is looked at below, see para **2.111** et seq).

Adaptations, translations and arrangements

2.19   A separate copyright subsists in adaptations and translations, which use original copyright works as their source. This separate copyright is justified by the fact that such works cannot be produced without the expenditure of additional skill and labour. Copyright did not subsist in a textbook which contained a number of excerpts from Plutarch's *Life of Alexander*, because insufficient skill and labour had been expended in selecting them. The court said, 'it is necessary that labour, skill and capital should be expended sufficiently to impart to the product some quality or character which the raw material did not possess, and which differentiates the product from the raw material' (*Macmillan & Co v K & J Cooper* (1923)). It is important to remember that adaptations, translations and arrangements, provided they have sufficient originality, may carry at least two copyrights: one in the underlying work and the other in the adaptation or arrangement. In *Redwood Music Ltd v Chappell & Co Ltd* (1982), the claimants owned copyright in the song, 'Zing'. The defendants had originally been licensed to produce arrangements of the song. The claimants' claim for copyright in all arrangements and adaptations of the song was rejected by the court. According to Goff J:

> *All arrangements had been so developed from the original song, decorated, transferred to a different medium or otherwise changed as to make them fall within the description of an original work and so attract an independent copyright. To secure such copyright, it is only necessary that the arranger's mode of expression be sufficiently different from the original not to appear to have been copied from it. There is no requirement that the ideas embodied in the arrangement be novel.*

However, the owner of the later copyright (in this case the 'arranger') cannot make the adaptation or exploit it without a licence from the owner of the copyright in the underlying work, as this would amount to infringement.

Artistic works (CDPA 1988, s 4)

2.20 Artistic works are defined as:

- a graphic work, photograph, sculpture or collage, irrespective of artistic quality;
- a work of architecture, being a building or a model for a building;
- a work of artistic craftsmanship.

In *Interlego AG v Tyco Industries* (1988), it was held that artistic copyright lay in the design drawings for a plastic brick and not in the written instructions which accompanied them. To quote Lord Oliver, the 'essence' of artistic copyright is that which is 'visually significant'. Graphic works include:

- any painting, drawing, diagram, map, chart or plan;
- any engraving, etching, lithograph, woodcut or similar work.

2.21 At present artistic works are protected regardless of artistic merit and so industrial drawings, as in the *Lego* case, attract copyright protection (although there are differences in how they may be infringed (s 51); see Chapter 7 on Industrial Design). Individual frames stored in the memory of a computer are graphic works. So are still images created for a cartoon film. However, a series of still images or individual frames is not in itself a separate graphic work (*Nova Productions Ltd v Mazooma Games Ltd & others* (2007), per Jacob LJ). Although, if they combined to produce a moving image, they may constitute a film and hence an original dramatic work (*Norowzian v Arks (No 2)* (2000), per Nourse LJ).

Some graphic works, for instance, a map or a plan, may also contain material which will attract literary copyright. Collage was new to the CDPA 1988 and is not defined. A sculpture includes a cast or model for the purposes of sculpture. Whether or not a work is a sculpture for the purposes of s 4 CDPA was recently considered in *Lucasfilms v Ainsworth* (2009) HC; (2010) CA; (2011) SC). In the High Court, Mann J set out a number of guidelines, derived from earlier cases, for determining whether a work is a work of sculpture. These included having regard to the ordinary meaning of the word 'sculpture', recognising that the concept goes beyond 'what one would normally expect to find in art galleries' and avoiding judgments based on artistic merit. In particular, Mann J noted that: 'It is the essence of a sculpture that it should have, as part of its purpose, a visual appeal in the sense that it might be enjoyed for that purpose alone, whether or not it might have another purpose as well. The purpose is that of the creator.' In *Lucasfilms*, the claimant commissioned the defendant to make a military style helmet to be worn by storm troopers in the movie, 'Star Wars'. The defendant based the helmets on paintings, drawing and models which he produced using sculpting techniques. He subsequently sold copies of these helmets to the public. One issue in the case was whether the helmet was a sculpture and, if so, who owned the copyright in it. Both in the High Court and the Court of Appeal, it was held that the helmet was not a sculpture because it was never intended to be a work of art; it was utilitarian and lacking in artistic purpose. This was true even though it was designed for use by a fictional character. The Supreme Court agreed. They endorsed the guidelines set out by Mann J, noting that the decision on whether a work is a sculpture will be a matter of judgment based on the facts in each case. The Supreme Court also agreed with the lower courts that the helmets were functional objects not sculptures. They were a mixture of 'costume and prop' in the production process, that is, in the making of a film. Given the iconic design of the helmet and its undoubted lack of utility in warding off enemy attacks, real or imagined, it is difficult not to sympathise with the argument of the claimant that the helmet should have been understood not as functional but as a work of art.

Works of architecture (CDPA 1988, s 4(1)(b))

2.22 A building is defined as including any fixed structure or part of a building or fixed structure (s 4(2)). The definition would include a contemporary addition to an old building, such as the Clore Gallery at Tate Britain in London. There is no need for these works to have artistic quality. In principle, the same protection is given to a monolithic office block as to the Lloyds' Insurance building in London, although it would, of course, be more difficult to maintain that the design for the former is original.

Artistic craftsmanship (CDPA 1988, s 4(1)(c))

2.23 This is the only description of work where courts may be called upon to make an artistic judgment. In *Hensher Ltd v Restawile Upholstery (Lancs) Ltd* (1976), a mock-up for a suite of furniture was held not to be a work of artistic craftsmanship. The House of Lords disagreed, however, as to why. Lord Reid suggested that a work was a work of art if it was appreciated as such by the public. Lord Kilbrandon said that it was the author's conscious intention to create a work of art which was the key. According to the court in *Vermaat and Powell v Boncrest Ltd* (2001), it must be possible to say of a work of artistic craftsmanship that the author was both a craftsman and an artist. The court defined a craftsman as 'a person who made something in a skilful way and who took justified pride in his workmanship'. An artist, on the other hand, was a person with creative ability 'who produced something with aesthetic appeal'. However, it was not necessary for the artistic contribution and the craftsmanship to emanate from the same individual. In *Lucasfilms*, the court was also asked to consider whether the helmet was a work of artistic craftsmanship. Mann J held that it was not. While the production of the helmet had necessitated a high level of craftsmanship, it was not a work of '*artistic* craftsmanship' as there had been no intention that it should 'appeal as a work of art'.

Artistic works and originality

2.24 Artistic works must be original to attract copyright (CDPA 1988, s 1(1)(a)). As with literary works, it has traditionally been the skill and labour which goes into the making of the artistic work that bestows originality. There is said to be the same idea/expression dichotomy that applies to literary works. In *Catnic Components Ltd v Hill and Smith Ltd* (1979), Buckley LJ said:

> What is protected is the skill and labour devoted to making the 'artistic work' itself, not the skill and labour devoted to developing some idea or invention communicated or depicted by the 'artistic work'. The protection afforded by copyright is not in my judgment any broader...where the 'artistic work' embodies a novel or inventive idea than it is where it represents a commonplace object or theme.

The amount of skill and labour necessary for subsistence of artistic copyright has been a matter of fact and degree. Copyright may subsist in very basic works, such as a drawing of a hand pointing to a cross on a ballot paper intended for illiterate voters. However, the subject of the illustration (in essence, the 'idea' behind it) was held not to be capable of copyright infringement. It was open to others to draw hands engaged in similar action for a similar purpose (*Kenrick & Co v Lawrence & Co* (1890)). Similarly, in *Hanfstaengl v Baines & Co* (1895), a painting of a courting couple at a stile was held not to be infringed by a sketch with the same theme, where the depiction of the couple and the landscape were quite different. In assessing the originality of an artistic work, a distinction is drawn between that which is visually significant, where the skill and labour employed are highly relevant, and that which is not, where the skill and labour employed are irrelevant. In *Drayton Controls (Engineering) v Honeywell Control Systems* (1992), the court compared two drawings of a valve. Knox J held that the later drawings were original because there was a change of shape which was visually significant. However, a mere scaling down of the original work would not have been visually significant and, therefore, not original. The decision in *Drayton* suggests that not all skill and labour can ensure a work is original for the purposes of copyright. A scaled-down drawing of an original work or a precise copy of a painting would not be. There must, in addition, be some element of material alteration or embellishment which is sufficient to make the work original (*Interlego AG v Tyco Industries Inc* (1988)). To date, there has been no case in the UK courts which has sought to apply the test for originality set out in *Infopaq* to artistic works. However, it is submitted that, following *NLA v Meltwater* (2011), it is likely that the traditional UK test for originality in relation to artistic works will remain relevant.

The idea–expression dichotomy in artistic works

2.25 It is necessary to exercise the same caution regarding the idea/expression dichotomy in artistic works as when dealing with original literary works. Like computer programs, works of art may embody a number of ideas, which the artist, through skill and effort, has put together in a particular way. The decision in *Kenrick & Co v Lawrence & Co* (1890), which concerned the pointing hand, suggests that the more general the idea expressed in the artistic work, the more difficult it will be to find infringement. *Kenrick* also illustrates the extent to which artistic works, far more than literary works, conflate the distinction between idea and expression. This was confirmed by the judgment of Lord Hoffmann in *Designers Guild Ltd v Russell Williams (Textiles) Ltd (No 2)* (2000). In this case both parties designed and sold wallpaper and fabrics. In 1994, DGL produced a fabric design, 'Ixia'. The design was characterised by vertical strips of alternating colours and scattered flowers. The stripes were painted with rough edges and brushstroke and the flowers were presented in an impressionistic style. In 1996, the defendants presented at a trade fair a fabric design, 'Marguerite', which also included stripes and scattered flowers in an impressionistic style. The claimants alleged copyright infringement. Among the questions raised by the case in the House of Lords was the distinction between idea and expression in artistic works. Lord Hoffmann took the view that every element of an artistic work 'unless it got there by accident or compulsion' is the expression of the idea on the part of the author.

2.26 Nowhere is this more true than in the currently fashionable 'conceptual art', where, by definition, the originality of the piece rests almost entirely on the concept (or idea) behind it, and not on its execution or expression. Consider, for example, an early work of conceptual art, Marcel Duchamp's 'Fountain'. This was a real urinal which the surrealist signed under a pseudonym and exhibited in a gallery. To what extent does copyright subsist in this work? Here, the real skill and effort went into the idea of the work, rather than its actual physical embodiment, which, at most, entailed locating the urinal and signing it. What of a pile of bricks or a sheep preserved in formaldehyde, both of which have been exhibited in museums? Do these works deserve any less protection than a Rothko or a Bacon? On the one hand, the decision in *Kenrick & Co v Lawrence & Co* (1890) suggests such works would have very narrow protection. It is submitted that another urinal signed by a different artist may well not infringe. However revolutionary (as it was at the time), the idea that a urinal may constitute a work of art would presumably merit no greater protection than the banal idea of painting a courting couple at a stile. On the other hand, to the extent that copyright subsists at all in such works, what is the law protecting but an idea? It may be that Duchamp's urinal falls into that category of work described by Lord Watson in *Hanfstaengl v Baines & Co* (1895), 'in which his [the artist's] design and the idea to which it gives birth, are both of them so novel and exceptional that it would be difficult, if not impossible, for another author to create the same idea without trenching upon his design'. But compare this view with Buckley LJ's comment in *Catnic Components Ltd v Hill and Smith Ltd* (1979) (cited in para **2.24**).

Artistic works compared

2.27 Some idea of what may constitute the variety of artistic works is to be found in *Creation Records Ltd v News Group Newspapers* (1997). Noel Gallagher, of the band Oasis, had organised a photo shoot at a hotel for an album cover, which involved a white Rolls Royce submerged in a swimming pool and other props. A newspaper photographer managed to infiltrate the grounds and took a photograph of the scene. The claimants' claim that the scene was itself a copyright work was rejected by the court. It was not a dramatic work, since 'there was no movement, story or action in the scene'. It was not an artistic work (a sculpture or collage). The scene had not been carved or modelled. It differed from the film set in *Shelley Films Ltd v Rex Features Ltd* (1994). It was simply a collection of *objets trouvés* and not the result, as the film set had been, of an exercise of artistic craftsmanship. It was not a collage within the definition of the *Oxford English Dictionary*, since it did not include a collection of unrelated things and the items were not stuck together. It differed from other examples of artistic creativity, in particular conceptual works, such as Carl Andre's piled bricks ('Equivalence 2'), an example which was raised by the claimants. In other words, simply describing the scene as a work of art did not make it so.

Secondary works

2.28 These works are also characteristically described as 'derivative', 'neighbouring' or 'supporting' works. In particular, they include sound recordings, films and broadcasts, and cable programmes (ss 5A, 5B and 6). Secondary works differ from primary works, such as literary and artistic works, in that the 'authors' of secondary works are typically the entrepreneurs who invest in their production. It is this investment, rather than any creative endeavour, that is primarily being protected by copyright. In the UK, where the history of copyright law has been as bound up with the interests of entrepreneurs (such as publishers) as it has with those of authors, secondary works have traditionally been treated no differently from primary works.

Sound recordings (CDPA 1988, s 5A(1)(a) and (b))

2.29 Sound recordings are:

- a recording of sounds, from which the sounds may be reproduced; or

- a recording of the whole or any part of a literary work, or a dramatic or musical work, from which sounds reproducing the work or part may be produced,

- regardless of the medium on which the recording is made or the method by which the sounds are reproduced or produced.

The definition is considerably broader than under the Copyright Act 1956, in order to embrace emerging technologies. Under s 5A(1)(a), sound recordings might encompass a broad range of sounds, including anything from natural sounds, such as animal sounds, to traffic noise, to a conversation overheard and recorded. The definition given in s 5A(1)(b) would fit, for example, a recording of a performance. Copyright would certainly subsist in parts of previous recordings which have been incorporated into 'rap' songs through 'sampling'. However, given that such songs are often highly original sound recordings in their own right, they would also have their own copyright, subject to any rights in the sample taken (Salmon, 'Sampling and sound recording reproduction – fair use or infringement?' [2010] *Entertainment Law Review* 174).

Film (CDPA 1988, s 5B(1))

2.30 Film means a recording on any medium from which a moving image may be produced. Again, this definition is very broad, and wider than under the Copyright Act 1956, which protected 'cinematographic' films. Film soundtracks are treated as part of the film. There is no necessity for the film or sound recording to be 'original' for copyright to subsist. Instead, copyright does not subsist in a sound recording or film which is, or to the extent that it is, a copy taken from a previous sound recording or film (s 5B(4)). This ensures that there will be no new copyright in a simple re-recording of, for instance, a rented DVD. It is important to note that a 'film' for the purposes of the CDPA 1988 is the actual recording, not the subject matter of the recording. A film of an original dramatic work, for instance a Mike Leigh film, in which, famously, much of the dialogue and action is wholly improvised, creates two copyrights–one in the film and one in the original dramatic work it records. The first time *Norowzian v Arks* came before the High Court in 1998, the court held, on the same facts as in the later case, that copyright in the film could be infringed only by a copying of the whole or part of the film in the sense of copying a whole or a part of the particular recording of the film. A re-shooting of a film sequence in which not a single still from the original copyright film had been included was not a copy for the purposes of the CDPA 1988. The later decision of the Court of Appeal took a different view. It held that copyright might subsist in the film itself, as a dramatic work, even if it is not the recording of an underlying dramatic work (see also *Nova Productions v Mazooma Games* (2007)).

Broadcasts (CDPA 1988, s 6)

2.31 These rights subsist without fixation. This section has been amended by the Copyright and Related Rights Regulations 2003. A broadcast is defined as an electronic transmission of visual images, sounds or other information, which is transmitted for simultaneous reception by members of the public, and is capable of being lawfully received by them, or is transmitted at a time determined solely by the person making the transmission for presentation to members of the public (s 6(1)(a) and (b)). Excepted from the definition of a broadcast is any internet transmission, unless it is taking place simultaneously on the internet and by other means, is a concurrent transmission of a live event, or it is a transmission of recorded moving images or sounds forming part of a programme service offered by the person responsible for making the transmission, being a service in which programmes are transmitted at scheduled times determined by that person (s 6(1A)). Police radio would not constitute a broadcast, because it is not for public consumption. However, a broadcast which can only be received through the use of decoding equipment, such as in pay-per-view, would be a broadcast protected by CDPA 1988, s 6(2). Where a wireless broadcast is made via satellite, the place from which the broadcast is deemed to be made is the place from which the signals are transmitted to the satellite (s 6(4)). A broadcast sent from the UK via satellite and picked up in the Netherlands will be subject to UK copyright law. Furthermore, the relaying of a broadcast by reception and immediate retransmission shall be regarded as a separate act of broadcasting from the making of the broadcast which is retransmitted (s 6(5A)) (see *Football Association Premier League (FAPL) v QC Leisure (QCL)* (2011), para **2.119**). Copyright does not subsist in a broadcast which infringes, or to the extent that it infringes, the copyright in another broadcast or in a cable programme (s 6(6)). Satellite broadcasts from countries outside of the European Economic Area (EEA) which do not provide the same level of copyright protection are dealt with in s 6A. In such circumstances, responsibility for making the wireless broadcast will fall to the person operating the 'uplink station' or, if that is not located in the EEA, to the commissioner of the broadcast if his place of business is in the EEA.

Published editions (CDPA 1988, s 8)

2.32 Essentially, this copyright protects the typographical arrangement (or layout) of a literary, dramatic or musical work against reprographic copying. It is concerned with the way the published edition looks, rather than its contents. It protects the whole edition of a work rather than separate parts of it. For instance, it will protect a newspaper as a whole, not the typographical arrangement of individual articles (*Newspaper Licensing Agency Ltd v Marks & Spencer plc* (2001)).

Authorship and ownership

2.33 The Copyright, Designs and Patents Act 1988 defines the author of a work as the person who creates it (s 9(1)). Authorship and ownership do not necessarily coincide.

Authorship of primary works

2.34 The definition of authorship of primary works is generally straightforward. The author is the individual who has expended the necessary effort, skill and labour in creating the work. In *Walter v Lane* (1900), copyright subsisted in the recording of Lord Rosebery's speech, because the reporter had expended skill and effort in transposing the spoken into the written word. In the same case, the court distinguished an 'amanuensis', who simply takes down words as they are dictated, and has no creative input. This individual would not be the author (or, indeed, the joint author) of the original literary work so produced.

Authorship in secondary works

2.35 The CDPA 1988 is more explicit when the question arises of the authorship in neighbouring works (s 9(2)(a)–(d)). The author is the individual (indeed, it is often a company) who has made the necessary commercial arrangements for their creation. This may seem reasonable in relation to broadcasts (the person who transmits the programme, providing he has responsibility for its contents, or the person who arranges for its transmission), typographical arrangements of a published edition (the publisher), and computer-generated works (the person making the necessary arrangements). But the rule is perhaps less easily justified in relation to sound recordings, where the author of a sound recording is the producer, although the sound engineer, particularly in relation to 'urban' music, may have had a major creative input (s 9(2)(aa)). The Copyright Term Directive (EC) 93/98), now the Copyright Term Directive (2006/116/EC), introduced important changes to the authorship of films. Previously, the author of a film had been the producer. The Directive provides that the principal director will be a joint author with the producer, thus belatedly giving directors in the UK the recognition that they have long received in France and other European countries as 'auteurs' (s 9(2)(ab)).

Joint authors

2.36 It is possible to have two or more joint authors of a copyright work, as long as the authors have collaborated and the contribution of one cannot be distinguished from that of the others (s 10(1)). There is no need for a common intention to produce a work of joint authorship, provided there is a common design to produce the work itself (*Robert James Beckingham v Robert Hodgens* (2003)). The onus is on the person asserting joint authorship to prove his case (*Brown v McAsso Music Production Ltd* (2005)). The joint author must make a significant and original contribution to the work although it need not be equal in magnitude to that of the other author(s) (*Brighton v Jones* (2004)). Thus in *Fisher v Brooker* (2007), the work at issue was the song, 'A Whiter Shade of Pale' recorded by the musical group Procol Harum in 1967 and still immensely popular today. The claimant played Hammond Organ for the group and claimed joint authorship of the song having written the organ parts, in particular a distinctive eight-bar introduction which is repeated throughout the four-minute song. The first defendant was the group's lead singer and had been credited with writing both the words and music for the song. He asserted, in turn, that the claimant had merely written an accompaniment to the song. According to Blackburne J, in the High Court, 'It is abundantly clear to me that Mr Fisher's instrumental introduction (i.e. the organ solo as heard in the first eight bars of the Work and as repeated) is sufficiently different from what Mr Brooker had composed on the piano to qualify in law, and by a wide margin, as an original contribution to the Work.' Fisher was therefore a joint-author.

2.37 In establishing joint authorship, the question of who 'pushed the pen' is not necessarily decisive. In *Cala Homes (South) Ltd v McAlpine East Homes Ltd* (1995), concerning copyright in architectural drawings, the High Court took the view that:

> *What is protected by copyright in a drawing or a literary work is more than just the skill of making marks on paper or some other medium. It is both the words or lines and skill and effort involved in creating, selecting or gathering together the detailed concepts, data or emotions which those works have fixed in some tangible form which is protected. It is wrong to think that only the person who carries out the mechanical act of fixation is the author.*

However, in *Robin Ray v Classic FM plc* (1998), the High Court held that for joint authorship what is required is 'something which approximates penmanship' in the sense that what is essential is a direct responsibility for what actually appears on paper. Situations where the putative joint author merely acts as a 'scribe' for the author are likely to be unusual. Nonetheless, the expenditure of skill and effort in itself is not determinate of authorship. The contribution by the joint author must be a contribution to the actual creation of the work. Thus, in *Fylde*, the claimant developed and manufactured, inter alia, software which the defendant, who claimed joint authorship, installed in his radios over a number of years. It was held that the expenditure of considerable time and effort by the defendant's employees in, for example, testing the program, making sure it performed well and setting specifications, did not amount to contributions to the 'authoring' of the software. In particular, according to the court, the expenditure of skill, time and effort in testing a program was analogous to the skill of a proofreader. It was not authorship skill. A similar situation arose in *Brighton v Jones* (2004). Jones wrote a successful play called *Stones in His Pockets*. Brighton, who directed its first production, claimed joint authorship on the basis of suggesting new episodes and dialogue changes during rehearsals. These were held not to be a sufficiently significant contribution to the play to establish joint authorship. Rather they went to its interpretation and presentation. Brighton was not a joint author.

Ownership (CDPA 1988, s 11)

2.38   It is generally the case that the author will be first owner of a copyright work, including works which are commissioned. There may also be joint-ownership of a work. In *Fisher v Brooker*, Fisher was also held to be a joint-owner of the work, 'A Whiter Shade of Pale'. As such, he was entitled to future royalties based on a 40 per cent share of the work, despite his lengthy delay in bringing the claim (*Fisher v Brooker* (2009) HL). There are two exceptions to the rule that the author(s) will also be the first owner. Where a literary, dramatic, musical or artistic work, or a film, is made by an employee in the course of his employment, his employer is the first owner, subject to any agreement to the contrary. Second, certain works will be Crown or Parliamentary copyright, or will be the copyright of certain international organisations.

Works created by employees (CDPA 1988, s 11(2))

2.39   To decide whether a work was created in the course of employment, it is necessary to ask whether the author was under a contract *of* service when the work was created, or alternatively whether the author was commissioned to create the work under a contract *for* service. In the latter case, copyright will stay with the author, subject to any contrary agreement. In *Beloff v Pressdram Ltd* (1973), the court cited with approval the dictum of Lord Denning that an employee is employed as part of the business and his work is an integral part of the business. *Beloff* concerned a journalist for the *Observer* newspaper. The court found that she was an employee of the *Observer*, although she also wrote books and gave broadcasts which did not fall within the terms of her employment. During the time of her employment, the claimant both produced works whose copyright belonged to the newspaper, and works, outside her duties to the newspaper, whose copyright belonged to her. Where it has been long-standing practice for copyright to belong to an employee of works created during the course of employment, for example as is frequently the case with university lecturers, the courts will imply such a term into the contract of employment (*Noah v Shuba* (1991); see also *Stephenson Jordan v McDonald & Evans* (1951)).

Commissioned works

2.40   Copyright in a commissioned work belongs to the author, in the absence of an express or implied term to the contrary (*Robin Ray v Classic FM plc* (1998)). Where the contract is unclear as to the rights of the commissioner to use the work, the courts may imply the grant of an appropriate right. If the lacuna can be satisfied by the grant of a licence rather than an assignment of copyright, then the court will imply the former. It follows that the ambit of the licence will also be the minimum required to secure for the commissioner the entitlement which the parties to the contract intended (*Ray*). There may, however, be situations where the court vests equitable ownership in the commissioner. In *Griggs Group Ltd v Evans* (2005), the manufacturers of 'Doc Martens' footwear commissioned an advertising agency to create a logo, combining two of their existing trade marks. The agency hired Evans, a freelance designer, to create the logo. Evans subsequently assigned copyright in the logo to an Australian company (the second defendant) which used it on their products. While it was agreed that the second defendant had the legal ownership of the copyright in the logo worldwide, the claimants argued that they were equitable owners of the copyright and, inter alia, asked that the copyright be assigned to them. Evans replied that he had only been commissioned by the claimants to produce the logo for point of sale use in the UK, not for all uses worldwide. Both the High Court and the Court of Appeal found that the second defendants held the copyright on trust for the claimants. According to Jacob LJ an opposite conclusion would be 'fantastic'. He noted:

> If an officious bystander had asked at the time of contract whether Mr Evans was going to retain rights in the combined logo which could be used against the client by Mr Evans (or anyone to whom he sold the rights) anywhere in the world, other than in respect of point of sale material in the UK, the answer would surely have been 'of course not'.

In *Richardson Computers Ltd v Flanders* (1993), a similar conclusion was reached in respect of customised computer software. Certainly, the frequent failure of those who commission works to determine who will own copyright in the ensuing product provides intellectual property lawyers with a steady and lucrative flow of business.

Qualifying works (CDPA 1988, ss 153–156)

2.41 Not all copyright works will be protected in the UK. They must be qualifying works. A work qualifies for copyright protection in the UK if:

- the author is a qualifying person;
- the work was first published in a qualifying country (or published simultaneously, that is, within 30 days of first publication);
- in the case of a broadcast, the UK was the country from which the broadcast was made.

A qualifying person includes a person who, at the time the work was made, is a British citizen or subject, or an individual domiciled or resident in the UK, as well as a citizen of, or a person domiciled or resident in, any extension country, which is a country that is a party to the Berne Convention or the Universal Copyright Convention. If the work is unpublished, first publication of a literary, dramatic or musical work occurs when the work is made or, if the making of the work extended over a period, a substantial part of the period.

Duration of copyright in primary works (CDPA 1988, s 12)

2.42 Copyright in a primary work lasts for the life of the author plus 70 years. The present term, which replaced the previous term of life plus 50 years, was the result of the Copyright Term Directive (EC) 93/98 (now 2006/116/EC), which was designed to ensure a uniform term throughout the EU. The effect of the Directive was that some works which had previously fallen out of copyright in the UK came back into copyright. Others which were about to fall out of copyright had their copyright extended. The length of protection afforded to copyright works has inexorably increased over the past two centuries and there has been considerable debate as to whether the broader public interest has been served by this latest extension to the copyright term. A key justification offered by the EU was that people now live longer and that their increased longevity should be recognised (although, it is, of course, the author's heirs rather than the author who will benefit). Others have argued that the previous life plus 50 years term was sufficient to ensure that the author, descendants and publisher were amply rewarded, and that the new longer term will stifle the free circulation of ideas (Laddie, 'Copyright: Over-strength, Over-regulated, Over-rated?' [1996] *European Intellectual Property Review* 253). There are special rules for primary works of an unknown authorship, works which are unpublished at the author's death, works of joint authorship and computer-generated works. The copyright in the latter expires 50 years from the end of the calendar year in which the work was made (s 12).

Duration of copyright in secondary works (CDPA 1988, s 13A and ss 13B–15)

2.43 Some secondary works, like computer-generated works, typically have a shorter term of protection than primary works, recognising that here copyright is protecting financial investment rather than creative endeavour. Broadly, typographical arrangements of published editions are protected for 25 years and broadcasts and sound recordings are protected for 50 years. As a result of the Copyright Term Directive, films have ceased to be protected as secondary works–in which the term of protection was 50 years. They are now protected like primary works, the term being 70 years from the death of the last to die of the following: principal director; author of the screenplay; author of the dialogue; and composer of the music specifically created for the film (s 13B). The Duration of Copyright and Rights in

Performance Regulations (SI 1995/3297) amended the protection afforded to sound recordings (s 13A). Until 2011, protection for sound recordings expired at the end of the period of 50 years from the end of the calendar year in which the recording was made, or, if during the period the recording was published, 50 years from the end of the calendar year in which it was first published. Following a campaign by a number of prominent recording artists of the 1960s, including Paul McCartney and Cliff Richard, who claimed a 'moral' entitlement to continue to profit from their recordings which were still commercially valuable, the European Parliament approved the Directive 2011/77/EU amending the Directive 2006/116/EC on the term of protection of copyright and certain related rights. This extends the term of protection for performers and sound recordings to 70 years. The Directive also contains 'use it or lose it' clauses, meaning that if record companies do not market a sound recording during the extended period, performers may get their rights back. According the EC this will allow the performer to find another record producer to market the recording, or in a nod to modern market realities perhaps sell it himself via the internet. In addition, record companies will also have to set aside 20 per cent of their earnings during this extended period to benefit session musicians. It is, of course, important to remember that there may be a number of rights in any given copyright work–and films are a good example–which will expire at uneven dates.

Infringement

2.44 There are two types of infringement. Primary infringement occurs when a person does, or authorises another to do, any of the restricted acts without the licence of a copyright owner (s 16(2)). Secondary infringement, which is mainly concerned with dealings in infringing works or facilitating their production, will be considered below at para **2.69**.

Primary infringement

Restricted acts

2.45 The owner of the copyright in a work has the exclusive right to do the following acts in the UK (s 16(1)):

- copy the work;
- issue copies of the work to the public;
- perform, show or play the work in public;

- communicate the work to the public;
- make an adaptation of the work, or do any of the above in relation to an adaptation.

The Copyright, Designs and Patents Act 1988 does not give a copyright owner a positive right to do any of the 'restricted acts', since in so doing it is quite possible he may infringe another's copyright. For instance, Y translates a play into French. Y will own copyright in her translation, but she has no right to copy it or issue copies to the public without the licence of Z, the owner of copyright in the play. Instead, the CDPA 1988 gives the copyright owner the negative right to stop anyone else from doing any of the restricted acts without his permission (or licence). Thus, Z can stop Y from publishing her translation without a licence. The relationship between the restricted acts and different kinds of copyright works is considered below (see para **2.61** et seq).

The elements of primary infringement

2.46 There are two defining elements to primary infringement. According to Denning LJ in *Francis, Day and Hunter Ltd v Bron* (1963), there must be a causal connection between the copyright work and the allegedly infringing work. In other words, the copyright work must be the source of the infringing work. Second, there must be copying of a substantial part of the copyright work.

The causal connection

2.47 For a work to be infringing, it must derive from the copyright work. It must be copied. If two works created independently are substantially the same, the first to be created will not be infringed by the second. The similarity may be coincidence, or perhaps result from the authors choosing the same subject, for instance photographs of the Manhattan skyline at night, where it is possible that the composition of resulting works will be similar. Alternatively, the two works may have derived from a common source. A great deal of historical writing depends upon the use of a limited pool of sources. If the second author uses the first author's work to identify the common source, there will be no infringement, since, by going back to the primary source, the second author will have expended his own skill and effort on his work (*Pike v Nicholas* (1869)).

Indirect copying

2.48 The infringing work need not be copied directly from the original work. Indeed, the infringing author may not even know of its existence. In *Solar Thomson*

Engineering Co Ltd v Barton (1977), the defendants asked a designer to design a spare part for its machinery. To avoid infringing copyright in the original design drawings of the spare (which belonged to the claimant), they gave the designer detailed instructions and the surrounding hardware, but did not show him the original drawing. He produced a design drawing which closely resembled the claimant's. The Court of Appeal held that the instructions were a sufficient causal link for copyright in the original design drawings to have been infringed. In *Plix Products Ltd v Winstone (Merchants)* (1986), the link between the copyright work and the infringing work was even more tenuous. The New Zealand Kiwifruit Authority (NZKA) had published written specifications for kiwi fruit containers, based on the claimants' designs. At the time, the claimants' packing case was the only one to have been approved by the NZKA, thus giving them an effective monopoly. The defendants, seeking to avoid a copyright challenge at all costs, and with legal advice, asked an Italian designer to come up with a container to fit the official specifications, without showing him the claimants' case. The resulting design was held to be infringing. The New Zealand Court of Appeal held it was possible to copy indirectly through the intermediary verbal instructions, provided the verbal description was sufficiently precise to provide a means whereby the copyist could appropriate the substantial features of the original.

Subconscious copying

2.49 It follows that the infringer need not be aware that he is copying to infringe. The copying may be subconscious. In *Francis, Day and Hunter Ltd v Bron* (1963), where the claimants claimed infringement of their song 'A Little Spanish Town', the composer of 'Why' did not remember ever hearing the former, and the Court of Appeal accepted that there had been no conscious copying. But it was said that if he had heard the work and subconsciously copied it, then 'Why' would constitute an infringing work.

A substantial part

2.50 Apart from a causal connection, in order to infringe, copying must be in relation to the work as a whole, or any substantial part of it (s 16(3)(a)). It is necessary, when judging substantiality, to assess the importance of the copied material to the original work and not to the allegedly infringing work (Lord Millet in *Designers Guild v Russell Williams (Textiles) Ltd (No 2)* (2000)). A 'substantial part' is defined qualitatively, not quantitatively (*Ladbroke (Football Ltd) v William Hill (Football Ltd)* (1964), per Lord Pearce). In *Hawkes & Son (London) Ltd v Paramount Film Service Ltd* (1934), the defendants infringed copyright in 28 bars of the 'Colonel Bogey' march, played during the opening of a school by the Prince of Wales, which the defendants filmed. Although the extract took up only 50 seconds or so of film time, the Court of Appeal held that these 28 bars, being the highly recognisable, 'essential' air of the march, constituted a substantial part (the CDPA 1988 now provides a defence of fair dealing, see para **2.73** et seq). At the other extreme, in *Warwick Film Productions Ltd v Eisinger* (1969), the defendant, the author of a film script on the trials of Oscar Wilde, borrowed heavily from a book by H on the same subject, which the claimants had also turned into a film. The borrowed passages were not original, since they had, in turn, been copied by H from a third book which was based on shorthand transcripts of the trials. The court held that, although the passages may have constituted a substantial part of the script quantitatively, they did not constitute a substantial part of the claimants' work for the purposes of infringement, because they were not original. Following *Infopaq*, the Court of Appeal considered the issue of what constitutes a substantial part for the purposes of finding infringement in *NLA v Meltwater* (2011). We have already looked at the facts. The Court of Appeal confirmed the judgment of Proudman J, that extracts of articles which Meltwater News provided to its clients, and which could not exceed 256 characters, could represent a substantial part of the articles if they contained elements which were the expression of the intellectual creation of the author (see para **2.17**).

Originality and infringement

2.51 The *Infopaq* judgment and the subsequent *Meltwater* judgment in the Court of Appeal appear to confirm the traditional approach of the UK courts that to constitute a substantial part of a copyright work, the part must be original in its own right, even when abstracted from the whole (*Ladbroke (Football Ltd) v William Hill (Football Ltd)* (1964), per Lord Pearce). Thus, in *Warwick*, H's book was held to be an original literary work by virtue of the skill and labour he had put into editing the source material. But by simply taking the source material, the defendants had not taken advantage of this skill and labour. They had not taken a substantial part of the work, because the part they had taken was not original.

Compilations

2.52 The principle that a substantial part must be original is clearly demonstrated in relation to compilations. Their originality lies not in the individual contents of the compilation but in the way the author has selected the contents and chosen to combine them in the work–it is this skill which is protected by copyright (*Ladbroke (Football Ltd) v William Hill (Football Ltd)* (1964) (see para **2.18**)). In *Ladbroke*, the court decided that the claimant's fixed-odds football betting coupons constituted an original literary work, that is, a compilation, by virtue of the skill, labour and judgement that had gone into their composition. However, as we have seen, the Court of Appeal, in *Football Dataco v Brittens Pools*, has now asked the Court of Justice to rule on whether the author's own intellectual creation in relation to database compilations ('the art 3 right') requires something beyond significant labour and skill from the author (see para **2.18**). If the Court of Justice rules that this is the case, and that the art 3 right cannot co-exist with a separate national copyright in a compilation, then it is arguable that cases, such as *Ladbroke*, would be decided differently in the future. The same might be true of the decision in *Independent Television Publications Ltd v Time Out Ltd* (1984), where the court held that it was the broadcasters' skill and labour in developing daily programme schedules, rather than their subsequent listing in the *TV Times* and *Radio Times*, that was worthy of protection (see also *Football League Ltd v Littlewoods Pools Ltd* (1959), per Upjohn J, in which Football League fixture lists were held to be protected by copyright). The consequence of *Independent Television* was to give the claimants an effective monopoly over publishing the television schedules, since they had generated them (but see para **2.121** on *Radio Telefis Eireann v EC Commission* (1995)).

The idea/expression dichotomy and infringement

2.53 It has been suggested that, as a general rule, copyright protects the form in which the idea is expressed rather than the idea itself. In *Ward (Moxley) Ltd v Richard Sankey Ltd* (1988), the defendant copied from the claimant the idea of designing a sleeve to fit around 'nestable' flowerpots. The defendant's drawing embodying this idea was the same as the claimant's drawing. The High Court held that this was not infringement. The defendant had infringed the claimant's copyright work neither indirectly through copying the dimensions of the claimant's pots (as in *Solar Thomson Engineering Co Ltd v Barton* (1977) (see para **2.48**)) nor directly through copying the claimant's drawings. It was simply the idea which had been taken.

Non-literal copying

2.54 It is possible to infringe a copyright work, or a substantial part of it, even though the infringing work is not an exact copy. For instance, the copy may be an adaptation. Is this tantamount to saying that there is, after all, copyright in ideas? One answer may be that, if the originality of a work resides in the way an idea is developed or a number of ideas are combined, then there may still be infringement even if there is no literal copying. In *Designers' Guild v Russell Williams (Textiles)* (2000), Lord Hoffmann identified two circumstances in which ideas will *not* be protected. First, ideas will not be protected when they have no connection with the literary, dramatic, musical or artistic nature of the work. Thus, if a literary work embodies an idea for an invention, the invention might be patented but the idea itself would not be protected by copyright. Alternatively, an idea will not be protected because although it is an idea of a literary, dramatic or artistic nature, it is commonplace and so is not a substantial part of the work. An example of the latter, cited by Lord Hoffmann, was the pointing hand in *Kenrick & Lawrence* (1890). However, if the originality of a work resides in the way an idea is developed or a number of ideas are combined, then there may be infringement without literal copying, provided what is taken represents a substantial part of the author's skill and labour. According to Lord Hoffmann in *Designers' Guild*:

> ...the original elements in the plot of a play or a novel may be a substantial part, so that copyright may be infringed by a work which does not reproduce a single sentence of the original. If one asks what is being protected in such a case, it is difficult to give any answer except that it is an idea expressed in the copyright work.

Whether or not an 'idea' is sufficiently detailed to be protected against copying is a question of degree (*Nova Productions v Mazooma Games* (2007)). According to Judge Learned Hand, referring to the idea/expression distinction, 'Nobody has ever been able to fix that boundary and nobody ever can' (*Nichols v Universal Pictures* (1930)).

2.55 Lord Scott addressed the issue of non-literal copying in his judgment in *Designers Guild Ltd v Russell Williams (Textiles) Ltd (No 2)* (2000). In this case, Lord Scott described the defendant's fabric design as an 'altered copy'. This was because the defendant's 'Marguerite' design was not an exact copy of the claimant's 'Ixia' design. Nor was any specific part of the 'Marguerite' design an exact copy of any corresponding part of the 'Ixia' design. Rather, in copying the claimant's design, the defendant had done so with 'modifications'. According to Lord Scott, an altered copy was infringing if it 'incorporated a substantial part of the independent skill, labour, etc contributed by the original author in creating the copyright work'. To determine whether there was infringement, it was necessary to look at the similarities between the works rather than their differences, considering the works as a whole. In this case, Lord Scott believed that the similarities between the two designs were sufficiently extensive to justify the trial judge's conclusion that the defendant had copied the claimant's design. It followed that the defendant had also incorporated a substantial part of the skill and labour of the claimant into its design. In particular, the designer's skill and labour had gone into putting together a number of artistic ideas from various sources to create an original artistic design (for the particular issues raised by the idea/expression in computer software, see para **2.98**).

A common source

2.56 Courts are frequently asked to decide whether the similarities between two works arise from their sharing the same general idea or, in the case of historical works, a common set of historical incidents, in which case there would be no infringement. In *Ravenscroft v Herbert* (1980), the defendant wrote a novel, *The Spear of Destiny*, about the fate of a spear said to have pierced the side of Christ. He took the idea from a work of 'non-fiction' by the claimant, who based his own book partly on 'orthodox' research and partly on 'mystical meditation'. There was some language copying, and the same characters, incidents and interpretation of the significance of the events were found in both works. Brigham J found that by taking not only the claimant's language, but also identical incidents of real and occult history, the defendant had appropriated to himself the 'skill and labour' of the author. An opposite result was reached more recently in *Baigent v Random House Group Ltd* ((2006) HC; (2007) CA)), which concerned the phenomenal bestseller, *The Da Vinci Code* ('DVC'). In 1982, the claimants Baigent and Leigh had published a book entitled *The Holy Blood and the Holy Grail* ('HBHG'). They contended that Dan Brown, the author of DVC, had infringed copyright in their work not by literal copying but by taking its central theme. In the course of the action they enumerated 15 central theme elements. These included the fact that Jesus married Mary Magdalene and had children; that Jesus' bloodline could be traced to a French royal dynasty, the Merovingians; that the Holy Grail was both a cup and a bloodline; and that a religious organisation, the Ordre de Sion, became custodians of the Holy Grail. HBHG also included a great deal of further material which the claimants did not claim as part of the central theme and were not to be found in DVC. When the case reached the Court of Appeal, Lloyd LJ enumerated a four-stage test for finding infringement:

- what relevant material was to be found in both works;
- how much, if any, of that had been copied from HBHG;
- whether what was copied was on the copyright side of the line between ideas and expression;
- whether any of the material that was copied and did qualify as expression, rather than ideas, amounted to a substantial part of HBHG.

Lloyd LJ held that the trial judge, Smith J had correctly concluded that DVC did not infringe HBHG. Smith J had found that there were 11 central theme elements in both books and that Brown had access to HBHG when he wrote parts of DVC which included this common material. Indeed, these parts of DVC were based on material in HBHG. Nonetheless, what was taken from HBHG amounted to generalised propositions at too high a level of abstraction to qualify for copyright protection. It was not the product of the application of skill and labour by the authors of HBHG in the creation of their literary work. As a result, 'It lay on the wrong side of the line between ideas and their expression.' Perhaps most crucially, the central theme itself did not amount to a substantial part of HBHG. Instead, it was a 'selection of features' put together for the purposes of showing infringement (because they were common to both books) rather than amounting to the central theme of the claimants' book. To have found otherwise, according to Mummery LJ in the same case, would have severely hampered scholarship. He noted:

> The literary copyright exists in HBHG by reason of the skill and labour expended by the Claimants in the original composition and production of it and the original manner or form of expression of the results of their research. Original expression includes not only the language in which the work is composed but also the original selection, arrangement and compilation of the raw research material. It does not, however, extend to clothing information, facts, ideas, theories and themes with exclusive property rights, so as to enable the claimants to monopolise historical research or knowledge and prevent the legitimate use of historical or biological material, theories propounded, general arguments deployed, or general hypotheses suggested (whether sound or not) or general themes written about.

Artistic works and infringement

2.57 As we have seen in the case of *Designers' Guild v Russell Williams (Textiles)* (2000), the infringement of artistic works presents similar difficulties for the courts seeking to draw a distinction between a general idea, which is not protected, and its expression, which is. But the general principles are the same as those applied to literary works. In *Bauman v Fussell* (1953), the claimant had photographed two cocks fighting. An artist painted a picture, the idea for which, he admitted, was taken from the photograph. The position of the cocks was the same in both works, although the colours in the painting were heightened to create, according to the Court of Appeal, 'a quite different effect'. The court endorsed the view of Dale J that the 'feeling and artistic character' of the painting were the work of the defendant, and that there was no infringement. In a dissenting judgment, Romer LJ suggested that the position of the birds was a substantial feature of the photograph, which had taken both skill and judgement to capture. By reproducing the position of the birds, he believed that the defendant had copied a substantial part of the photograph. In the case of paintings of well-known views or commonplace objects, copyright will subsist in the details of the design (*Hanfstaengel v Baines*). The more commonplace the subject, the closer a copy will have to come to infringe (*Kenrick & Co v Lawrence & Co* (1890) (see para **2.24**).

2.58 In determining whether a substantial part of an artistic work has been taken for the purposes of infringement, the correct approach is to consider the cumulative effects of the copied features, rather than to analyse and compare individual features from both works (*Designers Guild Ltd v Russell Williams (Textiles) Ltd (No 2)* (2000)). In the Court of Appeal, Morritt LJ had taken note of each of the features which the trial judge had considered were copied from the claimant's design, including, for example, the combination of the flowers and stripes. He had then asked whether the copying of each of these features constituted an infringement and concluded that, in each case, they did not. The combination of the flowers and stripes was held to be an idea, rather than the expression of an idea, and so its copying could not constitute an infringement. However, in the House of Lords, it was held that the correct approach was not to deal with the copied features in isolation, but to compare their cumulative effect. Taken together, the copying of these features amounted to the copying of a substantial part of the claimants' work and the trial judge was entitled to conclude that there had been infringement.

Authorisation

2.59 Copyright is infringed by any person who, without the licence of the copyright owner, authorises another to do any of the restricted acts (s 16(2)). Authorisation is a grant, or purported grant, which may be expressed or implied, of the right to do the restricted act. An example of what constitutes authorisation arose in *Pensher Security Door Co Ltd v Sunderland City Council* (2000). Sunderland City Council wanted a specific design of door to be installed in its council flats. In the course of taking tenders, the council specified a design which had originated from the claimant. The successful tender submitted a design similar to the claimant's design. The claimant alleged infringement. The Court of Appeal held, inter alia, that a person who commissioned another to produce an article to a particular design sanctioned and impliedly purported to grant him the right to make it to that design, and thus to authorise its production. In this case, the council was well aware that the design it accepted was similar to the claimant's design. Typically, the question of authorisation might also arise in relation to the manufacture and supply of the technological means for reproducing copyright works. In *CBS Songs Ltd v Amstrad Consumer Electronics plc* (1987), the defendant developed and sold a twin-deck tape recorder. The most obvious use for the recorder, which was underlined by the defendant's advertising, was to copy music cassettes. Nonetheless, it was not its only use, and infringement was not the inevitable result of the defendant's action. The House of Lords ruled that, since the defendant did not purport to have the authority to justify such taping (and nor would reasonable members of the public suppose that the defendant did), it did not amount to authorisation for the defendant merely to enable, assist or encourage others to infringe by giving them the 'power' to copy.

2.60 Some of the questions raised by *CBS* have, inevitably, been revisited following the growth in digital technology and the possibilities it offers for widespread copyright infringement. In *Twentieth Century Fox Film Corp v Newzbin* (2010), the claimant motion picture companies successfully sued the defendant for both primary copyright infringement and also authorising others to infringe copyright. Newzbin was a website on an internet discussion system called Usenet, which allows its users to upload and view messages on bulletin boards. Usenet supports both text and binary or non-text content. A film would constitute a large binary file but would normally be distributed across a significant number, perhaps hundreds or thousands, of messages. As a result, a user who wishes to download a copy of a film must first identify every one of these messages from a list of messages available on the Usenet server to which he has access and these must be assembled to form the whole copy, obviously a long and laborious process. Newzbin set out to facilitate this process, and in doing so developed a 'lucrative business'. A premium member of Newzbin, on payment of a fee, was given the ability to download the contents of files sourced by Newzbin. In particular, Newzbin indexed the contents of files and using about 250 editors identified all the individual messages which would comprise the content of a film or other binary work. It also produced an index, which listed so-called 'reports' by the name of the film or other work. The defendant claimed that this did not amount to copyright infringement since it merely indexed the contents of files and did not provide or upload any of files which would be found within Usenet. It also warned its editors that they 'may not do any act which would assist enable, incite or encourage any unlawful acts by any other person'. Similarly, the site carried a warning to users stating that, inter alia, it could only be used for lawful purposes. But Kitchin J found that in neither case had the defendant sought to enforce these warnings. Nor did the judge believe the defendant's assertion that it had no knowledge of infringing material being made available through its website, or that it would remove information relating to infringing material if it knew about it, or, indeed, that it would remove any editor responsible for posting data relating to infringing material and any member using Newzbin for the purpose of accessing such material. Rather Kitchin J took the view that the defendant had been aware for some years that the vast majority of films in the Movies category of Newzbin were likely to be protected by copyright, and that members of Newzbin who used its facilities to download those materials, including the claimants' films, were infringing copyright. Nor did the defendant take what would have been relative easy steps to filter this content. In relation to whether Newzbin had authorised infringement, Kitchin J took the meaning of authorization from the *Amstrad* case. He held that an allegation of authorisation by supply (as in this case) would depend upon all the surrounding circumstances, including the nature of the relationship between the alleged authoriser and the primary infringer, whether the equipment or other material supplied constituted the means used to infringe, whether it was inevitable it would be used to infringe, the degree of control which the supplier retained and whether he had taken any steps to prevent infringement. In this case, he held that Newzbin had authorised the infringement. He was satisfied that a reasonable member of Newzbin would deduce from the defendant's activities that it purported to possess the authority to grant any required permission to copy any film from the Movies category and that the defendant had sanctioned, approved and countenanced the copying of the claimants' films. More recently, a number of film companies obtained an injunction against British Telecom, an ISP, which will force it to block or impede access for its subscribers to the Newzbin site (*Twentieth Century Fox Film v British Telecommunications plc* (2011)). The injunction was obtained under s 97A CDPA 1988. This section, and others which relate to the circumvention of technological measures were introduced by Copyright and Related Rights Regulations 2003. These will be considered in the section on 'Copyright and the new technology' (para **2.93** et seq).

The restricted acts applied to copyright works (CDPA 1988, ss 16–21)

2.61 Different types of copyright work may be infringed in different ways. Examined below will be infringement by:

- copying (s 17);
- issuing copies to the public (s 18);
- performing, playing or showing a work in public (s 19);
- communicating to the public (s 20);
- making an adaptation (s 21).

Copying

2.62 Every description of copyright work may be infringed by unauthorised copying. What constitutes copying may differ, depending upon the type of work in question. Copying in relation to literary, dramatic and musical or artistic works means reproducing the work (or, of course, any substantial part of it) in any material form, including storing the work in any medium by electronic means. A photograph of a painting may infringe, and so may storing a literary, artistic or musical work in a computer memory. Copying of artistic works includes the making of a three-dimensional copy of a two-dimensional work and the making of a two-dimensional copy of a three-dimensional work. A photograph of a statue may infringe (subject to any fair dealing provision, see para **2.73** et seq), and so may the making of a statue from a drawing. Unauthorised copies of Popeye, in the shape of brooches, were held to be an indirect infringement of the Popeye cartoon drawings (*King Features Syndicate Inc v Kleeman Ltd* (1941)). An important exception is the making of an article or the copying of an article from a design document or model recording anything other than an artistic work (for example, an exhaust pipe for a motor vehicle; s 51(1)). This exception is discussed in Chapter 7 on Industrial Design. It is also not an infringement to produce a three-dimensional work from a set of instructions. In *Foley (Brigid) Ltd v Ellott* (1982), a garment made from a knitting pattern was held not to infringe the pattern, because it was not a reproduction of the work.

Issuing copies to the public and the rental right (CDPA 1988, s 18)

2.63 Every variety of copyright work is protected by the right of the copyright owner to issue copies of his work to the public for the first time. This is often called the 'distribution right'. Put generally, this right is exhausted if authorised copies are put on the market in the EEA. There are also lending and rental rights in literary, dramatic and musical works, most artistic works, as well as sound recordings and films. These rights enable the copyright owner to profit from the circulation of rental copies (for example, DVDs) beyond their first issue to the public, and to benefit from the distribution of works made available by public libraries (s 18A). They derive from the Directive on Rental, Lending and Neighbouring Rights (EC) 2006/115, which was implemented by the Copyright and Related Rights Regulations 1996.

Performing, playing or showing a work in public (CDPA 1988, s 19)

2.64 Literary, dramatic or musical works (but not artistic works) are infringed by their performance in public. Performances include lectures, addresses, speeches and sermons. Performance may be by any mode of visual or acoustic presentation, including the playing of a sound recording, or the showing of a film, broadcast or cable programme. Where the copyright is infringed by the work being performed, played or shown in public by means of audio-visual apparatus, the person who sends the images or sounds or who performs the work is not responsible for the infringement. It is the person who is in charge of the equipment who infringes (s 19). In addition, the Copyright and Related Rights Regulations 2003 (SI 2003/2498) have introduced a 'making available right' for performers. A performer's rights are infringed by a person who, without his consent, makes available to the public a recording of the whole or any substantial part of a qualifying performance by electronic transmission in such a way that members of the public may access the recording from a place and at a time individually chosen by them (CDPA 1988, s 182).

Public performances

2.65 What constitutes a public performance is determined by case law, and is widely defined. What have been termed quasi-domestic situations (such as a performance to a small number of doctors and nurses at Guy's Hospital) are largely excepted (*Duck v Bates* (1884)). The court is usually more concerned with the character of the audience (are they part of the likely paying customers for the copyright work at issue?) than with the context in which the performance takes place. So performances in clubs, shops and a factory (which relayed the radio show 'Music While You Work' to its luckless employees in order 'to raise productivity') have all been held to be in public (for the latter, see *Turner Electrical Instruments Ltd v Performing Right Society Ltd* (1943); see also Advocate General's opinion in *FAPL v QCL* (2011)).

Communication right (CDPA 1988, s 20)

2.66 The communication right was introduced by the Copyright and Related Rights Regulations 2003. The communication to the public of the work is an act restricted by the copyright in a literary, dramatic, musical or artistic work, a sound recording or film, or a broadcast. Its purpose is to ensure that the copyright owner will have the exclusive right to control the broadcasting of a work communicated to the public by electronic transmission and in such a way that members of the public may access it from a place and at a time individually chosen by them. For the infringement of the communication right, the relevant public will not be present at the place where the communication originates. This right is of particular relevance to works distributed via the internet. There is a limited exception to copyright infringement in relation to broadcasts, which applies to the showing or playing in public of a broadcast to an audience who have not paid for admission (CDPA 1988, s 72). An example would be a television in a public house or a radio broadcast in a shop. This exception was recently considered by the Court of

Justice in *FAPL v QCCL* (2011). According to the Court, 'communication to the public' covers transmission of broadcast works (in this case a football match) to the customers present in a public house.

Making an adaptation (CDPA 1988, s 21)

2.67 This restricted act relates only to literary, dramatic and musical works. Adaptation means a translation of the work, a dramatic work which is converted into a non-dramatic work or the reverse, a version of the work conveyed by pictures (in essence, a strip cartoon) or the arrangement or transcription of a musical work. An adaptation of a computer program means an arrangement or altered version of the program or a translation, which includes a version of the program which is converted into or out of computer language or code or into a different computer language or code, otherwise than incidentally in the course of running the program. Adaptation thus includes a number of acts already considered in relation to copying in general, such as turning a novel into a screenplay. It must relate to a substantial part of the copyright work to infringe. An unauthorised 'study-note' version of Shaw's play *St Joan*, a detailed scene-by-scene summary, was an adaptation, and not a synopsis. It reproduced a substantial part of the play and was infringing. A brief description of the play would not have infringed (*Sillitoe v McGraw-Hill Book Co (UK) Ltd* (1983)). It is, of course, possible for copyright to subsist both in the adaptation and in the original work, although the copyright in the former cannot be exploited without the licence of the owner of the copyright in the latter (*Redwood Music Ltd v Chappell & Co Ltd* (1982) (see para **2.19**)).

What is proof of copying?

2.68 To summarise: in order to find infringement, there must be copying of a substantial part of the copyright work. There must also be a causal connection between the copyright work and the infringing work. It is a question of fact whether the degree of similarity is sufficient to warrant the inference that there is a causal connection between the two works. In *Designers Guild Ltd v Russell Williams (Textiles) Ltd (No 2)* (2000), Collins J in the High Court based his finding of copying largely on the similarity between the two fabric designs. As was noted by Lords Bingham and Scott, it would have been surprising, under these circumstances, if he had not also found that the defendants had copied a substantial part of the claimant's design. The causal connection, itself, may be unconscious or indirect. A substantial degree of objective similarity, together with proof of access to the original work, is prima facie evidence of copying (*Francis, Day and Hunter Ltd v Bron* (1963)). The evidential burden may then shift to the defendant to show that his work was not copied.

Secondary infringement (CDPA 1988, ss 22–27)

2.69 Secondary infringement is concerned with dealing in infringing copies or providing the means for their manufacture. It includes possessing, selling, exhibiting or distributing infringing copies, and importing infringing copies into the UK. An article is an infringing copy if its making constituted an infringement of the copyright of the work in question or if it has been or is proposed to be imported into the UK and its making in the UK would have constituted an infringement of the copyright of the work in question, or a breach of an exclusive licence agreement relating to the work. A computer program which has previously been sold in any EEA member state, by or with the consent of the copyright owner, is not an infringing copy for the purposes of the CDPA 1988.

2.70 Secondary infringement differs from primary infringement in that it is necessary to show that the alleged infringer knows or has reason to believe that he is dealing with an infringing copy. This is an objective test. 'Reason to believe' means a knowledge of the facts from which a reasonable man would arrive at the relevant belief (*LA Gear Inc v Hi-Tec Sport plc* (1992); *Linpac Mouldings Ltd v Eagleton Direct Export Ltd* (1994)). It is no excuse for the defendant, who persists in dealing in the articles, to claim that his legal advisers had wrongly assured him that the articles were not infringing, once he has notice of the facts upon which the claim is based (*Sillitoe v McGraw-Hill Book Co (UK) Ltd* (1983)). On the other hand, he should be allowed sufficient time to investigate the facts in order to acquire the reasonable belief (*LA Gear*). The Copyright and Related Rights Regulations 2003 have introduced new provisions to deal with infringement and internet service providers. These are examined at para **2.109** et seq.

Permitted acts

2.71 Section 28 of the CDPA 1988 sets out a number of permitted acts in relation to copyright works. These cover circumstances in which it is possible to make use of a copyright work, or a substantial part of it, without infringing copyright. The aim of the permitted acts is to set the conditions in which a public interest in using the copyright works overrides the private interests of the copyright owner. Undoubtedly, the most important permitted acts are fair dealing for the purpose of research and private study, and fair dealing for the purpose of criticism, review and news reporting. The recent independent Hargreaves Review commissioned by the government to look at intellectual property and economic growth recommended a number of additions to the permitted acts, including introducing a limited private copying exception, which would allow consumers to format shift legitimately purchased content, for example music from a CD to an MP3 player, and an exception to copyright for the purpose of caricature, parody or pastiche. In July 2011, the Government announced that it planned to implement exceptions to copyright infringement for private copying and format shifting as well as for parody. Interestingly, in the United States, the Supreme Court has long recognised a fair use exception for parody, even if the parodic work has a commercial value of its own (*Campell v Acuff-Rose Music Inc* (510 US 578 (1994)).

Making temporary copies (CDPA 1988, s 28A)

2.72 This permitted act was introduced by the Copyright and Related Rights Regulations 2003, and is intended to protect 'browsing' and 'caching' on the internet. Copyright in a literary work, other than a computer program or a database, or in a dramatic, musical or artistic work, the typographical arrangement of a published edition, a sound recording or a film, is not infringed by the making of a temporary copy which is transient or incidental, which is an integral and essential part of a technological process, and the sole purpose of which is to enable a transmission of the work in a network between third parties by an intermediary or a lawful user of the work. This exception was considered in *Infopaq*. There the Court of Justice held that the conditions set out above are cumulative and should be interpreted strictly. It went on to hold that an act is transient when its duration is limited to that which is necessary to complete the technological process in question, where the process is automated and deletion will occur automatically once the process has come to an end. Furthermore, this exception will only apply if the temporary copy has no independent economic significance. The question of 'independent economic significance' was considered by Advocate General Kokott in *FAPL v QCL* (2011), which concerned the satellite transmission of football matches. The AG took the view that transient copies of a work created on a television screen which is linked to a decoder box do have independent economic significance, whereas transient copies created in a decoder's memory do not.

Fair dealing

2.73 According to Lord Denning MR in *Hubbard v Vosper* (1972), what constitutes fair dealing is 'impossible to define'. Nonetheless, a number of guidelines have emerged in the case law. The first concerns the amount of the work taken. The CDPA 1988 does not specify how much copyright material may be reproduced without falling outside the definition of fair dealing (although there are some specific rules for librarians). However, the amount should be commensurate with the purpose for which it is taken. This is a matter of impression or degree. It might justify the reproduction of the whole work, for example, an epitaph on a tombstone, or a large part of it (*Hubbard*, per Megaw LJ). In *Fraser-Woodward Ltd v British Broadcasting Corpn* (2005), the BBC broadcast a programme, 'Tabloid Tales', which was intended to be critical of celebrity journalism. To illustrate this critique, the programme used a number of photographs of Victoria Beckham, wife of the footballer David Beckham. Although apparently candid shots, according to the programme they had actually been posed. The photographer sued for copyright infringement and the broadcaster raised the defence of fair use for the purpose of criticism and review. In the course of his judgment in favour of the defendant, Mann J held that there had not been an excessive use of the works. Each photograph had been shown only for a few seconds. And although the entire photograph was reproduced, Mann J noted that any legitimate use of a photograph for the purposes of criticism and review was likely to entail the reproduction of a large part of the work.

Fair dealing and unpublished works

2.74 It is generally held not to be fair dealing for an unpublished work to be the subject of public criticism or review (*British Oxygen Co Ltd v Liquid Air Ltd* (1925); *Hyde Park Residence Ltd v Yelland* (2000)). However, the courts have also been willing to countenance exceptions. In *Hubbard*, Lord Denning gave the example of a company shareholder circular, which may be of general interest and therefore legitimate for the press to criticise. In *Hubbard*, itself, the Court of Appeal accepted that it was fair dealing for the defendant, a disenchanted member of the Church of Scientology, publicly to circulate bulletins sent by the church to its members, because the latter constituted a 'wide circle'. If a work is unpublished, but it has been 'leaked' by an unidentified source or obtained in breach of confidence, this will increase the likelihood of the court seeing the dealing as unfair (*Beloff v Pressdram Ltd* (1973)). In *Associated Newspapers Ltd v HRH Prince of Wales* (2006), the *Mail on Sunday* published extracts from the Prince of Wales' private diaries which described his controversial views of an official visit to Hong Kong. The Prince alleged that publication was both a breach of confidence and copyright infringement. The High Court and the Court of Appeal found for the Prince on both counts. In its defence to copyright infringement, the newspaper argued that publication was fair dealing both for the purposes of reporting current events and for criticism and review (see below paras **2.76** and **2.77**). In both the High Court and the Court of Appeal, it was held that since the diaries had been obtained in breach of confidence, it could not be argued that publication constituted fair dealing. Finally, a risk to the commercial value of the copyright work may demonstrate that the dealing is not fair, but this is not necessarily the case. It is a question of balance. In *Fraser-Woodward*, Mann J held that the use of the photographs was so fleeting it would not prejudice their value for later use. Whereas, in *Ashdown v Telegraph Group Ltd* (2001), where the newspaper reproduced extracts from a politician's unpublished memorandum, the dealing was held to be unfair in part because it was done for commercial motives and would compete with the author's own expectations of profiting from the memorandum's publication.

Research and private study (CDPA 1988, s 29)

2.75 This section has been amended by the Copyright and Related Rights Regulations 2003. It applies to literary, dramatic, musical and artistic works. Fair dealing with these descriptions of works does not infringe copyright if it is for the purposes of research and private study. Following the implementation of the Regulations, the exception will only apply if the research is for non-commercial purposes, and a sufficient acknowledgement of the copyright source is given (where practicable). Fair dealing for private study does not infringe copyright (CDPA 1988, s 29(1C)). Without such a provision, academic research would, of course, be severely hampered. Even before the recent amendments, it was not fair dealing to reproduce a copyright work for commercial purposes, even if one aim of the commercial enterprise was to facilitate private study for others, as might be the case with study notes for a play which reproduce a substantial part of the original work (see *Sillitoe v McGraw-Hill Book Co (UK) Ltd* (1983)). There are also a number of permitted acts in relation to computer programs (ss 50A, 50BA) (see para **2.107**).

Criticism and review (CDPA 1988, s 30)

2.76 This section applies to all copyright works, including a performance of a work. Fair dealing with a work for the purposes of criticism and review will not infringe copyright, provided it is accompanied by a sufficient acknowledgement, that is, the title and the author (not the owner) of the work. In addition, following the implementation of the Copyright and Related Rights Regulations 2003, the work must also have been made available to the public. A work has been made available to the public, if it has been made available by any means. But a work has not been made available to the public, if its availability is the result of an unauthorised act (s 30(1A)). Criticism may be not just of the work itself, but also of its underlying philosophy, so that in *Hubbard v Vosper* (1972), a disenchanted Scientologist might reproduce large chunks of the writings of its founder, L Ron Hubbard, in a book criticising the movement. The criteria for raising this defence should be interpreted liberally. These were discussed in *Pro Sieben Media AG v Carlton UK Television Ltd* (1999). Carlton broadcast a documentary, 'Selling Babies', intended to be a critique of cheque-book journalism. The programme featured the example of Mandy Allwood, then pregnant with eight children, who had sold exclusive rights to an interview to the claimant, a German television company. The interview was included in a news report, 'TAFF', which could be received in the UK. The Carlton documentary featured a 30-second excerpt from the interview. The claimant sued and the defendant claimed fair dealing for the purposes of criticism and review and reporting current events. The claimant succeeded in the High Court, but the decision was overturned on appeal. Walker LJ held that, in considering fair dealing for criticism and review, the test of fair dealing was an objective one, although the intentions of the user were still 'highly relevant'. Nonetheless, a sincere but misguided belief by a journalist that use was for criticism and review was not enough to support the defence. Walker LJ went on to say that criticism and review (and reporting current events) are of wide and indefinite scope. Criticism can be not just of style but also of a work's social and moral implications. It can be strongly expressed, even unbalanced. But in deciding whether the defence had been made out, the focus should be on the likely impact on the audience. Based on this criterion, the Carlton programme was made for the purpose of criticising cheque-book journalism, and the treatment of Allwood's story in particular (see also *Fraser-Woodward Ltd v British Broadcasting Corpn* (2005)).

News reporting (CDPA 1988, s 30(2))

2.77 Fair dealing with any sort of work (other than a photograph) for the purpose of reporting current events does not infringe copyright, provided it is accompanied by a sufficient acknowledgement (although this is not necessary for sound recordings, films or broadcasts where it is impractical to do so), and provided it has been made available to the public, but not through an unauthorised act (see for example, *Associated Newspapers Ltd v HRH Prince of Wales* (2006)). It was said by North J in *Walter v Steinkopff* (1892) that there is no copyright in the news, but only in the form in which it is expressed. Certainly, it has been widely accepted by the courts that newspapers and journals will pick up stories from each other, and rewrite them. But North J's maxim was perhaps most appropriate in the days of print journalism. Since the CDPA 1988, fair dealing has also applied to broadcasts, as well as more traditional copyright works. When BSkyB showed excerpts of BBC live broadcasts of the 1990 World Cup finals, there was, of course, no question of changing the form of the presentation–hence the importance of the fair dealing defence (*BBC v British Satellite Broadcasting Ltd* (1992)). Conflict has also arisen over newsworthy interviews, such as with Lady Ogilvy, a royal single mother, where again much would be lost if the exact words were not reproduced (*Express Newspapers plc v News (UK) Ltd* (1990)). It may even be necessary to refer to news which is not current in order to report on current events, and this, too, can be fair dealing (*Associated Newspapers plc v News Group Newspapers Ltd* (1986)). *Pro Sieben Media AG v Carlton UK Television Ltd* (1999) also looked at fair dealing for the purpose of news and current events. Walker LJ took the view that the criteria for judging this defence should be interpreted liberally, to include media coverage of the pregnancy and the sale of the interview. These were current events of real interest to the public, and, as with fair dealing for the purpose of criticism and review, it was the impact on the audience which was key to deciding if the defence succeeded. This generous approach was confirmed in *Ashdown v Telegraph Group Ltd* (2001) where the Court of Appeal defined 'current events' to include events of 'current interest' to the public, even if they had occurred some time in the past.

2.78 The criteria for establishing a defence of fair dealing for the purpose of reporting current events was summarised by the Court of Appeal in *Hyde Park Residence Ltd v Yelland* (2000). *Hyde Park* concerned a security video of Princess Diana and Dodi Fayed. The video, filmed at the Villa Windsor in Paris, the day before the couple were killed, was made under the responsibility of the claimant company, controlled by Dodi Fayed's father, Mr Al Fayed. A year later, stills from the video, which had been supplied without authority by M, an employee of the claimant, were published in *The Sun* newspaper. *The Sun* claimed that the purpose of publication was to prove that Mr Al Fayed had misrepresented both the length of the couple's visit and the claim that they were engaged. In a copyright action in the High Court, Jacob J accepted that the use was covered by both fair dealing and a public interest defence. In allowing the claimant's appeal, Aldous LJ concurred with the judgment in *Pro Sieben Media AG v Carlton UK Television Ltd* (1999) that it is appropriate to take into account the motives of the alleged infringer, the extent and purpose of the use, and whether the extent was necessary for the purpose of reporting current events. Furthermore, if the work had not been published or circulated to the public, that was also an important indication that the dealing was not fair. It followed that the court must judge fair dealing by the objective standard of whether a fair-minded and honest person would have dealt with the copyright work in the manner, for example, of the defendant, for the purposes of reporting current events. In this case, Aldous LJ believed that to view *The Sun*'s publication of the photographs as fair dealing would be to 'honour dishonour', not least because the information about the length of the stay at the villa was neither relevant to whether the couple were engaged, nor did its circulation require the publication of the stills. The fair dealing defence failed. The Court of Appeal then went on to consider the public interest defence.

Public interest

2.79 The public interest defence is recognised by CDPA 1988, s 171(3). A public interest defence was first developed in respect of breach of confidence, and gives an exception to the right of the confider to insist on confidence, if the breach is to disclose an iniquity (*Initial Services Ltd v Putterill* (1967); for confidential information, see para **3.50** et seq). In *Lion Laboratories Ltd v Evans* (1985), the Court of Appeal held the public interest defence might also be applied to claims of copyright infringement.

The legal basis for a public interest defence

2.80 In *A-G v Guardian Newspapers* (1988), the 'Spycatcher' case (which is discussed at length at para **3.55** et seq), Lords Griffiths and Jauncey suggested that it would be right to withhold copyright protection from Peter Wright's memoirs because publication of the memoirs of a former member of MI5 was against the public interest. This was not to say that there was no copyright in the work, but rather that it was against the public interest to permit it to be enforced. The House of Lord's opinion in Spycatcher suggests that the basis for a public interest defence in an action for copyright infringement is not the same as for a breach of confidence action. The Court of Appeal made this plain in *Hyde Park Residence Ltd v Yelland* (2000). It is not that the CDPA 1988 gives courts the power to enable an infringer to use another's copyright in the public interest. It does not. Rather, the courts have an inherent jurisdiction to refuse to enforce an action for copyright infringement where enforcement would offend against the public interest, or as was put by Aldous LJ, against the 'policy of the law'.

The necessary circumstances for a public interest defence

2.81 In *Hyde Park Residence Ltd v Yelland* (2000), Aldous LJ said it was impossible to define the circumstances in which a court would be entitled to use its inherent jurisdiction. However, such circumstances might arise if the work was immoral, scandalous or contrary to family life, or was injurious to public life, public health and safety or the administration of justice, or incited or encouraged others to act in such a way. In the *Hyde Park Residence* case, any relevant information could have been given to the public without infringing copyright in the stills and the public interest defence failed. It has been suggested that the Court of Appeal's decision narrows the scope of the public interest defence in relation to copyright infringement, and arose, perhaps, from a desire to curb the perceived excesses of the tabloid press. Indeed, in *Ashdown v Telegraph Group Ltd* (2001), Lord Phillips MR took the view that Aldous LJ had defined the public interest defence too narrowly by confining its application to circumstances where there had been serious wrongdoing on the part of the claimant. Instead, the Master of the Rolls held that the circumstances where public interest may override copyright 'are not capable of precise categorisation or definition'. Indeed, he took the view that, since the passage of the Human Rights Act 1998, the public interest in the right of freedom of expression might, albeit in rare cases, 'trump' the rights conferred by the CDPA 1988. In such cases a public interest defence was appropriate.

The Human Rights Act 1998 and freedom of expression

2.82 The European Convention on Human Rights was incorporated into UK law by the Human Rights Act 1998. Article 10 of the ECHR guarantees the right to freedom of expression: 'Everyone has the right to freedom of expression. This right shall include freedom to hold opinions and to receive and impart ideas without interference by public authority and regardless of frontiers.' On the other hand, ECHR, art 1 also acknowledges 'the right of every person to peaceful enjoyment of his possessions'. 'Possessions' have been understood to include copyright (*Ashdown v Telegraph Group Ltd* (2001)). The question then arises of whether and, if so, at what point, the right to freedom of expression will 'trump' copyright. One way of approaching the question would be to argue that internal safeguards built into the CDPA 1988 ensure that there need be no conflict between copyright and freedom of expression. These safeguards include the idea/expression dichotomy, the fair dealing defence and the public interest defence. However, others have argued that the passage of the HRA 1998 does, indeed, introduce an 'external' conflict between copyright protection and the rights guaranteed by the ECHR, which cannot be satisfied merely by the application of copyright law (Birnhack, 'Acknowledging the Conflict between Copyright Law and Freedom of Expression under the Human Rights Act' [2003] *Entertainment Law Review* 24).

The conflict between freedom of expression and copyright

2.83 The potential for conflict between freedom of expression and copyright protection was illustrated in *Ashdown v Telegraph Group Ltd* (2001). The claimant, Mr Paddy Ashdown, had been a Member of Parliament and leader of the Liberal Democratic Party. In 1997, he attended a meeting with the Prime Minister and afterwards dictated a minute of its contents. Of the two copies made, one remained with the claimant and the other, after being read by a small number of people, was shredded. It was the claimant's contention that the minute was confidential. The defendant newspaper obtained a copy of the minute, and in 1999 published three articles which contained verbatim quotations amounting to about 20 per cent of the minute. The claimant sued for copyright infringement. There was agreement that the minute was a copyright work and that the defendant had copied a substantial part of it. In its defence, the newspaper claimed fair dealing under s 30 and the public interest defence under s 171(3) of the CDPA 1988, as well as the right to freedom of expression guaranteed under ECHR, art 10. The newspaper argued that, when considering whether an actionable breach of copyright had occurred or what were the appropriate remedies in the event of a breach, the court must have regard to the right of freedom of expression conferred by art 10. In doing so, the court had to take account of the individual facts of each case to see whether a restriction of freedom of expression pursuant to the law of copyright could be justified. In the High Court, Sir Andrew Morritt V-C took what might be described as the 'internal' approach to any apparent conflict between copyright and freedom of expression. He held that the CDPA 1988 already struck the appropriate balance between the rights of copyright owners and the right to freedom of expression, and that it was not necessary to examine the facts further in the light of art 10. He then went on to apply the provisions of the CDPA and found that the newspaper had infringed the claimant's copyright. He also rejected both the fair dealing and public interest defences. The defendant appealed. By contrast, in the Court of Appeal, Lord Phillips MR acknowledged that there was a potential for conflict between copyright law and freedom of expression. In particular, he pointed out that copyright is 'antithetical' to freedom of expression, since it prevents all save the copyright owner from expressing information in the form of the literary work protected by copyright. In most cases no problem arose, because it was usually possible to publish the ideas and information conveyed in the literary work, although not in the same words. However, it was also important that citizens should be free to express ideas and convey information in the form of words of their choice. He concluded that, while freedom of expression does not confer the freedom routinely to use a form of expression devised by someone else, there were circumstances when the freedom to do so is important. These circumstances might be rare, but, when they did occur, freedom of expression would come into conflict with copyright, despite the exceptions found in the Act. In these circumstances, the court should apply the CDPA 1988 in a way that accommodates freedom of expression. The correct response would be to deny the claimant an injunction, although in principle the claimant should be indemnified for any loss, since 'freedom of expression should not normally carry with it the right to make free use of another's work'.

Applying the law in *Ashdown*

2.84 As we have seen, the Court of Appeal held that the public interest defence should be given a broad interpretation in the light of ECHR, art 10. Furthermore, the Court of Appeal agreed with the High Court, following *Pro Sieben Media AG v*

Carlton UK Television Ltd (1999), that it was possible to raise the exception for reporting current events, since the articles dealt with matters of current interest even though they were not current in time. Conversely, the exception for criticism and review did not apply, because the articles were neither criticising nor reviewing the copyright work (that is, the minute), but rather the actions of those involved. The Court of Appeal then considered whether there had been fair dealing by the defendant in relation to the current events exception. It suggested that it was necessary, when balancing the public interest in freedom of expression against the interests of copyright owners, to consider the principles which the courts had developed relating to fair dealing before the passage of the HRA 1998, always remembering that considerations of public interest were paramount. Here, it was relevant that the articles written by the newspaper would be in commercial competition with the claimant's future publication of the minute, since both were in the claimant's own words. It was also relevant that the claimant's work was unpublished and had been obtained in breach of confidence. Finally, the amount and importance of the work taken was also a serious consideration. Here, a substantial portion of the minute and, indeed, its most important elements had been taken. There had not been fair dealing. The court then turned to the impact of the HRA 1998 on the public interest defence. It asked whether the public interest in freedom of expression outweighed conventional standards for judging fair dealing. It held that the defendant may have been entitled to make some quotation from the minute in order to show that it had a copy and, thus, was able to give an authentic account of the meeting. But here the defendant had gone too far. It chose quotations, not for journalistic reasons, but in furtherance of its commercial interests, because these quotes would appeal to readers. This was not fair dealing, and the appeal was dismissed.

Moral rights (CDPA 1988, ss 77–89)

2.85   In the UK, it is fair to say that copyright law is primarily concerned with protecting the rights of the owner (not always the creator) to exploit a work economically. Moral rights recognise that the creator of a work also has a continuing interest in ensuring that his work is treated with respect, even if, by transferring copyright to another, he may no longer have an economic interest in it. Unlike copyright, moral rights are personal to the author of a work and may only transfer on death. They are quite distinct from copyright, and their breach leads to an action for breach of statutory duty, and not for infringement. There are four moral rights recognised by the CDPA 1988. The first is the right to be identified as the author of a literary, dramatic, musical or artistic work, or the director of a film (ss 77–79). This is sometimes called the 'paternity right'. The second applies to the same description of works, and is the right to object to derogatory treatment of the work, where derogatory treatment amounts to distortion or mutilation of the work, or is otherwise prejudicial to the honour or reputation of the author or director (ss 80–83). This is the so-called 'right of integrity'. The third also applies to the same description of works, and is the right against false attribution (s 84). The fourth is the right to privacy of photographs and films, and belongs to a person who has commissioned such a work for private or domestic purposes (s 85). It gives the commissioner the right not to have the work issued to the public, exhibited or shown in public, or broadcast. This right might prevent tabloid newspapers from publishing, say, a wedding photograph of an individual who later becomes famous. But it would have no effect on the printing of controversial paparazzi photographs of celebrities in perhaps even more private moments.

The weakness of moral rights

2.86 Moral rights have been criticised for leaning too far in the direction of protecting the economic interests of the copyright owner where these may conflict with the moral rights of the creator. The paternity right must be specifically asserted by the author or director to have effect. All of these rights may be waived by consent. Understandably, many authors are ignorant of their moral rights, or have little bargaining strength if the copyright owner asks for them to be waived (Waisman, 'What is there not to waive? On the prohibition against relinquishing the moral right to integrity' [2010] *Intellectual Property Quarterly* 225). Moral rights may be expensive to enforce, and the outcome of such an action may be uncertain. For the holder of moral rights in a copyright work, it may still be easier to seek redress through an action for passing off or defamation (see para **4.31** for an instance where the claimant was successful in passing off rather than for breach of moral rights (see *Clark v Associated Newspapers Ltd* (1998)). The CDPA 1988 also sets out numerous and important exceptions where moral rights do not apply. For instance, in the case of paternity and integrity rights, they do not apply where the works are made for the reporting of current events or for publication in newspapers, magazines or periodicals.

Dealing with copyright (CDPA 1988, ss 90–93)

2.87 Like other forms of property, copyright is transmissible by assignment, testamentary disposition or by operation of the law as personal or moveable property (s 90(1)). Assignments must be in writing (s 90(3)). Exclusive licences must also be in writing (s 92). Assignments or other transmissions of copyright may be partial, for example, limiting what the assignee may do with the copyright work, or the territory in which he may do it. Future, or prospective, copyrights may also be assigned (s 91). Feature films are frequently financed by the production company selling off a host of different rights before the films are even made. One distribution company may buy rights to exhibit the proposed film on terrestrial television in the Benelux countries, another the rights to theatrical exhibition in North America, a third the rights to show the film on aeroplanes and so on. Each licensee will be gambling, of course, that the film will be a success. Remember, however, that moral rights cannot be assigned, because of their personal nature (see para **2.85**).

Remedies

2.88 Infringement of copyright is both a civil and, in certain cases only, a criminal wrong. Civil actions may be brought in both the High Court, the Patents County Court and the County Court. The copyright owner or an exclusive licensee may sue for copyright infringement, although under certain circumstances the exclusive licensee may have to join the copyright owner to the action, and his damages may be limited to reflect the extent of his exclusive rights under the licence (ss 101–102).

Civil remedies

2.89 Claimants may seek interim injunctions and, at trial, damages or an account of profits. The CDPA 1988 specifies that damages are not available if the defendant did not know, or had no reason to believe, that copyright subsisted in the work. However, once copying is proved, this is unlikely to become an issue. On the other hand, the court may, unless the claimant has opted for an account of profits as the main remedy, order additional damages if the infringement is particularly flagrant and the benefit accruing to the defendant substantial (*Redrow Homes Ltd v Betts Bros plc* (1998)). The court may also order the delivery up of infringing copies, and articles specifically designed or adapted for making copies of a particular work (although in the latter case the person in possession must know or have reason to believe this was its purpose) (s 99). As with most cases involving intellectual property, the copyright owner will typically be as concerned with stopping dealings in infringing works as with collecting damages, and the interlocutory stage can be the most crucial period. Perhaps the most powerful, and controversial, weapon in his lawyer's armoury is the search order (formerly the Anton Piller order). The 1988 Act introduced the right of seizure (s 100), sometimes called a 'self-help search order'. In essence, this right allows an owner to seize, without a court order, infringing copies from public premises (but not the alleged infringer's own place of business), if the copy is exposed or otherwise available for sale or hire, and if he would be entitled to apply for a delivery-up order. This allows copyright owners to take speedy action where the dealings may be on a temporary basis. An obvious example might be traders selling pirated CDs outside rock concerts.

2.90 With respect to literary, dramatic, musical or artistic works, where a name purporting to be that of the author appears on copies of the published work or on the work when it was made, then the named person shall be presumed to be the author of the work (s 104). There is a similar provision in relation to films, sound recordings and computer programs (s 105). These presumptions do not apply in criminal proceedings. Lawyers should always alert their clients, who create copyright works, to these presumptions. Similarly, clients should also be encouraged to date and save all working papers. For instance, in the case of computer software, these might include flow-charts and earlier discarded programs, supporting the clients' claim, should his works be infringed, that they are original and of his own authorship.

Criminal offences (CDPA 1988, ss 107–111)

2.91 These may be brought either at the magistrates' court or the Crown Court (although the latter must be brought by the DPP). The primary purpose of the criminal sanctions is to protect copyright owners against commercial piracy of copyright works, such as DVDs and software. In recent years, internet piracy has also become an urgent problem for rights-holders (see para **2.101** et seq). The Copyright and Related Rights Regulations 2003 have broadened the definition of criminal offences to include infringement of a work by communicating it to the public, whether in the course of business or otherwise, to such an extent as to affect prejudicially the owner of the copyright, if the individual communicating the work knows or has reason to believe that, by doing so, he is infringing copyright in the work (s 107(2A)). It is also an offence to infringe a performer's 'making available right' with the requisite knowledge (s 198(1A)). The Copyright, etc and Trade Marks (Offences and Enforcement) Act 2002 has increased the penalty for dealing in materials infringing copyright, illicit recordings infringing performers' rights and unauthorised decoders to an unlimited fine and/or up to ten years in prison. The Act also increases police search and seizure powers and the powers of courts to order forfeiture of infringing goods. It rationalises the law by bringing these powers in line with those applicable to trade mark offences. It was noted during the passage of the Act that dealing in counterfeit goods may frequently involve both copyright and trade mark offences. There are also provisions in the CDPA 1988 for Customs and Excise to seize allegedly infringing goods upon their entry into the UK (s 111). Finally, the Copyright and Related Rights Regulations 2003 have introduced to the CDPA 1988 a number of offences relating to devices designed to circumvent technological measures to prevent copyright infringement. These are examined at para **2.104**.

Which jurisdiction?

2.92 The advantages of a civil action include the possibility of recovering damages and the speed at which pre-trial injunctive relief can be obtained. On the other hand, criminal prosecutions may involve no cost to the copyright owner and their resolution can be quicker than going to a full trial in a civil court. The threat of a criminal sanction may be an effective deterrent or negotiating counter with a recalcitrant infringer. Where copying is widespread within the industry, associations have grown up to help their members to combat copying. For instance, FAST (the Federation Against Software Theft) is an association of computer software suppliers, which takes civil action against infringers, and also co-ordinates action by trading standards officers and the police. Another is the Mechanical Copyright Protection Society, a collecting society for music publishers, which also brings criminal prosecutions. Organisations such as FAST will mount campaigns to raise public awareness of copyright infringement and its consequences, perhaps offering rewards to individuals who provide information leading to successful civil or criminal proceedings.

Copyright and the new technology

2.93 Two interrelated developments–the introduction of digital technology and the internet–have posed new challenges to traditional copyright protection. A host of new reproductive technologies have been introduced over the past century, for instance, sound recordings, film and videos. But their effects have all been accommodated to a greater or lesser extent within what is recognisably traditional copyright protection. It is widely accepted that the new reproductive technologies pose novel obstacles to a similar expansion of copyright. To understand why this is so, it is necessary to look briefly at their nature. The internet has been described as an 'end-to-end' technology. It has also been usefully described as having an 'architecture' characterised by three layers (Lessig, *The Future of Ideas* (2001)). The first layer is the 'physical' layer or network on which the internet applications (or software) operate. The second 'code' layer consists of the applications which are expressed in code (source code, object code) and embodied in software, which dictate how the internet functions. It is innovations in the code layer rather than the physical layer which have been key to the development of the internet. And, of course, code or software is the product of individuals and companies operating at the ends of the 'physical' network: hence the characterisation of the internet as 'end-to-end' technology. Finally, the third layer is the content layer. The content layer comprises the information which is 'placed' on the internet. Much of the content layer may consist of traditional copyright works: music, artistic or literary works, albeit expressed in a wholly different medium. Perhaps the most disruptive effect of the marriage of digital technology to the internet is that it has enabled private individuals to publish, reproduce and communicate copyright works to vast audiences without resorting to publishers, motion picture studios or record companies. Music-swapping networks, such as Kazaa and the now defunct Grokster, which operated peer-to-peer, exemplify both the enormous potential of this new technology to empower private individuals to distribute and access information, and the equally compelling threat that it poses to rights-holders who wish to protect their works from unauthorised use. The following section will look at the interaction between copyright law and the new technology, beginning with the protection afforded to software or code.

The protection of software

2.94 In order to understand the relationship between copyright and computer programs, it may be useful to set out, very generally, the basic technology and technical terms involved. A programmer writes a program in higher-level language, for example, BASIC, FORTRAN or COBOL. These languages are in human-readable form. This program is the source code. But computers work in binary code (a series of '0's and '1's and computer programs 'which tell the processor what to do' must be in binary form. A compiler, which is itself a computer program, converts the source code into binary code, which is machine-readable. This is the machine code or object code. Computers are programmed with a computer operating system. In order to carry out specific functions, an application program must be loaded into the computer, which tells the operating system what to do. Application programs may consist of a number of individual programs. Each program itself consists of a number of routines or sub-routines–in effect a set of instructions written in code–which the computer will execute. Usually, the programmer will begin by creating a flow-chart of the routines which will make up the program. He will then convert these routines into source code. Consumers of computer software will not normally have access to source code.

Software and the CDPA 1988

2.95 Computer programs and preparatory design material for computer programs, for example flow-charts, are defined as literary works (s 3(a) and (b)). The Software

Directive (Directive on the legal protection of computer programs 2009/24/EC, implemented by the Copyright (Computer Programs) Regulations (SI 1992/3233)) sought to harmonise EU copyright law in relation to computer programs. For instance, it is pursuant to the Directive that computer programs are specifically designated as literary works. However, like literary works, according to Art 1(2) of the Directive, only the expression of a computer program is protected, not the ideas and principles which underlie it. This has generally been interpreted by the courts to mean that programming languages, interfaces and the functionality of a program are not protected by copyright (see for example, *Navitaire Inc v easyJet Airline Co Ltd* (2004)). More recently, Arnold J has asked the Court of Justice to rule on how broadly the concept of a computer language should be interpreted (*SAS v WPL* (2010)) for the purposes of this exclusion and also the extent which interfaces are excluded from copyright protection. The Directive also gives a limited right to reverse engineering, in essence to decompile a computer program to achieve interoperability (s 50B). A computer-generated work is protected by copyright (see definition, s 178). Protection lasts for 50 years from when it was made and is owned by the person who 'arranged for its creation' (s 12(7); s 9(3)). However, it is important to remember that, like other 'literary' works, computer programs are frequently 'updated' or modified over time. This may create a fresh copyright in the modified program (*Ibcos Computers Ltd v Barclays Mercantile Highland Finance Ltd* (1994)).

Infringement

2.96 Like other literary works, a computer program is infringed by the taking of the whole or a substantial part of it. The CDPA 1988 also specifies that infringement by making an adaptation–in this case making an altered version or a translation–applies to computer programs (s 21(3)(ab)). A translation includes a version of the program in which it is converted into or out of a computer language or code, or into a different computer language or code otherwise than incidentally in the course of running the program (s 21(4)). The copying of computer programs is, of course, extremely easy, as the presence of pirated software in many British homes and businesses makes clear. Infringement may occur when the program is reproduced in any material form, including storage in any medium by electronic means, and this can include unlicensed storage on a memory stick or a magnetic hard drive or taking it out of storage (*Ocular Sciences Ltd v Aspect Vision Care Ltd* (1997)). The 1988 Act specifies that copying includes the making of copies which are transient or are incidental to some other use of the work (s 17(6)). As a result, merely running a program (which causes transient copies to be made in the RAM or temporary storage area of a computer) can constitute infringement. However, pursuant to the Software Directive, it is not an infringement for a lawful user of a copy of a computer program to make a back-up copy where it is necessary for use (s 50A).

Literal copying

2.97 Obviously, unlicensed copying of a computer program line-by-line, or disk-to-disk, will infringe, so long as a substantial part is taken. *Ibcos Computers Ltd v Barclays Mercantile Highland Finance Ltd* (1994 involved, inter alia, the copying of software, where the software constituted not just one but a suite of programs. Jacob J held that each individual program in the suite had copyright (and perhaps several, because each had been modified and updated), but also that the whole package, 'the program of all programs', had a separate copyright as an original compilation. The question of whether there was infringement then turned not just upon whether the defendant had copied literal pieces of code and the program structure within an individual program, which he had, but also whether he had taken the program structure and the design features as a whole, as these would be integral to the work as compilation. Again, the defendant was found to have infringed.

Non-literal copying

2.98 Non-literal copying occurs when what is copied is not the actual code (either source or object) of the program, but rather its function, structure or 'look and feel', for instance, the screen displays or menus. We have seen that art 1(2) of the Software Directive states that protection should not be given to the 'ideas and principles' which underlie a computer program. As usual, where literal copying is not at issue, the problem for the court is to decide whether what is copied is the idea behind the program or its expression. In *Navitaire v easyJet* (2004), the claimants had designed an online booking system ('OpenRes') for the defendant. The parties fell out, and the defendant developed its own online booking system ('eRes'), which was designed to have the same 'look and feel' as OpenRes. The defendants did not have access to the OpenRes source code, and the programs had a different architecture and language. There was no literal copying. Instead, the claimant alleged three areas of 'non-textual' copying of its software: its 'look and feel'; its user command structure; and certain display screens. The claimant succeeded only on the third claim. Pumfrey J found that the display screens, being constituted by complex codes which gave them a consistent appearance, qualified as artistic works and had been infringed. However, he did not find infringement in relation to the two other claims. He held that individual commands did not constitute copyright works, following the *de minimis* principle. Furthermore, the commands series were equivalent to a computer language, which was not protected under the Software Directive, rather than to a program, which was. Nor was the collection of commands protectable as a compilation as there was no author and no overall design to create a compilation. Turning to the 'look and feel' claim, the claimants alleged that the 'business logic' of OpenRes had been appropriated. The issue according to Pumfrey J was that, unlike traditional literary works, two completely different computer programs can produce an identical result. Furthermore, again unlike cases involving traditional literary works, the copyist in this case did not have access to the allegedly infringed work. In Pumfrey J's view what was being alleged was not 'non-textual' copying, but 'copying without access to the thing copied, directly or indirectly'. He identified the problems of establishing infringement in the present case as being 'a lack of substantiality' and 'the nature of the skill and labour to be protected'. The OpenRes program invited inputs, outputted results and created a record of passenger reservations, all of which were excluded from copyright protection. He concluded:

> What is left when the interface aspects of the case are disregarded is the business function of carrying out the transaction and creating the record, because none of the code was read or copied by the defendants. It is right that those responsible for OpenRes envisaged this as the end result for their program: but that is not relevant skill and labour. In my judgment this claim for non-textual copying should fail.

The approach to non-literal copying taken in *Navitaire* was approved by the Court of Appeal in *Nova Productions Ltd v Mazooma Games Ltd* (2007). The claimant produced computer games based on the game of pool, as did the defendant. In most respects the games were quite different, but there were some common features apart from their subject matter, including, for example, the ideas of a rotary controller and of synchronising the pulsing power meter with a power cue, which the claimant maintained had been copied by the defendant. As with *Navitaire*, in this case too the defendant had not had access to the claimant's code. In the Court of Appeal, Jacob LJ upheld the finding of the lower court that there had been no infringement because the defendant had copied the claimant's ideas and not their expression. In particular, he rejected the argument that software differs from other copyright works, because ideas are the 'building blocks' of a computer program. He noted, 'An idea consisting of a combination of ideas is still just an idea. That is as true for ideas in a computer program as for any other copyright work.'

The idea–expression dichotomy and software

2.99   More recently, in *SAS Institute v World Programming* (2010), Arnold J referred to the Court of Justice the question of where the line between idea and expression in software should be drawn. The claimant, SAS, developed analytical software known as the SAS System. This System, which is an extremely valuable asset, consists of an integrated set of programs which enable users to do a wide range of data programming, and especially statistical analysis. The System also enables users to run application programs (or scripts), which are written in SAS Language. The System can be extended by the use of additional components. Thousands of application programs have been produced using the SAS language. Before this dispute, the claimant's customers had to license the use of components in the System both to run their application programs and to create new ones. The defendant created World Programming System (WPS) to provide alternative software which enabled the execution of programs written in the SAS Language. WPS emulated the functionality of the SAS Components as much as possible, so that the applications programs of customers of SAS ran the same on both WPS and SAS System. WPL did not copy the source code. The claimant argued, inter alia, that its copyright had been infringed because: WPL copied its manuals for the SAS System; that in copying the manuals, when creating WPS, the defendant had indirectly copied the programs which made up the SAS Components; and that it copied the SAS manuals in producing its own documentation. On the last point, which involved literal copying of a literary work, Arnold J found infringement. However, in relation to the first two, he believed there had not been infringement, although he deferred a final decision until the matter had been considered by the Court of Justice. He accepted that copyright in a computer program might extend beyond protecting the source code, to protecting the design or the 'structure, sequence and organisation of a program'. But it was possible to produce a computer program with the same functionality as an existing program, which had a different design. In deciding what was to be protected by copyright, Arnold J held that one had to look at the nature of the skill and labour involved. Copyright in a computer program protects the skill, judgement and labour in devising the expression of the program, that is, its design and source code. Conversely, functionality fell on the wrong side of the line and would not be protected. Despite his own views, he nevertheless addressed the question to the Court of Justice as to whether and to what extent the functionality of a computer program attracts copyright protection.

Reverse engineering (CDPA 1988, s 50B), and observing, studying and testing software (s 50BA)

2.100 The decompilation (or reverse engineering) of software in order to achieve interoperability will not infringe copyright in the software. Interoperability means the ability of one computer program to interface with another program so that they may work together. However, decompilation may only be undertaken for the purpose of interoperability and for no other reason (*Mars UK Ltd v Teknowledge Ltd* (1999)). The Copyright and Related Rights Regulations 2003 have also introduced an exception to copyright infringement which covers the 'observing, studying and testing of computer programs' based on art 5(3) of the Copyright Directive. Under this provision, it is not an infringement for a lawful user of a copy of a computer program to observe, study or test the functioning of the program in order to determine the ideas and principles which underlie any element of the program if he does so while performing any of the acts of loading, displaying, running, transmitting or storing the program which he is entitled to do. Furthermore, these acts are permitted whether or not there is any agreement which purports to prohibit or restrict them (s 50BA; art. 9(1) Copyright Directive). In *SAS v WLP*, the claimant asserted that the defendant had breached its licensing terms when it purchased certain of SAS's manuals and used the information in them to create WLP. In the opinion of Arnold J, the license terms for the SAS manuals were null and void to the extent that they made it an infringement for the user to observe, study and test the manuals in order to determine the ideas and principles which underlay any element of the SAS System. Nonetheless, the question of whether art 5(3) entitled the defendant to carry out all the acts it had done, in relation to the manuals, was referred to the Court of Justice.

Software, copyright and the internet

2.101 It has already been suggested that the development of the internet has rested, not on radical changes to the physical networks on which it operates, but on the development of applications at its 'ends'. For some, it is precisely the nature of this 'end-to-end' technology which has allowed the internet to grow with such speed and in such an innovative fashion. They would argue that this has been the consequence of an unlimited number of individuals writing, distributing and applying code freely, and collaborating with others in so doing. Furthermore, these individuals apparently did not need the economic incentive to create, which is supposedly provided by copyright protection. A material outcome of this argument has been the growth of the Free Software and Open Code Software Movements. Each is dedicated to the idea that code should be made publicly available rather than be protected by copyright laws. For example, the Free Software Movement develops code and places it in the public domain. It can be used by anyone, with the proviso that they agree to the terms of the General Public License, which dictates that any improvements made to the software will be similarly placed in the public domain. The most prominent success of the Free Software Movement has been the development of the Linux operating platform, which is widely used including by major companies, such as IBM. Yet IBM and other companies have dedicated huge resources to the development of software, which has proved immensely popular with the public. They would argue that not only does copyright protection allow them to recoup their investment, but also that consumers of their software welcome the assurance that dealing with a named company provides. While there may be a strong argument that the collaborative production of software outside copyright protection has been a driving force behind the development of the internet, similar arguments are perhaps less persuasive when applied to the protection of its content. It is to the interrelation between copyright law and the content of the internet that this chapter now turns.

The internet and the protection of the content layer

2.102 It has already been noted that a characteristic of the new technology is that copying is frequently inexpensive, quick and easy, and indeed that the copied works are of high quality, as is the case with MP3 technology and DVDs. Second, much of this technology is interactive, allowing the consumer enormous leeway as to when and where to access the copyright works. Third, it operates across national boundaries. In the case of music search engines like Grokster, these characteristics are often combined, posing new and possibly intractable problems for rights-holders. The Information Society Directive was intended to update the EU copyright regime to reflect these new developments in reproductive technology. It allows Member States to ratify the WIPO Copyright Treaty and the Phonograms and Performance Treaty. In the USA, these same treaties were ratified by the 1998 Digital Millennium Copyright Act (DMCA).

The Information Society Directive

2.103 The Information Society Directive harmonises the basic rights relevant to the use of copyright material in the so-called 'information society', namely, the rights of reproduction (copying), distribution and communication to the public by electronic transmission, including digital broadcasting and online services. It also limits the scope of permitted exceptions to these rights and provides legal protection for anti-circumvention measures. Its stated purpose is to provide 'increased legal certainty' and 'a high level of protection of intellectual property', thus fostering 'substantial investment in creativity and innovation'. In order to implement the Directive, the UK has introduced a new communication right (see para **2.66**). The exceptions to copyright infringement are dealt with in art 5 of the Directive. There is a mandatory exception for temporary copying, for example, browsing and caching on the internet (s 28A; see para **2.72**). Article 5(2)–(4) lists a further 20 optional 'fair use' exceptions. The list is exhaustive. Among the more notable innovations is that reproduction for research is allowed only where its purpose is neither directly nor indirectly commercial (CDPA 1988, s 29; see para **2.75**). There is a similar narrowing of the exception for teaching and scientific research to non-commercial purposes. There are also exceptions, inter alia, for reporting of current events, criticism and review, all of which are currently recognised in UK copyright law.

Circumvention of technological measures (CDPA 1988, s 296ZA)

2.104 Perhaps the most controversial aspect of the Directive, and the one which contributed to its delayed implementation in the UK, is art 6 which deals with technological measures used by rights-holders to protect their works against copyright infringement and unauthorised use. According to the Directive, Member States must provide adequate legal protection against circumvention of effective technological measures. The Copyright and Related Rights Regulations 2003 have introduced a series of provisions to implement this aspect of the Directive. Section 296ZA applies where effective technological measures have been applied to a copyright work other than a computer program, and a person (B) does anything which circumvents these measures knowing, or with reasonable grounds to know, that he is pursuing this objective. A person who will have the same rights against B as a copyright owner, in respect of infringement of copyright, is a person issuing to the public copies of, or communicating to the public, the work to which effective technological measures have been applied, or the copyright owner or his exclusive licensee, if he is not the same person. Technological measures are defined as any technology, device or component which is designed, in the normal course of its operation, to protect a copyright work other than a computer program. Such measures are 'effective' if the use of the work is controlled by the copyright owner through an access control or protection process such as encryption, scrambling or other transformation of the work, or a copy-control mechanism which achieves the intended protection. Protection is defined as the prevention or restriction of acts that are not authorised by the copyright owner of that work and are restricted by copyright. However, use of the work does not extend to any use of the work that is outside the scope of the acts restricted by copyright (s 296ZF). It follows that the protection will not (and, indeed, should not) extend to permitted acts (see para **2.107**).

Offences in relation to circumvention

2.105 It will be an offence if a person, inter alia, manufactures, imports or, in the course of business, sells, advertises, possesses or distributes any such device, product or component which is primarily designed to facilitate the circumvention of effective technological measures. It will also be an offence if a person distributes otherwise than in the course of business such devices to such an extent as to affect prejudicially the copyright owner. A person also commits an offence if he provides, promotes, advertises or markets, in the course of business or otherwise than in the course of business to such an extent as to affect prejudicially the copyright owner, a service the purpose of which is to enable or facilitate the circumvention of effective technological measures. The latter two offences are almost certainly aimed at internet users who, for example, share music files, not for their own gain, but on a scale which affects the profits of the rights-holders. Penalties include imprisonment for up to two years and fines.

Devices designed to circumvent technological measures (CDPA 1988, s 296ZD)

2.106 This section applies where effective technological measures have been applied to a copyright work other than a computer program. It applies to a person (C) who, inter alia, manufactures, imports, distributes, sells or lets for hire, or has in his possession for commercial purposes a device, product or component, or provides services which are promoted, advertised or marketed for the purpose of circumvention of, or have only a limited commercially significant purpose or use other than to circumvent, or are primarily designed, produced, adapted or performed for the purpose of enabling or facilitating the circumvention of effective technological measures. As with s 296ZA, those who have rights against C include persons who issued public copies of, or communicated to the public, the work to which effective technological measures have been applied. Unlike s 296ZA, the remedies against such actions are civil (see ss 101–102; see also *CBS Songs Ltd v Amstrad Consumer Electronics plc* (1987), at para **2.59**). There is similar protection against circumvention of technical devices applied to computer programs (s 296).

Fair dealing and anti-circumvention measures

2.107 The increasing use of anti-circumvention measures by rights-holders to prevent either access to, or reproduction of, their works goes to the heart of the principles behind copyright protection. It has been generally accepted that copyright laws are intended to produce a balance between the rights of creators to profit from their creations and the rights of the public to have limited access to them. The 'all or nothing' nature of anti-circumvention measures is seen by some as directly challenging the ability of the public to benefit from fair use exceptions. It was noted above that the protection afforded to anti-circumvention devices does not extend to use of a work which is outside the scope of the acts restricted by copyright. In practice, however, technological protection measures introduced by the rights-holder may well make fair use of a copyright work impossible unless the user actively circumvents them. Rights-holders may, of course, introduce voluntary measures or agreements which would allow users to undertake permitted acts, where it will be necessary to circumvent technological protection measures to do so. The Copyright and Related Rights Regulations 2003 introduce a remedy where effective technological measures prevent permitted acts (s 296ZE). In such circumstances, individuals or representatives of a class of individuals may issue a notice of complaint to the Secretary of State, who may then investigate to discover whether voluntary measures are in place and, if not, may direct that the rights-holder gives the complainant the means to carry out the permitted act. The Secretary of State may publicise any failure by the rights-holder to comply with his directions. Failure to comply is a breach of statutory duty. It remains to be seen whether these provisions will have the desired effect. Private individuals, unable to undertake a permitted act because of technological protection measures, may find the road to redress a daunting one to take. Certainly, there is no suggestion that when faced with illegitimate obstacles from rights-holders, the public can use its own anti-circumvention devices with impunity (Foged, 'US v EU Anti-Circumvention Legislation: Preserving the Public's Privileges in the Digital Age' [2002] *European Intellectual Property Review* 525; Akester, 'The new challenges of striking the right balance between copyright protection and access to knowledge, information and culture' [2010] *European Intellectual Property Review* 372).

Electronic rights management (CDPA 1988, s 296ZG)

2.108 This section concerns information used by rights-holders to identify, track and assist with the utilisation of their works. This information will generally be associated with a copy of a copyright work or appear in connection with its communication to the public. Remedies are provided to a rights-holder if a person knowingly and without authority removes or alters such information, knowing or having reason to believe that by so doing he is, inter alia, enabling or concealing an infringement of copyright. Alternatively, remedies are also available if a person knowingly or without authority distributes, imports or communicates to the public copies of a copyright work from which electronic rights management information has been altered or removed, if that person has reason to believe he is enabling, etc an infringement of copyright.

Protection on the physical layer: internet service providers (ISPs)

2.109 It is obviously the case that a significant amount of content which gets routed through the internet is infringing. The E-Commerce Directive (Directive on

Electronic Commerce (EC) 2000/31), among other things, seeks to regulate the activities of ISPs in relation to such material. Articles 12–15 of the Directive impose on ISPs limited liability for copyright infringement. ISPs are exempted from liability where they act as a 'mere conduit' between the information provided by a recipient of their service and the provision of access to a communication network (art 12). They are not liable for mere caching (that is, the automatic, intermediate and temporary storage of information) (art 13). Nor are they liable for hosting (or storing) information provided by a recipient of their service, provided the ISPs do not have actual knowledge of illegal activity or information and provided that, when supplied with such knowledge, they act expeditiously to disable access to it (art 14). There is also no general obligation to monitor information to see if it is infringing (art 15). Faced with the actual knowledge of allegedly infringing material, ISPs must act expeditiously to remove it or disable access to it. But how will they know when to act? (This question was considered in relation to trade marks in *Google France Sarl v Louis Vuitton Malletier SA* (2010) and *L'Oreal v eBay* (2011), at para **5.89**.) The Copyright and Related Rights Regulations 2003 introduce a power for the courts to grant an injunction against an ISP where it has actual knowledge of a person using its service to infringe copyright (s 97A) or, in the case of performers, their property right (s 191JA). In determining whether an ISP has actual knowledge, the court shall take into account all relevant circumstances, including whether the ISP has received notice from the rights-holder. As we have seen, in *Twentieth Century Fox v BT* (2011), the latter has, as a result of an injunction, been obliged to block access to Newzbin's website. In granting the injunction, Arnold J made the following observations about s 97A: that it applied to ISPs whose users were merely passive recipients of infringing material, as was the case here; that if users are using the ISP, in this case, BT, to infringe copyright, then BT is also infringing copyright by making works available which can be accessed over BT's network; and that the requirement for actual knowledge should not be interpreted too restrictively. It is enough that BT knows that its service is being used to infringe. It is not necessary to know the details of actual infringers. In the course of this decision, Arnold J acknowledged that it will no doubt lead to a growing number of actions by rights-holders against ISPs, but he believed it would not 'open the floodgates'. Rather, rights-holders would concentrate their efforts on the more egregious offenders. Others are concerned that this decision will inhibit an ISP's willingness to host material which may not, in fact, be infringing to the detriment of free speech, if they are unsure whether it is infringing or not.

The future

2.110 The Information Society Directive has been criticised for being too protective of rights-holders, although its stated purpose, in this direction, was quite explicit

(Doherty and Griffiths, 'The Harmonisation of European Union Copyright Law for the Digital Age' [2000] *European Intellectual Property Review* 17). More generally, fears have been expressed that changes to copyright law pursuant to the introduction of digital technology and the internet have upset the balance between rights-holders and the public which is seen to lie at the heart of the justification for copyright. An equally interesting question is whether copyright law, however it is amended in response to the new technology, is capable of providing a practical means for preventing large-scale copying via both the internet and by digital technology more generally. It is certainly true that the long-term development of copyright law has occurred in a context where it was most likely to be deployed against commercial copiers. This has now changed. Private individuals have the ability to produce high-quality copies of copyright works and distribute them at minimum cost. The Recording Industry Association of America (RIAA) has filed civil law suits against what they term 'major offenders', that is, private individuals who have been swapping music through peer-to-peer networks. These have included a claim against a 12-year-old schoolgirl for over $150,000 per song. The stated aim of the RIAA in launching these claims was not simply to bring these individuals to book, but also to deter the approximately 40 million others in the USA alone who use such networks, and to educate them as to the illegality of their activities. Some have argued that by using copyright law in this way the result will have the opposite effect of undermining the legitimacy of copyright laws among the general public (Litman, *Digital Copyright* (2001)). In the UK, the government has responded to the challenge posed to copyright by digital technology by passing the Digital Economy Act (DEA) 2010. By the government's own account, the DEA 2010 is in large measure a response to the concerns of rights-holders in the 'creative industries', in particular music and film. Among its most controversial provisions is one that would force ISPs to disclose to rights-holders the personal details of their customers who download infringing material. It is envisaged that, in the first instance, these users would be sent warning letters. However, if a mass notification system does not result in a substantial reduction in illegal downloading, then more severe measures might follow, such as the slowing down of a user's internet access or its suspension. There is some scepticism that these measures will be effective against large-scale infringers in any event, who would be adept at hiding their own internet addresses, and that it might instead punish entire households where only one member is misusing the internet in this way. On a more positive note, rights-holders have also developed effective new ways to profit from digital technology by, for instance, using the internet as a powerful marketing tool for their products, as in the case of iTunes and e-books. However, it is also the true that despite the increasing opportunities to legally access and purchase copyright material on the internet, illegal downloading remains widespread.

Databases

2.111   The Database Directive was incorporated into UK law by the Copyright and Rights in Database Regulations (SI 1997/3032). A database is defined in s 3A of the CDPA 1988 as a collection of independent works, data or other materials which:

- are arranged in a systematic or methodical way; and

- are individually accessible by electronic or other means.

In the UK, these had traditionally been protected as compilations (see para **2.18**). The Regulations introduced a new two-tier system of protection for databases. A database will be protected as an original literary work if the selection or arrangement of the data constitutes the author's own intellectual creation (s 3A(2)). An 'original' database will have the full term of copyright protection, which is afforded to literary works, of 70 years from the death of the author (see para **2.42**). The Regulations also introduced a new *sui generis* 'database right', which is based, not on originality, but on whether the compilation of the database involved a substantial investment in the obtaining, verification or presentation of its contents. Investment can be financial, human and/or technical, and it may be judged qualitatively or quantitatively. The database right protects the raw data contained in the database rather than its arrangement. It carries a far shorter 15-year period of protection. However, if the database is 'substantially changed', it may go on to attract a further 15-year term, and so on. It is possible for a single database to be protected both by copyright, if it is original, and by the database right if its creation involved a 'substantial investment'. Traditionally, the English courts have been slow to offer protection to the basic information which goes to make up compilations. The introduction of the database right raised fears that it might limit the availability of basic information, necessary, for example, for scientific or other scholarly research, for very considerable periods indeed.

Databases and infringement

2.112   According to the Copyright and Related Rights Regulations (SI 1996/2967), an original database right is infringed by the taking of a substantial part. Protection extends to the selection and arrangement of the contents, but not the contents themselves. A 'second tier' database will be infringed if, without the consent of the owner, a person extracts or re-utilises all, or a substantial part of, the contents of the database. Extraction is defined as 'the permanent or temporary transfer of any contents to another medium by any means or in any form', and 're-utilisation' means making its contents available to the public by any means. Repeated and systematic extraction or re-utilisation of insubstantial parts of the database may amount to extraction or re-utilisation of a substantial part, and hence be infringing.

A substantial part and database infringement

2.113 The Court of Justice has looked at a number of issues relating to the database right in *British Horseracing Board Ltd (BHB) v William Hill Organisation Ltd* (2005). BHB is the governing authority of the British horseracing industry. Among other things, it creates fixture lists and compiles other data related to horseracing. Since 1993, a company called Weatherbys has compiled an electronic database of this information on behalf of BHB, which is licensed to third parties, through a number of means including an electronic Raw Data Feed, supplied by a company called Satellite Information Services Ltd (SIS). William Hill (WH), one of the largest bookmakers in the UK, had a contract with Weatherbys for much of the information, but not the Raw Data Feed. However, WH began displaying information from the Raw Data Feed through a contract with SIS. Three other actions were brought by Fixtures Marketing Ltd, which creates the list of football fixtures for English and Scottish football, against betting companies in Greece, Finland and Sweden, respectively, for using some information, but not all, from the football fixtures list for their betting operations.

The judgment in *BHB*

2.114 In these four cases, which the Court of Justice considered together, a number of questions were posed relating to the scope of database protection. First, on its wording, the database right confers protection on a database maker who makes a 'substantial investment' in 'obtaining, verifying or presenting the contents of the database'. But what is a substantial investment? The Court of Justice made clear it is not the investment made in creating the database–but in obtaining and verifying its data. In relation to the football fixture list, the investment went into the organisation of the leagues and in horseracing into the organisation of the time, place or name of the race, and so on. This investment was not protected. Thus, in *BHB*, while there may have been substantial investment by BHB in creating data, the investment in verifying the data once created was minimal. Second, the Court of Justice was asked what constitutes a 'substantial part' for the purposes of infringing a database right. According to the Court of Justice, it can be quantitative or qualitative. It is qualitatively substantial if it is 'the human, technical and financial efforts put in by the maker of the database in obtaining, verifying and presenting the data' which constitutes a substantial investment. It is not sufficient that the information itself has substantial economic value as, for example, BHB argued. What WH took from the BHB database may have been valuable information in and of itself, but it was not a qualitatively substantial part because BHB had not invested substantially in obtaining and verifying it. In assessing a quantitively substantial part, the volume of data extracted from the database or re-utilised must be assessed in relation to the contents of the whole database. In the case of BHB, the Court of Justice held that the amount of information taken was not a quantitively substantial part. Third, the Court of Justice considered what constituted a 'repeated and systematic' infringement (art 7(5) of the Database Directive). BHB said WH took information from the database systematically and, if combined, this information would constitute a substantial part. The Court of Justice said art 7(5) was meant to prevent repeated acts which would lead to the reconstitution of the database or a substantial part of it. In the case of BHB, WH's re-utilisation of insubstantial parts of the database did not add up to a substantial part. Finally, the Court of Justice held that infringement could occur even if the material was obtained indirectly (as was the case in BHB), or if the database had been made available to the public. However, there was no infringement if the public merely consulted the database, although the court did not explain how in the digital environment it is possible to consult a database without copying it, at least momentarily. When the case returned to the Court of Appeal, it was held that WH had not infringed BHB's database (*British Horseracing Board Ltd v William Hill Organisation Ltd* (2005)).

Exceptions to the database right

2.115 The database right allows a fair dealing exception for the purpose of research or private study. On the other hand, if the research is for commercial purposes, then the exception does not apply (art 6(2)(b)). There is also a lawful user exception. This exception allows a person who has a legal right to use a database, or any part of it, to do anything which is necessary for the purposes of access to, and use of, the contents of the database, or of that part of the database (CDPA 1988, s 50D(1)). The lawful user exception cannot be overcome by a contractual term which purports to prohibit or restrict it (s 50D(2)). However, despite the fair dealing provisions, there continue to be some who question whether there should be any protection for raw data, albeit even of a limited kind. For these critics, the *BHB* decision was welcome at least in relation to what are called 'sole-source' databases, such as the racing and football fixture lists (and one could also include television listings and telephone numbers), since others, not just their creators, will now be able to exploit that information (Davison and Hugenholtz, 'Football Fixtures, Horserace and Spin Offs: The ECJ Domesticates the Database Right' [2005] *European Intellectual Property Review* 113). Indeed, more recently, in *Attheraces Ltd v British Horseracing Board* (2007), the Court of Appeal held that BHB had not abused its dominant position under EU competition law (art 102 TFEU) through excessive pricing of the licensing of its pre-race data. Perhaps inevitably, given the international nature of the internet, the question has also arisen as to where an act of extraction and re-utilisation of data from a database actually occurs. Thus if data is extracted from a database in one Member State (A) which is uploaded by a webserver in Member State (B) and then sent to proprietors of internet sites in A for storage and display, does extraction and re-utilisation occur in A or B, or both. This question has now been addressed to the Court of Justice by the Court of Appeal in *Football Dataco v Sportradar* (2011).

Copyright in its international context

2.116 Secondary infringement is concerned with dealings in infringing copies. It can occur when infringing copies are imported into the UK. This raises the question of parallel imports. In relation to copyright works, parallel imports are copyright works which have been placed on the market in one country (X) with the rights-holder's consent, but are subsequently imported into a second country (Y) without the rights-holder's express consent. Often this will happen because these goods are available more cheaply in country X than in country Y. Suppose Z imports 100 *Avatar* DVDs into the UK which were made in a Chinese factory without the licence of any rights-holder in the UK or abroad. These would be infringing copies, and Z, provided he had the requisite knowledge, would be a secondary infringer. But what if the same DVDs were produced under licence from the rights-holder for the Far East, including China, and imported into the UK as parallel imports? These would not be infringing copies in China, because they were produced with the consent of the relevant rights-holder. Could the separate rights-holder for *Avatar* in the UK, nonetheless, prevent their importation as infringing copies? The CDPA 1988 provides that an article is an infringing copy if it has been, or is proposed to be, imported into the UK and its making in the UK would have constituted an infringement of copyright in the work in question, or a breach of an exclusive licence agreement relating to the work (s 27(3)). It is submitted that, under these circumstances, the *Avatar* DVDs produced under licence in China are infringing copies in the UK and their importation constitutes an act of secondary infringement (for a case involving the importation of Bee Gees records from Portugal on similar facts, see *Polydor Ltd v Harlequin Record Shops Ltd* (1980)).

Parallel imports and the EU (CDPA 1988, s 27)

2.117 Once goods have been placed on the market with the copyright owner's consent in one EEA country, they can be freely imported into another EEA country (*Deutsche Grammophon GmbH v Metro-SB-Grossmärkte GmbH & Co KG* (1971)). The rights attached to copyright have been exhausted. The CDPA 1988 applies the exhaustion of rights principle expressly to computer programs, but it applies equally to other copyright works. As with trade marks (see para **5.119** et seq) and patents (see para **6.105**), in dealing with the exhaustion of rights in relation to copyright, the Court of Justice differentiates between the specific subject matter of copyright which is protected and cannot be exhausted, and the exercise of those rights which can, because they may stand in the way of the free movement of goods within the EU. The specific subject matter of copyright works has been held to be the right to reproduce the protected work. In fact, a copyright work often has a bundle of rights attached to it, which may include, not only the reproduction right, but also the performance right and the rental right, and not all of these rights may be exhausted on first sale by the copyright owner. In *Warner Bros Inc v Christiansen* (1988), C bought videos of a James Bond film in the UK and imported them into Denmark for video hire. In Denmark, there was a rental right but there was not, at the time, a similar rental right in the UK. It was held that the Danish licensee had the right to collect royalties from C for the rental of the video in Denmark. Recently, the question of exhaustion of rights has arisen in relation to satellite broadcasts.

The EU and competition law

2.118 The same concerns of the EU to balance the protection of industrial and commercial property (which includes intellectual property), whose extent is generally territorial, with the free movement of goods within the European Economic Area arises in relation to competition law.

Article 101 TFEU

2.119 Exclusive licences will not necessarily fall under the umbrella of art 101 TFEU (formerly art 81 of the Treaty of Rome). In *Coditel SA v Cine-Vog Films SA* (1982), the Court of Justice recognised that it is in the nature of the film industry that there may well be a division of rights by way of exclusive licences in order to finance films, and this was not likely to prevent, restrict or distort competition. The correct interpretation of art 101 also arose in *Football Association Premier League v QC Leisure* (2011). The claimant makes available live English premiership games to viewers throughout the world. It films the games and licenses the broadcasting rights. These rights are divided territorially and only one broadcaster is appointed within each territory. Each broadcaster undertakes in the licensing agreement to encrypt the satellite delivered game, and there are authorised decoder cards whose circulation is limited to each of the territories in question. Among the issues arising in the case was the fact that a publican in the UK, Karen Murphy, had purchased a decoder card which had been put on the market in Greece and which enabled her to screen games in the UK which were broadcast by foreign satellite channels not licensed for broadcast in the UK. The claimant alleged that by doing so both the suppliers of the equipment and the cards and also the publican had, inter alia, infringed its copyright, in particular its communication and reproduction rights. Among the findings of the Court of Justice was that freedom of competition within the EU means that an 'illicit device' covers neither foreign decoding devices which are marketed with a broadcaster's authorisation but which are used against its will outside the geographical area for which they are issued nor devices which are licensed only for private purposes. For the same reason, Member States cannot prevent importation of foreign decoding devices which give access to encrypted satellite broadcast from another Member State, even if it includes subject matter legally protected in that State. The Court went on to hold that the clauses of an exclusive licence agreement concluded between a holder of intellectual property right and a broadcaster constitute a restriction on competition outlawed by art 101 TFEU, where they oblige a broadcaster not to supply decoding devices enabling access to the rightsholder's protected subject matter with a view to their use outside the territory covered by that licence agreement.

Article 102 TFEU

2.120 The general approach which has been taken is that protection of the specific subject matter of the copyright–for example, in *Volvo AB v Veng (UK) Ltd* (1988) (see, in relation to patents, para **6.109**) a refusal by Volvo to license the production of spare parts–would not, in itself, be an abuse of a dominant position under Art 102 TFEU (formerly art 82 of the Treaty of Rome). There would need to be some particular abusive behaviour such as, in the case of car parts supply, overcharging or refusing to supply spare parts to non-franchise dealers.

2.121 The relationship between art 102 TFEU and copyright was clarified in the 'Magill' case (*Radio Telefis Eireann v EC Commission* (1995)). Magill sought to publish a weekly TV listing magazine in the Irish Republic and Northern Ireland. Copyright in the information was owned by the BBC and other English and Irish television companies, which published their own listings and also gave listings to newspapers on the basis that they were only published 24 hours in advance of broadcast. The television companies refused to license the information to Magill, in effect preventing Magill's listings magazine from competing with theirs. It should be remembered from the earlier case of *Independent Television Publications Ltd v Time Out Ltd* (1984) (see para **2.52**) that such listings were protected in the UK (although not in other EU countries) as compilations and that, since the information contained in the compilations was generated by the television companies, copyright protection gave them a de facto monopoly over that information and, therefore, television listings in general. The EU found the television companies to be in breach of art 86 (now art 102 TFEU), a decision which was confirmed by the General Court. Eventually, 'Magill' reached the Court of Justice. The Court of Justice ruled that the television companies were abusing their dominant position by using their monopoly to prevent competition in the market for weekly television listings. The Court of Justice confirmed that, while refusal to license per se did not represent an abuse, on the particular facts of this case, it did. The essential subject matter of the copyright was not at issue–rather, they were using their copyright in the listings to prevent competition in the market for television listings. The Court of Justice took a similar approach in *Micro Leader Business v EC Commission* (2000). This case concerned the refusal by Microsoft to allow its French language software, which was marketed in Canada more cheaply, to be imported and sold in France. The Court of Justice held that whilst, as a rule, the enforcement of copyright by its holder, as in the case of prohibiting the importation of products from outside the EU into a member state, is not a breach of art 82 (now art 102 TFEU), such enforcement could in certain 'exceptional' circumstances involve abusive conduct.

2.122 Article 102 TFEU may also be used to change the terms of intellectual property licences. The *Microsoft case* (Commission's 23rd Annual Report on Competition Policy) involved licences for MS-DOS and Windows software. Certain aspects of the licences were challenged under art 82 (now art 102 TFEU). For example, Microsoft calculated its licence fees on the basis of the number of PCs sold by the licensee. This meant that even if the licensee sold a PC that did not contain MS-DOS or Windows, it would still have to pay Microsoft a royalty. Article 82 (now art 102 TFEU) was used to prevent Microsoft from extracting royalties on this basis.

SELF-TEST QUESTIONS

1   Jake, a reporter for the Daily Scoop, is asked to 'ghost write' the autobiography of the movie star, Maxine. They work closely together. The book, which is published on the internet, incorporates passages from the transcript of Maxine's infamous divorce trial. It is a huge success and Jake decides to adapt the book for the screen. The film is to be produced by XRated Films and Jake will direct. Jake learns that a rival, Greg, is also writing a book about Maxine, based in large measure on

the internet edition of Jake's book. Cine Corp has produced its own film based on Maxine's life story, but purporting to be about a fictional movie star, Marilyn. Advise Jake about the copyright position of the book, the screenplay and the film, in the light of the activities of Greg and Cine Corp.

2   To what extent will *Infopaq International A/S v Dansk Dagblades Forening* (2009) influence the protection afforded to copyright works in the UK?

3   Is copyright the appropriate means for protecting computer programs and digital works?

4   Do fair dealing and the public interest defence provide a sufficient balance between copyright protection and the public interest in the dissemination of information?

FURTHER READING

Akester, P, 'The New Challenges of Striking the Balance Between Copyright Protection and Access to Knowledge, Information and Culture' [2010] European Intellectual Property Review 372.

Aplin, T, *Copyright Law in the Digital Society: The Challenges of Multimedia* (Hart, 2005).

Birnhack, M, 'Acknowledging the Conflict between Copyright Law and Freedom of Expression under the Human Rights Act' [2003] *Entertainment Law Review* 24.

Browes, R, 'Copyright: Court of Appeal Considers Fair Dealing Defence and Rejects Common Law Defence of Public Interest' [2000] *European Intellectual Property Review* 289.

Copinger and Skone James on Copyright (16th edn, Sweet & Maxwell, 2010).

Cullabine, J N, 'Copyright in Short Phrases and Single Words' [1992] *European Intellectual Property Review* 205.

Davies, G, *Copyright and the Public Interest* (2nd rev edn, Sweet & Maxwell, 2002).

Davison, M J and Hugenholtz, P B, 'Football Fixtures, Horserace and Spin Offs: The ECJ Domesticates the Database Right' [2005] *European Intellectual Property Review* 113.

Derclaye, E, 'Infopaq International A/S v Danske Dagblades Forening (C-5/08): Wonderful or Worrisome? The Impact of the ECJ Ruling in Infopaq on UK Copyright Law' [2010] *European Intellectual Property Review* 247.

Doherty, M and Griffiths, I, 'The Harmonisation of European Union Copyright Law for the Digital Age' [2000] *European Intellectual Property Review* 17.

Edwards, L and Waelde, C, *Law and the Internet* (Hart, 2009).

Foged, T, 'US v EU Anti-Circumvention Legislation: Preserving the Public's Privileges in the Digital Age' [2002] *European Intellectual Property Review* 525.

Gravells, N P, 'Authorship and Originality: The Persistent Influence of *Walter v Lane*' [2007] *Intellectual Property Quarterly* 267.

Laddie, Sir H, 'Copyright: Over-strength, Over-regulated, Over-rated?' [1996] *European Intellectual Property Review* 253.

Landes, W M and Posner, R A, 'An Economic Analysis of Copyright Law' [1989] *Journal of Legal Studies* 325.

Lawson, E, 'Fisher v Booker: "Whiter Shade of Pale" Organist Matthew Fisher Wins Case in House of Lords–but with a Sting in the Tail' [2009] *Entertainment Law Review* 296.

Lessig, L, *The Future of Ideas: The Fate of the Commons in a Connected World* (Random House, 2001).

Litman, J, *Digital Copyright* (Prometheus Books, 2001).

Stokes, S, 'The Development of UK Software Copyright Law: From John Richardson Computers to Navitaire' (2005) *Computer and Telecommunications Law Review* 129.

Waisman, A, 'What is There Not to Waive? On the Prohibition Against Relinquishing the Moral Right to Integrity' [2010] *Intellectual Property Quarterly* 225.

3 Confidential information

SUMMARY

- The juridical justification for a law of confidence and its development
- The three elements of the law of confidence
- Element 1: confidential information
- The form of confidential information; the springboard doctrine
- Types of confidential information
- Element 2: the confidential obligation
- The limited purpose test; information given to third parties
- Other relationships of confidence: employees and confidential information
- Element 3: unauthorised use or disclosure
- The public interest defence and other defences
- The Human Rights Act 1998, privacy and breach of confidence
- Remedies

The law of confidence: an introduction

3.1 The law of confidence has been seen as necessary to upholding certain standards, both in public and private life (see, for example, *Coco v AN Clark (Engineering) Ltd* (1968)). According to Sir John Donaldson MR in *A-G v Guardian Newspapers Ltd* (1988), the 'Spycatcher' case:

> There is an inherent public interest in individual citizens and the state having an enforceable right to the maintenance of confidence. Life would be intolerable in personal and commercial terms, if information could not be given or received in confidence and the right to have that information respected and supported by the force of law.

In fact, the law of confidence has most often been used to protect commercial or trade secrets, such as customer lists or industrial know-how, where economic interests will also be at stake. But the law of confidence may apply equally to any information, provided it has the necessary quality of confidence (see para **3.7** et seq). Prominent cases have concerned, for example, the private lives of the famous and the relatively obscure and, in the 'Spycatcher' case, the details of the UK's espionage operations. However, it is also important to remember that there may be occasions when the public interest would appear to demand the publication of secrets which otherwise would have the necessary quality of confidence. There has been considerable debate as to when public interest should override confidentiality, none more so than during the 'Spycatcher' case itself (see para **3.55** et seq). More recently, the incorporation of the European Human Rights Convention (ECHR) into UK law through the Human Rights Act 1998 (HRA 1998) has had a significant impact upon the balance between confidentiality and the public interest, particularly in cases concerning personal privacy (see para **3.60** et seq).

The nature of the law of confidence

3.2 The juridical justification for a law of confidence has been located in equity and in contract. More controversially, some have argued that it also has some basis in the law of property.

The equitable basis

3.3 It has been said that 'the equitable jurisdiction in cases of breach of confidence is ancient' (*Coco v AN Clark (Engineering)* (1968)). In two mid-nineteenth century cases, the courts clearly identified an equitable jurisdiction for breach of confidence actions, which would operate regardless of any contractual relationship between the parties. In both *Prince Albert v Strange* (1849) and the almost contemporaneous case of *Morison v Moat* (1851), a number of causes of action were advanced to justify the protection of confidential information, including breach of trust and contract, but in both cases the courts also identified breach of confidence as a separate cause of action. The ability of the court to act independently in equity in the absence of express or implied contractual obligations of confidentiality was confirmed in a number of key twentieth-century decisions, which again roughly coincided. According to Lord Greene MR in *Saltman Engineering Co Ltd v Campbell Engineering Co Ltd* (1948): 'If a defendant is proved to have used confidential information directly or indirectly obtained from a plaintiff without the consent, express or implied, of the plaintiff, he will be guilty of an infringement of the plaintiff's rights.' He went on to say that the obligation to respect confidence is not limited to cases where the parties are in a contractual relationship.

The Court of Appeal judgment in *Seager v Copydex Ltd* (1967) confirmed that the court would act independently of the law of contract. The claimant, during preliminary negotiations with the defendants, revealed to them secret information about a carpet grip which he had invented. The negotiations broke down, but the defendants produced a carpet grip of their own which apparently made use of the claimant's information. There was no contract between the parties. In his judgment, Lord Denning MR stated:

> The law on this subject does not depend on any implied contract. It depends upon the broad principle of equity that he who receives information in confidence shall not take unfair advantage of it. He must not make use of it to the prejudice of him who gave it without obtaining his consent.

In the third major case, *Coco*, Megarry J said: 'I think it quite plain from the *Saltman* case that the obligation of confidence may exist where, as in this case, there is no contractual relationship between the parties.' He described the applicable law as 'the pure equitable doctrine of confidence, unaffected by contract'.

Confidential information as property

3.4 Confidential information may have considerable economic value, but it is not a form of property. In *Douglas v Hello* (2005), which concerned the publication by an unauthorised third party of the wedding photographs of Michael Douglas and Catherine Zeta-Jones, the Court of Appeal held that they had no proprietary interest in the information contained in the photographs, a view which was confirmed by Lord Walker in the House of Lords. He noted, 'information, even if it is confidential, cannot properly be regarded as a form of property' (*OBG v Allan* (2007)). Nor is confidential information recognised as property for the purpose of the Theft Acts, although, of course, one can steal the physical medium upon which it is recorded (*Oxford v Moss* (1979)). What is at issue is the right to protect the confidentiality of the information, not its physical embodiment.

Contractual obligations

3.5 Any competent lawyer will advise a client to seek a confidentiality agreement, before he discloses commercially valuable confidential information to another party. Limitations to express contractual terms might arise if publication of the information is held to be in the public interest (*Hubbard v Vosper* (1972)). Or an express contractual term might be held to be void or unenforceable if, for example, it is drawn too widely and, therefore, unreasonably restricts the actions of one party. A typical example might be a contractual term which applies to an employee once he leaves his employment (see para **3.40** et seq). Conversely, in certain circumstances, the courts will imply a contractual term in the absence of an express obligation to respect confidentiality (*Saltman Engineering Co Ltd v Campbell Engineering Co Ltd* (1948); *Wessex Dairies Ltd v Smith* (1935)). It is also possible for the court to identify both equitable and contractual obligations based on the same set of facts (*Robb v Green* (1895); *Saltman*). The relationship between the equitable and contractual bases giving rise to a breach of confidence is examined in greater detail in the discussion of employee confidentiality (see para **3.32**).

The elements of a breach of confidence action

3.6 There are three elements which will normally be required for a breach of confidence action to succeed. These were set out by Megarry J in *Coco v AN Clark (Engineering) Ltd* (1968). They are:

- the information must have the 'necessary quality of confidence about it';

- the information must have been imparted in circumstances where the confidant ought reasonably to have known that the information had been imparted in confidence (although recently, particularly in cases involving privacy, this condition has been held not necessarily to obtain (see para **3.60** et seq);

- there must be unauthorised use or disclosure of that information to the detriment of the party communicating it.

Each of these elements will be looked at in turn.

Element 1: the confidential information

3.7 Confidential information must 'have the necessary quality of confidentiality about it' (*Saltman Engineering Co Ltd v Campbell Engineering Co Ltd* (1948), per Lord Greene). But no single and clear definition of what constitutes 'confidential information' is to be found in the case law. Generally, the courts have offered a negative definition. In *Saltman*, Lord Greene stated that confidential information 'must not be something which is public property and public knowledge' (see also *Seager v Copydex Ltd* (1967), per Lord Denning). According to Lord Denning in *Woodward v Hutchins* (1977), it should not already be in the 'public domain'. In this case, the Court of Appeal held that an incident on a 'jumbo jet' during which Tom Jones, the recording artist, 'got high', which was known to all the passengers, was in the public domain. In *Coco v AN Clark (Engineering) Ltd* (1968), Megarry J said, 'However confidential the circumstances of communication, there can be no breach of confidence in revealing to others something which is already common knowledge.' Generally, the law of confidence will not protect 'trivial tittle-tattle' (*Coco*), although there may be exceptions in cases concerning personal privacy (see para **3.75**). Nor will the law protect 'useless' information, such as a betting system based on the age of the moon (*McNicol v Sportsman's Book Stores* (1930)). Generally, once any information is in the public domain it is no longer confidential (for exceptions, see para **3.12**). This statement, of course, begs the question of when does information enter the public domain? Or, put another way, when does it become sufficiently accessible to the public, that it is no longer confidential? According to Scott J in *A-G v Guardian Newspapers Ltd* (1987) ('Spycatcher'), the answer will depend upon the circumstances of the case. The court may, for instance, take a different view depending upon whether it is dealing with commercial information, government information or personal information, such as may be contained in photographs of a private event (see para **3.77**). Each of these categories is considered separately below, although there are some broad principles which apply to them all.

Material in the public domain

3.8 A body of information which has been constructed by combining in a novel way information which is in the public domain may possess the necessary quality of confidence (*Coco v AN Clark (Engineering) Ltd* (1968)). To endow such information with the necessary quality of confidence, some product of the human brain, whether it be termed skill, ingenuity or originality, must have been applied to its creation. In *Coco*, the information related to the design of a moped engine, but the claimant failed to convince the court that his ideas were not 'common to the moped world'. More recently, it was suggested that confidentiality would not reside in a substantial collection of data, all of which was in the public domain (in this case a list of features of contact lenses), because even though it had presumably required time and effort to compile, it had required no particular skill (*Ocular Sciences Ltd v Aspect Vision Care Ltd* (1997)). In *Schering Chemicals Ltd v Falkman Ltd* (1981), the information at issue was available to any member of the public who was prepared to undertake a lengthy and painstaking trawl through the scientific literature. The defendant, who had not made such a search, was held to have breached confidentiality (see also *Vestergaard Frandsen A/S v Bestnet Europe Ltd* (2009) as per Arnold J).

Dissemination by the confider

3.9 Whether information has the necessary quality of confidence may depend upon not just how or how widely the confidential information is disseminated but also upon who publishes it. A number of cases have considered when action by the confider destroys the confidentiality of his own information. It has been held that publication of a patent specification including confidential information will destroy the latter's confidentiality. In *Mustad & Son v Allcock & Co Ltd* (1928), the claimant brought proceedings for breach of confidence after D, the ex-employee of a company it had purchased, disclosed confidential details of its fish-hook manufacturing machine to a competitor. Before the case came to court, the claimant applied for and was granted a patent which covered the confidential information. The House of Lords found that the patent disclosed the 'essential part' of the claimant's machine to the world, and so the claimant's action had destroyed the confidentiality of the information at issue. The 'secret, as a secret, had ceased to exist' (see also *Franchi v Franchi* (1967)). However, in *Cranleigh Precision Engineering Ltd v Bryant* (1964), the defendant, a director of the claimant, learned of a patent which affected the claimant's design, a fact he withheld from the claimant. He purchased the patent and then set up a rival company. He was found liable for breach of confidence, despite his argument that the information contained in the patent specification was in the public domain. Here the information covered by the patent had not been published by the claimant, as was the case in *Mustad*. Rather, the defendant had used confidential information which had been available to him as a director of the company to take advantage of the patent himself. In *Dunford and Elliott Ltd v Johnson and Firth Brown Ltd* (1977), a company failed to impose an obligation of confidence on two share-holders over a confidential financial report because, inter alia, it had revealed the report to all its institutional shareholders.

Accessibility through analysis or reverse engineering

3.10 Placing a product on the market will not in itself destroy the confidentiality of information, which may be derived by reverse engineering of the product or by other analyses of it, provided it would require substantive work to acquire such information (*Ackroyds (London) Ltd v Islington Plastics Ltd* (1962)). This was the view taken in *Terrapin v Builders' Supply Co (Hayes) Ltd* (1967). The claimants designed and marketed a novel type of portable building, which the defendants manufactured on their behalf. The defendants, making use of confidential information from the claimants, manufactured and marketed similar buildings once their contract with the claimants had expired. The defendants argued that by publishing detailed brochures and putting their buildings on the market so that a purchaser might analyse them, the claimants had destroyed any confidentiality. This argument was rejected. The court found that a member of the public, without the benefit of the confidential information, would have had to employ considerable effort in order to analyse the buildings in this way. The information was not, therefore, accessible to the public. Conversely, it was held that encrypted information in a commercially available computer program did not have the necessary quality of confidence about it. Any purchaser with the skills to decrypt the program would have access to the information. The fact that the information was encrypted did not make it confidential (*Mars UK Ltd v Teknowledge Ltd* (1999)). More recently, in *EPI Environmental Technologies Inc v Symphony Plastic Technologies plc* (2004), the court held that a party to a confidentiality agreement covering the make-up of certain products, which were in the public domain, was not in breach of confidence for analysing those products using material in the public domain (see also *Vestergaard v Bestnet* (2009) HC; (2011) CA).

The form of confidential information

3.11 Unlike the situation in copyright, the law of confidence will protect information even if it has not been recorded in any material form. Confidential information may be communicated orally (*Seager v Copydex Ltd* (1967)). It may also, unlike in copyright, consist of an idea, rather than something written down. However, for an idea to be protected as confidential it must be substantially original; it must be clearly identifiable (as an idea of the confider); it must have commercial potential; and it must be sufficiently well developed to be capable of actual realisation (*De Maudsley v Palumbo* (1996)). For example, in *Fraser v Thames Television Ltd* (1983), the claimants had an idea for a television series based on their own experiences in a female rock band, 'Rock Bottom'. They disclosed their idea to the defendant over an extended lunch. The subsequent highly successful series, 'The Rock Follies', which was made without the claimants' permission, not only had lead characters closely modelled on those in the real band, but also featured a number of their real-life experiences. It was held that the content of the idea was clearly identifiable, original, of potential commercial attractiveness and capable of reaching fruition. It was, therefore, protectable under the law of confidence. More recently, in *Burrows v Smith* (2010), the claimant claimed confidentiality in an idea for a computer game which involved moving a ball from one side of an environment to another by laying a track or path in front of the ball. The game drew on features from other computer games. However, the idea was held to be sufficiently original to attract confidence because of the novel way these features were combined. By contrast, in *De Maudsley v Palumbo* (1996), the claimants had an idea for a night club which they communicated to the defendants at a party. Among its features were to be a 'high tech' industrial setting, a VIP lounge and all-night opening. The defendants subsequently opened the club as 'The Ministry of Sound'. The claimants, who had no share in it, sued the defendants for breach of confidence. Knox J held that before the status of confidential information can be achieved by a concept or idea, it is necessary to go beyond simply identifying a desirable goal. A considerable degree of particularity is required to show that an idea is capable of being realised as a finished product in the relevant medium. This did not exclude simplicity, but vagueness and simplicity were not the same

The springboard doctrine 1: when does it arise?

3.12 Suppose information given by company A to company B in confidence subsequently becomes public. B will be in a better starting position to compete with A than will other traders, who must wait for the information to enter the public domain. Similarly, what if company A gives confidential information to company B which the latter realises can be gleaned from the publicly available information if sufficient effort is expended, as was the situation in *Terrapin v Builders' Supply Co (Hayes) Ltd* (1967)? Here again, by exploiting the confidential information, B can gain a competitive advantage, both against A and also against other potential competitors, who will be put to the effort of collecting the information themselves. In other jurisdictions, such behaviour may fall foul of specific laws against unfair competition or misappropriation, or, as in the USA, trade secrets laws. In the absence of such laws in the UK, the law of confidence offers the best protection against these practices. In *Terrapin*, it was held to be wrong that a person, who has obtained information in confidence, should, in either of the two situations outlined above, be allowed to use it as a springboard for activities detrimental to the confider. In *Seager v Copydex Ltd* (1967), where the defendants had copied the claimant's carpet grip, the details of which had been given in confidence, the Court of Appeal considered the situation where the information was in part public and in part private. Lord Denning stated that the confidant should not get a start over others. He must either go to the public source to get the material in the public domain, 'or, at any rate, not be in a better position than if he had gone to the public source' (see also *EPI Environmental Technologies Inc v Symphony Plastic Technologies plc* (2004)).

The springboard doctrine 2: when does it expire?

3.13 The springboard doctrine has now become an accepted part of the law of confidence, but it also gives rise to difficult questions concerning the appropriate remedies for its breach. These questions were addressed by Arnold J in the recent case of *Vestergaard v Bestnet* (2009) (for the facts, see para **3.14** below). In *Vestergaard*, Arnold J surveyed the authorities relating to the springboard doctrine and summarised those situations where he believed an injunction was an appropriate remedy. He took the view that the springboard doctrine could not be used to justify an injunction to restrain a defendant from the continued misuse of confidential information, once that information was in the public domain. This was so even if it was the defendant who had published the information in breach of confidence (see for example, *AG v Observer* (1988) as per Lord Goff). Arnold J also looked at three other possible scenarios where the springboard doctrine might be said to apply. In the first, the information concerned has a limited degree of continuing confidentiality, although that same information could be gathered from sources in the public domain. In this case, a limited injunction might be granted which would last until it was likely that the confidential information would have passed into the public domain either through reverse engineering or through research into public sources (see for example, *Terrapin v Builders' Supply* (1967) at para **3.10**). However, Arnold J believed that it should not be so long lived that it would enable a claimant to profit at the expense of a defendant. In the second, a defendant is continuing to benefit from the past misuse of confidential information, which is no longer confidential. Arnold J believed that here the situation was less clear. Arnold J suggested that in most commercial situations an appropriate remedy would be an account of profits rather than an injunction. In the third scenario, the defendant is profiting from a product which derives from information which may or may not still be confidential. According to Arnold J, if a product derives from information which is still confidential then an injunction may be appropriate. However, if the product was derived from information which was but is no longer confidential then a more appropriate remedy might be a financial one (*Ocular Sciences Ltd v Aspect Vision Care Ltd (No 2)* (1997) as per Laddie J).

Vestergaard: the judgment

3.14 In *Vestergaard*, the claimant, VF, manufactured insecticidal fabrics, in particular, mosquito nets, some of which were particularly long lasting. The defendants were two former employees of VF (the Head of Production and Sales Manager, respectively) and a scientist, Dr Skovmand, who had acted as consultant to VF for a number of years and was, in effect, its Head of Development. The defendants set up a company in competition with VF which also sold mosquito nets called Netprotect. They later sold a different version of Netprotect called WHOPES II. Netprotect was based on information drawn from the claimant's database, Fence. At the first trial, Arnold J found all three defendants had acted in breach of confidence. Not only did they owe a duty of confidence to the claimant, but Arnold J also held that the Fence database contained confidential information which the defendants had misused (although, in the case of the Sales Manager, this finding was later successfully challenged in the Court of Appeal, see para **3.47**). In relation to Netprotect, Arnold J held that although it would have been possible to recreate its formula using material in the public domain, Dr Skovmand did not do so. Rather he used detailed results from the Fence database as the basis for Netprotect, saving considerable time and trouble. However, in relation to WHOPES II, Arnold J took a different view, holding that this product although based on the Fence database was sufficiently different from the original formula that it might have been developed by Dr. Skovmand, or indeed any other expert, using trial and error from material in the public domain. The second trial concerned the appropriate remedies. VF asked, inter alia, for injunctions to prevent the further sale of Netprotect and WHOPES II (*Vestergaard v Bestnet* (2009)). Arnold J held that VF was entitled to an injunction to prevent the defendants from using information contained in the Fence database, provided it did not apply to information which was in the public domain or might be so in the future. Once it had entered the public domain then the correct remedy was a financial one. VF was also entitled to an injunction to prevent the sale of the first Netprotect product. However, the claimant did not succeed in obtaining an injunction against the manufacture and sale of WHOPES II. This was because, as we have seen, not only did WHOPES II differ substantially from Netprotect, but also in the five or so years between the two products, Dr Skovmand would have been able to develop WHOPES II independently of the claimant's trade secrets. His knowledge of these trade secrets may have saved him time, but the granting of an injunction would be a disproportionate remedy. Arnold J's findings in this regard were subsequently upheld by the Court of Appeal in *Vestergaard Frandsen S/A v Bestnet* (2011). For an application of *Vestergaard*, in particular in relation a refusal to give injunctive relief for information already in the public domain, see *BBC v HarperCollins Publishers Ltd* (2011).

Commercial secrets

3.15 These may include confidential information which is exchanged in the course of a business relationship, such as the situation in *Seager v Copydex Ltd* (1967) (para **3.3**), or private information such as details of an individual's wedding which may be licensed to a third party for publication (*Douglas v Hello* (2006)). In *Andrew Gray v News Group Newspapers* (2011), the claimants were a well-known comedian and a sports broadcaster, whose phone calls were tapped by a private investigator. The court held that the information thus obtained was commercial information because it was possible to sell it to media outlets for considerable sums of money.

Trade secrets

3.16 Unlike in the USA, the UK courts have not given a general definition of trade secrets as such. A definition was offered by Megarry J in *Thomas Marshall*

(Exports) Ltd v Guinle (1978). The owner must believe that the release of the information injures him or helps his rivals. He must believe the information is not in the public domain. In both cases, his belief must be reasonable. Finally, the information must also be judged in the light of the particular trade practices to which it pertains. However, the subjective elements of Megarry J's definition set it apart from the objective definitions of confidential information which have predominated in the case law and, hence, it is by no means authoritative. The extent to which the law of confidence protects trade secrets which arise in the course of employment and the particular obligations of confidentiality owed by an employee to an employer are looked at separately below (see para **3.32** et seq).

Personal secrets

3.17 Personal information may be protected by an obligation of confidence (*Coco v AN Clark (Engineering) Ltd* (1968)). The passage of the Human Rights Act 1998 has had a considerable impact upon the law relating to personal privacy. The relationship between the law of confidence and personal privacy is examined below (para **3.60** et seq).

Immoral material

3.18 In *Stephens v Avery* (1988), the court accepted that a duty of confidence would not be enforced if it related to matters which had a 'grossly immoral tendency'. It also accepted that there is no clear social consensus as to what constitutes immoral sexual conduct. Recently, in a controversial decision, Eady J held that an individual who engaged in sadomasochistic sexual acts for money owed a duty of confidence to the other participants (*Mosely v Newsgroup Newspapers Ltd* (2008); see para **3.76**).

Government secrets

3.19 In the past half-century, there have been a number of occasions when the state has sought to use the law of confidence to block publication of its secrets. The use of the law of confidence in this way has been criticised. It has been argued that 'state secrets' constitute a different category of information from confidential information. Indeed, since 1911, 'state secrets' have been granted particular protection by the Official Secrets Acts (1911–89). The fact that successive governments have successfully employed the law of confidence to prevent publication of their secrets has, therefore, been seen by many as a worrying extension of its use.

The judgment in *A-G v Jonathan Cape Ltd* (1975), which concerned the publication of the diaries of a former cabinet minister, Richard Crossman, was the first to hold that the law of confidence might be used to protect government secrets. However, the court tempered this extension of the law of confidence by introducing a public interest test, which is not applicable to commercial secrets. Not only must it be shown that the information at issue has the necessary quality of confidence, but also that it is in the public interest that the government should continue to keep the information secret. In the Crossman case, it was held that there was a public interest in the maintenance of the doctrine of joint responsibility in the cabinet, which might be prejudiced by the premature disclosure of views by individual members. However, there was no public interest in preventing publication of proceedings which, as in this case, were over ten years old. The Australian case of *Commonwealth of Australia v John Fairfax & Sons Ltd* (1980) followed the Crossman decision. In this case, it was recognised that government secrets could be the basis of an obligation of confidence, but also that, 'unless disclosure is likely to injure the public interest, it will not be protected'. The apparent tension between the state's interest in secrecy and the public interest in disclosure was considered at length in *A-G v Guardian Newspapers Ltd* (1988) ('Spycatcher'), which concerned an attempt by the government to prevent a number of newspapers from publishing revelations by a former British spy, Peter Wright. The 'Spycatcher' case will be looked at in detail below, when the public interest defence is fully considered (see para **3.50** et seq). In fact, the decision by the House of Lords to allow publication by at least some of the defendants rested primarily on a recognition that the information at issue had already entered the public domain. The Freedom of Information Act 2000 extended public access to information held by the government and other official bodies. There are, however, some notable restrictions to access, including information relating to the security services, and information which may be withheld by public authorities on the basis of risk or reasonable expectation of prejudice.

Professional confidences

3.20 There are a number of other relationships in which an obligation of confidence may be generated, including a number of professional relationships, for example, that between solicitors and their clients. In *Tournier v National Provincial and Union Bank of England* (1924), Bankes LJ stated that:

> The privilege of non-disclosure to which a client or a customer is entitled may vary according to the exact nature of the relationship between the client or the customer and the person on whom the duty rests. It need not be the same in the case of the counsel, the solicitor, the doctor and the banker although the underlying principle may be the same.

Where personal information is relayed in the context of such a relationship, but is subsequently broadcast without the identity of the confider being put at risk, this may not constitute a breach of confidence (*R v Department of Health, ex p Source Informatics Ltd* (1999); see para **3.26**).

Element 2: the confidential obligation

3.21 The second element of a breach of confidence action is that the information must have been imparted in circumstances where the confidant ought reasonably to have known that the information had been imparted in confidence. In other words, a duty of confidence arises from the particular relationship between the parties.

The origins of the duty of confidence

3.22 Where the parties are in a contractual relationship, there may be an express contractual term which establishes a relationship of confidence. Or the court may imply such a term. But an obligation of confidence may also arise in equity. According to Megarry J in *Coco v AN Clark (Engineering) Ltd* (1968), 'Where there is no contract, the information must have been imparted in circumstances importing an obligation of confidence' (see also *Marcel v Metropolitan Police Comr* (1991)). As a result, it has been suggested that the obligation of confidence 'affects the conscience of the person who receives the information with knowledge that it has originally been communicated in confidence' (*A-G v Guardian Newspapers Ltd* (1987), per Sir Nicolas Browne-Wilkinson V-C). Similarly, in *R v Department of Health, ex p Source Informatics Ltd* (1999), Simon Brown LJ concluded:

> To my mind the one clear and consistent theme emerging from all these author-
> ities is this: the confidant is placed under a duty of good faith to the confider and
> the touchstone by which to judge the scope of his duty and whether or not it has
> been fulfilled or breached is his own conscience, no more or no less.

This remains an objective criterion. The question posed is what would affect the conscience of a reasonable man? Conversely, however secret and confidential the information, there can be no binding obligation of confidence if the information 'is blurted out in public' or is communicated in other circumstances which obviously undermine any duty to hold it confidential. The breadth and dura-tion of the obligation of confidence depends on all the circumstances of the case ('Spycatcher', per Scott J).

Limited purpose test

3.23 The question arises of how to determine whether the information was communicated in circumstances which gave rise to an obligation of confidence. The most common test recognised by the courts is to ask whether the information was given for a limited purpose only. In *Saltman Engineering Co Ltd v Campbell Engineering Co Ltd* (1948), the claimants were the owners of drawings of tools for leather punches, which they gave to the defendants, who manufactured the tools for them. The defendants used the drawings to manufacture tools on their own behalf. It was held, inter alia, that the defendants had an equitable obligation to keep the drawings confidential, because they knew that they had been given to them for a limited purpose only, that is, for the manufacture of tools for the claimants' use (see also *Ackroyds (London) Ltd v Islington Plastics Ltd* (1962). *Standard Life Assurance Ltd v Topland Col Ltd* (2010) concerned information which had been given to the Serious Fraud Office (SFO) by the defendants in the course of a criminal investigation into their conduct. The court held that the SFO did not breach the defendants' confidentiality by passing this information on to the claimant in a civil action against the defendants because the claimant would be able to obtain this same information during the discovery stage of the action in any event.

3.24 The general view has been that the limited purpose test is an objective one. In other words, it is not necessary for the defendant actually to know that the confidential information was imparted for a limited purpose. It is sufficient if, given the circumstances in which the information was imparted, he *ought* to have known. The circumstances might include the confider's own attitude or behaviour in confiding the information, that is, did the confider act in a way commensurate with the information being confidential? For instance, if the confider was an employer, did he ensure that his employee was aware that he was being given confidential information? The objective nature of the test was considered in an interesting Australian case, *Smith, Kline & French Laboratories (Australia) (SKF) Ltd v Secretary to the Department of Community Services and Health* (1990). The applicant, SKF, imported a controlled drug, Cimetidine, into Australia. To obtain approval to import the drug, SKF sent information relating to the drug to the relevant government department. Some years later, Alphapharm, which manufactured and imported generic drugs, also sought to import Cimetidine into Australia. The department, in order to evaluate the generic product, intended to make use of the information supplied by SKF. SKF claimed that the information had been made available to the department for the sole purpose of assessing its own application. It sought an injunction to prevent the department from using it for any other purpose. It was held by the court that the information was confidential, thus satisfying the first part of Megarry J's trilogy. But was the department bound by the obligation of confidence? SKF alleged that the department knew or ought to have known of the limited purpose for which it was supplied. It was found, on the facts, that the department did not *actually* know that the data was supplied on the understanding that it would not be used to evaluate generic data; but *ought* it to have known? The court assumed that the test was objective. The obligation of confidence arose, not only where the defendant knew, but where he ought to have known in the circumstances. In this case, the court found that although there was an 'implicit' understanding on the part of both SKF and the relevant departmental secretary that the information would not be revealed to third parties, there was no similar understanding on the part of SKF as to what else the department might do with the information. The court would not impute to the department the placing or the acceptance of an obligation which restricted the manner in which it might discharge its functions, as would be the case if SKF had succeeded. In other words, in the circumstances, it could not be held that the department 'ought to have known' that it should not use the information for the further purpose of evaluating the generic drug.

An objective test

3.25 It was also suggested in *Coco v AN Clark (Engineering) Ltd* (1968) that a general test of whether information is given in confidence should be objective. Megarry J said:

> It may be that hard-worked creature, the reasonable man, may be pressed into service once more; for I do not see why he should not labour in equity as well as law. It seems to me that if the circumstances are such that any reasonable man standing in the shoes of the recipient of the information would have realised that upon reasonable grounds the information was being given to him in confidence, then this should suffice to impose upon him the equitable duty of confidence.

'Anonymised' information

3.26 What if the information given to the confidant is clearly confidential, in that it reveals personal information about the confider, and is subsequently 'anonymised' so that identification of the confider is no longer possible? Is the confidant still bound by an obligation of confidence? This was the issue addressed in *R v Department of Health, ex p Source Informatics Ltd* (1999). The appellants, Source Informatics, compiled databases of drugs dispensed by pharmacists, for the use of the pharmaceuticals industry. The pharmacists' databases included the name of the patient, the date of the prescription, the drug and the dosage prescribed. When pharmacists gave this information to the appellant, the name of the patient and any other information by which he might be identified was excised. The DoH argued, inter alia, that the information contained on the prescriptions was confidential and that it was given to the pharmacist for the sole purpose of obtaining drugs. Hence, any use of the information for another purpose without consent would involve a breach of confidence. For its part, the appellant asked the Court of Appeal for a declaration that the DoH was wrong in law and that disclosure by a doctor or pharmacist to a third party of anonymous information did not constitute a breach of confidence. The Court of Appeal agreed that even in its anonymised state the information given to the appellant was not in the public domain. However, the relevance of this must, according to the Court of Appeal, depend entirely upon which interest is at stake in protecting confidentiality. Here the interest at stake was to protect the confider's personal privacy. The patient had no property in the information as such and no right to control its use, provided that his privacy was not put at risk. It was necessary to ask: Would a reasonable person's conscience be troubled by the proposed use to be made of the patients' prescriptions? The court concluded that 'the pharmacists' consciences ought not reasonably to be troubled by co-operation with Source's proposed scheme'. In providing the information, the pharmacists' duty of confidence 'will not have been breached'.

Confidential information given to third parties

3.27 According to Lord Keith in *A-G v Guardian Newspapers Ltd* (1988), 'It is a general rule of law that a third party who comes into possession of confidential information which he knows to be such, may come under a duty not to pass it on to anyone else.' If this were not the case, the confidant might remove the obligation of confidence by wrongly disclosing the information to a third party. In *Schering Chemicals Ltd v Falkman Ltd* (1981), the claimants marketed a drug, Primodos. The second defendant was given confidential information about the drug by the claimant, so that he might do public relations work. In fact, he planned to use the information in a television documentary made by Thames Television, the third defendant. Thames was aware of the circumstances in which the second defendant had acquired the information. The Court of Appeal upheld an interlocutory injunction against both the second and third defendants. According to Lord Denning, if the second defendant was in breach of duty, then Thames could not take advantage of his breach. In *Fraser v Thames Television Ltd* (1983) (para **3.11**), Hirst J held that to fix a duty of confidence, the third party must know the information was confidential. He said, 'Knowledge of a mere assertion that breach of confidence has been committed is not sufficient.' There is a wide range of cases where a third party has been held liable, encompassing situations where the confider and confidant are linked by contract or where the obligation of confidence lies in equity. In the early case of *Prince Albert v Strange* (1849), the defendant,

Judge, was restrained from exhibiting copies of etchings, which Strange, who had obtained them 'surreptitiously', had given to him. Typically, a third party case might involve the communication of personal information to the press, such as in *Argyll v Argyll* (1964), where a newspaper was restrained from publishing marital secrets. Another common situation arises when an employee confides confidential information relating to his former employment to his new employer. In 'Spycatcher', the government sought to prevent newspapers from printing confidential information passed on to them by an ex-secret agent. In this case, Scott J posed the question as to whether there can be circumstances where a duty of confidence is owed by the original confidant, but will not necessarily lie on every third party who comes into possession of the confidential information, because it may be that a public interest in publishing the information will apply to the latter and not to the former. Sir John Donaldson agreed that the newspapers' duty to the government was not necessarily the same as that of the ex-spy. However, if the confidant's breach causes the information to enter the public domain, then the third party will have no obligation to keep it confidential.

3.28 There are two situations where a third party who receives information may be in breach. First, he may know the information is confidential at the time it is given to him or, second, he may find out only later. In the first case, the third party may be fixed with three different kinds of knowledge. The first is actual knowledge (for example, Judge, in *Prince Albert v Strange* (1849) (para **3.27**). The second is imputed knowledge. This has often been imputed to companies which have been formed by confidants to exploit the confidential information that they have obtained (for example, in *Cranleigh Precision Engineering Ltd v Bryant* (1964) (para **3.9**)). The third is constructive notice, where the third party is affixed with notice if he wilfully fails to make proper inquiries. Here the third party will be held to be in a similar position to the confidant, who knew or *ought to have known* that information given to him was for a limited purpose. It is submitted that third party constructive notice is established by an objective test: Are the circumstances such that a reasonable person in his position would have made inquiries at the time he acquired the information? For instance, in *London and Provincial Sporting News Agency v Levy Ltd* (1928), the claimants were turf commission agents who informed subscribers of the betting prices offered at race meetings. The subscribers were under contract not to pass on the information. A subscriber (a bookmaker) passed the information to a second turf commission agent who, in turn, passed it to a news agency. It was held that the latter two defendants knew or ought to have known that the information came from the claimants, 'or at any rate that they had a very certain suspicion that it was the plaintiffs' news and had deliberately refrained from asking a direct question'. In the second situation, where the third party acquires the information but is unaware that it is confidential or that it has been given in breach of confidentiality, his liability arises only from the date at which he is informed or given notice of the fact that the information was confidential.

Confidential information obtained improperly

3.29 If information has been obtained improperly or surreptitiously, the courts have been willing to accept that the recipient of such information may well be bound by a duty of confidence. As early as 1913, Swinfen Eady J stated that 'the principle upon which the Court of Chancery has acted for many years has been to restrain the publication of confidential information improperly or surreptitiously obtained...' (*Ashburton v Pape* (1913)). It has been widely recognised that it would be inequitable if a confidant were to be held accountable under the law of confidence for disclosing information which was willingly communicated to him by the confider, while an individual who engages in dishonesty or subterfuge to obtain what he knows to be confidential information is not. This is especially so when, in the case of industrial espionage or media 'snooping', for example, the acquisition of confidential information can prove immensely profitable. The Australian case of *Franklin v Giddins* (1978) set out the judicial basis for potentially broad protection. Here the defendant had stolen a cutting from the claimant's uniquely high-yielding nectarine tree. The court found that the defendant had behaved 'unconscionably and in contravention of the claimant's rights' and that the latter was entitled to equitable relief. However, the extent to which the law of confidence in the UK will protect secrets gained outside a confidential relationship remains uncertain. *Malone v Metropolitan Police Comr* (1979) took a narrow approach. The claimant's telephone had been tapped by the police, who used the information gained to prosecute him unsuccessfully for handling stolen goods. Malone sought a declaration that the tapping of his telephone by the police had been unlawful, and an injunction to restrain future tapping. Sir Robert Megarry V-C, in rejecting the application, took the view, inter alia, that the claimant had no right of privacy in his conversation. Nor did he believe that there was a general right to confidentiality in telephone conversations. Even if there were, he considered that the interception by the police had been justified, since it was of material assistance in an attempt to uncover a criminal act. He reasoned that to use the telephone involved an inherent risk that the user will be overheard by an 'unknown' individual, in the same way as if confidential information is imparted on a bus or train. In such circumstances, he did not see why someone who overheard the secret should be under any legal obligation to keep it confidential. Indeed, he went further and, perhaps surprisingly, concluded that no realistic person would rely on the telephone to protect his confidentiality against those who might overhear the conversation 'by tapping or otherwise' (see now the Interception of Communications Act 1985).

3.30 There was some criticism of the decision in *Malone v Metropolitan Police Comr* (1979) for circumscribing the remit of the law of confidence in this way. Later cases have suggested the courts' willingness to take a more expansive view. In *Francome v Mirror Group Newspapers Ltd* (1984), the defendant newspaper had acquired tapes of telephone conversations of the claimant, a leading jockey, from an undisclosed source. The tapes were alleged to show breaches of Jockey Club rules and of the criminal law by the claimant. The claimant successfully obtained an interlocutory injunction against the *Mirror* newspaper to prevent publication of the tapes. In the Court of Appeal, Fox LJ distinguished *Malone*, which was concerned with authorised tapping by the police, against the present situation, where the phone had been tapped illegally. In this case, it could not be said that the claimant had accepted the risk that his conversations would be overheard in the same way he might have accepted the risk that he would be overheard because of accidents or imperfections in the telephone system itself. Following this reasoning, Fox LJ considered that there was a serious issue to be tried and granted the injunction.

3.31 In *A-G v Guardian Newspapers Ltd* (1988), Lord Goff even suggested that a duty of confidence might exist where an individual comes across confidential information 'innocently', such as 'when an obviously confidential document is wafted by an electric fan out of a window into a crowded street', or 'a private diary, is dropped in a public place, and is picked up by a passer by'. Whether Lord Goff would have applied the same rule to personal and commercial information is an open question. *Francome v Mirror Group Newspapers Ltd* (1984) suggests that where there is no relationship between the parties, the court's view as to whether or not there is an obligation of confidence might be based upon how the information was acquired. Following the introduction of the HRA 1998, this question has been revisited, particularly in the context of cases involving personal privacy. For instance, guidelines set out by Lord Woolf CJ in *A v B* (2002) suggest that the court will consider all the circumstances of the relationship between the parties at the time of the alleged breach. According to Lord Woolf, it is possible that an obligation of confidence will have to be 'inferred from the facts', an approach confirmed by the House of Lords in *Campbell v MGN* (2004) (see para **3.67** et seq).

Other relationships of confidence: employees and confidential information

3.32 The law has long recognised that an obligation of confidence may arise out of particular relationships. Examples are the relationships between a doctor and patient, a priest and penitent, a solicitor and client, a banker and customer. The relationship which has generated the most amount of case law, reflecting its central importance both economically and socially, is the relationship between employer and employee. It is this relationship which is examined below.

3.33 The general rules of the law of confidence will apply to the employee/employer relationship. However, the relationship between employee and employer also gives rise to a number of particular problems concerning the use of information. Typically, an employer will wish to limit, as far as possible, the ability of an employee to compete using information acquired during the course of his employment. On the other hand, an employee, particularly a former employee, may well seek to use this same information in pursuit of his own interests even if these conflict with those of his (ex-)employer. The conflict engendered by the competing claims of employer and employee frequently focuses on the boundary between what the employer will claim is his confidential information and what the employee will claim is, in reality, the general knowledge or 'know-how' of his trade or business, which he should be allowed to take elsewhere. In balancing these competing claims, the courts have drawn a distinction between the duty owed by employees and former employees. In the first situation, the courts have emphasised the duty which is owed to an employer by an employee. In the second, they have, by contrast, sought to protect the ex-employee's freedom to earn a livelihood without unreasonable constraint.

Duties during employment

3.34 The duty of confidence may be based in equity as well as in contract. In the context of employment, where the parties are linked by a contract of employment, the duty of confidence is founded on that contractual relationship (*Vokes Ltd v Heather* (1945)). In the absence of any express term, an undertaking by the employee to serve his employer with 'good faith and fidelity' will be implied into the contract of employment (*Robb v Green* (1895), per Smith LJ). Since the last century, the courts have viewed the duty of confidence, during the course of employment, as a central aspect of the general duty of good faith or fidelity (*Faccenda Chicken Ltd v Fowler* (1986)). Fundamental to the general duty of good faith and fidelity is the duty of an employee not to compete during the duration of the employment contract, including, as a general rule, the duty not to compete in his spare time. In the latter circumstance, the courts are likely to identify a conflict if the employee knows of trade secrets which may be useful to a competitor, and if he occupies a position with the employer where the expectation would be that he owes an exclusive duty to him. So a 'manual worker' working by the hour may be under less constraint as to how he uses his spare time than a more senior employee (*Thomas Marshall (Exports) Ltd v Guinle* (1978)). In certain limited circumstances, an employee may make preparations while he is employed in order to compete with his employer after he has left. But these will not include taking away a card index file of customers (*Roger Bullivant Ltd v Ellis* (1987)) or, as in *Wessex Dairies Ltd v Smith* (1935), soliciting customers on the final day of employment in order to set up a rival milk round. It has also been held that it is wrong to memorise lists of names of customers for later use (*Printers and Finishers v Holloway Ltd* (1964)). However, merely recalling rather than memorising information will not be restrained (*Coral Index Ltd v Regent Index Ltd* (1970)). An employee may even have a positive duty to disclose information, which may be of benefit to his employer, which he encounters during his term of employment. This was the conclusion reached in *Cranleigh Precision Engineering Ltd v Bryant* (1966) (para **3.9**). The extent of this positive duty will again depend upon the position of the employee. For instance, in *Cranleigh*, the defendant was managing director of the company, and therefore owed a fiduciary duty to his employer which went beyond the general duty of good faith and fidelity. A similar duty may not extend to an employee in a less responsible position.

The *Faccenda Chicken* case

3.35 In 1986, in *Faccenda Chicken Ltd v Fowler*, the Court of Appeal reviewed the general principles behind breach of confidence cases involving employees. In his judgment, Neill LJ considered both the extent of the employees' duties and the nature of the information which was owed protection. Although the case was concerned with a post-termination breach, the judgment has a wider relevance. The facts are relatively straightforward. The defendant, Fowler, was employed as a sales manager by the claimant company, which marketed fresh chickens. Fowler had the novel and profitable idea of using a fleet of travelling salesmen to sell fresh chickens direct to retailers from refrigerated vans. Subsequently, Fowler resigned from the claimant and set up a competing business covering the same geographical area. He also employed a number of the claimant's former salesmen. During their employment with the claimant company, Fowler and the other salesmen had acquired information concerning customers' names and addresses, routes, the quality and quantity of the goods, and the prices charged. The claimant contended, inter alia, that the defendants had abused the confidential information they had acquired during their employment. At first instance, Goulding J had divided workplace information into three general categories:

- easily accessible information which was not confidential;
- confidential information which an employee could not use or disclose during his employment, but which, in the absence of an express covenant, he was at liberty to use subsequently;
- 'trade secrets' which he was not at liberty to disclose or use, either during his employment or after.

Goulding J placed the information carried away by Fowler in the second category. But since there was no express covenant, Fowler was held not to be liable. The claimant appealed. The Court of Appeal reached the same conclusion as the trial judge, but disagreed on one vital point. Neill LJ held that there was no second category of information which could be protected by an express restrictive covenant. Instead, there were two categories of information: trade secrets which would be protected post-employment either by an express or implied contractual term and the rest, including information which may have had the necessary quality of confidence while the employee was employed, but ceased to do so once he had left. In this case, the information at issue did not amount to a trade secret, and so did not remain confidential post-employment.

The *Faccenda* definition of 'trade secrets'

3.36 It has been suggested that the subjective approach of Megarry J's definition of trade secrets in *Thomas Marshall (Exports) Ltd v Guinle* (1978) does not fit with the general run of case law (see para **3.16**; also the comments of Carnwath J in *Lancashire Fires Ltd v Lyons & Co Ltd* (1996)). In *Faccenda Chicken Ltd v Fowler* (1986), Neill LJ did not attempt to define trade secrets per se. He cited examples of trade secrets or their 'equivalent', including 'secret processes of manufacture such as chemical formulae' or 'designs and special methods of construction'. He also left the category open by adding, 'other information which is of a sufficiently high degree of confidentiality to amount to a trade secret', including, albeit in circumstances different from those obtaining in this case, information about prices. Neill LJ then went on to identify four factors which are relevant to differentiating between trade secrets and other information, including 'merely confidential information', which would not be protected post-employment. The first is the nature of the employment. An employee who is accustomed to handling confidential information as part of his job may be expected to protect trade secrets better than one who is not. The second is the nature of the information. Is it the sort of information which meets the standard of a trade secret? In *Faccenda*, the example was offered of information which was given only to a limited number of employees. Third, did the employer impress upon the employee the confidentiality of the information? Merely saying that information is confidential does not make it so, but a warning that the information is confidential will assist the court in finding that it is. Finally, Neill LJ in *Faccenda* identified the fourth question to be whether the confidential information could be easily isolated from other information which the employee acquires during his employment. In *Faccenda*, the Court of Appeal found that the information about prices could not be isolated from the other information which was not protectable post-employment. The controversy surrounding the *Faccenda* view that, post-termination, only 'trade secrets' can be protected is examined at para **3.43**. But first it is necessary to look at how the courts have sought to draw a distinction between confidential information, however defined, and the know-how and general knowledge which the employee is able to take away from his employment.

Confidential information versus 'know-how'

3.37 In the Court of Appeal decision on employee secrets, *FSS Travel and Leisure Systems Ltd v Johnson* (1998), Mummery LJ cited with approval (as had Neill LJ in *Faccenda Chicken Ltd v Fowler* (1986)) the distinction drawn by Cross J in *Printers and Finishers Ltd v Holloway* (1964) between trade secrets which are 'owned' by the employer, and the general skill and knowledge which an employee is entitled to take with him. In *Printers and Finishers*, the defendant was a manager of the claimants' flock-printing factory. While still in their employment, he contacted another company, V, about setting up a competing flock-printing plant. In addition, he showed employees of V around the claimants' 'secret factory', showed them samples of the claimants' products, and ordered a 'cyclone' machine of the claimants' design for the use of V. The claimants sought to restrain the defendant from misusing their confidential information. According to Cross J, if the contested information could 'fairly be regarded as a separate part of the employee's stock of knowledge which a man of ordinary honesty and intelligence would recognise to be the property of his old employer and not his own to do as he likes with', then that information would be protected as confidential. By contrast, general knowledge of the claimants' plant and process, of the difficulties encountered in production and ways around them which the employee has discovered 'for himself by trial and error during the employment' were not trade secrets. In this case, according to Cross J, the defendant's 'skill in manipulating a flock-printing plant' which he had acquired during his employment could not be separated from 'his general knowledge of the flock-printing process' and Cross J doubted whether 'any man of average intelligence and honesty would think that there was anything improper in his putting his memory of particular features of his late employers' plant at the disposal of his new employer'.

3.38 Clearly, the distinction between confidential information and know-how is not always an easy one to make. It was examined once more by the Court of Appeal in *FSS Travel and Leisure Systems Ltd v Johnson* (1998). The claimant specialised in producing computer programs for the travel industry. The defendant, J, was employed as a computer programmer. There was a term in J's contract that for a period of one year after leaving the claimant's employment, he would not engage in any competing business. J left and took up employment with a competitor. The claimant sought to enforce the post-termination covenants. At first instance, it was held, inter alia, that the claimant had trade secrets to protect, but that the scope of the restrictive covenant was unreasonable. The claimant appealed. The Court of Appeal dismissed the appeal, but on the ground that there was no confidential information capable of being protected. According to Mummery LJ, the determination of whether the employee's knowledge constitutes confidential information or know-how is a question of fact, to be decided by examining all the evidence, considering not only the four factors which had been identified in *Faccenda Chicken Ltd v Fowler* (1986) (see para **3.36**) but also the extent to which the information is in the public domain and the likely damage to the employer if the information is disclosed. During his employment, J had acquired skill, experience, know-how and general knowledge relating to the computer systems, rather than a separate identifiable body of objective trade secrets to which the claimant was entitled. The express covenant was, therefore, invalid, as the latter had no trade secrets legitimately protectable by the imposition of a covenant. The Court of Appeal emphasised that the claimant's lack of precision in its pleadings, and the absence of solid evidence of trade secrets was fatal to its case.

The *Faccenda* test for trade secrets applied

3.39 The four *Faccenda* factors for determining whether information constitutes a trade secret, protectable post-termination, were examined by Arnold J in *Vestergaard v Bestnet* (2009) (see para **3.14**). As we have seen, Dr Skovmand (S) was employed by the claimant as its Head of Development. One question for the court in the main judgment was whether the information taken from the Fence database which S had used in developing the rival product, Netprotect, amounted to trade secrets which would be protected after S ended his employment with VF. Arnold J concluded that it did. First, it was the in nature of S's duties that he was engaged in developing new products for VF. And indeed new inventions might and did result from his carrying out of those duties. Second, the information on the Fence database, which consisted of recipes for nets and the results of experiments, constituted trade secrets. Third, as well as an express confidentiality agreement between S and VF, there was also abundant evidence that both VF and S regarded the information in the Fence database, and in particular the recipes, as confidential information. Indeed, both VF and S took extensive steps to prevent misuse of that information by third parties, including inter alia the use of codes. Fourth, Arnold J also held that the information in the Fence database might be separated from S's general skill, knowledge and experience including the general skill, knowledge and experience he gained during the course of his work for VF. He concluded that all these factors suggested the information contained in the database, particularly the recipes, constituted VF's trade secrets.

Post-employment obligations

3.40   The duty of good faith and fidelity owed by a former employee is not as great as the duty owed by an employee during his employment. During employment, there is an implied term in the contract of employment that the use or disclosure of confidential information, even though it may not amount to a trade secret, will be a breach of the duty of good faith. By contrast, post-employment, the implied term will cover the obligation not to use or disclose trade secrets, but it will not cover all the information acquired by an employee during the course of his employment. It will not cover Goulding J's second category in *Faccenda*, that is information which is 'confidential' in the sense that it would be a breach of an employee's duty of good faith to disclose it while he is employed. In *Printers and Finishers Ltd v Holloway* (1964), Cross J gave as an example of this sort of information the printing instructions which were given to the defendant by the claimant. During his employment, it would have been a breach of confidence for the defendant to disclose these instructions to 'a stranger'. But, according to Cross J, many of these instructions were not really 'trade secrets'. While the defendant was clearly not entitled to take a copy of the instructions away with him, 'in so far as he carried them in his head', he was entitled to use them for his own benefit or for the benefit of a future employer. In effect, upon leaving his employment, they had become part of his general knowledge or know-how.

Post-employment restrictive covenants

3.41   Since the judgment in *Faccenda*, there has been much debate as to whether Goulding J's second category of information, while not protected by an implied term, can be or should be protectable post-employment by an express term in a restrictive covenant. In *Faccenda*, Neill LJ disagreed with Goulding J, and clearly expressed the opinion that a restrictive covenant would only restrain an ex-employee if it could be shown he was divulging a trade secret, or the equivalent of a trade secret. Before examining the dissent from this finding, it is useful to look at the nature of restrictive covenants themselves.

3.42   In dealing with restrictive covenants, the courts have always been concerned to ensure that they will not be used unreasonably to prevent competition, as this is assumed to be broadly against the public interest (*Herbert Morris Ltd v Saxelby* (1916); *Faccenda*). The public interest at stake is 'that a man should be free to exercise his skill and experience to the best advantage for the benefit of himself and of all those who desire to employ him' (*Herbert Morris*, per Lord Atkinson). Accordingly, the courts will not uphold a restrictive covenant whose sole aim is to protect an employer generally from competition, rather than to protect some specific subject matter for which the employer can legitimately claim protection, such as trade secrets (*Stenhouse Australia Ltd v Phillips* (1973), per Lord Wilberforce; *FSS Travel and Leisure Systems Ltd v Johnson* (1998); *TFS Derivatives Ltd v Simon Morgan* (2004)). It follows, according to Neill LJ in *Faccenda*, that a trade secret can be protected post-employment by an express term in a restrictive covenant. However, the second category of information identified by Goulding J, which is less than a trade secret, cannot. To allow such protection would unreasonably expand the scope of the subject matter of restrictive covenants and inhibit competition. In effect, according to the Court of Appeal in *Faccenda*, Goulding J's second category of information becomes, post-employment, an aspect of the know-how and general knowledge which is acquired by the employee as part of his job and which cannot be subject to restraint.

Faccenda criticised

3.43 Neill LJ's austere view, arguably obiter, that only trade secrets may be protected by express or implied contract terms post-employment was challenged both by legal commentators and in later cases. Following *Faccenda*, there was widespread surprise that a suitably worded restrictive covenant, which was reasonable in its scope, could not prevent a former employer from deploying his know-how to compete with his employer, at least for a limited period or within a limited geographical area. (Critics of the Court of Appeal cited *Printers and Finishers Ltd v Holloway* (1964) in support of the idea that it could, whereas in *Faccenda*, Neill LJ cited the same case as authority that it could not!) In *Balston Ltd v Headline Filters Ltd* (1987), Scott J questioned whether the Court of Appeal was right to disagree with Goulding J. He observed that he did not believe that the Court of Appeal in *Faccenda* could have 'intended to hold that confidential information that could not be protected by an implied term of a contract of employment ipso facto could not be protected by a suitably limited express covenant'. The same point was taken up by the Court of Appeal in *Lancashire Fires Ltd v Lyons & Co Ltd* (1996), where Bingham LJ suggested, again obiter, that a covenant to prevent a former employee working for a competitor was a reasonable way of protecting Goulding J's second category of information. However, in this case the information at issue was held to fall into Goulding J's third category of employee know-how, and, hence, the point was not pursued.

Faccenda approved

3.44 A different approach, which it is submitted better overcomes any problem that may be posed by the *Faccenda* decision, was taken by the Court of Appeal in *Lansing Linde Ltd v Kerr* (1990). Here the approach was to enlarge the category of information which might be protected post-termination by allowing for a flexible view of what might constitute a 'trade secret' (although, to be fair, Neill LJ had, himself, left the category open). In *Lansing Linde*, the claimant company, which manufactured, distributed and sold forklift trucks, employed the defendant as a divisional director. The defendant signed a contract which restrained him from working for any competitor, worldwide, for 12 months following termination. After he left the company, he became managing director of a competitor. The claimant sued for breach of contract and to enforce the restrictive covenant. The Court of Appeal considered the question of whether the defendant was in possession of confidential information which could be protected post-termination. According to Staughton LJ, a trade secret will generally be information used in a trade or business, its owner must limit the dissemination of it or at least not encourage or permit its widespread publication, and its publication must cause real harm to its owner. Therefore, it can include not only secret formulae for the manufacture of products, as mentioned in *Faccenda*, but also a much wider variety of information, including, as in this case, the names of customers and the goods which they buy. These may not be trade secrets in 'ordinary parlance', but they still justified post-termination restrictions. Here, it was held that the defendant did have 'trade secrets' (or 'confidential information') which could be protected, but the protection claimed was too wide. According to Butler-Sloss LJ, also in *Lansing Linde*:

> ...we have moved into the age of multi-national businesses and world wide business interests. Information may be held by very senior executives, which, in the hands of competitors, might cause significant harm to the companies employing them. 'Trade secrets' has, in my view, to be interpreted in the wider context of highly confidential information of a non-technical or non-scientific nature, which may come within the ambit of information the employer is entitled to have protected, albeit for a limited period.

The Court of Appeal in *FSS Travel and Leisure Systems Ltd v Johnson* (1998) (para **3.38**) appears to have followed *Faccenda* and *Lansing Linde* by giving protection only to trade secrets following termination, but maintaining a highly flexible approach to what these might be. It should be remembered that in this case, as in *Lansing Linde*, the Court of Appeal was considering an express term in a restrictive covenant and came to the conclusion that it was unenforceable because the information it sought to protect did not constitute a 'trade secret'. By contrast, in *Poeton (Gloucester Plating) Ltd v Horton* (2000), the Court of Appeal found that the knowledge of out-of-tank electroplating, which the defendant had picked up during his employment, might have constituted a 'trade secret'. However, it could not be isolated from the more general knowledge he had also acquired. As a result, it was not protectable post-employment in the absence of a specific restrictive covenant. Following *FSS Travel* and later decisions, it seems likely that the criticisms of *Faccenda* aired in *Balston Ltd v Headline Filters Ltd* (1987) and *Lancashire Fires Ltd v Lyons & Co Ltd* (1996) are unlikely to be repeated.

Element 3: unauthorised use or disclosure

3.45 The third element required for a breach of confidence action is that there must be unauthorised use of the confidential information, and that use must be to the detriment of the party communicating it (*Coco v AN Clark (Engineering) Ltd* (1968)). Breach can be either by use or by disclosure. Whether or not a breach has occurred is a matter of fact and evidence. Three elements need to be shown:

- that the confidant has used or disclosed the confidential information;
- that the information was obtained from the confider directly or indirectly;
- that the use or disclosure went beyond the purpose for which the information was confided.

There has been some controversy, however, as to whether it is also necessary to show detriment, and this is considered separately at para **3.49**.

Misuse and unauthorised disclosure compared

3.46 In *Saltman Engineering Co Ltd v Campbell Engineering Co Ltd* (1948), Lord Greene MR stated:

> *If a defendant is proved to have used confidential information, directly or indirectly, obtained from the plaintiff without the consent, express or implied, of the plaintiff he will be guilty of infringement of the plaintiff's rights.*

In *Saltman*, the confidential information consisted of a set of drawings given by the claimants to the defendants, in order for the latter to manufacture tools for leather punches on the claimants' behalf. The defendants were found to have breached the relationship of confidence, because they used the drawings to make tools and punches on their own behalf. Their use went beyond that authorised by the claimants. The line between breach by disclosure and breach by use may be a thin one. The former might arise when an ex-employee sells his employer's trade secrets to a third party, and the latter when he makes use of these same trade secrets to compete on his own account. In *Thomas Marshall (Exports) Ltd v Guinle* (1978), Sir Robert Megarry V-C examined the relationship between use and disclosure. The claimant, which bought and sold textile products, employed the defendant as a managing director. There was an express clause in the defendant's contract not to 'disclose' during or after employment any confidential information relating, inter alia, to the trade secrets of the claimant. Sir Robert Megarry V-C found that the defendant had breached his implied duty of fidelity and his fiduciary duty as director. The defence argued that the express clause only prevented 'disclosure' of business secrets, and not the defendant's own use, and was able to point to another clause which explicitly prevented both 'use' and 'disclosure'. On this argument, the defendant succeeded. But Sir Robert Megarry V-C stated:

> I can conceive of methods of use which would amount to making a disclosure. If an employee were to use his secret knowledge in such a way as to make it plain to others what the secret process or information was, that might well amount to a disclosure. The mode and circumstances of use may be so ostentatious that they plainly constitute a disclosure. But apart from such cases, I do not think a prohibition on disclosure prevents use.

The defendant's state of mind

3.47 To be fixed with a duty of confidence, it must be shown that the defendant knew or ought to have known the information was given to him in confidence. The question of whether or not this is an objective test has been looked at above (para 3.16). Once it has been established that the defendant had the requisite knowledge, his state of mind at the time of the breach is irrelevant. A defendant may be found liable even if he was unaware that his act amounted to a breach. In *Seager v Copydex Ltd* (1967), the claimant had disclosed his 'Invisgrip' carpet grip to the defendants during prolonged negotiations over his earlier 'Klent' grip. After the negotiations broke down, the defendants sought to patent an 'Invisigrip' which, like that of the claimant's, had a special 'V-tang' shape. It was the defendants' belief that, so long as they did not infringe the claimant's patent, they had done nothing wrong. In the Court of Appeal, Lord Denning acknowledged that the defendants 'were quite innocent of any intention to take advantage' of the claimant, but nonetheless he found them in breach for using the information 'unconsciously'. Other defendants have been held liable even though the breach of confidence had simply been 'by error or oversight' (*Interfirm Comparison (Australia) Pty Ltd v Law Society of New South Wales* (1975)). However, in *Vestergaard v Bestnet* (2011), the Court of Appeal held that there was no liability for breach of confidence where the defendant had not been in actual receipt of the confidential information. In the main judgment, Arnold J had found Mrs Sig, the Sales Manager for Bestnet, liable for breach of confidence, even though she had had no access to the Fence database. Nor had she known that it had been used to develop Netprotect. He reasoned that since Mrs Sig was under an express contractual obligation of confidence, this continued post employment in relation to trade secrets. Relying upon *Seager v Copydex*, he went on to hold that Mrs Sig was liable even though she was not conscious that what she had done amounted to the misuse of confidential information. Mrs Sig appealed. On appeal, counsel for VF, also relying on *Seager v Copydex*, argued further that once the law imposes an obligation of confidence, whether in equity or as a matter of contract, that obligation is broken even where the obligee uses the information unknowingly. In other words the obligation is one of strict liability. In this case, Mrs Sig was using the information when she placed orders for Netprotect with suppliers. Jacob LJ disagreed. He distinguished *Seager v Copydex* because in that case the defendants were using information which had actually been imparted to them, whereas Mrs Sig was not. He went further to suggest that implying a term of strict liability, such as suggested by VF's counsel, could not be justified in any event. He opined that there 'was no business reason to imply a term of that harsh extent'.

The extent of misuse

3.48 In the case of both patents and copyright, infringement will follow only if a certain level of copying is identified. In the case of copyright, the copying must be of a substantial part of the copyright material. For patent infringement, there must be copying of the essential elements of the patent. There are, however, no fixed rules as to how much confidential information must be misused or disclosed to found an action for breach of confidence. This may mean that an action for breach of confidence has certain advantages, as was illustrated by *Cantor Fitzgerald International v Tradition (UK) Ltd* (1999). The claimant company was an inter-dealer broker in bonds. Its former managing director joined with a number of other former employees who had been responsible for developing the claimant's bond-trading computer systems to work for a rival company, Tradition. The system used by Tradition had similarities to the claimant's, and the claimant alleged breach of confidence and copyright infringement. Although the claimant succeeded in showing copyright infringement of two of its program modules, it failed to do so in respect of its source code, which the court found had actually been reproduced in the defendants' system. Nonetheless, the defendants had disclosed the claimant's source code to Tradition while its system was being set up, and this was found to be a breach of confidence. Furthermore, it is also true that, while a breach of confidence action will not protect trivial tittle-tattle, it will protect ideas, which may not be protected by copyright (see *Fraser v Thames Television Ltd* (1983), para **3.11**).

Must there be detriment?

3.49 It is unlikely that a claimant will bring an action for breach of confidence unless he expected to suffer from, or had already suffered by, the defendant's actions. However, despite the fact that Megarry J's third element specifies that for a breach to occur the unauthorised use must be of 'detriment' to the confider, there is by no means agreement on this point. Even *Coco v AN Clark (Engineering) Ltd* (1968) is unclear. Megarry J himself says he can 'conceive of cases' where a claimant might bring an action without suffering detriment. He gives as an example a case where the information might show the claimant in a favourable light, but injure a relation or friend whom the claimant wishes to protect. In *Seager v Copydex Ltd* (1967), Lord Denning suggested that breach of confidence involves 'prejudice' to the confider. During the 'Spycatcher' case, Lord Keith raised the question once more (*A-G v Guardian Newspapers Ltd* (1988)). He made the obvious point that detriment is usually present in commercial cases. But his comments suggest that the necessary detriment in the case of personal secrets can be so minimal as to be practically meaningless. It was sufficient that the confider did not want the information to be given to people whom he would prefer not to know, even though the disclosure would not be positively harmful to himself. Indeed, Lord Keith went further and suggested that since 'as a general rule' it is in the public interest that confidences should be respected, then the general detriment which a breach causes to this broad public interest may be sufficient, even if there is no specific detriment to the confider. In the same case, Lord Goff suggested it was still an open question, since, although detriment would 'nearly always form part of the case', it 'may not always be necessary'. Meanwhile, Lord Griffiths required detriment or potential detriment in both personal and commercial cases. In fact, the question of detriment is unlikely to be an issue in commercial cases, which would almost by definition involve some financial loss to the claimant, while in cases of personal secrets, the courts are often willing to assume detriment if the other elements of breach of confidence are present. The exception arises in cases involving public information, where the state must positively show why the information should remain confidential. This issue is looked at below.

Defence 1: the public interest defence

3.50 It has been suggested that behind the law of confidentiality lies the belief that there is a public interest in ensuring that 'confidences should be preserved and protected by the law' (*A-G v Guardian Newspapers Ltd* (1988), per Lord Goff). It has also been long maintained by the courts that in certain circumstances, for example, if the confidence concerns an 'iniquity', the obligation of confidence should not be recognised. More recently, the courts have taken the view that on occasion the public interest in knowing certain information may out-balance the public interest in information remaining confidential. The so-called 'public interest' defence has been recognised in relation to information which emanates from government and the public sector, as well as information arising from commercial and personal relationships. The passage of the Human Rights Act 1998 has also had an impact on the public interest defence, most obviously, but not exclusively, in the area of personal privacy. Thus, s 12(3) of the HRA 1998 has been interpreted to mean that the threshold for granting an interim injunction in cases involving a breach of confidence may be higher where freedom of the press is at issue (*Cream Holdings v Banerjee* (2004) HL, see para **3.81**).

The origins of the defence

3.51 The origins of the public interest defence are usually traced to the judgment of Sir William Page-Wood V-C in *Gartside v Outram* (1856), who held that an employee has a duty to the public to disclose information regarding fraudulent practices by his employer, there being 'no confidence as to the disclosure of an iniquity'. Later, in *Weld-Blundell v Stephens* (1920), the Court of Appeal affirmed that in certain circumstances, such as when confidential information relates to a proposed or contemplated crime or a civil wrong, the duty of confidence may be overridden by a duty to the public to disclose.

The defence in contract and equity

3.52 Initially the defence of iniquity or public interest derived from a contractual analysis of the duty of confidence. The courts would not imply a term of confidentiality into a contract whose enforcement would be contrary to public policy. In *Initial Services Ltd v Putterill* (1967), the claimants ran a laundry. The defendant, who was their sales manager, left and took with him documents which he handed to the *Daily Mail*. These documents and information supplied by the defendant suggested, inter alia, a price-fixing agreement between the claimant and other laundries, which should have been registered under the Restrictive Trade Practices Act 1956, but was not. The allegations were published by the *Daily Mail*. The claimants claimed that by disclosing the information to a third party, the defendant was in breach of an implied term of his contract of employment. Lord Denning accepted that, while there was an implied duty of confidence in the contract, it was subject to exceptions, including 'any misconduct of such a nature that it ought in the public interest to be disclosed to others'. Such was the case here, and the defendant was held to have a reasonable defence to the action. However, it is now well established that the defence will also apply where the obligation of confidence is an equitable one (*Fraser v Evans* (1969)). The present balancing exercise, in which the court will weigh up on a case-by-case basis whether or not public interest lies in disclosure of information or in maintaining its confidentiality, has arguably moved the defence away from any narrow dependence upon either contractual or equitable principles (see, for example, the criticisms offered by Gummow J in the Australian case of *Corrs v Collector of Customs* (1987)).

The scope of the defence

3.53 In *Gartside v Outram* (1856), Sir William Page-Wood V-C appeared to limit the defence to the situation in which the confidence concerned an 'iniquity'–hence its original sobriquet of the 'iniquity defence'. In *Initial Services Ltd v Putterill* (1967), Lord Denning said that the defence had a far broader scope, covering 'any misconduct of such a nature that it ought in the public interest to be disclosed to others, including crimes, frauds, misdeeds, both those actually committed and those in contemplation'. Two years later, in *Fraser v Evans* (1969), Lord Denning said that, '[iniquity] is merely an instance of a just cause and excuse for breaking confidence'. In *Beloff v Pressdram Ltd* (1973), Ungoed-Thomas J said that the defence covered:

> …matters carried out or contemplated, in breach of the country's security, or in breach of law, including statutory duty, fraud, or otherwise destructive of the country or its people, including matters medically dangerous to the public; and doubtless other misdeeds of similar gravity.

3.54 By the time *Lion Laboratories Ltd v Evans* (1984) was decided, the defence was already being referred to as 'the public interest defence' rather than 'the iniquity defence'. In *Lion Laboratories*, the question arose as to whether 'a just cause or excuse' had to rest on actual misconduct on the part of the confider. The claimant manufactured the Lion Intoximeter, which the UK police used exclusively when 'breathalysing' motorists. Two ex-employees had contacted a national newspaper with evidence, including internal correspondence, which raised doubts as to its reliability. The claimants obtained an *ex parte* injunction against the ex-employees and the newspaper restraining them from disclosing the information. The defendants appealed, contending that the judge had not given sufficient weight to the public interest in allowing publication of the material when granting the injunction. In response, the claimant argued that, since the confidential information did not show any misconduct on its part, the defendants could not rely on the public interest defence. It was held by the Court of Appeal, in discharging the injunction, that there need be no evidence of wrongdoing to raise the public interest defence. The defence rested upon showing that 'there was a legitimate ground for supposing it is in the public interest for [the information] to be disclosed'. Stephenson LJ then went on to perform a balancing exercise, weighing up the public interest in disclosure against non-disclosure. In this case, the Court of Appeal, unlike the High Court, found that the balance came down squarely in favour of disclosure.

The 'Spycatcher' case

3.55 The decision in *Lion Laboratories Ltd v Evans* (1984) suggested that the public interest defence no longer rested upon the unconscionableness of maintaining the confidentiality of details relating to particular behaviour (or, more properly, misbehaviour) on the part of the confider. Instead, it is submitted it is now possible to see the defence as having evolved into a pure balancing exercise between competing public interests. This was the approach taken by the courts in the 'Spycatcher' case (*A-G v Guardian Newspapers Ltd* (1988); for a more recent case, see *LRT v Mayor of London* (2001)). In 'Spycatcher', the A-G sought to prevent a number of English newspapers from publishing details of the UK's espionage operations as revealed in *Spycatcher*, a book written by a disenchanted agent, Peter Wright, and, in the case of *The Sunday Times*, from serialising the book. In denying an injunction, the House of Lords based their decision on the fact that the material, which had been widely disseminated abroad, no longer had the necessary quality of confidence. However, along the way, the courts at every level considered the public interest defence in some detail.

3.56 Although various conclusions were reached as to whether the public interest demanded the publication of some or all of this material, there was a broad consensus that it was necessary to proceed through a balancing exercise. According to Lord Goff, the most important limiting principle to the scope of an obligation of confidence is that:

> ...the public interest in preserving confidentiality, may be outweighed by some other countervailing public interest which favours disclosure. This limitation may apply...to all types of confidential information. It is this limiting principle which may require a court to carry out a balancing operation, weighing the public interest in maintaining confidence against a countervailing public interest favouring disclosure.

Lord Goff went on to state that, although this limiting principle was once 'narrowly stated' as applying to 'crime or fraud', 'it is now clear that the principle extends to matters of which disclosure is required in the public interest'. Accordingly, the balancing exercise did not merely involve weighing up whether it is better for the public if the information is disclosed, but whether the danger to the public is of such gravity as to make disclosure vital. There was also a general view expressed that to justify an iniquity defence it was insufficient to argue that publication of the allegations of iniquity, if true, would justify an iniquity defence or that allegations of iniquity had been made. It must be shown that they are likely to be true or, alternatively, that there is a prima facie case that the allegations have substance or that a reasonable attempt has been made to verify their truth. On a related point, the Court of Appeal has recently held that it was not a defence to breach of confidence if a third party published information which it knew to be confidential under an honest but mistaken belief that publication was in the public interest (*Campbell v Mirror Group Newspapers Ltd* (2002)).

The balancing exercise in 'Spycatcher'

3.57 By applying the balancing principle to the facts in 'Spycatcher', it was held by Scott J in the High Court and Bingham LJ in the Court of Appeal that, while in relation to Peter Wright's breach of confidence, the most 'pressing social need' would be to maintain the principle that spies do not publish their memoirs, in relation to the newspapers, public interest in freedom of the press might be said to favour publication.

To whom should disclosure be made?

3.58 In 'Spycatcher', the disclosure of the confidential information by the newspapers was made to the general public. Behind the public interest defence lies the principle that limited disclosure may be sufficient to satisfy the public interest. Until recently, it had been settled law that only if proper channels of complaint are lacking or fail to take action may wider dissemination be justified. In *Initial Services Ltd v Putterill* (1967), Lord Denning said that disclosure should be '...to one who has a proper interest to receive the information'. In this case, he held that the defendant was arguably justified in making his disclosure to the public at large through the press. Conversely, in *Francome v Mirror Group Newspapers Ltd* (1984), the Court of Appeal took the view that, pending trial, disclosure to the police and the Jockey Club about the claimant's alleged misconduct would be sufficient to satisfy the public interest. In reaching this conclusion, Lord Donaldson MR made the still apposite observation that newspapers are apt to confuse their own interest in publishing a story with that of the public interest. According to Lord Goff in 'Spycatcher', alleged iniquity in the Secret Service was a 'classic example' where disclosure was sufficient, as there are 'a number of avenues for proper complaint'. These had been enumerated in the judgment of Lord Donaldson, and included the Prime Minister and the Leader of the Opposition. Lord Donaldson doubted that these controls would, in themselves, be insufficient to support the public interest, but conceded that, at bottom, 'if the newspapers seriously concluded that parliamentary control had broken down and that the allegation of significant wrongdoing was supported by compelling evidence, I would accept their right and duty to make the allegation public'.

Defence 2: the confidential information is insufficiently identified

3.59 An action for breach of confidence will fail if the claimant does not identify the information at issue sufficiently clearly (*John Zink Co v Wilkinson* (1973)). In *Ocular Sciences Ltd v Aspect Vision Care Ltd* (1997), Laddie J gave two reasons for this rule. First, when a claimant seeks an injunction, the injunction might be of uncertain scope and, hence, difficult to enforce. Second, the defendant must know what case he has to meet in order to mount a defence. For instance, he may wish to argue that certain items were in the public domain (see also *CMI-Centers GmbH v Phytopharm plc* (1998)). Similarly, it may be an abuse of process to cite information in the action which is not, in fact, confidential (*Searle & Co Ltd v Celltech Ltd* (1982)). In *Ocular Sciences*, the claimants had previously used the defendant company and its directors to manufacture contact lenses. In their statement of claim, the claimants listed as confidential information 'more or less everything' to do with manufacturing contact lenses. During the trial, they dropped their claims to the confidentiality of many of these items. Laddie J held that the claimants had made 'reckless claims' to confidentiality, although he granted an injunction to prevent disclosure of a far more limited category of information which he accepted was, in fact, confidential.

The Human Rights Act 1998, breach of confidence and invasion of privacy

3.60 The incorporation of the ECHR into English law by the HRA 1998 has had a considerable impact on the law of confidentiality in three interrelated areas: the protection of personal privacy, the right to freedom of expression and the scope of the public interest defence. There are two articles of the ECHR which have immediate relevance to the law of confidentiality in these areas. The first is art 8, which concerns the right to privacy. The second is art 10, which concerns the right to freedom of expression. In addition, HRA 1998, s 12 relates to any relief that may be granted which might affect the exercise of the right to freedom of expression.

Finally, HRA 1998, s 6(1) dictates that it is unlawful for a public authority to act in a way which is incompatible with a Convention right.

Personal secrets before the Human Rights Act 1998

3.61 In the UK, the 'tabloid' newspapers have long competed by publishing personal information about the famous and not-so-famous. Increasingly, social networking sites such as Facebook and Twitter have allowed members of the public to engage in similar activity. Although there has been considerable discussion over a long period as to whether personal privacy laws should be introduced, which was particularly intense following the death of Princess Diana in 1997, arguments that they would be an unjustifiable incursion into press freedom have so far prevailed. In the absence of a right to privacy, the law of confidence provided one line of defence for individuals against unwarranted press intrusion into their private lives. In *Argyll v Argyll* (1964), the leading modern case, the claimant sought to prevent her former husband, the Duke of Argyll, and a national newspaper from publishing details of her private life which she had revealed to the Duke during their marriage. Ungoed-Thomas J held that marital secrets were protected by an obligation of confidence. Indeed, even subsequent adultery by one spouse, resulting in divorce, did not relieve the other spouse from the obligation to preserve earlier confidences. In *Tchenguiz v Imerman* (2011), the Court of Appeal confirmed that a wife had an obligation of confidence to her husband in relation to information which outside of marriage would have been held to be either confidential or private. This information might include a private diary or, here, details of her spouse's financial assts. Conversely, marital secrets received less protection in *Woodward v Hutchins* (1977), which involved a number of pop stars. They sought to prevent the defendants, their former public relations officer and a national newspaper, from revealing personal details of their lives, such as, according to one headline, why Mrs Tom Jones threw her jewellery from a car window and that Tom Jones 'got high' on a jumbo jet. In discharging an injunction, Lord Denning in the Court of Appeal held, inter alia, that because the defendants had sought publicity for certain favourable aspects of their lives, they were in no position to claim that other, less favourable aspects, were confidential. It was also true that much of the information was already in the public domain (see para **3.7**). The Court of Appeal appeared to be influenced by the fame of the claimants, and the judgment was criticised, not least because it seemed to allow a well-known individual no defence of confidentiality if he chose to reveal only certain aspects of his private life. Critics of the *Woodward* decision found the approach in *Stephens v Avery* (1988), which also concerned intimate personal confidences, preferable. The claimant had a lesbian affair with a Mrs Telling, who was later murdered by her husband. She told Mrs

Avery, a friend, details of the affair in confidence. Mrs Avery gave the information to a Sunday newspaper. The claimant sued Mrs Avery and the newspaper for breach of confidence, and the defendants sought to have the action struck out. In rejecting the defendants' application, Sir Nicolas Browne-Wilkinson V-C held that it was unconscionable for a person who had received information, including information regarding a sexual relationship, in confidence, to reveal that information, irrespective of the particular relationship between the parties. Nor did he believe that information relating to sexual conduct was 'mere tittle tattle'.

The absence of a right to privacy

3.62 Before the passage of the HRA 1998, it was an accepted principle of English law that there was no free-standing right to privacy (*Kaye v Robertson* (1991)). The common law of confidentiality would protect personal secrets, provided the three prerequisites for a breach of confidentiality could be proved. However, it was less clear whether the law of confidence would protect information which was not confided by one person to another, but where it related to an aspect of an individual's private life which he did not choose to make public (*Campbell v Mirror Group Newspapers Ltd* (2002), per Phillips MR). The results of the lack of a free-standing right to privacy could appear inequitable. In *Kaye*, a well-known television actor, who suffered horrific injuries in a car accident, was photographed and interviewed by the press in his hospital room. The journalists claimed that he had consented to the interview. The claimant subsequently complained that he had been too ill to have given informed consent, and sought to prevent publication of both the photographs and the interview. The case was brought on the grounds, inter alia, of malicious falsehood and libel. In the course of its judgment, the Court of Appeal, which was sympathetic to the claimant's plight, noted the lack of a right to privacy in English law. According to Glidewell LJ:

> If ever a person has a right to be let alone by strangers with no public interest to pursue, it must surely be when he lies in hospital recovering from brain surgery and in no more than partial command of his faculties. It is this invasion of his privacy which underlies the plaintiff's complaint. Yet it alone, however gross, does not entitle him to relief in English law.

Immediately following the passage of the HRA 1998, there was some expectation that a free-standing right to privacy had been imported into English law. However, no such right was recognised by the courts. Instead, through a number of decisions in the years following, the courts sought to re-fashion the tort of breach of confidence, under the influence of the HRA 1998, to provide protection against intrusions into private life. It is submitted that the end result of this refashioning has, in effect, been to introduce something tantamount to a new tort of invasion of privacy into UK law, despite the initial reluctance of the courts to take such a step without explicit legislative sanction.

Privacy and the tort of invasion of privacy post HRA 1998

3.63 The first case to raise the issue of whether the UK had acquired a right to privacy under the HRA 1998 was *Douglas v Hello! Ltd* (2001). The film actors, Michael Douglas and Catherine Zeta Jones, were married in New York in 2000. They sold the exclusive rights to photographs of their wedding to *OK!* magazine for £1m. It was agreed that the couple would select which photographs would be published. Before the wedding, *Hello!* magazine had unsuccessfully competed for these same rights. Despite tight security arrangements which the actors had been obliged to institute under their agreement with *OK!*, a freelance photographer gained access to the wedding and took unauthorised (and apparently unflattering) photographs, which *Hello!* bought for publication in the UK and other European countries. In the High Court, the claimants succeeded in obtaining an injunction against publication which was subsequently lifted by the Court of Appeal. The claimants based their claim on a number of causes of action, including breach of confidence, which they claimed rested both on a breach of trust and on a breach of privacy. In turn, *Hello!* argued, inter alia, that there had been no breach of confidence, as the photographs did not constitute information, and that the claimants had no right of privacy under UK law. The Court of Appeal found that the photographs had been taken in breach of a duty of confidence and that evidence suggested that *Hello!* had been put on notice that the information was confidential. As a result, there was a serious issue to be tried (per Brooke LJ). However, although Sedley LJ suggested, obiter, that the law of confidentiality had developed to the point where it would recognise and appropriately protect the right of personal privacy, the Court of Appeal came to no conclusion as to whether there was, in fact, a right to privacy in the UK. Two years later in *Wainwright v Home Office* (2003), which involved the strip-searching of two individuals during a prison visit, the question arose as to whether the courts should now recognise a new tort of invasion of privacy which had developed from previous domestic case law. Lord Hoffmann in the House of Lords held that there was no general tort of invasion of privacy in UK law. He differentiated between identifying privacy as a value which underlies the existence of a rule of law, and privacy as a principle of law in itself. He concluded by rejecting 'the invitation to declare that since at the latest 1950 there has been a previously unknown tort of invasion of privacy', and he believed that the creation of a new right of privacy was best left to the legislature.

Privacy, freedom of information and the public interest (1): *A v B*

3.64 The Douglases' action against *Hello!* magazine eventually reached the Court of Appeal (see para **3.77**). More recently, *OK!* magazine's own claim against *Hello!* was heard by the House of Lords (see para **3.78**). However, in the meantime, a number of cases were decided which further developed the law relating to privacy. In these cases, unlike in *Douglas v Hello*, the courts were asked not only to look at the protection afforded to privacy following the passage of the HRA 1998, but also at the balance to be struck where there was an apparent conflict between arts 8 and 10 of the ECHR. In *A v B* (2002), the claimant was a successful footballer. B published a Sunday newspaper, in which it intended to publish articles detailing A's affairs with a lap dancer and a nursery school teacher. Both women had supplied the newspaper with details of the affairs and the latter, C, was the second defendant in the action. A was married with children, and his wife was unaware of the affairs. A had obtained an injunction in the High Court to prevent publication of the articles. The defendants successfully applied to the Court of Appeal to have the injunction discharged. In his judgment, Lord Woolf described the circumstances in which the law of confidence would protect the privacy of an individual. He held that a duty of confidence would arise where the party subject to the duty was in a situation where he either knew or ought to know that the other party could reasonably expect his privacy to be protected. The necessary relationship could be expressly created. More often, its existence would have to be inferred from the facts. Whether a duty of confidence did exist would depend upon all the circumstances of the relationship between the parties at the time of the threatened or actual breach. Thus, if the alleged intrusion into privacy occurred in a situation where the person could reasonably expect his privacy to be respected, then that intrusion would be capable of giving rise to liability for breach of confidence unless the intrusion could be justified. However, in situations where the alleged intrusion was the result of the reporting of the information to a third party by a party to the relationship (a material factor in situations where two people had shared a sexual relationship outside of marriage), difficulties arose. One party might wish to exercise her art 10 right to freedom of expression, which would impact on the other's right to maintain confidentiality. The weaker the claim for privacy, the more likely it would be outweighed by the competing claim to freedom of expression.

A v B: applying the principles to the facts

3.65 Lord Woolf CJ held that Jack J in the High Court had erred on a number of points in granting the injunction. Jack J had assumed that A was entitled to the same protection in respect of his 'transient' relationship with C and D as would be available if the information had concerned a married relationship. Lord Woolf took the view that there was a significant difference between the confidentiality that existed in marriage from that in the 'category' of relationships in which A was involved in this case (see also *Theakston v MGN Ltd* (2002)). It was necessary to take into account the degree of intimacy, the relationship within which it occurred, and other circumstances, including the location. The fact that C and D chose to disclose their relationship to B affected A's right to protection, since the opposite would not acknowledge C and D's right to freedom of expression. Furthermore, the High Court should not have rejected the idea that there was a public interest in the proposed publication, since footballers were role models, particularly to young people. It followed that, while A had not courted publicity, 'the fact is that someone holding his position was inevitably a figure in whom a section of the public and the media would be interested'. Indeed, the courts should not ignore the fact that if newspapers do not publish information which the public is interested in, there would be fewer newspapers, and this would not itself be in the public interest. Lord Woolf concluded that relationships of the sort A had with C and D are 'not the categories of relationships which the court should be astute to protect when the other parties to the relationships do not want them to remain confidential', and a pre-trial injunction would be an unjustified interference with press freedom.

3.66 The decision in *A v B* (2002) aroused controversy. Critics noted that when Lord Woolf suggested that the public interest in publishing may simply reside in the fact that information of interest to the public sells more newspapers, which is itself in the public interest, he appeared to blur the traditional distinction in confidence actions between what is of interest to the public and what is in the public interest to publish. It also seemed hard that individuals who become role models by default, for instance because they played football well, should be placed on a similar footing with regard to an invasion of their private lives as those who deliberately present themselves as role models. Finally, if *Stephens v Avery* (1988) had been commended for affording equal protection in confidentiality to sexual relationships, 'irrespective of the relationship between the parties', the decision in *A v B* seemed to represent a retreat from this morally neutral stance.

Personal privacy and the public interest defence (2): *Campbell v MGN*

3.67 The case of *Campbell v Mirror Group Newspapers Ltd* (2002) looked again at the relationship between personal privacy, press freedom and public interest. The claimant, Naomi Campbell, was an internationally famous fashion model who, according to Lord Phillips MR in the Court of Appeal, had 'courted, rather than shunned, publicity'. The defendant, the *Mirror* newspaper, published articles which exposed the fact that she was a drug addict and was attending meetings of Narcotics Anonymous. Photographs of Ms Campbell on the street leaving one of these meetings were also published. The information in these articles, which had come from an anonymous source, contradicted Ms Campbell's own, earlier public claims that she was not a drug addict. The claimant brought proceedings for damages for breach of confidence and for compensation under s 13 of the Data Protection Act 1998 (see para **3.79**). In the High Court, she succeeded on both counts and was awarded modest damages. On appeal, the claimant conceded that the *Mirror* was entitled to publish information that she was a drug addict and that she was receiving treatment, given that she had previously publicly stated she was not, but not the more detailed information concerning her therapy or the photographs. The defendant conceded that this latter information was confidential, despite the claimant's high profile. However, it argued, inter alia, that since the claimant had publicly denied that she had taken drugs, it was entitled to publish the information in the public interest. In the Court of Appeal, Phillips LJ held that a reasonable person of ordinary sensibilities would not find such information offensive (although a different view might be taken of the photographs). In other words, it was too peripheral to shock the conscience and justify the court's intervention, and therefore its publication did not amount to a breach of duty of confidence. Furthermore the Court of Appeal held that the publication of details of Ms Campbell's treatment was necessary to demonstrate that Ms Campbell had initially deceived the public concerning her drug-taking (see also *Campbell v Frisbee* (2002) and *Woodward v Hutchins* (1977)). Ms Campbell appealed to the House of Lords.

3.68 The House of Lords, in an important judgment, reversed the decision in the Court of Appeal, although the judgment was not unanimous (*Campbell v MGN Ltd* (2004)). Their Lordships agreed on the general principles to be applied in an action concerned with an invasion of privacy and on how the rights enshrined in arts 8 and 10 should be balanced. However, they differed on the correct application of these principles to the facts of this particular case. The House of Lords agreed that the question to ask in assessing whether the information is private is whether the person to whom the information relates has a reasonable expectation of privacy. On the balance between arts 8 and 10, the House of Lords held that when faced with an apparent conflict between a right to privacy and to freedom of expression, the courts must undertake a balancing exercise (as per Lord Goff, 'Spycatcher'). Any interference with the public interest in disclosure had to be balanced against the interference with the right of the individual to respect for her private life. According to Lord Hope, the test to be applied is: whether publication of the material pursues a legitimate aim and whether the benefits that will be achieved by its publication are proportionate to the harm that may be done by the interference with the right to privacy. In Baroness Hale's formulation, both the right to privacy and the right to freedom of expression can be interfered with if four conditions are fulfilled: the interference must be in accordance with the law; it must pursue a legitimate aim; it must meet a 'pressing social need'; and it must be proportionate to the legitimate aim pursued.

Campbell: applying the principles to the facts

3.69 On the facts of this case, Lords Hoffmann and Nicholls, in the minority, held that the *Mirror's* right to publish trumped the claimant's right to privacy. They took the view that the *Mirror* had a right to set the record straight both about her treatment and to publish the photographs, and this outweighed any 'residual right to privacy'. They stressed the importance of allowing a proper degree of journalistic margin for the press to deal with a legitimate story in its own way, and publishing the treatment details and photographs added 'colour and conviction'. The majority of the court disagreed, taking the view that Ms Campbell had a strong claim for protection on grounds of privacy in relation to her treatment for drug addiction. According to Lord Hope, publicity about treatment would cause distress, even to those who in other circumstances court publicity. On this test, the information was 'easily identifiable as private'. Furthermore, setting the record straight about the claimant's addiction was not the same as giving details of her treatment, since as to the latter there was no falsehood to be corrected. Nor was there a compelling need for the public to know the details, since they were not used to support the integrity of the story but to attract interest. The balance tipped further towards the protection of the claimant's privacy because of the publication of photographs with the text. These greatly added to the intrusion into her private life. It was irrelevant that the pictures had been taken in a public place (for a European Court of Human Rights decision on this, see *Peck v United Kingdom* (2003). They were not just street scenes, but had been taken deliberately and in secret. Assuming the claimant to be a person of ordinary sensibilities, it would have been distressing for her to see the photographs. The publication of the details of the treatment and the photographs were a gross intrusion in her private life which outweighed the right of the defendants to freedom of expression. Baroness Hale concurred that the photographs were an additional invasion of the claimant's privacy. They were covert pictures of a 'private' activity. As such, they could be contrasted with a photograph showing how the model looks 'when she pops out to the shops for a bottle of milk'. There would be nothing essentially private about this latter information which, given Ms Campbell's profession, would be a legitimate object of public interest.

Invasion of privacy following Campbell

3.70 A number of general propositions emerged from the House of Lords' decision in *Campbell*. Both the right to privacy and the right to freedom of expression are 'vitally important' and neither takes precedence over the other. The question to ask, in assessing whether information is private, is whether the person to whom the information relates has a reasonable expectation of privacy, assuming that he or she is an individual of ordinary sensibilities. There need be no pre-existing relationship of confidence between a claimant and a third party for an obligation of confidence to arise in relation to private information. Information may be private even if it derives from behaviour which occurs in a public place (see *Peck v UK* (2003)). Thus, the information concerning Ms Campbell's drug treatment was private information, although the photographs which showed her entering Narcotics Anonymous were taken on a public thoroughfare. In *Re S (A Child)* (2005), Lord Steyn summarised the general principles identified in *Campbell* thus:

> First, neither Article [8 or 10] has as such precedence over the other. Secondly, where the values under the two Articles are in conflict, an intense focus on the comparative importance of the specific rights being claimed in the individual case is necessary. Thirdly, the justifications for interfering with or restricting each right must be taken into account. Finally, the proportionality test must be applied to each. For convenience, I will call this the ultimate balancing test.

Lord Steyn's approach has subsequently been referred to as 'the new methodology' (see *Mosley v News Group Newspapers* (2008), para **76**).

The invasion of privacy and the influence of the ECHR

3.71 The invasion of privacy through the taking of unauthorised photographs was central to the case of *Von Hannover v Germany* (2004), which followed the *Campbell* decision in the House of Lords. In this case, Princess Caroline of Monaco sought to prevent the publication of photographs of her private life, some of which were taken in public places. The European Court of Human Rights (ECtHR) held that an assessment of whether there had been an invasion of the Princess' privacy was not dependent upon whether or not the photographs had been taken in a public place. Furthermore, it was relevant, although not decisive, that photographs taken by the 'tabloid press' had over time created a 'climate of continual harassment' for the claimant. The ECtHR noted that Princess Caroline was a well-known person who had received a great deal of public attention, although crucially she did not exercise any official function. But it held that there was a fundamental distinction between reporting information which contributed to a 'debate of general public interest', for example about politicians exercising their functions, and reporting details of the private life of an individual who did not have an official position. The former was vital for the public's right to be informed. However, in the case of the latter, where the purpose of publication was to satisfy public curiosity about an individual, albeit one who was well known to the public, that individual had a reasonable expectation of privacy. In this case, the ECtHR concluded that balancing the right to freedom of expression against the right to privacy for the Princess, it was the Princess who had an overriding 'legitimate expectation' of protection of her private life.

The protection of privacy in the UK following *Von Hannover*

3.72   *Von Hannover* was followed by both the High Court and the Court of Appeal in *McKennitt v Ash* ((2005) HC; (2006) CA) and in *HRH Prince of Wales v Associated Newspapers Ltd* ((2006) HC; (2006) CA). In *McKennitt v Ash*, the claimant was a folk-singer and the defendant published a book entitled, *Travels with Loreena McKennitt: My Life as a Friend*. The defendant had been a close friend and a member of the claimant's crew for many years. The claimant alleged that the publication of the book was in breach of confidence. In particular, the claimant objected to information being made public about her personal relationships and feelings. In defence, it was claimed that either the information was not confidential or that the information was in the public interest. This case differed from the situation in *Campbell v MGN* in that there was a pre-existing relationship between the claimant and the defendant. In the High Court, Eady J found for the claimant. The information was confidential and the defendant had disclosed it in breach of confidence. Nor was there a countervailing right to freedom of expression. Following *Von Hannover*, he held that even where there is a genuine public interest, alongside a commercial interest, in the media publishing articles or photographs of well-known figures, such interests would sometimes have to yield to the individual's right to the effective protection of his or her private life. In relation to such private information, it may remain confidential even if it has had a limited distribution to the public and even if the information is trivial. However, it was necessary to make a judgment in all the circumstances as to whether publication of such information, trivial or otherwise, would be an intrusion into the claimant's privacy. The Court of Appeal upheld Eady J in finding that the claimant had a reasonable expectation of privacy in relation to the details of her private life. It also looked at the defendant's argument that some of the material published was 'shared information'. It noted that the situation here differed from that in *A v B*, in that it was a relationship of confidence rather than 'casual sex' and from *Woodward v Hutchins* where, unlike McKennitt, who 'carefully guards her personal privacy', the claimants were not particularly sensitive to personal information being made public. In this case, although the defendant had the shared experiences with the claimant, these could remain confidential. In turning to the defendant's art 10 claim, Buxton LJ held that the UK courts should have regard to the judgment in *Von Hannover*. In particular, the principles enunciated in *Von Hannover* overrode the interpretation of arts 8 and 10 as set out by Lord Woolf in *A v B*. Just because an individual is of interest to the public, there is no automatic public interest in allowing information about that individual being made public. Even if an individual has made some private information public, as had McKennitt, she should be able to choose to keep other information private. He also expressed his doubts that such a rule would be obviated if the individual were a role model as suggested by Lord Woolf.

3.73 In *HRH Prince of Wales v Associated Newspapers Ltd* ((2006) HC; (2006) CA), the claimant, the Prince of Wales, kept a journal in which he recorded his experiences. The journal was circulated to a limited circle of acquaintances in an envelope marked 'private and confidential'. G who was employed by the claimant and who was under a contract to keep confidential information acquired in the course of her employment gave copies of the journal to the defendant. Excerpts which covered the Prince's visit to Hong Kong were published in the *Mail on Sunday*. These excerpts included unflattering comments that the Prince had made about the behaviour of the Chinese at a banquet. The Prince argued that the publication was both an invasion of his right to respect for his private life under art 8 and also a breach of confidence. The newspaper claimed its right to freedom of expression under art 10. The High Court found for the claimant and the defendant appealed. The Court of Appeal dismissed the appeal. It held that the claimant had a reasonable expectation of privacy and publication interfered with his right under art 8. Furthermore, there was clearly a relationship of confidence between the claimant and G and these factors, taken together, heavily outweighed any claim by the defendant that publication of the diary was in the public interest. According to Phillips LJ, the public interest in a democratic society in ensuring that employees respect a duty of confidence placed upon them by their employers may at times supersede in importance the public interest in freedom of information, and this was such an occasion.

Campbell and *Von Hannover* compared

3.74 The judgment in *Von Hannover* gave rise to some debate. Some argued that an unjustified intrusion into private life might arise simply from the photographing of an individual carrying out activities in a public place, where in the case of a public individual such activities did not relate to his or her public role. Others argued against such an absolutist view and suggested instead that key to the *Von Hannover* decision was that the photographing of the Princess occurred within a continuing campaign of press harassment, although the subsequent ECtHR decision, *Sciacca v Italy* (2006), suggests that press harassment was not decisive in the *Von Hannover* case. Furthermore, the absolutist view of *Von Hannover* might appear to conflict with the House of Lords' decision in *Campbell v MGN*

(2004), since, in the latter case, it was held that the right of an individual not to be photographed in a public place did not arise unless there were particular circumstances such as harassment, distress or disclosure through the photographing of private or confidential information. In the case of *Campbell*, for example, the photographs were an intrusion into Ms Campbell's private life because of their connection with her medical condition. Had she merely been buying milk on a public street, there would have been no such intrusion.

Privacy and public spaces: *Murray v Express Newspapers*

3.75 The question of to what extent a reasonable expectation of privacy is compatible with mundane activities in a public place was revisited in *David Murray (by his litigation friends Neil Murray and Joanne Murray) v Express Newspapers plc, Big Pictures (UK) Ltd [BPL]* (2007). The claimant in this case was the infant son of J K Rowling. He was secretly photographed while his parents pushed him in a buggy on an Edinburgh street. These photographs were subsequently published in the first defendant's newspaper. The child's parents brought a claim on his behalf for infringement of his right to privacy. In the High Court, Patten J held that photographs fell within that category of information which, because it was relatively innocuous and distressed neither the child nor his parents, did not constitute an invasion of privacy. According to Patten J, under the current law, there 'remains an area of conduct in a public place which does not raise a reasonable expectation of privacy'. In the case of *Murray*, he believed it included a ride in a pram on a public street. The claimant made a successful appeal to the Court of Appeal. In reaching its decision, the Court of Appeal emphasised the importance of the fact that the action was brought on behalf of the child and was not concerned with the privacy of the parents, not least because the child, David, might have had a reasonable expectation of privacy where the mother did not. The Court of Appeal then set out questions that needed to be asked in an action for breach of privacy.

> The first question is whether there is a reasonable expectation of privacy. This is of course an objective question. As we see it, the question whether there is a reasonable expectation of privacy is a broad one, which takes account of all the circumstances of the case. They include the attributes of the claimant, the nature of the activity in which the claimant was engaged, the place at which it was happening, the nature and purpose of the intrusion, the absence of consent and whether it was known or could be inferred, the effect on the claimant and the circumstances in which and the purposes for which the information came into the hands of the publisher.
>
> If the answer to the first question is yes, then the next question would be:

> *how the balance should be struck as between the individual's right to privacy on the one hand and the publisher's right to publish on the other. If the balance were struck in favour of the individual, publication would be an infringement of his or her Art 8 rights, whereas if the balance were struck in favour of the publisher, there would be no such infringement by reason of a combination of Arts 8(2) and 10 of the ECHR.*

The Court of Appeal concluded, in contrast to Patten J, that David had a reasonable expectation of privacy. It was significant that he was a child and that his parents had sought to protect him from media intrusion. This was so, even though the photographs showed no more than could be seen by anyone in the street. The key fact here was that the photographs would be widely disseminated and hence might increase the risk of further intrusion. The Court of Appeal also went on to say that it was not possible to generalise, as Patten J had done, and hold that routine acts in public did not attract a reasonable expectation of privacy. It would depend on the circumstances. Thus, the position of an adult might be very different from that of a child. The Court believed that this conclusion was compatible with the reasoning in *Von Hannover*. However, it has been pointed out since that the *Murray* decision did not resolve the possible differences between *Campbell* and *von Hannover* (see para **3.74**), since it concerned the ordinary acts of a child and not an adult in a public place, as had both the latter cases. And some might suggest that the situation has been further complicated by the decision of the Court of Appeal in *KGM v News Group Newspapers Ltd* (2011) which held that art 8 could be engaged if the information at issue related to family life, but it should not always be assumed that this would lead to a reasonable expectation of privacy. It would depend upon the particular facts of the case.

Privacy, freedom of expression and contributing to a debate of general interest

3.76 In *von Hannover*, it was stated that one measure of whether the right to freedom of expression outweighed the right to privacy was if the published information contributed to a debate of general interest. From this perspective, the decision in *Murray* was relatively uncontroversial, not least because it concerned the privacy of a young child. The same cannot be said for *Mosley v News Group Newspapers* (2008). For many, not least in the media, the balance between privacy and freedom of expression was far more difficult to draw in this case. The claimant, Max Mosley, was president of the FIA, which oversees Formula 1 motor racing. His father, Oswald Mosley, had been a notorious fascist politician in the 1930s. In 2008, the defendant's newspaper, the *News of the World*, published an article entitled: 'FI BOSS HAS SICK NAZI ORGY WITH 5 HOOKERS', which was accompanied by images of the claimant involved in sadomasochist activities with a number of women. Video footage was also placed on the paper's website. The claimant sued for breach of confidence and infringement of his right to privacy. He accepted that sadomasochistic activities had taken place, but maintained that it was expected of the participants, who knew each other, that they would keep such occasions confidential. One of the participants, Woman E had told a reporter about the event. The claimant argued that the reporter must have known that he was given the information in breach of confidence, not least because he gave Woman E a concealed camera to film it. For its part, the defendant argued that the claimant had no reasonable expectation of privacy. However, even if he did, it was outweighed by the defendant's right to freedom of expression because the activities involved Nazi or concentration-camp role play and were illegal, involving assaults and brothel keeping. Finally, because of the claimant's public position, the public had a right to know of his activities. In his judgment, Eady J followed the two-step test in actions for breach of privacy, which he described as the 'new methodology' (see para **3.70**). He also looked to Lord Goff's judgment in *Spycatcher* as providing a guide to balancing art 8 and art 10, when both are engaged (see para **3.56**). On the question of whether there was a reasonable expectation of privacy or a duty of confidence, Eady J noted that it has been generally recognised by the courts that sexual activity engages art 8. Furthermore, this engagement was not undermined by the nature of the sexual activity involved, or whether it was paid or unpaid. He concluded that the claimant had a reasonable expectation of privacy and that Woman E had an obligation of confidence. Eady J also held that there was no countervailing public interest in publication. Regarding the question of criminal activity, he held that art 10 does not always act as a defence if the crime is technical or trivial. There must be proportionality. In this case the activities would not have been prosecuted. He accepted that had there been a 'Nazi theme' to the event, there might have been a public interest in revealing this, at least to the FIA, but there had been no Nazi theme and hence no public interest in publication. Finally, and most controversially, he turned to the defendant's argument that the activities involved had been 'immoral, depraved and adulterous' as a reason for publication. Eady J took the view that this too was unsupported. He did not think it was for the media to expose sexual conduct merely on grounds of prurience or in the course of a moral crusade, or where there was no significant criminal conduct involved. He concluded: 'The fact that a particular relationship happens to be adulterous, or that someone's tastes are unconventional or "perverted", does not give the media *carte blanche*. Despite involving a public figure, the revelations did not contribute to a debate of general interest.' The claimant succeeded on all counts. It is submitted that although Eady J would maintain that his findings necessarily avoided any moral judgment of the behaviour involved, for many in the media, his failure to condemn such behaviour was itself a moral judgment and hence open to criticism (McLean and Mackey, 'Mosley v News Group Newspapers

Ltd: how sadomasochism changed the face of privacy law: a consideration of the Max Mosley case and other recent developments in privacy law in England and Wales' [2010] *European Intellectual Property Review* 77).

Privacy and commercial secrets: *Douglas v Hello*

3.77 The question of the relationship between personal and commercial secrets was raised in *Douglas v Hello* when it returned to the High Court for trial (*Douglas v Hello! Ltd* (2003)). The trial took place before the House of Lords decision in *Campbell v MGN* (2004) and a subsequent appeal by *OK!* was heard afterwards. The case had been complicated by the fact that in order to pre-empt the publication of the unauthorised photographs by *Hello!*, *OK!* had published the authorised photographs first. On this basis, *Hello!* claimed that the information contained in their photographs was in the public domain. In the High Court, Lindsay J upheld both the Douglases' and *OK!*'s claim for breach of confidence. The claimants' image was a valuable trade asset capable of protection as a trade secret. Alternatively, the claimants were the holders of a 'hybrid' confidence. In other words, they were holders of private and personal information, which they intended to turn into a commodity through sale. In either case, the photographic representation of the wedding had the necessary quality of confidence. Both the photographer and *Hello!* were aware that the wedding was private and both were therefore bound by an obligation of confidence. The fact that the claimants had intended to make the photographs public did not negate the obligation of confidence, as the defendants had argued. The claimants were entitled to a perpetual injunction against their publication and damages. The Court of Appeal upheld the judgment in favour of the Douglases but not *OK!*. Phillips LJ began by acknowledging that an action for breach of confidence was the correct vehicle for protecting the art 8 right to privacy in the UK, but added: 'We cannot pretend that we find it satisfactory to be required to shoe-horn within the action for breach of confidence claims for publication of unauthorised pictures of a private occasion.' He found that the Douglases' wedding was clearly private, as *Hello!* would have known, and fell to 'be protected by the law of confidence'. It was true that information which is in the public domain might no longer be protected by the law of confidence, but this was not necessarily true of photographs. Insofar as they did more than convey information and intruded on privacy by enabling a viewer to focus on intimate person details, there would be a fresh intrusion of privacy when each additional viewer saw the photographs. Furthermore, even if a person authorises the publication of selected personal photographs of a private occasion, he may reasonably feel distress at the publication of unauthorised photographs taken at the same occasion. Turning to the Douglases' commercial claim, Phillips LJ saw no reason why an individual, who had information which he created or which was private or personal from which he intended to profit and from which he could reasonably deny access to third parties, should not succeed in an action for breach of confidence, if the information was used or published to his detriment when the third party was or ought to have been aware that the information was confidential and published it without authority. In this case, *Hello!* was aware that these were unauthorised photographs of a private occasion and they were published to the detriment of the Douglases. *Hello!* was therefore liable for breach of confidence.

Commercial secrets licensed to third parties: *Douglas v Hello*

3.78 As we have seen, in the High Court, *OK!* succeeded in its claim for breach of confidence. However, the Court of Appeal held that in relation to a claim by *OK!*, there was no breach of confidence. According to Phillips LJ, the right of the Douglases to the private information about their wedding was not an intellectual property right. Confidential information was not property, and so could not be owned or transferred. Rather *OK!* merely had a licence to publish certain photographs. The photographs published by *Hello!* were not those which had been licensed by the Douglases, but others which the Douglases rightly claimed invaded their privacy. As such, *OK!*, itself, had no right of action for breach of a commercial confidence. Claims by *OK!* magazine based on the economic torts of unlawful interference with business and conspiracy to injure also failed. *OK!* magazine appealed to the House of Lords (*Douglas v Hello! Ltd (No 10) (2007)*). By a majority verdict, the House of Lords reversed the decision of the Court of Appeal in relation to the claim for breach of confidence. Lord Hoffmann held for the majority that the fact that *OK!* had paid £1m for the benefit of the obligation of confidence imposed on those present at the wedding should not be lost sight of. He noted that, 'Provided that one keeps one's eye firmly on the money and why it was paid, the case is, as Lindsay J held, quite straightforward.' The fact that the information concerned the personal life of the Douglases was irrelevant. What mattered was that the Douglases were in a position to impose an obligation of confidence in respect of the photographs. Nor did it matter that the photographs were intended for publication, since there was no reason why an obligation of confidence should not be upheld in order to enable someone to be the only source of publication, if that were something worth paying for. In addition, the fact that *OK!* published photographs of the wedding a few hours earlier than *Hello!* did not mean that the information in the photographs published by *OK!* was in the public domain. Instead, each picture should be treated as a separate piece of information which *OK!* would have the exclusive right to publish. In his dissenting judgment, Lord Nicholls focused on the question of whether the information in the photographs published by *OK!* lacked the necessary quality of confidence. He believed that secret information could not lie in the difference between the unapproved and the approved photographs, because there was nothing in the former which was not included in the later. As a consequence, the publication of the unapproved photographs was not a breach of confidence. Lord Walker concurred with this view, noting that the confidentiality of information should depend on its nature and not its market value. For similar reasons, the decision of the majority in this case has caused some concern among commentators. Some have suggested that it is tantamount to establishing an 'image right' in the UK, since it would allow celebrities and others to licence their images to third parties for their exclusive use. Others are concerned that by focusing on the inaccessibility of the event rather than upon whether the information, itself, was confidential the House of Lords has dangerously widened the remit of a breach of confidence action (Michalos, '*Douglas v Hello: The Final Frontier*' [2007] *Entertainment Law Review* 241).

The Data Protection Act 1998

3.79 The Data Protection Act 1998 (DPA 1998) regulates the processing of information about individuals. In particular, it is intended to protect individuals against prejudice resulting from the processing of their data, including an invasion of their privacy. An individual who suffers damage or distress through contravention of the Act is entitled to damages. Newspapers, as data processors, have been held to come within the scope of the DPA 1998. Can a claim for a breach of the Act therefore be used as an alternative to a claim for breach of confidence? This question was raised in *Campbell v Mirror Group Newspapers Ltd* (2002). In the High Court, Moreland J held that the *Mirror* had failed to comply with the terms of the DPA 1998, in that it had not obtained the photographs of Ms Campbell fairly, that the processing was unlawful as a breach of confidence, and that the standards of fair processing had not been followed. The newspaper argued that it fell within the exemptions set out in DPA 1998, s 32, which applies to data processed for the purpose of publication, including by journalists, where publication would be in the public interest. Moreland J held that, while s 32 might offer protection during processing of data, no such protection was available after publication. The Court of Appeal disagreed. It held that both publication of data as well as its processing before publication could fall within the scope of s 32. In this case, there was a public interest in publishing the articles. The defendants fell within the s 32 exemption. However, the Court of Appeal did not comment on the High Court's conclusion that the articles had contravened the DPA 1998 in the first instance. Following *Campbell v MGN*, it has been suggested that, although the DPA 1998 was intended to protect personal privacy, it may be used by celebrities who have a commercial interest in protecting their personal image against newspapers seeking to publish unauthorised photographs which are not confidential (Calleja, '*Campbell v Mirror Group Newspapers:* The Price of Fame?' [2003] *Entertainment Law Review* 48).

Remedies

3.80 Given the 'private' nature of the information which by definition forms the sub-ject of a breach of confidence action, it is not surprising that search orders are particularly suited for uncovering evidence of a breach. Indeed, the *Anton Piller* case (see para **1.34**) was itself an action for breach of confidence. As with other breaches of intellectual property rights, the primary concern of the claimant, in a breach of confidence action, is typically to bring the breach to an end as quickly as possible, with damages only a secondary consideration. Again, like other breaches of intellectual property rights, if the claimant obtains an interim injunction, the defendant is likely to abandon its use of the confidential infor-mation. As a result, an interim injunction usually brings a breach of confidence action to an end, without the need for a trial and consequent remedies.

Interim injunctions

3.81 Generally, the principles enunciated in *American Cyanamid Co v Ethicon Ltd* (1975) apply to an action for breach of confidence (*Francome v Mirror Group Newspapers Ltd* (1984)). There is an exception, however, where an action involves the competing claims of a right to confidentiality and the public interest in pub-lishing information. This exception arises because of the enactment of s 12 of the HRA 1998, and in particular s 12(3) which imposes a threshold test which has to be satisfied before a court may grant interlocutory relief in such cases. Section 12(3) reads:

> No such relief [which might affect the exercise of the Convention right to free-dom of expression] is to be granted so as to restrain publication before trial unless the court is satisfied that the applicant is likely to establish that publica-tion should not be allowed.

In *Cream Holdings Ltd v Banerjee* (2005), the House of Lords held that s 12(3) sets a higher threshold for the grant of interim relief against the media than the *American Cyanamid* test of 'a serious question to be tried'. 'Likely', in the context of s 12(3), means 'more likely than not to succeed at trial'. The House of Lords cautioned, however, that this higher threshold would not be appropriate in all cases. There might be some cases where a lesser degree of likelihood of success would be the more appropriate test, if, for example, the potential adverse effects of disclosure on the claimant would be particularly grave, or where a short-lived injunction is needed to enable the court to hear and consider an application for interim relief pending the trial or any other permanent outcome.

Injunctions

3.82 It is possible to identify two common situations where the question of an injunction might arise. Where the breach of confidence is continuing, the court will normally order injunctive relief. In the second situation, the breach has already occurred, and as a result of the defendant's actions the information has now become public. Is it appropriate for the defendant to be restrained, by use of an injunction, from making further disclosure or use of the information? The authorities are by no means decisive on this issue. In *Terrapin Ltd v Builders' Supply Co (Hayes) Ltd* (1967), it was suggested that there could be a continuing obligation not to use the information as a springboard despite the fact that it was now public knowledge. In *Coco v AN Clark (Engineering) Ltd* (1968), the question was raised but not answered. In *A-G v Guardian Newspapers Ltd* (1988), Lord Goff took the view, obiter, that once the subject matter of the breach of confidence action had been 'destroyed' (that is, had been made public), an injunction to prevent further disclosure of the information was generally inappropriate. The proper remedy for the claimant was in damages or an account of profits. He took the same view towards the defendant who is continuing to benefit from the use of the information, having previously employed his unique access to it as a springboard; he doubted that an injunction would be appropriate, suggesting instead that a remedy might lie in a constructive trust or restitution. In *Roger Bullivant Ltd v Ellis* (1987) (see para **3.34**), the court dealt with the latter situation by granting a time-limited injunction. More recently, in *Vestergaard v Bestnet* (2009), Arnold J preferred Lord Goff's approach. Even if the continued use of the confidential information, in this case concerning the production of mosquito nets, produced an 'unfair advantage for the defendant', where the information was no longer confidential, the proper remedy was not an injunction but the imposition of a financial penalty (see para **3.14**). By contrast, in *Douglas v Hello* ((2006) CA), the claimants were granted a perpetual injunction against publication of the photographs acquired by *Hello!*, even though the authorised photographs of the wedding were already in the public domain.

An injunction 'against the world'

3.83 Unusually, a claimant might seek an injunction, not just against an identified defendant or defendants, but *contra mundi*. This was the situation in *Venables* *v News Group Newspapers Ltd* (2001). The claimants had been convicted of the murder of a two-year-old boy. They had been 10 years old at the time of the murder and were now about to be released under new identities. They applied to the Family Division of the High Court for an injunction 'against the world', but in particular the media, to prevent the disclosure of information which would enable them to be identified. The defendants were a newspaper group. The injunction was granted. The judge, Dame Butler-Sloss held, inter alia, that the information regarding the claimants had the necessary quality of confidence and that a duty of confidence could arise independently of a relationship between the parties. The need to protect the claimants' anonymity trumped the right to freedom of expression under art 10, not least because, if the claimants were identified, there might arise a real threat to their lives. The fact that the court had a positive obligation to protect the claimants' rights under ECHR, arts 2 and 3 (which include the right to life) was sufficient for the limitations to freedom of expression set out in art 10(2) to outweigh art 10(1).

Anonymised orders and super-injunctions

3.84 There has been considerable controversy surrounding both the granting of orders which anonymise the names of the parties involved, such as for example in *A v B* (2002), and also the granting of so-called super-injunctions. In the case of the latter, these consist of an additional order which prevents a defendant from making public the existence of the proceedings at issue. Like anonymised orders, super-injunctions are generally, although not always, granted in respect of cases involving an invasion of privacy. Much of the controversy has been provoked by the extent to which both anonymisation and, in particular, super-injunctions derogate from the well-recognised principle that it is in the public interest that court proceedings should take place in public. In the case of *Ntuli v Donald* (2010), the Court of Appeal considered the circumstances in which anonymisation and a super-injunction might be granted. In the High Court, Eady J had granted an anonymised claimant an injunction restraining the defendant and others from publishing the fact that an injunction had been issued. The claimant, Howard Donald, was a member of the popular 'boy-band', Take That. He was unmarried and had two children. The defendant, Adakini Ntuli, had a relationship with Donald. When the relationship, which lasted a number of years ended, Ntuli threatened to sell her story to the press. The injunction allowed Ntuli to make known only the existence of the relationship, which in any event was in the public domain, but not any 'intimate', 'personal' or 'sexually explicit' details, except to family and close friends. The Court of Appeal upheld the fact that these details could not be made public, but overturned both the anonymisation and the super-injunction. In his judgment, Maurice Kay LJ accepted that there were times that to insist upon open justice would lead to a greater injustice. But he went on:

> *This is an essentially case-sensitive subject. Plainly [the claimant] is entitled to expect that the court will adopt procedures which ensure that any ultimate vindication of his Article 8 case is not undermined by the way in which the court has processed the interim applications and the trial itself. On the other hand, the principle of open justice requires that any restrictions are the least that can be imposed consistent with the protection to which [the claimant] is entitled.*

In this case, he was unpersuaded that the claimant had shown that lifting both the super-injunction and the anonymisation order would be invasive of his private or family life.

3.85 An opposite result was reached in *JIH v News Group Newspapers Ltd* (2011). This case concerned a famous sportsman who, while he had a long-term and 'conventional relationship', also had sexual relationships with at least two other women. It was one of these relationships which the defendant newspaper planned to make public. The parties came to an agreement that the identity of the claimant would not be made public and nor would any hearing that took place be reported and asked the court to approve this in a consent order. However, in the High Court, Tugendhat J refused to do so without being persuaded that this was an appropriate course. He took this view because he believed that the parties, in a private agreement, could not 'waive the rights of the public'. Upon hearing the arguments, he refused to grant anonymity to the claimant. The claimant appealed. In the Court of Appeal, the Master of the Rolls set out a number of principles which underlie an anonymity order or a super-injunction. These include the fact that no special treatment should be afforded to public figures and that such orders should be made only if there are no less restrictive or more viable alternatives. In this case, the Master of the Rolls upheld the claimant's appeal. In particular, he took the view that if the nature of the private information is made public, then the order should be anonymised. Conversely, if the name of the claimant is made public then the nature of the private information should not be disclosed. To find otherwise, would mean that the nature of the information about an identified claimant would be disclosed by default. Here, since the nature of the information had been made public, then the claimant should retain his anonymity.

The future of art 8 actions

3.86 There has been some disagreement as to whether super-injunctions are a recent development and whether their number is increasing. It has also been noted that super-injunctions, and indeed injunctions in privacy cases more generally, are almost certainly out of reach of any who are not both rich and famous (and generally male). Certainly, this seems to be the view of much of the media and a number of prominent politicians. Furthermore, the existence of super-injunctions has fed a more general concern that it should be Parliament rather than the judiciary which introduces a law of privacy to the United Kingdom. In addition, some have gone further to argue that any such law should, as in the United States, privilege freedom of expression over the right to privacy, particularly in relation to those already in the public eye. Counter arguments have been made to the effect that the Human Rights Act does not allow for the privileging of freedom of expression over the right to privacy; that no law could cover all those situations where it would be necessary to achieve a balance between them; and that, in any event, courts are not generous in their granting of such injunctions. For example, in the recent case of *LNS v Persons Unknown* (2010), the courts refused to grant a super-injunction to the footballer John Terry to prevent the publication of details of an extra-marital affair. This refusal was based on the fact that Terry had yet to show that his confidence had been breached or that there was any real threat to publish these details in breach of his right to privacy. As a result, there was no party against whom the injunction could be served. Nor did Tugendhat J believe that Terry would necessarily be able to succeed at trial when the issue of freedom of expression was raised. Perhaps, also of importance, was that Terry was worried less about the effect that publication would have on his private life and more on the commercial disadvantage which might result from losing sponsorship deals. Some have taken this decision to show that the courts will be wary of granting super-injunctions except in very particular circumstances. However, this has not served to quell disquiet about their existence among media outlets (Eady, 'Injunctions and the protection of privacy' [2010] *Civil Justice Quarterly* 411).

Damages/an account of profits

3.87 In cases where breach of confidence is based on contract terms, either express or implied, the courts may award compensatory damages (*Nichrotherm Electrical Co Ltd v Percy & Co* (1957)). However, where the breach is an equitable one, the situation is less clear. Courts have traditionally had discretion to award an account of profits, typically an equitable remedy, which is generally designed to satisfy the principle that no one should be permitted to profit from his own wrongdoing (*A-G v Guardian Newspapers Ltd* (1988), per Lord Goff). It follows that for an account to be ordered there will be knowledge on the part of the defendant. An account of profits has been ordered in commercial cases (*Satnam Investments Ltd v Dunlop Heywood & Co Ltd* (1999)). In 'Spycatcher', Lord Keith thought it appropriate that *The Sunday Times* should be ordered to account to the Crown for the profits accruing from its publication of Peter Wright's memoirs. More recently, in *A-G v Blake* (2000), the House of Lords, Lord Hobhouse dissenting, held that in exceptional circumstances an account of profits might be ordered for breach of contract. The defendant, Blake, was a former member of the security services who had been convicted of spying and sentenced to 42 years' imprisonment, from which he had escaped in 1966. He lived in Moscow and in 1990 wrote his memoirs, for which he was to receive substantial payment from the publisher. He had signed an undertaking not to disclose any official information gained during the course of his employment, whether or not it was confidential. The lower courts found that the information disclosed in his memoirs was no longer confidential and there was no public interest in preventing its publication. Should Blake, however, be allowed to benefit from the breach of his undertaking? The House of Lords thought not. In his leading judgment, Lord Nicholls identified the exceptional circumstances which justified an account of profits in this case. They included the fact that no member of the security services should have a financial incentive to break an undertaking, and the fact that much of the appeal of Blake's book resulted from its account of previous breaches of his undertaking.

3.88 Since the nineteenth century, courts have also had discretion to award damages for future loss instead of, or together with, an injunction. In fact, the courts have also ordered damages for past infringement, that is, where an injunction may be inappropriate. The legal basis for such an award has remained a point of contention. In *Seager v Copydex Ltd* (1967), it was held that the remedy of an account of profits was inappropriate, and an enquiry as to damages was ordered. The court may have been influenced by the fact that it did not believe the defendants had acted deliberately. In *Seager v Copydex Ltd (No 2)* (1969), the court held that the basis for assessing the amount of damages should be, by analogy with tort of conversion, on the basis of what a willing purchaser would have paid a willing vendor for the information. In cases where personal, rather than commercial, information has been disclosed, the amount of damages is obviously hard to determine and seldom compensates the plaintiff for his or her distress. Courts have also ordered the delivery up or destruction of infringing material in breach of confidence actions. In *Franklin v Giddins* (1978), where the defendant had taken cuttings from the claimant, the court ordered the delivery up of the resulting nectarine trees.

SELF-TEST QUESTIONS

1   Barbara is a factory foreman at Bedlow Ltd, which manufactures mattresses. Over the years, she has come to understand the production process well and has adjusted the machinery to produce more hard-wearing mattresses. Her husband, Alan, is sales manager. He has had an excellent and long-term relationship with Bedlow's customers. By accident, Alan has received a letter meant only for Bedlow's directors outlining a plan to introduce a revolutionary new mattress, while Barbara has overheard one director on the telephone, making plans to join an Italian rival. Alan is aware that this same director has been 'insider dealing' with

Bedlow's shares. Meanwhile, Barbara and Alan have been offered better-paying jobs by Sleepy Ltd, Bedlow's main British rival. Naturally, Sleepy would be interested in all the relevant information which Barbara and Alan have about the mattress business and Bedlow. How much of this information can Barbara and Alan safely reveal, and to whom, without a breach of confidence?

2   In your opinion, does the public interest defence provide an acceptable balance between the need for personal privacy and the need for certain information to be published for the public good?

3   What particular difficulties are presented by the relationship between employer and employee in relation to confidentiality? How have the courts dealt with these difficulties?

FURTHER READING

Aplin, T, 'Commercial Confidences after the Human Rights Act' [2007] *European Intellectual Property Review* 411.

Aplin, T, 'The relationship between breach of confidence and the "tort of misuse of private information"' [2007] *King's Law Journal* 329.

Calleja, R, 'Campbell v Mirror Group Newspapers: The Price of Fame?' [2003] *Entertainment Law Review* 48.

Conaglen, M, 'Thinking about proprietary remedies for breach of confidence' [2008] *Intellectual Property Quarterly* 82.

Eady, D, 'Injunctions and the protection of privacy' [2010] *Civil Justice Quarterly* 411.

Hull, J, *Commercial Secrecy: Law and Practice* (Sweet & Maxwell, 2008).

Hunt, C, 'Rethinking surreptitious takings in the law of confidence' [2011] *Intellectual Property Quarterly* 66.

McLean A & Mackey C, '*Mosley v News Group Newspapers Ltd*: how sadomasochism changed the face of privacy law: a consideration of the Max Mosley case and other recent developments in privacy law in England and Wales' [2010] *European Intellectual Property Review* 77.

Michalos, C, '*Douglas v Hello*: The Final Frontier' [2007] *Entertainment Law Review* 241.

4 Passing off

SUMMARY

- Development and definitions of passing off
- Unfair competition and the relationship with trade marks
- The first element of passing off: goodwill
- What is not protected by passing off and the definition of a trader
- The second element of passing off: misrepresentation
- Types of actionable misrepresentation
- The definition of distinctiveness
- The third element of passing off: damage
- Defences to passing off
- Character/personality merchandising
- Remedies

Passing off: development and definitions

4.1 Passing off may be defined as a misrepresentation in the course of trade by one trader which damages the goodwill of another. The three essential elements of passing off, the 'classical trinity', are: goodwill, misrepresentation and damage.

The origins of passing off

4.2 Passing off is a common law tort. Its origins lie in the tort of deception. However, passing off does not now depend upon any fraudulent intent by the defendant. In *Perry v Truefitt* (1842), the basic underlying principle of a passing-off action was stated to be: 'A man is not to sell his own goods under the pretence that they are the goods of another man...'. Another summation was given by Lord Halsbury in the later case of *Reddaway & Co Ltd v Banham & Co Ltd* (1896), where he stated that, 'nobody has the right to represent his goods as the goods of somebody else'. Over the past century, passing off has developed on a case-by-case basis. Different factual situations have led to an expansion of the law. As Lord Oliver observed in *Reckitt & Colman Products Ltd v Borden Inc* (1990), the 'Jif Lemon' case: 'this is not a branch of the law in which reference to other cases is of any real assistance except analogically'.

The development of passing off

4.3 It is generally accepted that the modern form of passing off was first defined by Lord Parker in *Spalding & Bros v AW Gamage Ltd* (1915). He said:

> ...the basis of a passing-off action being a false representation by the defendant, it must be proved in each case as a fact that the false representation was made. It may, of course, have been made in express words, but cases of express misrepresentation of this sort are rare. The more common case is where the representation is implied in the use or imitation of a mark, trade name, or get-up with which the goods of another are associated in the minds of the public, or, of a particular class of the public. In such cases the point to be decided is whether, having regard to all the circumstances of the case, the use by the defendant in connection with the goods of the mark, name, or get-up in question impliedly represents such goods to be the goods of the plaintiff, or the goods of the plaintiff of a particular class or quality, or, as it is sometimes put, whether the defendant's use of the mark, name, or get-up is calculated to deceive. It would, however, be impossible to enumerate or classify all the possible ways in which a man may make the false representation relied on.

Spalding extended passing off to encompass situations beyond the limited nature of the misrepresentation described in *Perry v Truefitt* (1842). In *Spalding*, the claimant produced moulded footballs, of an inferior quality, which it abandoned in favour of sewn footballs. The moulded balls were sold to waste rubber merchants. The defendant acquired the moulded balls. It sold them off, with advertising which imitated the claimant's own publicity for the sewn balls. In this case, the misrepresentation was not that the defendant's goods were those of the claimant. They were. Rather, this was a misrepresentation by the defendant as to the quality of the claimant's goods.

The extended form of passing off

4.4 The most important development after *Spalding* came with the so-called 'drinks' cases, of which the 'Champagne' case, *Bollinger v Costa Brava Wine Co Ltd* (1959), was the first. The successful claimants were a number of French champagne producers and importers who objected to the sale in England, by the defendant, of so-called 'Spanish champagne', an alcoholic beverage produced in Spain. Central to this 'extended form of passing off' is that protection is being given to the goodwill in a name or word which has come to mean a particular product, in this case the generic 'Champagne', rather than the product of a particular trader (see para 4.40). The 'Champagne' case was followed by the 'Sherry' and 'Whisky' cases (*Vine Products Ltd v Mackenzie & Co Ltd* (1967); *John Walker & Sons Ltd v Henry Ost & Sons Ltd* (1970)).

Lord Diplock's definition in *Advocaat*

4.5 The 'extended' form of passing off in the 'drinks' cases was confirmed in *Warnink BV v Townend & Sons (Hull) Ltd* (1980), the 'Advocaat' case, which also provided the authoritative modern formulation of passing off. In Lord Diplock's words:

> *Spalding v Gamage and the later cases make it possible to identify five characteristics which must be present in order to create a valid cause of action for passing off: (1) a misrepresentation (2) made by a trader in the course of trade, (3) to prospective customers of his or ultimate consumers of goods or services supplied by him, (4) which is calculated to injure the business or goodwill of another trader (in the sense that it is a reasonably foreseeable consequence) and (5) which causes actual damage to a business or goodwill of the trader by whom the action is brought or (in a quia timet action) will probably do so.*

Quia timet means an action for an injunction to prevent damage for which money is no remedy. Lord Diplock warned that an action for passing off did not necessarily follow, even if all five factors are present (although they would describe a situation which 'morally' might be considered 'dishonest trading'). In his famous phrase, he noted that, 'in seeking to formulate a general proposition of English law, however, one must be particularly careful to beware of the logical fallacy of the undistributed middle.' He explained: 'It does not follow that because all passing-off actions can be shown to present these characteristics, all factual situations which present these characteristics give rise to a cause of action for passing off.' It is Lord Diplock's formulation which has been generally followed. Nonetheless, in the same case Lord Fraser offered his own less general definition which did identify three necessary conditions for passing off. These were that goodwill must be in England, misrepresentations must be about the defendant's goods and not the claimant's (although see reverse passing off at para **4.45**), and the claimant must be a member of a clearly identifiable class which is entitled to make the representation about its own goods. Each of these conditions will be examined later in this chapter.

The classic definition of passing off: the 'Jif Lemon' case

4.6 In *Reckitt & Colman Products Ltd v Borden Inc* (1990) ('Jif Lemon'), Lord Oliver endorsed Lord Diplock's definition and reduced it to three key elements: good-will, misrepresentation and damage. He said:

> First the plaintiff must establish a goodwill or reputation attached to the goods or services which he supplies in the mind of the purchasing public by which the identifying 'get-up' (whether it consists simply of a brand name or a trade description or the individual features of labelling or packaging) under which his particular goods or services are offered to the public, such that the get-up is recognised by the public as distinctive specifically of the plaintiff's goods or services. Secondly, he must demonstrate a misrepresentation by the defendant to the public (whether or not intentional) leading or likely to lead the public to believe that goods or services offered by him are the goods or services of the plaintiff…Thirdly, he must demonstrate that he suffers or, in a quia timet action, is likely to suffer damage by reason of the erroneous belief engendered by the defendant's misrepresentation that the source of the defendant's goods or services is the same as the source of those offered by the plaintiff.

Lord Oliver's 'classic' definition of passing off continues to be authoritative and was even applied in *Consorzio del Prosciutto di Parma v Asda Stores Ltd* (1998), the 'Parma Ham' case, whose facts reflect more closely the extended form of passing off. Lord Oliver's formulation was also preferred to that of Lord Diplock by Millett LJ in *Harrods Ltd v Harrodian School Ltd* (1996), the 'Harrods' case (which is considered at para **4.13**).

Passing off and unfair competition

4.7 There is, in English law, no recognised general tort of unfair competition. As Laddie J stated in *Chocosuisse v Cadbury Ltd* (1998), the 'Swiss Chalet' case: 'in its current state of development the common law does not recognise a general right in one trader to complain of damaging dishonest practices committed by his competitors'. As a result, over the years, the law of passing off has become an important element in preventing some forms of unfair competition. However, there has been continued debate as to how far it might be stretched, and whether passing off can, practically, compensate for the lack of a general law of unfair competition. In 'Advocaat', Lord Diplock warned that it should not be stretched too far, in case it might be used to hamper genuine competition. Passing off should not, for instance, provide a general remedy against damagingly inaccurate statements by rival traders. A similarly cautious approach was taken by Lord Scarman in *Cadbury-Schweppes Pty Ltd v Pub Squash Co Pty Ltd* (1981), the Australian 'Pub Squash' case. The claimant launched a lemon-flavoured soft drink, 'Solo', in a yellow can designed to look like a beer can. In a substantial advertising campaign, the claimant emphasised the masculine nature of the drink and its nostalgic similarity to squash 'which pubs used to make'. The defendant launched a similar product, 'Pub Squash', in a yellow can, with a similarly themed, macho and nostalgic, advertising campaign. A novel question in the case was whether confusion, which arose as the result of an advertising campaign, could amount to passing off. The court held that it could, but that there was no passing off because the can and the advertising were easily distinguishable. In his judgment, Lord Scarman noted the need for balance between competition and laws to prevent unfair competition. He stated:

> But competition must remain free; and competition is safeguarded by the necessity for the plaintiff to prove that he has built up an 'intangible property right' in the advertised descriptions of his product, or, in other words, that he has succeeded by such methods in giving his product a distinctive character accepted by the market. A defendant, however, has done no wrong by entering a market created by another and then competing with its creator. The line may be difficult to draw; but, unless it is drawn, competition will be stifled.

4.8 Despite these strictures, there has been some argument that recent decisions, which appear to downplay the importance of a misrepresentation damaging to the claimant's goodwill as a necessary element in passing off, demonstrate a trend towards the metamorphosis of passing off into a tort of unfair competition. This view was greatly strengthened by comments made obiter by the Court of Appeal in the case of *Arsenal Football Club plc v Reed* (2003). It was suggested by Clarke LJ that the 'cause of action traditionally called passing of' is now 'best referred to as unfair competition'. He added that the traditional form of passing off, as enunciated in such cases as *Reddaway & Co Ltd v Banham & Co Ltd* (1896), 'is no longer definitive of the ambit of the cause of action'. In particular, he cited with approval Cross J's statement in *Vine Products Ltd v Mackenzie & Co Ltd* (1967), which was, in turn, a comment on the decision in *Bollinger v Costa Brava Wine Co Ltd* (1959), the 'Champagne' case. Cross J said that in such a case there was:

*not, in any ordinary sense, any representation that the goods of the defendant
are the goods of the plaintiffs, and evidence that no-one has been confused or
deceived in that way is quite beside the mark. In truth the decision [in Bollinger]
went beyond the well-trodden paths of passing off into the unmapped area of
'unfair trading' or 'unlawful competition'.*

However, recently in *L'Oreal SA v Bellure NV* (2007), Jacob LJ made it clear that
the UK had neither an independent tort of unfair competition, nor had the action
for passing off metamorphosed into such a tort by dropping the requirement of
misrepresentation by the defendant. Indeed, his own view was that a general tort
of unfair competition would be 'anti-competitive', since there would be real difficulties in drawing the line between fair and unfair competition. Nor was it right
for judges to introduce a tort of unfair competition, when the legislature had
failed to do so (for the facts of *L'Oreal v Bellure*, see para **5.53**; Davis, 'Why the
United Kingdom should have a Law against Misappropriation' [2011] *Cambridge
Law Journal* 561).

Other remedies against unfair competition

4.9 Other torts, such as breach of confidence, injurious falsehood and trade libel,
as well as the Trade Marks Act 1994, the Competition Act 1998, implementing
arts 81 and 82 of the Treaty of Rome, the Enterprise Act 2002 and the Business
Protection from Misleading Marketing Regulations 2008 all play a role in com-
bating various forms of unfair competition. In particular, the tort of malicious or
injurious falsehood (trade libel) covers some of the ground left vacant by passing
off. The difference between these torts is that trade libel relates to false statements about the claimant's goods, whereas passing off is concerned with misrepresentations about the defendant's goods which damage the claimant's goodwill
(although reverse passing off is a possible exception to this rule, see para **4.45**).
Unlike passing off, in the case of trade libel the relevant misrepresentation must
be deliberate or reckless (Davis, 'Unfair Competition Law in the United Kingdom'
in Hilty and Henning-Bodewig, *Law Against Unfair Competition* (2007) 183).

The relationship with trade marks

4.10 The protection offered to a trader by a passing-off action, on the one hand, and
by a registered trade mark, on the other, may overlap at many points. The areas
of overlap as well as the important contrasts between passing off and registered
trade marks are, where relevant, highlighted in this chapter (and also in Chapter 5
on Trade Marks). However, it is worth emphasising at the outset that perhaps the
fundamental difference between them is that in passing off there is no property in

the relevant name or other indicia, as there is in a registered trade mark. Instead, passing off protects the claimant's ownership of his goodwill or reputation, which may be damaged by the defendant's misrepresentation. Nonetheless, passing off will on occasion protect identifying insignia that trade marks will not. Changes to trade mark law, introduced by the Trade Marks Act 1994, increased the overlap with passing off. These include the possibility of protecting identical or similar registered trade marks with a reputation on similar and dissimilar goods (see para **5.48** on trade marks). Also, the category of registrable marks was enlarged to include any which may be represented graphically, including, inter alia, shapes. Nonetheless, it is clear that, in some respects, the protection offered by passing off may still be wider than that endowed by trade mark registration. For instance, in *United Biscuits (UK) Ltd v Asda Stores Ltd* (1997), the 'Penguin/Puffin' case, where the defendant marketed a biscuit whose packaging was similar in a number of respects to the Penguin biscuit, the claimant was able to obtain an injunction to prevent passing off, but failed in trade mark infringement, because the precise marks, the Penguin and the Puffin, were not sufficiently similar. It is arguable that traditionally judges have been willing to provide more extensive protection to traders under passing off, for instance, in cases involving descriptive names, precisely because the law of passing off does not provide the potentially indefinite monopoly endowed by trade mark registration.

The first element of passing off: goodwill

4.11 Goodwill is the first element in the 'classical trinity' necessary to establish an action for passing off. Goodwill is personal property, and it is the claimant's goodwill which is the property right protected by a passing-off action. According to Lord Diplock in *Star Industrial Co Ltd v Yap Kwee Kor* (1976): 'A passing-off action is a remedy for the invasion of a right in property not in the mark, name or get-up improperly used, but in the business or goodwill likely to be injured by the misrepresentation made by the passing off of one person's goods as the goods of another.' (See also *Reddaway & Co Ltd v Banham & Co Ltd* (1896), per Lord Herschell; *Spalding & Bros v AW Gamage Ltd* (1915), per Lord Parker.) Note the contrast with trade mark law, where the claimant's property is in the 'mark, name or get-up', provided it is validly registered as a trade mark.

The meaning of goodwill

4.12 Goodwill was defined by Lord Macnaghten in *IRC v Muller & Co's Margarine Ltd* (1901) as 'the benefit and advantage of the good name, reputation and connection of a business. It is the attractive force which brings in custom.' In the same case, Lord Lindsey described goodwill thus:

> I understand the word to include whatever adds value to a business by reason of situation, name and reputation, connection, introduction to old customers, and agreed customers, and agreed absence from competition, or any of these things, and there may be others that do not occur to me.

This definition was adopted by Lord Diplock in *Star Industrial Co Ltd v Yap Kwee Kor* (1976).

The difference between goodwill and reputation

4.13 Although goodwill and reputation are often used interchangeably in relation to passing off, there is strong authority for the proposition that the two do not mean the same, and that passing off protects the former and not the latter. As Millett LJ put it in *Harrods Ltd v Harrodian School Ltd* (1996): 'Damage to goodwill is not confined to loss of custom, but damage to reputation without damage to goodwill is not sufficient to support an action for passing off.' In the 'Harrods' case, the claimant was the proprietor of the 'world famous' department store. It sought to restrain the defendant from running a private preparatory school, named 'The Harrodian School', in premises which had previously housed the 'Harrodian Club', originally established for the store's employees. The claimant certainly had a worldwide reputation, but it was held that the defendant's activities would not damage its goodwill, as such. As Millett LJ stated: 'The name "Harrods" may be universally recognised, but the business with which it is associated in the minds of the public is not all embracing. To be known to everyone is not to be known for everything.' An earlier case where the unsuccessful claimant was held to have had a reputation, but no goodwill, was *Anheuser-Busch Inc v Budějovický* (1984), the 'Budweiser' case. In 'Budweiser', the claimant, an American brewing company, whose beer was sold almost exclusively on American airforce bases, was unable to restrain a Czech company from selling beer under the same name in England. In his judgment, Oliver LJ acknowledged that the American company had a reputation as brewers of beer among a substantial section of the British public, but, in the absence of carrying on a business in England, it did not have the relevant goodwill (for what constitutes the 'relevant' goodwill, see para **4.16**). In *Lego Systems v Lemelstrich* (1983), the court took a more expansive view of the overlap between reputation and goodwill. In this case, the claimant manufactured and distributed children's construction kits made from coloured plastic. The defendant had, for many years, sold gardening equipment including sprinklers made from coloured plastic, under the name 'Lego', although not in the UK.

It sought to expand its market into the UK, and the claimant, who alleged passing off, succeeded in obtaining an injunction. The court found that the claimant had established a 'high' reputation in the mark 'Lego' which extended beyond the field of toys. Indeed, its reputation was wide enough to extend to goods such as gardening equipment, so there was a real risk that the public would be led to believe that there was a business connection between the parties (see also *BBC v Talksport Ltd* (2000)).

Dealings with goodwill

4.14 Goodwill is a form of property and can be assigned, licensed, bequeathed, etc. However, goodwill cannot be separated from the business that generated it. It cannot, for instance, be assigned alone. In *IRC v Muller & Co's Margarine Ltd* (1901), it was said: 'Goodwill regarded as property has no meaning except in connection with some trade, business or calling...In the wide sense, goodwill is inseparable from the business to which it adds value, and, in my opinion, exists where the business is carried on.' By contrast, registered trade marks can be assigned, licensed, etc by their proprietors separately from the business to which they attach, so long as they do not become deceptive (see para **5.107** et seq).

The goodwill must be in England

4.15 Goodwill is local in character and divisible. If the claimant carries on business in a number of countries, then he will have separate goodwill in each country (*Star Industrial Co Ltd v Yap Kwee Kor* (1976), per Lord Diplock). Traditionally, it has been the case that to bring an action for passing off in the UK, the claimant must have goodwill in this country (*MedGen v Passion for Life Products Ltd* (2001)). This was made clear in *Anheuser-Busch Inc v Budějovický* (1984). Section 56 of the Trade Marks Act 1994 has, to some extent, altered the situation, since it offers limited protection to 'well-known' trade marks which are not registered in the UK, whether or not the proprietor of the mark carries on a business or has any goodwill in the UK (see para **5.70**).

What constitutes goodwill

4.16 The courts will decide whether or not a claimant has the relevant goodwill, not on the basis of whether he actually has a place of business in this country, but rather on whether he 'carries on business' in England, in the sense of there being a sufficient number of customers for his product (*Anheuser-Busch Inc v Budějovický* (1984) ('Budweiser'); also *Athlete's Foot Marketing Associates v Cobra Sports Ltd*

(1980)). Customers do not necessarily mean persons who have a direct relationship with the claimant, such as an agent, but also include the ultimate consumers of his goods on the market ('Budweiser'). In *Panhard v Levassor* (1901), the claimants, who produced cars in France, had neither business nor an agency in England. They could not import their cars into England because of certain patent restrictions. However, the cars were bought in France by an importer, who re-sold them in England, and private individuals also went to Paris to buy the cars. The court held that 'England was one of their markets' and that they had the necessary goodwill to bring a passing-off action. Conversely, in 'Budweiser', the claimant's beer was available to the general public only irregularly, but was regularly supplied to US bases. This was held to be insufficient to constitute carrying on business in this country.

Goodwill in services

4.17 A trader who supplies goods abroad may prove goodwill in England by showing he has home-grown customers for his goods. However, a claimant who supplies his services abroad may have greater difficulty in demonstrating the necessary goodwill. In *Alain Bernardin v Pavilion Properties Ltd* (1967), the claimant owned a Paris nightclub, the 'Crazy Horse Saloon', which it advertised in England and from where it also drew customers. In this case the claimant failed to gain an injunction against the defendant, who deliberately copied the claimant's name and its advertising for its UK business. The case of *Pete Waterman Ltd v CBS United Kingdom Ltd* (1993) threw doubt on the 'Crazy Horse' decision. The claimant produced hit records, and by 1987 was known to the public as 'The Hit Factory'. It did not trade as 'The Hit Factory', but had released some records under that name. The defendant opened a recording studio in London which it proposed to call 'The Hit Factory'. The defendant was in partnership with a New York recording company, trading as 'The Hit Factory' since 1970, which drew large numbers of British recording stars and record companies to use its services in the USA. Browne-Wilkinson V-C held that the presence of customers in England was sufficient to constitute carrying on a business with local goodwill, even if the service was provided abroad. Thus, the defendant had acquired sufficient goodwill in England to defeat the claimant's action for passing off. He suggested that the 'Crazy Horse' case had been wrongly decided. The approach taken in the 'Hit Factory' decision was confirmed by the Court of Appeal in *Hotel Cipriani v Cipriani (Grosvenor Street)* (2010). The claimants owned a 'world famous' hotel in Venice, often known simply as the 'Cipriani'. The defendant, a member of the Cipriani family, opened a restaurant in London, called 'Cipriani London', or simply 'Cipriani'. He had been running a similarly named restaurant in New York for some time. Lloyd LJ held that the claimant had acquired a sufficient number of customers in the England to show local goodwill through its marketing efforts and from the fact that a significant number of telephone bookings were made in England by individuals and by travel agents or tour operators. On the other hand, the defendant failed to show he had concurrent goodwill in England, as he did not have 'any significant English custom at the relevant time.' Lloyd LJ, noted that in future the test of direct bookings might become outmoded as establishments allowed customers to book through their own or shared websites. It is submitted that the widespread availability of air travel combined with the commercial possibilities of the internet will inevitability make it easier for foreign-based traders to establish goodwill in England for both goods and services.

Who owns goodwill

4.18 This is a question of fact in each case. It is not necessary for the public to know which individual or company may own the goodwill. It is enough if they think that the claimant's goods derive from a particular source (*Reckitt & Colman Products Ltd v Borden Inc* (1990) ('Jif Lemon')). In *Edge & Sons Ltd v Niccolls & Sons Ltd* (1911), the claimant had manufactured 'washing blues' and 'tints' for many years, which it had sold on a stick without an identifying label or name on the wrapper. It had also advertised that its 'blues' always had a stick. The defendant who had also sold 'blues' and 'tints' for many years, in a different shape and get-up, began selling its products on a stick, but with 'Niccolls' prominent on the label. The House of Lords found passing off. When the defendant began to sell its products in the same get-up but with its name on the bag, the public would think that they were getting the claimant's goods and that the defendant and the claimant were the same (although, of course, they did not know the claimant's identity).

Goodwill can be local

4.19 A passing-off action may protect local goodwill. In *Associated Newspapers, Daily Mail and General Trust v Express Newspapers* (2003), the claimants published the national *Daily Mail* newspaper and the defendant planned to launch a London evening newspaper, called the *London Evening Mail*. The claimants succeeded in an action for passing off. The defendant had argued, inter alia, that there were a number of regional newspapers which also incorporated the word 'mail' in their titles. Laddie J held that it was sufficient that the claimants had goodwill and reputation in London and the south-east of England, which is where the defendant's newspaper would be distributed. He directed that any injunction should be drafted to reflect the geographical extent of the claimants' goodwill. Conversely, in *Chelsea Man Menswear v Chelsea Girl Ltd* (1987), the claimant, who had shops in Leicester, Coventry and London, but was known more widely, sold clothes under the label, 'Chelsea Man'. The defendant, who had a nationwide chain of shops, called 'Chelsea Girl', opened 'Chelsea Man' shops. The claimant obtained a nationwide injunction in the face of the defendant's argument that it should be confined to the three shop locales. It was held that, since the defendant intended to use the name 'Chelsea Man' nationwide, the claimant was entitled to a nationwide injunction (see also *Clock Ltd v Clock House Hotel Ltd* (1936)).

Shared goodwill

4.20   Goodwill may be shared. Shared goodwill might arise in a jointly owned partnership, through the division of a business on the death of the original owner (*Dent v Turpin* (1861); *Sir Robert McAlpine Ltd v Alfred McAlpine plc* (2004)), or if two companies sell the same product under similar identifying insignia, perhaps because of an earlier distribution agreement. In *Associated Newspapers, Daily Mail and General Trust v Express Newspapers* (2003), the defendant had argued that other newspapers, apart from the claimants', also had goodwill attaching to the word 'mail' and, thus, it was not distinctive of the claimants' goods. Laddie J disagreed. He held that it was quite possible for several traders to have a shared reputation in a mark. He went on to say:

> If, as appears to be the case, the claimant has a reputation in The Mail, Daily Mail and The Mail on Sunday as an indication of newspapers from a particular source, the fact that others may have reputations in other newspaper titles which incorporate the word 'mail' does not deprive it of the right to protect that reputation.

Shared goodwill and the extended form of passing off

4.21   The most obvious example of shared goodwill is to be found in the 'drinks-type' cases and their successors. In these cases, it has been suggested that goodwill attaches both to the product and to each producer individually. In *Warnink BV v Townend & Sons* (1979) ('Advocaat'), it was held, obiter, that each member of the class must have built up his own goodwill in the product before he could sue. However, in *Chocosuisse v Cadbury Ltd* (1998) ('Swiss Chalet'), Laddie J suggested that, although this held true for classic passing-off cases, it was unrealistic in the context of the extended form of passing off. Even new producers should be assumed to have a stake in the collective goodwill. The 'Swiss Chalet' case suggests that the class sharing a reputation can be a large one, and the product itself can be broadly (even indefinitely) defined. The claimants, who produced and sold chocolate made in Switzerland, obtained an injunction against the defendant, who sold an English chocolate bar, which was marked 'Swiss Chalet' and carried a picture of the Matterhorn and a chalet. In the High Court, Laddie J held that the relevant goodwill was shared by the producers of any Swiss-made chocolate, no matter how recent their entry into the market. The question then arises as to what products might embody the necessary goodwill for a passing off action. Would the extended form of passing off extend, for example, to products such as bread or milk? In 'Advocaat', Lord Diplock stated that:

> ...the larger the class of traders, the broader must be the range of products to which the descriptive term used by members of the class has been applied, and the more difficult it must be to show that the term at issue had acquired a public reputation and goodwill as denoting a product endowed with recognisable qualities which distinguished it from others of inferior reputation which competed with it in the same market.

In the 'Swiss Chalet' case, Laddie J held that, in order to establish the requisite goodwill, it was sufficient that Swiss chocolate was perceived as having a distinctive reputation, even though the public may not be agreed as to those qualities which made it so. In confirming Laddie J's judgment, the Court of Appeal agreed that it was necessary for the claimants to show that the words 'Swiss chocolate' had been taken by a significant section of the public in England, at the time of the action, to mean only chocolate made in Switzerland and that Swiss-made chocolate had a discrete reputation, distinct from other chocolates, which the manufacturers were entitled to protect. The Court of Appeal endorsed Laddie J's view that the claimants' chocolate had such a reputation. The question of what generic products can claim the necessary goodwill for passing off was at the centre of the recent case, *Diageo N. America Inc v Intercontinental Brands (ICB)* (2010) HC; (2010) CA. The claimant was a leading producer and distributor of vodka. The defendant marketed a drink under the name, 'Vodkat', which was a mixture of vodka and neutral fermented alcohol. The claimant successfully sued for passing off in the High Court and the defendant appealed. The defendant argued, inter alia, that vodka, unlike, for example, champagne or Swiss chocolate, had insufficient goodwill to qualify for protection under the extended form of passing off as it lacked 'quality' or, as was put by the defendant, 'cachet.' Patten LJ held that the real question was not whether the product had cachet but whether it was distinctive, in the sense that customers had come to value it for its inherent qualities rather than for its status. He agreed with Arnold J in the High Court that vodka had a following which created sufficient goodwill in its name to establish an action in passing off. The Court of Appeal identified vodka's distinctive qualities as residing in the fact that it was a 'clear, tasteless, distilled, high strength spirit'. It is certainly the case that similarly precise characteristics could not be attributed to bread or milk.

What is not protected by passing off

4.22 Lord Oliver's formulation in *Reckitt & Colman Products Ltd v Borden Inc* (1990) ('Jif Lemon') suggests that what is protected by passing off is the goodwill attached to the goods or services which the claimant supplies by association with the identifying name or get-up, and not the name or get-up itself (see also *Harrods Ltd v Harrodian School Ltd* (1996)). Traditionally, it had been this principle which differentiated the protection given by passing off from that given by trade mark registration. In 'Jif Lemon', the claimant had sold lemon juice in yellow plastic squeeze packs for many years. They were embossed with the word 'Jif', and they also had a green paper label printed with the word 'Jif'. The product had come to be known as 'Jif Lemon'. The defendant began selling lemon juice in yellow lemon-shaped containers which had a green cap (the claimant's cap was yellow). The claimant obtained an injunction. The point in 'Jif Lemon' was not that the claimant had a proprietary right to the lemon-shaped container. Instead, it had acquired goodwill in the product, which was known to its buyers by the distinctive get-up in which it was sold. However, recent decisions have suggested that courts are increasingly willing to protect identifying insignia against damage caused by loss of distinctiveness, or dilution, quite apart from actual damage to goodwill. (This trend is discussed in para **4.61**.)

The origin of goodwill

4.23 The length of time it takes to establish goodwill sufficient to bring an action for passing off is a question of fact in each case. Put simply, if the claimant shows that he has the requisite goodwill, then the length of time for which it has subsisted is irrelevant. In some instances, the courts have considered actions brought before the claimant has begun actual trading, but where he has already acquired sufficient goodwill, for instance, through pre-launch advertising (*My Kinda Bones Ltd v Dr Pepper Store Co Ltd* (1984) concerned advertising of 'The Chicago Rib Shack', which had not yet opened). In others, the claimant may have traded for some time but be held not to have the necessary goodwill. This is particularly true where the name at issue is primarily descriptive. For instance, despite using the name 'The Gold AM' for six months for a radio station, the claimants, in *County Sound plc v Ocean Sound Ltd* (1991), were held not to have acquired the requisite goodwill because of the descriptive nature of the name. The station played 'golden oldies'.

Assessing goodwill

4.24 The relevant date for assessing goodwill is the date upon which the allegedly infringing activities started (*Phones 4u Ltd v Phone4u.co.uk Internet Ltd* (2006), CA; see also *DaimlerChrysler AG v Javid Alavi (t/a Merc)* (2001)). In the 'Merc' case, the claimant manufactured the Mercedes-Benz car and sold clothing marked 'Mercedes' and 'Mercedes-Benz', but did not have significant sales in the UK until the late 1990s. The defendant had been selling clothing under the mark 'Merc' since 1967. The court held that by the time proceedings began, the defendant had acquired his own goodwill in the mark 'Merc', and it was not possible to limit his reputation through a passing-off action.

The end of goodwill

4.25 Goodwill will not necessarily dissipate when a business closes. Provided the claimant intended and still intends to recommence trading, it may be possible to bring an action for passing off. In *Ad-Lib Club Ltd v Granville* (1970), the claimant had run a successful night club called the 'Ad-Lib Club', which it had been forced to close, some four years before, because of noise complaints. It was looking for alternative premises when the defendant opened its own club, 'Ad-Lib'. The claimant claimed that customers of the latter would be confused. The court held the claimant still retained sufficient residual goodwill in the name to be entitled to an injunction. Remarkably, in *Jules Rimet Ltd (JRCL) v Football Association Ltd (FA)* (2007) the period of non-use was not four but forty years. This case concerned 'World Cup Willie', a cartoon lion dressed in a Union flag shirt which had been created by the FA for the 1966 World Cup. Although very popular at the time, the mascot had not subsequently been exploited by the FA. In 2005, JRCL sought to register Willie as a trade mark. Its application was opposed by the FA on the basis that it had a prior right in passing off. The court agreed that Willie still embodied sufficient goodwill to provide the basis for a successful passing off action. Indeed, evidence of the mascot's continuing goodwill was the fact that JRCL sought to register it as a trade mark in the first place (see also *Sutherland v V2 Music Ltd* (2002)).

Who is a 'trader'?

4.26 For the purposes of passing off, 'trader' is given a wide definition. Generally, provided the claimant can show that there are goods and services supplied to customers, that there is trading activity calculated to generate goodwill, and further, that there will be prospective loss of income from the damage done to this goodwill by the relevant misrepresentation, then this will be sufficient. However, even 'non-trading' organisations such as clubs and charities are entitled to protection from passing off (*Burge v Haycock* (2001)). Traders have been held to include the late politician and diarist, Alan Clark, ballroom dancers and an association of accountants, whose damage, through the defendant's misrepresentation, would have been loss of subscriptions from present or future members (*Society of Accountants and Auditors v Goodway* (1907)). In *Burge*, the Court of Appeal held that the Countryside Alliance, a political group lobbying in support of rural pursuits, could prevent a former member of the extremist British National Party from falsely describing himself as a member of the Alliance in a local election. According to the Court of Appeal, effectively overturning the earlier High Court decision in *Kean v McGivan* (1982), it was unnecessary in an action for passing off for the claimant to carry on a commercial activity. In this case, the Alliance had valuable goodwill in its name which was entitled to protection by the courts.

The second element of passing off: misrepresentation

4.27 Misrepresentation is the second element in passing off. To be actionable in passing off, the misrepresentation must be a material misrepresentation. The deception must be more than momentary and inconsequential (*Cadbury-Schweppes Co Pty Ltd v Pub Squash Pty Ltd* (1981)). In other words, the claimant must demonstrate that it is a reasonably foreseeable consequence of the defendant's misrepresentation that his business or goodwill will be damaged (*Reckitt & Colman Products Ltd v Borden Inc* (1990), per Lord Jauncey). It is worth noting that not all damaging misrepresentations are actionable in passing off. For instance, if Trader A dishonestly claims that a rival Trader B's goods are substandard or overpriced, this may be damaging to Trader B, but it is not, on the face of it, a misrepresentation which is relevant to a passing-off action.

The nature of a material misrepresentation

4.28 The misrepresentation may be express or implied, although express misrepresentations are rare (*Spalding AG v AW Gamage Ltd* (1915), per Lord Parker). The classic misrepresentation, as described by Lord Oliver in *Reckitt & Colman Products Ltd v Borden Inc* (1990), is one by the defendant to the public (whether or not intentional), leading or likely to lead the public to believe that the goods or services offered by him are the goods or services of the claimant. More generally, a material representation may be any misrepresentation where there is use by the defendant of the claimant's indicia as a result of which the defendant's goods or services are 'associated' in the minds of the public with those of the claimant. As summed up by Buckley LJ in *Bollinger v Costa Brava Wine Co Ltd* (1959), a relevant misrepresentation is one calculated to mislead the public into a mistaken belief that 'the goods or services of the defendant or the defendant's business are or is either (a) the goods or services or business of the plaintiff or (b) connected with the plaintiff's business in some way which is likely to damage the plaintiff's goodwill in that business…'.

The difference between confusion and misrepresentation

4.29 Confusion alone does not necessarily amount to a material misrepresentation. In *Phones 4u Ltd v Phone4u.co.uk Internet Ltd* (2007), Jacob LJ summarised the difference between confusion and a material misrepresentation as 'whether what is said to be deception rather than mere confusion is really likely to be damaging to the claimant's goodwill or divert trade from him'. An example of confusion rather than misrepresentation arose in *HFC Bank v HSBC Bank plc* (1999). Here, the claimant operated a bank called HFC, which attracted customers through credit brokers, retail agreements and credit card business. The defendant, formerly known as Midland Bank, was a high street bank owned by HSBC Holdings. In December 1998, it re-branded itself as HSBC. The court held that if the use of HSBC were to constitute a 'relevant' or 'material' misrepresentation, then it would have to be shown that its use had led to some HFC customers or potential customers not only to be exposed to the Midland Bank in circumstances which might not otherwise have occurred but also to enter into a transaction with the bank in the belief that it was HFC. The court could envisage no circumstances in which, where the identity of the bank mattered to the customers, the customer would enter into such a transaction without being disabused of such confusion. In other words, while there might be an initial misrepresentation, it would not be a material one (see also *BP Amoco plc v John Kelly Ltd* (2001)).

Passing off and 'initial interest confusion'

4.30 Recently, the courts have recognised what is termed 'initial interest confusion' as a material misrepresentation in passing off. Initial interest confusion arises when a claimant can show that consumers have been confused even if that confusion has dissipated by the time of purchase. It is submitted that, as a result, *HFC Bank v HSBC Bank* might be decided differently today. Thus, in *Phones 4u*, the claimants had since 1995 owned and operated a nationwide chain of shops under the name, Phones 4u, which sold mobile phones and arranged customer contracts. It also had a domain name, 'phones4u.co.uk'. In 1999, the defendant registered the domain name 'phone4u.co.uk'. It sold mobile phones from this site, although, in 2000, it offered to sell its domain name to the claimant for a considerable sum. The Court of Appeal found that, by the time the defendant commenced trading, the claimant had substantial goodwill in the name, Phones 4u. A considerable number of people sought to contact the claimant, via the defendant's website. Once on the site, the defendant offered to sell them phones, but also stated it was unconnected with the claimant's business. It was found in the Court of Appeal that, despite this disclaimer, customers or potential customers were being deceived into contacting the defendant's website, under the assumption that it was connected with the claimant and, once there, the defendant sought to take advantage of this initial deception. As a result, the claimant's trade and goodwill would be damaged and passing off was made out. Initial interest confusion was also recognised in *Och-Ziff Management Europe Ltd v Och Capital LLP* (2010). The claimant was part of a leading asset management group. The defendant was an independent investment house. The claimant alleged both infringement of its registered marks, 'Och-Ziff' and 'Och', and also passing off. In response, the defendant argued that since the two businesses were not in competition, a customer who initially confused them, would be disabused of any such confusion by the time of his entering into a contract with the defendant. Arnold J held that, while this was undoubtedly the case, such a misrepresentation would still be damaging to the claimant's goodwill (for trade marks, see para **5.47**) (O'Byrne and Allgrove, 'Initial interest confusion recognized by the English courts' [2011] *Journal of Intellectual Property Law and Practice* 147).

An actionable misrepresentation

4.31 An actionable misrepresentation is made by a trader to prospective customers or ultimate customers of his goods and services (*Warnink BV v Townend & Sons (Hull) Ltd* (1979), per Lord Diplock). It is a general rule that customers must be taken as they are found (*Reckitt & Colman Products Ltd v Borden Inc* (1990) ('Jif Lemon'), per Lord Oliver). Customers will not be assumed to be 'morons in a hurry', to quote Foster J in *Morning Star Co-operative Society v Express Newspapers* (1979). But, according to Lord Oliver in 'Jif Lemon', it is no defence that the public would not be misled if they were more 'literate, careful, perspicacious or wary'. The amount of attention that a customer might be expected to exercise must be judged in the context of the type of goods or services concerned, the market in which they are sold, and the habits and characteristics of the customers in that market ('Jif Lemon', per Lord Oliver). In other words, as with so much in passing off, it will depend upon the facts of the particular case. In 'Jif Lemon', the defendant had distinguished its goods from those of the claimant by a different coloured label. The House of Lords made the assumption that the customer for this particular product, which typically would be sold in the supermarket, would look for the distinctive lemon shape and not read the label. It followed that the addition of the label would be insufficient to avoid deception. Conversely, potential customers 'wishing to borrow quite large sums of money from a bank could reasonably be expected to pay rather more attention to the details of the entity with which they are…seeking to do business' (*HFC Bank plc v HSBC Bank plc* (1999)). So, too, might customers of specialist articles sold to the trade. However, in *Ravenhead Brick Co Ltd v Ruabon Brick and Terra Cotta Co* (1937), the court found that it was precisely the knowledgeable purchaser who would be most likely to make the connection between the claimant's 'Rus' bricks and the defendant's 'Sanrus' bricks, because only he would be aware of both. In *Alan Kenneth Clark v Associated Newspapers Ltd* (1998), the 'Alan Clark Diaries' case, the *Evening Standard* produced a weekly parody of the MP's well-known diaries entitled 'Alan Clark's Secret Political Diaries', which carried a photograph of the claimant, followed by a further heading saying, in effect, that the column was how the *Standard*'s journalist imagined the claimant would record the events which followed. One question was whether this was sufficient to alert the reader to the fact that this was a parody, and not the work of the claimant. The court found, inter alia, that the *Evening Standard*, being an evening paper read by many on their journey home, was not the sort of publication which is 'read word for word'. As a result the defendant's disclaimer was not sufficient to avoid confusion among a number of the public.

How many customers must be deceived?

4.32 It is necessary for a substantial number of customers to be misled or to be likely to be misled, but not all of the potential public (*Neutrogena Corpn v Golden Ltd* (1996), per Morritt LJ). There may still be passing off even if many people are not misled (*Alan Kenneth Clark v Associated Newspapers Ltd* (1998)). In *Chocosuisse v Cadbury Ltd* (1998), Laddie J concluded that the number of people who would be confused into thinking that the defendant's chocolate was Swiss chocolate was less than the number who would not. Since the former group was, nonetheless, substantial in number, this was sufficient. Similarly, in *Numatic International Ltd v Qualtex Ltd* (2010), which concerned vacuum cleaners, Floyd J accepted that a moderate amount of care would be exercised by purchasers, but 'there will clearly be a spectrum of carefulness of purchaser ranging from the meticulous to the hurried and distressed'. Although he believed some purchasers would make careful enquiry to ensure they got their intended cleaner, others would not. It was sufficient if the latter group was misled.

Evidence of deception

4.33 Although the presence of customer confusion may not be sufficient to establish a case in passing off, it has been suggested that evidence of actual confusion is always relevant, and may be decisive in judging whether passing off has occurred (*Dame Vivienne Westwood OBE v Anthony Edward Knight* (2011)). Claimants may produce evidence of actual customer confusion. It is also common to produce survey evidence, although the courts are often wary of this (see for example, *Numatic v Qualtex*). Experts may also be called, but there is conflicting authority as to whether their evidence should cover only the circumstances of the trade and their own likely confusion, or whether they may give an opinion on the likelihood of others being confused. The authorities are rehearsed in *Dalgety Spillers Foods Ltd v Food Brokers Ltd* (1994) (see also *Taittinger SA v Allbev Ltd* (1993), the 'Elderflower Champagne' case, at para **4.41**). By contrast, in many passing-off actions, the claimant may not be able to produce evidence of deception. This need not be fatal to the case. As was acknowledged in *Harrods Ltd v Harrodian School Ltd* (1996), an absence of confusion may often be readily explained and is rarely decisive. However, if the alleged passing off has been continuing for some time, the inability of a claimant to provide evidence of confusion may be telling. In *Arsenal Football Club plc v Reed* (2001), Matthew Reed had been selling Arsenal memorabilia outside the football club for 31 years. The memorabilia carried the insignia of the club, which the claimant had also registered as trade marks. The claimant, which carried on substantial merchandising activities, sued for trade mark infringement and passing off. AFC was unable to produce any evidence of confusion. It then asked Laddie J to infer confusion. He would not. According to Laddie J, this was precisely the kind of case in which evidence of confusion might arise, particularly from customers who complained to AFC that they 'were being overcharged', because the same goods were available more cheaply from Mr Reed 'a few yards away'. Instead, Laddie J took the view that those customers who wanted to support AFC by buying 'official' merchandise would not be confused into buying Mr Reed's products. Conversely, a large number of the public would view the Arsenal insignia on Mr Reed's goods as a badge of allegiance, and would be indifferent as to its source. They, too, would not be confused. Nonetheless, it is always up to the court to decide, even if there is no evidence of confusion whatever, whether or not passing off has been established (*Electrolux Ltd v Electrix Ltd* (1953); *Spalding AG v AW Gamage Ltd* (1915), per Lord Parker; *HFC Bank plc v HSBC Bank plc* (2000)). Thus, in *Phones 4u Ltd v Phone4u.co.uk Internet Ltd* (2007), no evidence was adduced that the defendant's misrepresentation had diverted sales from the claimant, despite the fact that they had been trading 'side by side' for five years. However, in the Court of Appeal it was held that such lack of evidence did not undermine the claimant's case. Indeed, it was noted by Jacob LJ, that the more perfect the deception the less likely there is to be evidence of it.

Passing off and fraud

4.34 There is no need for a defendant to have deliberately set out to deceive the public, if that is the probable result of his misrepresentation. However, the courts will see the reasons why the defendant chose to adopt a particular indicia as highly relevant. As stated by Kerr LJ in *Sodastream v Thorn Cascade Co Ltd* (1982), 'it is a question which falls to be asked and answered' (cited in *Harrods Ltd v Harrodian School Ltd* (1996) and *United Biscuits (UK) Ltd v Asda Stores Ltd* (1997) ('Penguin/Puffin')). In the 'Penguin/Puffin' case, the defendants consciously designed the get-up of the Puffin biscuit to avoid deception, yet nonetheless with the idea of 'matching', 'challenging' or 'parodying' the Penguin get-up. Walker J concluded that, 'while aiming to avoid what the law would characterise as deception, they were taking a conscious decision to live dangerously', and that was not something the court was bound to disregard.

Instruments of fraud

4.35 A claimant will usually obtain an injunction against a defendant where passing off is established or threatened. It is also possible to obtain an injunction where the defendant equips himself or intends to equip another with an instrument of fraud, that is, *the means* of passing off by himself or by another. In *BT plc v One in a Million Ltd* (1998), the defendants had registered a large number of internet domain names which were the names or trade marks of well-known commercial enterprises, without their consent. These included BT, Virgin, J Sainsbury and Marks & Spencer. The defendants admitted that they had registered the domain names for profit, planning to sell them to the owners of the goodwill in the names or to others. They advertised the names on the internet. An injunction was granted in the High Court on the grounds, inter alia, that the defendants had created an instrument of deception (or fraud). The defendants appealed, arguing, inter alia, that there should be no injunction unless they had, themselves, threatened passing off. The Court of Appeal found that the defendants had registered the names because of the value of their goodwill and not because, as the defendants unconvincingly claimed, they could be used in some legitimate way by a third party. The registrations were made with the purpose of appropriating the claimants' goodwill or with the intention of threatening dishonest use by the defendants or another to whom the registrations might be sold. Accordingly, the Court of Appeal found that the domain registrations were instruments of fraud. The Court of Appeal also found passing off. An internet search for the owner of the domain name 'Marks & Spencer', for example, would reveal the owner to be the defendants, leading the searcher to assume a connection between the two. This misrepresentation would lead to damage, because it would erode the exclusive goodwill in the name 'Marks & Spencer' (see also, *Phones 4u Ltd v Phone4u.co.uk Internet Ltd* (2007)). In *L'Oreal v Bellure* (2007), Jacob LJ held that there can be no instrument of deception, if what is complained of does not inherently tell a lie, even if 'down the line' it says something dishonest about a product honest in itself (Davis, 'Passing off and joint liability: the rise and fall of instruments of deception' (2011) *European Intellectual Property Review* 203).

Types of actionable misrepresentation

4.36 In *Spalding AG v Gamage Ltd* (1915), Lord Parker stated that it would be 'impossible to enumerate or classify all the possible ways a man may make the false representation relied on'. An operative misrepresentation may arise even when the claimant and the defendant are not competing in the same line of business (*Warnink BV v Townend & Sons (Hull) Ltd* (1979); *Och-Ziff v Och Capital* (2011)). However, it may be easier to establish such a misrepresentation when the parties' trading activities are similar or overlap. If they do not, then the likelihood of confusion may depend upon the scope of the 'field of recognition' of the claimant's reputation (*Lego Systems v Lemelstrich* (1983)). Some of the more common types of actionable misrepresentation to be found in the case law are set out below.

The defendant's goods are the claimant's

4.37 Probably the most common form of passing off, it is likely to arise when the name, mark or get-up of the defendant's products or services is the same or similar to that of the claimant as in the classic 'Jif Lemon' case (see also, *McDonald's Hamburgers Ltd v Burger King (UK) Ltd* (1987)). A defendant may also deceive the public by adopting the claimant's style of promoting or advertising his products and so lead the public to assume that his product is that of the claimant. This was the position in *Cadbury-Schweppes Pty Ltd v Pub Squash Co Pty Ltd* (1981) (see para **4.7**), where the defendant adopted the same advertising theme of nostalgia and manly outdoor pursuits as the unsuccessful claimant. In his judgment, Lord Scarman noted that passing off:

> …is now wide enough to encompass, not only the name or trade mark of a product or business, but other descriptive material, such as slogans or visual images, which advertising could lead the market to associate with the plaintiff's product provided that such material has become part of the goodwill of the product. The test is whether the product has derived from the advertising a distinctive character which the market recognises.

Misrepresentation as to quality

4.38 The defendant may sell the claimant's goods, but pass off inferior goods as if they were of superior quality, as in *Spalding AG v Gamage Ltd* (1915) (see para **4.3**). In *Revlon Inc v Cripps & Lee Ltd* (1979), the defendants imported 'Flex' shampoo, which had been put on the market by an associated company of the claimant in the USA. The imported shampoo was medicated, whereas the 'Flex' shampoo sold in England was not. The Court of Appeal held that the anti-dandruff shampoo was not of inferior quality, and that a 'reasonably perspicacious' member of the public would understand that it was different from the British version. Passing off also failed, because the Court of Appeal found there had been no misrepresentation as to the origin, class or quality of the goods. A misrepresentation may arise when the defendant sells the claimant's second-hand goods as if they were new (*Gillette Safety Razor Co v Diamond Edge Ltd* (1926)), or goods which have passed their 'sell by' date as if they were fresh (*Wilts United Dairies Ltd v Thomas Robinson Sons & Co Ltd* (1958)). In both cases, the defendants will have passed off one class of the claimant's goods as if they were another class.

Misrepresentation as to origin

4.39 What if the goods sold by the defendant are precisely the same as those of the claimant, but have been sold without the claimant's authorisation? This was the situation in *Primark Stores Ltd v Lollypop Clothing Ltd* (2001). The claimant sold jeans to which were attached labels and swing tags with its marks, 'Denim Co' and 'Primark'. The defendant had obtained jeans from the claimant's supplier, made to the claimant's specifications. It was also suggested that the supplier may have attached the claimant's labels to the goods before they were acquired by the defendant. The court held that passing off had occurred. Even if the goods had been ordered by the claimant, they were not its goods and anyone selling them would be making a false representation that they were (Kwan, 'Infringement of Trade Mark and Passing Off by Dealing in Genuine Articles' [2003] *European Intellectual Property Review* 45.)

The extended form of passing off

4.40 Here the defendant misrepresents the quality of his own goods, thereby purporting to render them competitive with a class of products of that quality, rather than with the goods of a particular trader. In the first case to recognise the extended form of passing off, *Bollinger v Costa Brava Wine Co Ltd* (1959), the 'Champagne' case, the claimants were producers and importers of champagne, who sought to restrain the defendant from selling 'Spanish champagne'. The court held that champagne was distinctive of wine produced in the Champagne region of France. As a substantial number of the public would know little about the actual nature of champagne, but view it as a wine with a 'high reputation', they would be misled by the defendant's representation of its product. Other 'drinks' cases followed (see para **4.4**). In *Warnink BV v Townend & Sons (Hull) Ltd* (1979), the claimant had sold the Advocaat drink in the UK since 1911. By 1976, sales totalled 75 per cent of the market. Before 1974, practically all the Advocaat sold in the UK was made in Holland, and consisted of eggs, spirit and sugar, but no wine. In 1974, the defendant began to market 'Old English Advocaat' which was made from eggs and fortified Cyprus wine. In his judgment, Lord Diplock approved the extended form of passing off, the principles of which, established in the 'Champagne' case, were that 'a person competing in a trade may not attach to his product a name or description with which it has no actual association, so as to make use of the reputation and goodwill which has been gained by a product genuinely indicated by the name or description…'.

4.41 The 'Advocaat' case also made it clear that the extended form of passing off might stretch beyond products whose reputation resides in a particular locality. In 'Advocaat', it was the composition of the product which was at issue. Later, in *Taittinger SA v Allbev Ltd* (1993), the claimants objected to the marketing of a (very inexpensive) non-alcoholic sparkling drink as 'Elderflower Champagne' in a champagne-style bottle. The Court of Appeal held that, while the vast majority of the public would not be confused into thinking the beverage was champagne, they might nonetheless believe it was a product that was associated in some way with the champagne houses (particularly in the light of the proliferation of low-alcohol and non-alcohol drinks being introduced by the drinks trade). It has been argued that this decision extends the scope of passing off beyond the traditional 'drinks' cases, where one product might be taken for another (see para **4.61**). There is a further argument that *Chocosuisse v Cadbury Ltd* (1998) also extended the scope of passing off. In this case, Laddie J held that Swiss chocolate manufactured in Switzerland in accordance with Swiss food regulations was sufficiently identifiable as a class of goods with a public reputation, whether or not the public appreciated the identifying characteristics of the class, or, indeed, had quite different views as to what those were. Nonetheless, the court held that despite the uncertainty as to the precise misrepresentation made, it was still a material one.

A business relationship

4.42 The defendant may deceive the public into thinking there is a business relationship between his goods or services and those of the claimant, with the effect that it damages the claimant's reputation and, therefore, his goodwill. In *Ewing v Buttercup Margerine Co Ltd* (1917), the claimant had shops which sold margarine under the name 'Buttercup'. The defendants were planning to sell margarine under the same name, but wholesale. As a result, it was unlikely that customers of the claimants would also be customers of the defendants. However, according to Lord Cozens Hardy MR:

> I should be very sorry indeed if we were so to limit the jurisdiction of the court... I know of no power and can see no principle for holding that a trader may not be injured, and seriously injured, in his business as a trader by a confusion which will lead people to conclude that the defendants are really connected to the plaintiffs or a brand of the plaintiffs or in any way mixed up with them.

Similarly, in *Phones 4u Ltd v Phone4u.co.uk Internet Ltd* (2006), the claimant was unable to provide evidence that it had lost sales to the claimant (see para **4.30**). Indeed, it appeared that the defendant's trade was exiguous. Nonetheless, there was ample evidence that customers or potential customers of the claimant believed they were communicating with the claimant when they accessed the defendant's website and this was held by Jacob LJ to amount to a 'damaging misrepresentation' (see also, *Och-Ziff v Och Capital* (2010)). In *United Biscuits (UK) Ltd v Asda Stores Ltd* (1997), where the product at issue was the supermarket's own-brand biscuit, Walker J did not believe that a substantial number of the public would take the Asda Puffin for the McVities' Penguin. It was enough that the general public might be led to 'suppose', 'assume' or 'guess' that the claimant was in some way responsible for the defendant's goods, in that the two were made by the same manufacturer.

4.43 However, not all connections which might be drawn by the public are relevant. In *Harrods Ltd v Harrodian School Ltd* (1996), the Court of Appeal held that it was not enough that the public might think that Harrods sponsored or backed the school. Millett LJ noted that it was common practice for traders to sponsor sporting or artistic events or teams, but the public would not assume that the sponsor controlled or was responsible for the organisation of the event or the performance of the team. The relevant connection must be one by which the claimants would be taken by the public to have made themselves responsible for the quality of the defendant's goods or services. Kerr LJ dissented, and said a belief in sponsorship was enough (see also *British Legion v British Legion Club (Street) Ltd* (1931)). A sponsorship connection was, indeed, held to be sufficient in the more recent case of *Unilever plc v Griffin* (2010). The defendant was a representative of the extremist British National Party. Its pre-election party political broadcast featured a picture of the iconic 'Marmite' jar together with the slogan, 'Love Britain Vote BNP'. The claimant which manufactured Marmite alleged copyright and trade mark infringement as well as passing off. In relation to the alleged passing off, Arnold J held that the use of the Marmite jar was likely to lead at least some viewers to believe that Unilever had sponsored or endorsed the BNP and as a result its goodwill would be damaged. The 'Harrods' judgment was also distinguished by the Court of Appeal in *Dawnay Day & Co Ltd v Cantor Fitzgerald International* (1999). In *Dawnay Day*, the Court of Appeal suggested that the extent to which the public might expect control or responsibility may differ, depending upon the business concerned. The claimant group of companies, Dawnay Day (DD), which traded in stocks and bonds, included a company, Dawnay Day Securities Ltd (DDSL), which subsequently went into liquidation. The administrator sold DDSL's business to the defendant, who started a new company trading as Dawnay Day Securities (DDS). The Court of Appeal held, inter alia, that it was a sufficient misrepresentation that DDS was part of the claimant's group, even if there was no further misrepresentation that the claimant had any particular control over the quality of DDS's services. The Court of Appeal pointed out that it was characteristic of a brokerage business that some trading companies within a group are closely controlled, while others have almost complete autonomy.

A licensing relationship

4.44 One way the public may be deceived into concluding there is a relevant trade connection between the goods of the claimant and the defendant is if they mistakenly take them to have been made under licence. This issue is central to the problem of character merchandising, which is discussed at para **4.66** et seq.

Reverse (or inverse) passing off

4.45 In these cases, the defendant misrepresents the claimant's goods or services as his own, reversing the classic misrepresentation that the defendant's goods are those of the claimant. It is generally accepted that reverse passing off is not a separate tort, but would fall within the ambit of passing off as set out by Lord Diplock in *Warnink BV v Townend & Sons (Hull) Ltd* (1979). This was confirmed in *Bristol Conservatories Ltd v Custom Built Ltd* (1989). The defendant's salesmen showed prospective customers photographs of conservatories as examples of its own work, which were actually photographs of the claimant's conservatories. The Court of Appeal held that the defendant, by its misrepresentation, was seeking to induce customers to purchase conservatories in the belief that they would actually get a conservatory from the 'commercial source' (that is, the claimant) which had designed and constructed those shown in the photographs. In fact, previous cases had recognised misrepresentations analogous to that in *Bristol Conservatories*, without characterising them as a reversal of the classic misrepresentation. For instance, in *Copydex Ltd v Noso Products Ltd* (1952), the defendant advertised its adhesive 'as shown on television', when in fact it was the claimant's product which had been advertised on television, albeit anonymously. The High Court granted an interlocutory injunction, but was unsure whether the defendant's conduct amounted to passing off. It is submitted that the decision in *Bristol Conservatories* confirms that it was (see also *Samuelson v Producers Distributing Co Ltd* (1931)). Interestingly, the *Bristol Conservatories* decision recognised that the misrepresentation left no room for customer confusion. Since the products were not compared side by side, the prospective customer was not called upon to judge the difference between them. Because reverse passing off is, by definition, characterised by an absence of confusion, it has been argued that it approaches a new tort of unfair competition, in that the defendant is not damaging the claimant's goodwill as such, but appropriating the value that the claimant has in it. In *Bristol Conservatories*, the court held that the claimant's goodwill arose only when the defendants showed the photographs of its conservatories to prospective customers and was simultaneously misappropriated (Carty, 'Inverse Passing Off: A Suitable Addition to Passing Off?' [1993] *European Intellectual Property Review* 370).

Common field of activity/competition

4.46 It is now generally accepted that there is no need for a defendant in a passing-off action to carry on business which competes with that of the claimant, or which may compete with any 'natural extension' of the claimant's business (*Harrods Ltd v Harrodian School Ltd* (1996), per Millett LJ). In other words, there is no need for a common field of activity between the claimant and the defendant. In the early case of *McCulloch v May* (1947), it had been held that a common field of activity was necessary (see para **4.66** et seq on character merchandising). However, this case went against the spirit of earlier decisions. For instance, in *Eastman Photographic Co Ltd v John Griffiths Cycle Corpn Ltd* (1898), the claimant manufactured Kodak cameras, including cameras specifically designed for cyclists, and the defendant was enjoined from selling Kodak bicycles. In *Warnink BV v Townend & Sons (Hull) Ltd* (1979), Lord Diplock confirmed that there could be passing off even though 'the plaintiff and the defendant were not competing traders in the same line of business'. In *Mirage Studios v Counter-Feat Clothing Co Ltd* (1991), the 'Ninja Turtles' case, the 'so-called' requirement that a common field of activity is necessary was held to be discredited. Instead, it was necessary for the claimant to show, not a common field of activity with the defendant, but that there is likely to be confusion between common customers of the parties. For instance, in *Lego Systems v Lemelstrich* (1983) (see para **4.13**), the claimant made plastic construction kits and the defendant made plastic garden hoses. There was evidence that the public could be deceived into thinking that the claimant had diversified into garden equipment. Realistically, however, the presence of a common field of activity may assist the claimant in persuading the court that there has been an operative misrepresentation. By contrast, only a slight overlap, or its absence, will make this far more difficult. In the *Lego* case, Falconer J stated:

> In the law of passing off as it has recently developed, there was no limitation in respect of the parties' fields of activity. Nonetheless, the proximity of the defendants' field of activity to that of the plaintiffs would be relevant as to whether the acts complained of in a particular case amounted to a misrepresentation.

(For another example, see *Stringfellow v McCain Foods (GB) Ltd* (1984), para **4.69**, concerning a night club and oven chips.) It follows that the absence of a common field of activity will also make it more difficult for a claimant to persuade the court it has suffered, or is likely to suffer, damage from any confusion that does result (*Stringfellow*, per Stephenson LJ).

The definition of distinctiveness

4.47 Passing off involves the use by the defendant of a mark, trade name, a get-up, or any other indicia which are associated in the minds of the public with the claimant's goods or services, or, in other words, which are distinctive of them. It is a matter of fact in each case whether the indicia are sufficiently distinctive of the claimant's goods so that their use by the defendant will lead to confusion in the minds of the public. In principle, any indicia can be distinctive. The following discussion looks at marks (which might include, inter alia, personal names, descriptive and fancy names, titles of books, newspapers or other works), get-up and other distinguishing features (see para **4.66** et seq for the related subject of character merchandising).

Distinctiveness in trade marks and passing off

4.48 Until the Trade Marks Act 1994 (TMA 1994), there was a wide disparity between indicia which had been held to be distinctive in passing off, and the more limited range of marks which could be protected by registration. For instance, the classic Coca-Cola bottle, like other containers, was not capable of trade mark registration, but arguably would have been protected in passing off. Since the passage of the TMA 1994, many of these limits have been breached. Nonetheless, trade mark actions are still relatively limited, since a registered mark is only infringed by use of an identical or similar sign (see para **5.36** et seq), whereas a passing-off action may take into account any indicia, alone or in combination, which the claimant maintains has become distinctive of his goods or services. A good example of the contrast can be found in *United Biscuits (UK) Ltd v Asda Stores Ltd* (1997). The claimant had registered the pictorial mark of a penguin for chocolate biscuits, and used a picture of a penguin together with the word 'Penguin' in black lettering on its packaging. The defendant sold chocolate biscuits using both a picture of a puffin and the word 'Puffin' in black lettering. The Penguin and Puffin marks were held to be insufficiently similar for a finding of trade mark infringement. However, taken as a whole, the get-up of the packaging, including the use of the birds, together with other unregistered elements such as colour and materials, were held to be sufficiently similar so that the public would be confused into thinking that the products were associated in some way. An injunction was granted.

Descriptive words

4.49 As is the case with registered trade marks, a fancy or made-up word or an imaginative device will more readily distinguish the goods or services of a trader than a purely descriptive word or a plain get-up (*Cellular Clothing Co v Maxton and Murray* (1899)). Not only is it difficult for a claimant to prove that a descriptive mark has become distinctive, but also, as a matter of public policy, the courts are traditionally reluctant to grant protection in passing off where the mark at issue is descriptive and, therefore, one which other traders may wish to use. This is so even if confusion may result from the use of a purely descriptive word or a word which is common to the trade by more than one trader. Of course, in this case there will be no cause of action in passing off, because there will have been no relevant misrepresentation (*Reckitt & Colman Products Ltd v Borden Inc* (1990), per Lord Jauncey).

Descriptive marks and secondary meanings

4.50 However, even a purely descriptive name or other indicia may, through use, become associated by the public with the claimant's goods or services, so that they may be said to be descriptive of only the claimant's goods. They will have acquired, in the words of the courts, a 'secondary meaning'. In such circumstances, a passing-off action may well succeed. According to Lord Herschell in *Reddaway & Co Ltd v Banham & Co Ltd* (1896):

> To succeed in such a case he [the plaintiff] must demonstrate more than simply the sole use of the descriptive term. He must demonstrate that it has become so closely associated with his goods as to acquire the secondary meaning not simply of goods of that description but specifically of goods of which he and he alone is the source.

In *Reddaway*, the claimant manufactured belting with the descriptive name 'camel hair'. It was found that the words had acquired the secondary meaning of belting manufactured by the claimant. By contrast, in *Cellular Clothing Co v Maxton and Murray* (1899), the claimant failed to establish a secondary meaning in the term 'cellular', which was descriptive of its clothing. Where a claimant uses a descriptive mark, the court will accept very small differences in the defendant's own mark as sufficient to avert the relevant confusion. In *Office Cleaning Services Ltd v Westminster Window and General Cleaners* (1946), the claimant, trading under the name 'Office Cleaning Services', was unable to secure an injunction against the defendant, trading as 'Office Cleaning Association'. The House of Lords believed that a certain amount of confusion was inevitable, but this was a risk the claimant ran by choosing a wholly or partly descriptive name. On the other hand, the public might be expected to exercise greater discrimination when faced with a descriptive name on a product. In trade mark law, descriptive marks which acquire distinctiveness through use may be registered (see para **5.24** et seq). By contrast, a fundamental principle in passing off is that the relevant trader has no ownership in a distinctive mark (or get-up), as such, but rather the right to stop its use by other traders in a deceptive way (*Reddaway*, per Lord Herschell). As a result, it may be more difficult to show acquired distinctiveness for the purposes of trade mark registration since, because registration endows a monopoly, the public interest will demand that a high level of distinctiveness be proved (*Phones 4u Ltd v Phone4u.co.uk Ltd* (2006), per Jacob LJ). Realistically, however, if a descriptive mark is shown to have acquired distinctiveness in passing off, the trader may well end up with a de facto monopoly in his mark in any event (*Reckitt & Colman Products Ltd v Borden Inc* (1990), per Lord Jauncey).

Generic names in passing off

4.51 When a trader introduces a new product, there is a risk that the name he gives to it might come to be taken by the public as denoting all similar products, as well as his own. In other words, it may become the product's generic name. A generic name will lack the distinctiveness necessary to a successful passing off action (*British Vacuum Cleaner Co Ltd v New Vacuum Cleaner Co Ltd* (1907)). In *McCain International v Country Fair Foods* (1981), the claimant introduced a new product, chips that could be cooked in an oven, onto the UK market. It sold the product under the name 'McCain Oven Chips'. About a year later, the defendants marketed their own product under the name 'oven chips', with and without their brand names. The claimant obtained an injunction in the High Court and the defendants appealed. The Court of Appeal decided for the defendants. The claimant's argument that the term 'oven chips' was distinctive of its products was rejected. Instead, the Court of Appeal held it to be a descriptive name. The claimant's case was weakened by the fact that it had always advertised its product as 'McCain Oven Chips', even before its competitors had entered the market. As a result, the court found that 'oven chips' had not acquired a secondary meaning. The Court of Appeal noted that, where a person introduces a new product to the market, gives it a descriptive name and has a monopoly over the product, he cannot then claim a monopoly on the name. He can only require that other traders who enter the market distinguish their products from his–which the defendants had done. Other examples are 'Chicago Pizza' in *Chicago Pizza Pie Factory (My Kinda Town) v Soll* (1983) and, of course, *Cellular Clothing Co v Maxton and Murray* (1899). It is also possible for 'fancy' or made-up names, which bear no relation to the product itself, to become generic (for example, linoleum: *Linoleum Manufacturing Co v Nairn* (1878)). A trader who introduces a new product is always well advised to give it both a generic name and a brand name under which it is sold. An example is the brand name 'Librium' for the tranquilliser, chlordiazepoxide. Indeed, pharmaceutical companies routinely give new drugs both a generic name (often difficult to remember and pronounce!) and a brand name, in the expectation that customers will almost certainly refer to the product by its easier brand name, when ordering the drug.

Generic names and extended passing off

4.52 There is one group of passing-off cases where the generic name is given protection, that, is in the extended form of passing off. In the 'drinks-type' cases, protection is given to a name or word which has come to mean a particular product, rather than a product from a particular trader. The word is entirely descriptive of the product. However, the drinks-type cases differ from other cases involving the use of generic names. In the drinks-type cases, the defendant uses the name deceptively to describe his goods which are not of the same quality as those of the claimant and, as a result, damages, or potentially damages, the claimant's goodwill. In other cases involving generic names, it is precisely because they accurately describe the defendant's goods as well as those of the claimant, as in 'oven chips', that a passing-off action will fail. In *Warnink BV v Townend & Sons (Hull) Ltd* (1979), a product of a particular character or composition had been marketed under a descriptive name, 'Advocaat', under which it had gained a reputation that distinguished it from competing products of a different composition. Therefore, the goodwill in the name enabled those entitled to make use of it to be protected against deceptive use by competitors (see also, *Diageo v ICB* (2010)).

Get-up

4.53 Get-up may be broadly defined as the visual features which distinguish a trader's goods, most notably the packaging of goods. As defined by Lord Jauncey in *Reckitt & Colman Products Ltd v Borden Inc* (1990): 'Get-up is the badge of the plaintiff's goodwill, that which associates the goods with the plaintiff in the mind of the public.' Features of get-up which may be imitated include colour (*BP Amoco plc v John Kelly Ltd* (2001)), the shape of the product or its container ('Jif Lemon' is an example of the latter), the style of lettering and so on. In *Hoffman-La Roche v DDSA Pharmaceuticals* (1969), the claimant, who sold the drug chlordiazepoxide ('Librium') in distinctive green and black capsules, was granted an injunction against the defendant, who used the same colour combination for the same drug. Often, the success of a passing-off case will rest on the defendant's use of a combination of features which together distinguish the claimant's get-up (as in *United Biscuits (UK) Ltd v Asda Stores Ltd* (1997) ('Penguin/Puffin')).

Get-up common to the trade

4.54 As with names and other marks, passing off will protect only those features of get-up which are distinctive of the claimant, and not those which are common to the trade. In *Reckitt & Colman Products Ltd v Borden Inc* (1990), Lord Jauncey observed: 'Any monopoly which a plaintiff may enjoy in get-up will only extend to those parts which are capricious and will not embrace ordinary matters which are in common use.' In 'Jif Lemon', the get-up at issue was the yellow plastic, lemon-shaped container. This was found not 'to be common to the trade' because the lemon-shaped package was not in general use and so it was capable of protection. Nor was it 'available to the trade', since the House of Lords found that having come to distinguish the claimant's goods in the minds of the public, its use by the defendants would be deceptive. According to Romer LJ in *Payton & Co v Snelling, Lampard & Co* (1899), 'When one person has used certain leading features, though common to the trade, if another person is going to put goods on the market, having the same leading features, he should take extra care by the distinguishing features he is going to put on his goods, to see that the goods can be really distinguished.' Interestingly, Lord Bridge in 'Jif Lemon' expressed his concern that the judgment gave a de facto monopoly to the claimant in lemon-shaped containers, which would not have been registrable as trade marks. Since the TMA 1994, of course, it is possible to register shapes.

Get-up and the shape of the goods

4.55 Can the shape of the goods themselves be protected in passing off? In *Reckitt & Colman Products Ltd v Borden Inc* (1990), it was suggested that there was nothing in law that would prevent this result, provided the shape of the object had become distinctive of the particular trader. Arguably, the courts will be reluctant to endow a monopoly over the actual shape of a product if it is necessary for the product to function. However, by adding capricious, decorative or other distinctive features to such a product, a rival trader may be in a position to sell his own version without passing it off as the original ('Jif Lemon', per Lord Jauncey; also *Edge & Sons Ltd v Niccolls & Sons Ltd* (1911)). In 'Jif Lemon', the product itself was the lemon juice and the lemon-shaped container was the packaging, so the question did not arise. In *Numatic v Qualtex* (2010) the question was whether the shape of the defendant's vacuum cleaner was sufficiently similar to that of the claimant's so that the public would assume that they came from the same source. The court recognised that it might be difficult to show that the shape of a product has acquired a secondary meaning since the public would not normally conclude that all products with the same shape (here the court used the example of a red cricket ball) come from the same source. However, in this case, the combination of features of its vacuum cleaner was held to be distinctive of the claimant's goodwill. These features included, inter alia, the name 'Henry', the cleaner's tub-like shape, its black lid which some consumers recognised as a bowler hat and a printed smiling face, from whose nose the hose emerged. The cleaner was also known for its reliability. The court concluded that the similar design of the defendant's cleaner, even lacking both the distinctive smiling face and the name 'Henry', would give rise to a misrepresentation.

The name of the trader need not be known

4.56 The distinguishing indicia need not call to the minds of the public the actual name of the trader to whose goods they attach (*Edge & Sons Ltd v Niccolls & Sons Ltd* (1911); *Reckitt & Colman Products Ltd v Borden Inc* (1990)). As Lord Carswell CJ observed in *BP Amoco plc v John Kelly Ltd* (2002):

> Whether the public is aware of the plaintiff's identity as the manufacturer or supplier of the goods or services is immaterial, as long as they are identified with a particular source which is in fact the plaintiff. For example, if the public is accustomed to rely upon a particular brand name in purchasing goods of a particular description, it matters not at all that there is little or no public awareness of the identity of the proprietor of the brand name.

In *United Biscuits (UK) Ltd v Asda Stores Ltd* (1997), Parker J noted that the public would not know that Penguin biscuits were made by the claimant, but would assume that they came from a single, reliable source.

Passing off and brand 'lookalikes'

4.57 It is now common for supermarkets to sell goods under their own brand name or label alongside the goods of other brand owners. It is certainly true that the supermarket's packaging of its 'own brand' goods is frequently designed to resemble that of famous brand names or a brand leader. Perhaps the most well-known example of such marketing resulted in a dispute between Coca-Cola and J Sainsbury over the latter's product, 'Classic Cola' in 1994. Many would argue that the supermarkets are taking advantage of the brand owner's goodwill, which may be identified with their well-known packaging. Others suggest that a certain uniformity of packaging allows shoppers to make speedy and informed choices in supermarkets. A number of European countries have laws to counter 'misappropriation' of this type. However, there is no comparable law in the UK. (Kelly, 'Protecting the goods: dealing with the lookalike phenomenon through the enforcement of IP rights in the United Kingdom and Ireland' [2011] *European Intellectual Property Review* 425). As a result, passing off remains the main barrier against such practices. This was made clear in *United Biscuits (UK) Ltd v Asda Stores Ltd* (1997). In this case, the court accepted there was passing off, because a substantial number of the public would assume there was a connection between the two products in that the two were made by the same manufacturer, although they would not suppose that the Asda Puffin was the McVitie's Penguin. However, the law of passing off does not always provide brand owners with a remedy for such practices. It may, in particular, be difficult to show an actionable misrepresentation, that is, that consumers are deceived into buying the 'own-brand' product in mistake for the original. In fact, there may be no such confusion. Consumers may be well aware that they are buying the supermarket's product, but are nonetheless attracted to it by its similarity of packaging with a brand leader coupled with its lower price. The recent *Gowers Review of Intellectual Property* (2006) suggested that the government consider introducing a statutory remedy to protect against what it termed 'copycat' packaging.

The third element of passing off: damage

4.58 The third element in passing off is damage (or the likelihood of damage). The damage is to the claimant's goodwill, which is the property protected by a passing-off action. Traditionally, in passing-off cases, there has been a need to establish a real likelihood of more than minimal damage to the claimant's goodwill (*Warnink BV v Townend & Sons (Hull) Ltd* (1979); *Harrods Ltd v Harrodian School Ltd* (1996)). In many cases, where the claimant has proved both goodwill and a relevant misrepresentation by the defendant, the court will go on to infer that there will be a real likelihood of damage. However, as with all generalisations in passing off, the courts' willingness to make this assumption will depend upon the facts of a particular case. For example, the court will look to see whether the parties share a common field of activity (see para **4.46**). More recently, courts have been willing to find passing off where the damage has been, not to the claimant's goodwill, but rather to the distinctiveness of its insignia. Below are set out some of the more common types of damage which have been recognised by the courts.

Damages for lost business

4.59 This is most likely to occur if the parties are in direct competition with each other and the defendant represents his goods as those of the claimant (for example, *Reddaway & Co Ltd v Banham & Co Ltd* (1896)). It may or may not be the case that the defendant's goods are inferior to those of the claimant. In a number of the drinks cases, the defendant's product was inferior (for example, *Warnink BV v Townend & Sons (Hull) Ltd* (1979) (para **4.40**)). However, in *Chocosuisse v Cadbury Ltd* (1998) (see para **4.22**), the defendant's chocolate was not necessarily inferior. A related head of damage is where the defendant sells the claimant's inferior goods as if they were superior (*Spalding AG v AW Gamage Ltd* (1915) (see para **4.3**). In *Gillette UK Ltd v Edenwest Ltd* (1994), the claimant was entitled to damages where the defendant had unwittingly sold counterfeit Gillette blades.

Damage by association

4.60 Here, damage is caused by the defendant's misrepresentation that there is some connection between the parties. In *Och-Ziff v Och Capital* (2010), Arnold J found that this was the type of damage which might arise from 'initial interest confusion' (para **4.30**). Where the quality of the defendant's reputation is inferior to that of the claimant, the courts may be more ready to assume the likelihood of damage. In *Annabel's (Berkeley Square) v Schock* (1972), the claimant, who ran a well-known and 'respectable' night club, won an injunction against the defendant, who had set up an escort agency, also named 'Annabels'. While escort agencies are not illegal, the Court of Appeal recognised that they had 'an indifferent public image' which might affect the claimant's reputation. There are also examples where the defendant's reputation is not necessarily inferior to that of the claimant, but the court has recognised a risk that, as was put by Millett LJ in 'Harrods', the claimant may nonetheless 'lose control over his own reputation' (see also *Warwick Tyre Co Ltd v New Motor & General Rubber Co Ltd* (1910)). One risk might, of course, be that the defendant's reputation will deteriorate in the future because some, at present unforeseen, 'evil might befall' him. For instance, in *British Legion v British Legion Club (Street) Ltd* (1931), the defendant opened a British Legion Club in Street, which was not connected to the national organisation, which ran its own clubs. It was suggested by the court that if 'evil befell' the defendant in the future, for instance, if it were in trouble over licensing laws, the claimant might suffer damage. In *Lego Systems v Lemelstrich* (1983), it was suggested that a customer dissatisfied with the defendant's garden equipment might not buy the claimant's bricks.

Damages for loss of distinctiveness

4.61　In the extended form of passing off, the damage to the claimant's goodwill may be caused directly through lost sales to the defendant, or indirectly through the damage to the reputation of the mark in question. In *Warnink BV v Townend & Sons (Hull) Ltd* (1979), Lord Diplock recognised these two forms of damage. The claimants' trade and goodwill would suffer directly in the loss of sales and indirectly in the debasement of the reputation attaching to the name 'Advocaat'. What is notable about Lord Diplock's formulation is that, although the damage may be direct or indirect, it is still damage to the claimants' goodwill which is at issue. The persistent question is whether the extended form of passing off may be said to go further and offer a remedy purely for loss of distinctiveness in the mark itself. In other words, does it protect against 'dilution' of the reputation in the name or other indicia? Key to the dilution approach is that there is no need for public confusion for such damage to occur. In *Taittinger SA v Allbev Ltd* (1993) (see para 4.41), the Court of Appeal recognised that the claimant would suffer damage both from public confusion that the defendant's product was champagne or that there was some connection between the parties' drinks. However, Gibson LJ went further to state that if the defendant was allowed to market 'Elderflower Champagne', 'there would take place a blurring or erosion of the uniqueness that now attends the word "champagne" so that the exclusive reputation of the champagne houses would be debased'. In the same case, Sir Thomas Bingham MR appeared to endorse this argument, although it was probably obiter. Some take the view that the decision in 'Elderflower' marked a new departure for passing off (Russell, 'The Elderflower Champagne Case: Is This a Further Expansion of the Tort of Passing Off?' [1993] *European Intellectual Property Review* 379). In *Harrods Ltd v Harrodian School Ltd* (1996), Millett LJ warned that, although erosion of a mark's distinctiveness has been recognised as a form of damage to the claimant's goodwill in the business to which the name is connected, care should be taken to ensure that it did not become an 'unacceptable' extension to passing off. He went on to observe that his discomfort arose from the fact that the degeneration of a distinctive brand name into a generic term is not necessarily dependent upon confusion, although the law of passing off 'insists both upon the presence of confusion and damage'. By contrast, in his dissenting judgment, Sir Michael Kerr suggested that the reputation in a trader's name may be such that it constitutes part of the goodwill of his trade, and may therefore be in the nature of a property interest. A later Court of Appeal case to canvas this same territory was *BT plc v One in a Million Ltd* (1998) (see para **4.35**). The Court of Appeal held that the registration of distinctive names, such as 'Marks & Spencer', made a representation to persons who consulted the register that the registrant was connected to, or associated with, the name registered and, thus, with the owner of the goodwill in the name. This amounted to passing off. Damage lay in an erosion of the exclusive goodwill in the name. It is difficult not to see this decision as recognising that passing-off actions may protect damage to the distinctiveness of a name as such, without any obvious evidence of confusion. Dilution was also recognised as a head of damage by Laddie J in *Irvine v Talksport Ltd* (2002). And in *Och-Ziff v Och Capital* (2010), Arnold J held that the principle that passing off protects against a misrepresentation which erodes the distinctiveness of an 'indication' is 'well established'. (The protection afforded by trade mark registration against dilution is considered at para **5.52** et seq.)

Defences to passing off

4.62 The three most important defences in a passing-off action are:

- use of own name;
- honest concurrent use;
- delay.

Each of these is looked at below.

Use of own name

4.63 The general rule is that a trader cannot use his own name if the effect would be to pass off his goods as those of another. This is true even if the use is innocent. There is a very limited defence (and exactly how limited is a matter for debate) that a trader may use his own name as a trade name, provided that he does so honestly and that he does nothing more than cause confusion with another's business (*Rodgers & Sons Ltd v Rodgers & Co* (1924); also *Parker-Knoll Ltd v Knoll International* (1962) and *Asprey and Garrard Ltd v WRA (Guns) Ltd* (2001)). Furthermore, use must be of the defendant's full name and not of nicknames or abbreviations (*Biba Group Ltd v Biba Boutique* (1980)). Companies are even less likely to succeed with this defence. In *Asprey*, the Court of Appeal held that the 'own name' defence had never been meant to apply to the names of new companies, 'as otherwise the route to piracy would be obvious'. Interestingly, the TMA 1994 allows a broader defence. Use by a person of his own name and address will not infringe a registered trade mark, provided the use is in accordance with honest business practices. Such use also extends to companies (on trade marks, see para **5.73**).

Honest concurrent use

4.64 Sometimes two traders may use a name or mark concurrently. If the name or mark is distinctive of both traders (rather than having lost its distinctiveness altogether as a result), then a situation may arise in which the law recognises the right of both traders to continue such use. In *Habib Bank Ltd v Habib Bank AG Zurich* (1981), the court found that where two traders had concurrently made use of the same name, there may be 'a factual situation in which neither of them can be said to be guilty of any misrepresentation'. Clearly, where concurrent use is long-standing, a claimant may find it difficult to prove either an operative misrepresentation or the likelihood of damage.

Delay

4.65 There is no 'time limit' for bringing a passing-off action, as long as the claimant can prove all the elements of passing off. In *DaimlerChrysler AG v Javid Alavi (t/a Merc)* (2001), Pumfrey J suggested, obiter, that 'there must come a time after which the court would not interfere with a continued course of trading which might have involved passing off at its inception but no longer did so ...'. He added that, 'logically, this point would come six years after it could safely be said that there was no deception' and that the defendant had established independent goodwill. Certainly, if a claimant delays, he may find it more difficult to persuade the court that there is an operative misrepresentation or that there is the likelihood of damage. In *Bulmer v Bollinger* (1971), the champagne houses failed to prevent the defendant from using the name 'champagne perry' for cider, a name which it had used for 18 years, because the claimants were unable to show that, in all that time, there had been any confusion, or that they had suffered any damage because of the defendant's actions. In some circumstances, delay by the claimant may give rise to a defence of acquiescence or estoppel, if the claimant's actions, on the particular facts of the case, are found by the court to have been 'unconscionable' or 'inequitable' (*Habib Bank Ltd v Habib Bank AG Zurich* (1981)).

Character and personality merchandising

4.66 Character merchandising involves merchandising products by reference to fictional characters, while personality merchandising involves similar activities in relation to real individuals. A number of countries, including the USA, have introduced separate publicity rights for famous individuals. In the UK, however, those who engage in character or personality merchandising have most frequently resorted to the law of passing off to protect their interests. One reason for this has been that, until the passage of the TMA 1994, trade mark registration had offered limited protection to both character and personality merchandising. Under the TMA 1938, trade mark proprietors were forbidden to traffic in their marks. In effect, this provision prevented merchandisers from registering famous names or characters as trade marks if their intention was to deal in the marks primarily as commodities in their own right, rather than to identify or promote merchandise in which they were interested (*Re American Greetings Corpn's Application* (1984)). There were also stringent restrictions on the licensing of marks. It was assumed, before its passage, that the TMA 1994 would offer more extensive protection to character and personality merchandising, by sweeping away the anti-trafficking provisions and allowing registration of marks for licensing purposes alone. Although these changes have widened the area of legal protection offered to such merchandising, the *Elvis Presley Trade Marks* (1999) decision suggests that the protection offered under trade mark law, particularly in relation to personality merchandising, remains limited, and passing off will continue to play a role (discussed in relation to trade marks at para **5.112**).

Character/personality merchandising and passing off: the basis for protection

4.67 It is important to remember that in UK law there is no protection offered to a name, or even to a fictional character 'as such'. There can be no copyright in a name (*Du Boulay v Du Boulay* (1869)). To succeed in passing off, it is necessary to demonstrate, not only that there is a material misrepresentation, but also that there is goodwill, that is, an economic interest, which will be damaged. It is quite possible for an individual to have a business to which his name is connected and in which his goodwill can be damaged. For instance, cases which involve false attribution of authorship may be placed in this category. In *Alan Kenneth Clark v Associated Newspapers Ltd* (1998), it was Alan Clark's reputation and goodwill as an author which was put at risk by the defendant's parody, and so, too, were prospective sales of his published works and the market value of his rights to exploit his works (see also *Marengo v Daily Sketch* (1946)). The problem has been that not all famous people, or, indeed, those who create fictional characters, can show a business with goodwill, even as they may wish to complain that the use of a name or character, the same or similar to their own, implies a connection or even an endorsement that does not exist.

Character/personality merchandising: the common field of activity

4.68   In passing-off cases, until relatively recently, the courts have sought to identify a common field of activity between the real character or the merchandising of a fictional character and the defendant. In the early case of *McCulloch v May (Produce Distributors) Ltd* (1947), Uncle Mac, a children's radio presenter, tried to restrain the defendant from selling a breakfast cereal, also named 'Uncle Mac'. He failed, because the court could find no common field of activity between the claimant and the defendant. In later cases, the need for a common field of activity continued to restrict the protection given in passing off. In *Wombles Ltd v Wombles Skips Ltd* (1975), the claimant owned the copyright in the books and drawings of the Wombles, fictional characters known for their tidiness. The claimant's business was to license copyright reproductions. The defendant leased rubbish skips under the name 'Wombles Skips Ltd'. The claimant unsuccessfully argued that use of the 'Womble' name by the defendant was bound to lead some to believe the defendant was connected to the claimant. The High Court held that there had to be a common field of activity, or one that a reasonable man might assume, and that there was none in this case. An important consideration for the court was that the name only was taken. It has been argued that the court might have taken another line if the Womble image was also used by the defendant. In *Tavener Rutledge Ltd v Trexapalm Ltd* (1975), the defendant company was licensed by the producers of a popular television series featuring the detective, Kojak, well known for his affection for lollipops, to use the name 'Kojak' on merchandise, including Kojak Lollies. It was sued by the claimant company, which sold 'Kojakpops', in which it had built up considerable goodwill and reputation, but without a licence from the creators. The claimants succeeded. Again, it was held that there was no copyright in the name as such, even though it was an invented one. Furthermore, the court could find no common field of activity between the television company, which licensed the name, and the claimant confectioners. The court held that it was not enough to show that the public would think that the television company had given a licence to the claimant. The public must also assume the licensed goods would be of a certain quality. However, Walton J did suggest that, in future, as the public became more familiar with character merchandising, a simple misrepresentation that the claimant had licensed the defendant might be sufficient.

Character/personality merchandising: the move away from a common field

4.69   In *Warnink BV v Townend & Sons (Hull) Ltd* (1979), it was made plain that there is no need for a common field of activity to succeed in passing off. Similarly, the trend in character merchandising cases has been to move away from a common field of activity to look instead for an operative misrepresentation. This was the approach taken by the Court of Appeal in *Stringfellow v McCain Foods (GB) Ltd* (1984). The claimant, Peter Stringfellow, owned a famous night-club, 'Stringfellow'. The defendant manufactured oven-ready chips named 'Stringfellows', advertised by a boy dancing in a kitchen with 'disco' lighting. The Court of Appeal looked for an operative misrepresentation and held there may have been some members of the public who would think the two were connected. However, because there was no evidence that the claimant had been able to exploit any merchandising rights in his name, he was unable to prove damage, and the action failed. Here, the absence of a common field of activity was still relevant, because its absence meant the court was less likely to find confusion and, therefore, damage.

Character/personality merchandising: the 'Ninja Turtle' case

4.70 The decision in *Stringfellow v McCain Foods (GB) Ltd* (1984) pointed the way to *Mirage Studios v Counter-Feat Clothing Co Ltd* (1991). The claimants licensed the reproduction of fictitious, humanoid cartoon characters, the 'Teenage Mutant Ninja Turtles', but manufactured no goods themselves. The unfortunately named defendant made drawings of humanoid turtle characters using the concept, but not copying the claimant's drawings, and licensed them for use on clothing. The claimant sued for copyright infringement and passing off. The court held there was a case to answer in passing off. Echoing the prediction in *Tavener Rutledge Ltd v Trexapalm Ltd* (1975) ('Kojak'), Browne-Wilkinson V-C took the view that the public would be aware of the licensing industry, and would assume a connection between the claimant and the defendant. Accordingly, the operative misrepresentation was that the reproduction on the defendant's goods had been licensed by the claimant. However, since they were not, the goods were not 'genuine'. The damage was to the image, which, by being placed on inferior goods, would reduce the value of the claimant's licensing rights. The licensing business in the copyright was held to have the relevant goodwill.

4.71 In his judgment, Browne-Wilkinson V-C approved a line of Australian cases, which, as early as 1969, had rejected the need for a common field of activity in passing-off cases involving character/personality merchandising. In the Australian cases, it had been sufficient that there had been wrongful appropriation of a claimant's reputation by falsely representing that he had endorsed a product. This was the position in *Henderson v Radio Corpn Pty Ltd* (1969), where the claimants were well-known ballroom dancers, who had not so far licensed their name or image. The defendant used their picture, without a licence, on a gramophone record, 'Strictly Dancing'. In finding for the claimants, who had alleged passing off, the court held that there was no need to show a common field of activity or damage. This principle was extended to fictional characters in *Hogan v Koala Dundee Pty Ltd* (1988) and *Pacific Dunlop Ltd v Hogan* (1989), where the character in question was 'Crocodile Dundee'. In the latter case, a television advertisement for shoes caricatured a knife-fight scene from the film, *Crocodile Dundee*. In its judgment, the court held that there was no need for the public even to assume a licensing relationship for passing off to succeed. Passing off was established merely because an erroneous belief was created that the claimant may have approved the advertisement. It is submitted that the decision in *Mirage Studios v Counter-Feat Clothing Co Ltd* (1991) actually stopped far short of the Australian destination. The operative misrepresentation in 'Ninja Turtles' was the public's assumption that there was a licensing arrangement between the parties. The second 'Crocodile Dundee' case jettisoned the need even for such a minimal assumption.

Beyond the 'Ninja Turtles'

4.72 It is possible to distinguish *Mirage Studios v Counter-Feat Clothing Co Ltd* (1991) from earlier passing-off decisions involving character merchandising, because the claimant's business was licensing, not just a name or an image, but a piece of intellectual property, that is, the copyright in the turtle drawings. In *Elvis Presley Trade Marks* (1999), the Court of Appeal confirmed that it was this fact that was the distinguishing feature of the 'Ninja Turtles' decision and also the basis for its limited application (see para **5.113** for a discussion of the trade marks issue). In *Elvis Presley*, the estate of the late singer sought to register his name for use on toiletries. The Court of Appeal refused registration on the grounds that the names, 'Elvis' and 'Elvis Presley', were too descriptive to function as trade marks. It also took the opportunity to comment on the implications of the 'Ninja Turtles' case. In his leading judgment, Walker LJ rejected the idea, advanced by the applicant, that (following the 'Ninja Turtles') it was now a general rule that a trader should not make unauthorised use of the name of a well-known person or character on his merchandise. Walker LJ emphasised that the 'Ninja Turtles' decision was justified only on its particular facts, of which the most important was that the claimant had copyright in the drawings and a substantial business in licensing them. Another clear implication of the *Elvis Presley* judgment was that, in character/personality merchandising cases, the claimant will still need to show that the public will assume a licensing connection between the parties. It will not be taken for granted by the courts. The *Elvis Presley* decision confirmed the approach taken in *Halliwell v Panini* (1997), a High Court case involving the Spice Girls. The defendant published an 'unofficial' sticker collection, consisting of photographs of the girl band, entitled 'The Fab Five'. The band was unable to obtain an injunction preventing its distribution. According to the court, it did not believe that members of the public would buy the collection believing that it was authorised by the claimants.

False endorsement

4.73 More recently, in *Irvine v Talksport Ltd* (2003), the courts recognised that a claimant who is falsely depicted as having endorsed a product may succeed in passing off. In this case, the claimant, Eddie Irvine, was a Formula 1 racing car driver, who was runner-up in the 1999 World Championships. He had, since 1996, built up a worldwide reputation in the sport, which was accompanied by a growing business in endorsing products. The defendants had, until 1999, been known as 'Talk Radio', but at the end of that year decided to concentrate on live sports coverage and re-brand themselves as 'Talksport'. They initiated a marketing campaign which included sending a number of boxed sets to likely advertisers to promote their Grand Prix coverage. These boxes included a brochure which had a picture of Eddie Irvine holding a radio, on which the defendant's logo appeared. The picture had been doctored. In the original photograph, he had been holding a mobile phone. The doctored photograph clearly gave the impression that Mr Irvine was 'listening intently to the radio, and hence (given the logo) to Talk Radio'. Irvine sued the defendant for passing off. In his judgment in the High Court (*Irvine v Talksport Ltd* (2002)), Laddie J suggested that the width of protection offered by the law of passing off had widened since the decision in *McCulloch v May (Produce Distributors) Ltd* (1947). To establish passing off, it was not necessary to show that the claimant and defendant shared a common field of activity, or that damage would be confined simply to a loss of sales. Passing off now protected the goodwill in a claimant's name or reputation against others whose actions might blur or tarnish the exclusivity of either. In the present commercial environment, famous people might well have a reputation, not only in their own field of endeavour, but they might also use that reputation to endorse unrelated products for considerable sums. According to Laddie J, the 'endorsee is taking the benefit of the attractive force which is the reputation or good will of a famous person'. He believed that the law of passing off should now recognise this commercial reality. Indeed, he added that there was nothing to stop the law of passing off applying in a false endorsement case. The claimant simply needed to show, first, that he had a significant reputation or goodwill at the time of the acts complained of. Second, the claimant had to prove that the actions of the defendant gave rise to a false message, which would be understood by a not insignificant section of his market, that his goods have been endorsed, recommended or are approved of by the client. Both these elements were present in this case. Irvine was a famous sportsman and, by virtue of his fame, he had been paid to endorse a variety of products. Furthermore, a 'not insignificant' number of those who received the publicity brochure would think that Irvine had endorsed or recommended Talk Radio. As a result, Irvine would suffer damage from the loss of earnings, both for this and for future endorsements. Irvine succeeded in his action for passing off. The approach taken by Laddie J to false endorsement was later approved by the Court of Appeal (although the Court of Appeal overruled his approach to the calculation of damages, see para **4.74**). Interestingly, in *Irvine*, Laddie J differentiated between 'character merchandising' cases, in which category he included *Elvis Presley Trade Marks* (1999), and cases of false endorsement. He suggested that in the former, where the characters were either fictitious or (as in the case of Elvis Presley) deceased, there would be no question that they were actually endorsing the product. Rather, their images would simply be used for 'commercial purposes'. Bearing in mind that before the most recent James Bond film was released, its producers had already been paid several million pounds by manufacturers eager to have the secret agent 'endorse' their products, it is submitted that the distinction between character merchandising and false endorsement may not always be an easy one to make (Bains, 'Personality Right: Should the UK Grant Celebrities a Proprietary Right in Their Personality?' Part II [2007] *Entertainment Law Review* 205).

Damages and 'false endorsement'

4.74 In *Irvine v Talksport Ltd* (2002), Laddie J had held that the principles established for the assessment of damages for infringement of patents were applicable. He then assessed the damages as a reasonable fee for Irvine's endorsement of the defendant's radio station. The reasonable fee would be based upon what the defendant would have to pay the claimant in order to do lawfully what it had done unlawfully. Irvine had argued that he would not have 'bothered to get out of bed' for less than £25,000. However, Laddie J had based his assessment of damages, not on what Irvine claimed he would have asked, but rather upon what he believed was a reasonable sum for the defendant to pay. He accepted the defendant's evidence that, given the limited nature of the advertising campaign, a reasonable fee would have been £2,000. Irvine appealed. The Court of Appeal allowed the appeal. Laddie J had erred in rejecting Irvine's evidence. The Court of Appeal accepted that Irvine would have asked for £25,000 to make the endorsement. It was this sum that the defendant would have had to have paid to make lawful what it had done unlawfully. Irvine was awarded damages of £25,000.

Remedies

4.75 Passing-off actions may be brought in the county court, the Patents County Court, and the High Court, although in *McCain International v Country Fair Foods* (1981), the Court of Appeal took the view that the most appropriate forum was the Chancery Division of the High Court. As in other actions involving intellectual property, a claimant who brings a passing-off action is interested first and foremost in stopping the defendant's activities as quickly as possible. Damages will usually be a secondary consideration. If the claimant is successful in obtaining an interim injunction, it is unlikely that the case will continue to trial. Usually, the defendant, whatever his own view about the rights and wrongs of the case, will prefer to change his marketing approach rather than refrain from marketing the product until the issues are resolved at trial. If passing off is proved, the usual remedies–damages, delivery up, and so on–are available.

Actions for passing off and trade mark infringement

4.76 The protection offered by registered trade marks is generally considered superior to that offered by passing off. Trade mark registration endows its proprietor with exclusive use of the mark. By contrast, for a passing-off action to succeed, it is, of course, necessary for Lord Oliver's trilogy to be present. Nonetheless, passing off remains a useful adjunct to an action for trade mark infringement, and the two are often combined. Typically, this is because in trade mark actions it is open to the defendant to argue in its defence that the trade mark at issue is invalid or should be revoked. If the defendant is successful, it may yet be possible for the claimant to fall back on the claim of passing off.

SELF-TEST QUESTIONS

1   'Firenzo' is a cheap and cheerful sparkling wine produced in northern Italy by a number of producers. It is sold in brown glass bottles with a pinched waist, although different producers have different labels. It is sold only over the internet from the 'Firenzo' Italian website but it has a large number of customers in the UK. Three years ago a UK company, X, started selling 'Florenzo' wine, which is also cheap, but is not sparkling. It, too, is sold in a brown glass bottle with a pinched waist. However, the labels are identical on all the bottles, and show the name 'Florenzo' clearly. 'Florenzo' wine is sold in supermarkets and over the internet, with a statement that 'This wine is made in England.' Over the years the popularity of 'Florenzo' has increased and it is now sold in large numbers. Murray Madson, a

famous football player, was photographed at a restaurant drinking 'Florenzo' wine from the bottle. X has put this photograph on their website. Advise whether Madson and the producers of 'Firenzo' can bring actions for passing off against X.

2   To what extent has passing off moved beyond protecting damage to the claimant's goodwill to protection against other forms of 'unfair' competition?

3   Discuss the development of passing off in relation to character and personality merchandising. Do you think the UK should have a personality right?

FURTHER READING

Carty, H, 'Inverse Passing Off: A Suitable Addition to Passing Off?' [1993] *European Intellectual Property Review* 370.

Carty, H, 'The Common Law–The Quest for the IP Effect' [2007] *Intellectual Property Quarterly* 237.

Davis, J, 'Unfair Competition Law in the United Kingdom' in Hilty and Henning-Bodewig, *Law Against Unfair Competition: Towards a New Paradigm in Europe?* (Springer, 2007).

Davis, J, 'Passing Off and Joint Liability: The Rise and Fall of "Instruments of Deception"' [2011] *European Intellectual Property Review* 203.

Davis, J, 'Why the United Kingdom should have a Law against Misappropriation' [2010] *Cambridge Law Journal* 561.

Hoffman, F, 'The right to publicity in German and English Law' [2010] *Intellectual Property Quarterly* 325.

Kelly, G, 'Protecting the goods: dealing with the lookalike phenomenon through the enforcement of IP rights in the United Kingdom and Ireland' [2011] *European Intellectual Property Review* 425.

Kwan, G, 'Infringement of Trade Mark and Passing Off by Dealing in Genuine Articles' [2003] *European Intellectual Property Review* 45.

O'Byrne, P and Allgrove, B, 'Initial Interest Confusion recognized by the English courts' [2011] *Journal of Intellectual Property Law and Practice* 147.

Russell, F, 'The Elderflower Champagne Case: Is This a Further Expansion of the Tort of Passing Off?' [1993] *European Intellectual Property Review* 379.

Wadlow, C, *The Law of Passing Off* (3rd edn, Sweet & Maxwell, 2005).

5

Trade marks

SUMMARY

- The Trade Marks Act 1994 and the function of trade marks domestic registration and the routes to international protection
- The definition of a trade mark
- Absolute grounds for refusal of registration
- Relative grounds for refusal of registration
- Infringement, comparative advertising and exclusions from trade mark protection
- Trade marks and the internet
- Losing the mark: revocation and invalidity
- Licensing, assignments and character merchandising
- Civil and criminal remedies
- Trade marks and the international context: exhaustion of rights and competition law

Introduction: the law and function of trade marks

5.1 Trade mark law in the UK is governed by the Trade Marks Act 1994 (TMA 1994). Registered trade marks were introduced into the UK by the Trade Marks Act of 1875. The 1994 Act represented the first major overhaul of trade mark law in almost 50 years, replacing the Trade Marks Act 1938 (TMA 1938). It incorporates into UK law the First Council Directive of 21 December 1989 to approximate the laws of the Member States relating to trade marks (the TM Directive) (2008/95/EC; formerly EEC 89/104). The TMA 1994 is organised into four parts. Part I covers substantive trade mark law and much of its wording is taken verbatim from the Directive. Part II deals with international matters, including the Community Trade Mark (CTM), the Madrid Protocol and the Paris Convention for the Protection of Industrial Property. Parts III and IV include administrative, supplementary and general provisions relating to the Registry's powers, to legal proceedings, and to definitions.

5.2 Because the TMA 1994 implements the TM Directive, it would be fair to say that it is the protection of trade marks, of all the intellectual property rights, which is now the most uniform across the EU (and the European Economic Area). The move towards a uniform EU trade mark regime has been further encouraged by the introduction of the Community Trade Mark. In the case of both the CTM Regulation (Council Regulation (EC) No 207/2009; formerly Council Regulation (EC) 40/94) and the TM Directive, the final word in interpretation lies with the Court of Justice. The internationalisation of trade mark law, at least as far as the EU is concerned, is far advanced. Such internationalisation is appropriate in an age of global marketing and e-commerce, when a growing number of trade marks have a fame which crosses national boundaries and when the most valuable–Coca-Cola, IBM, Microsoft and Google–are known worldwide. Despite these developments, however, trade mark protection remains essentially territorial. Thus, a UK registered trade mark is protected only in the UK. Obviously, this can present major problems, for example when such a mark is used on the internet in an infringing manner. The value of trade marks lies in their ability to play a number of roles in modern commerce. Below, we look at the various functions of trade marks, which are protected by registration.

The function of trade mark protection: (i) an indicator of origin

5.3 Traditionally, the justification for trade mark protection has been to protect the trade mark's function as an indicator of origin of the goods and services to which it attaches. This means, at its simplest, that the registered trade mark 'X' on a soft drink should reliably tell the consumer that all drinks marked 'X' originate from a single proprietor and not from any other enterprise. This protection is taken to be both for the benefit of the proprietor against his competitors and as a guarantee of quality for the buying public. The essential function of registered trade marks and their specific subject matter (that is, the rights conferred on the proprietor by registration) have been confirmed by the Court of Justice in a number of cases (for an example, see *Arsenal Football Club plc v Reed* (2002)). They were summarised by the Advocate General in *Bristol-Myers Squibb v Paranova* (1996):

> In so far as the trade mark protects the interest of its proprietor by enabling him to prevent competitors from taking unfair advantage of his commercial reputation, the exclusive rights conferred on the proprietor are said, in the language of the Court's case law, to constitute the specific subject-matter of the trade mark. In so far as the trade mark protects the interest of consumers by acting as a guarantee that all goods bearing the mark are of the same commercial

origin, this is known in the Court's terminology, as the essential function of the trade mark. These two aspects of trade mark protection are of course two sides of the same coin.

5.4 In recent years, the role of trade marks has substantially changed. For a number of reasons, the perceived link between many trade marks and the origin of the goods or services to which they attach has become increasingly attenuated. For example, the TMA 1994 made licensing of trade marks and assignments substantially easier (see para **5.107** et seq). For another, the ownership of many well-known brands is becoming concentrated in a relatively small number of companies, many of which operate across national boundaries. For instance, it has been reckoned that just three companies account for the ownership of nearly one-third of all branded products sold in UK supermarkets. As a result, the trade mark 'X' on a soft drink may not mean it is produced by X Soft Drinks Ltd, but by its brand owner, a large multinational, which may also produce a number of competing brands as well as the supermarket's 'own brand' product. Second, the role of the trade mark as a guarantor of quality is also arguably less crucial to a wide range of goods and services. One impetus for early trade mark legislation had been to enable the consumer to choose between products of a certain quality which carried a known trade mark and others of more dubious (and in the case of foodstuffs, occasionally lethal) attributes. However, consumer legislation has ensured that, in many countries, the public can expect a certain minimum quality for a wide range of goods and services, whatever mark attaches to them. As a result, the competition between goods and services has increasingly come to reside, not in their differing quality, but in the relative attractiveness of the trade marks they carry. An obvious example is the competition between different athletic shoes (many of which are made in the same factories in the developing world), which is based on the wide range of associations which their trade marks carry, beyond the simple message of where they originate.

The function of trade mark protection: (ii) brand attractiveness

5.5 It is now generally recognised that many trade marks are to be valued for other qualities apart from their role as an indicator of origin. For instance, the Advocate General in *Arsenal Football Club plc v Reed* (2002) suggested that a distinctive mark might also indicate quality, reputation, the renown of the producer or even a way of seeing life. Furthermore, marks which have acquired such extrinsic qualities may be extremely valuable, even more so if they are internationally recognised. Indeed, the extrinsic attractiveness of a mark is often acquired only as the result of vast and expensive advertising campaigns, with, again, the relationship between athletic shoes and major sporting events being a case in point.

It is scarcely surprising, therefore, that the implementation of the TM Directive initiated intense debate over the extent to which it should be interpreted to give protection to the extrinsic advertising value of trade marks, as divorced from their function as indicators of origin. It is a debate that will figure largely in the chapter which follows. But it is, perhaps, useful to begin with a brief discussion of the background.

5.6 In the Benelux countries, the Uniform Benelux Trade Mark Law, even before the implementation of the TM Directive, recognised this second function of trade marks. It introduced the concept of 'dilution' into trade mark protection. Registered trade marks would be protected in situations where the public was not confused as to the origins of two identical or similar marks. Under Benelux law, registered trade marks would also be protected where the use of two identical or similar marks created a simple association in the public mind between one mark and another, because such an association might be detrimental to the first registered mark's exclusivity or diminish its attractiveness and, hence, 'dilute' its reputation and consequently its value. With the implementation of the TM Directive, many commentators took the view that it was simply good sense to recognise this altered role for trade marks and to follow the Benelux approach throughout the EEA. Others feared that this would give far too much opportunity to wealthy owners of famous brands to corner large areas of language and shapes, and that it would be anti-competitive. Unfortunately, the wording of the TM Directive was ambiguous as to the extent to which it was intended to introduce 'dilution' into EU trade mark law, perhaps because Member States were themselves divided on the issue. Hence, the debate as to which way the law would fall has been central to interpreting the TM Directive, the CTM Regulations and, in the UK, the TMA 1994.

Trade marks and the public interest

5.7 Trade mark registration places under private control for an indefinite period certain uses of the mark which would previously have been available to society at large. The monopoly will only bite if the proprietor uses the mark in the course of trade (for example, a private individual may still use the colour green for his living room wall, even though only BP may have exclusive use of it for service stations). Nonetheless, such use is no longer commonly available. As has been suggested, the creation of trade mark monopolies has been justified by the benefit to the public of knowing the trade origins of the goods they buy, and to proprietors (who may have invested a good deal in the promotion of their marks) of being able to prevent others from trading on their reputation (see *Bristol-Myers Squibb v Paranova* at para **5.3**). Nonetheless, in the past, successive TM Acts have been based on the assumption that the public interest and trading interests may not always coincide, and have sought to hold a balance between them. For instance, under the TMA 1938, the conditions for licensing trade marks were tightly controlled to protect the trade mark's role as an indicator of origin. In general, the UK courts adopted a similar balancing approach in interpreting the legislation. In *Coca-Cola Trade Marks* (1985), the Court of Appeal refused registration of the Coca-Cola bottle even though it was clearly acting as an indicator of origin. In part, its decision was based on a conviction that giving indefinite protection to functional objects such as containers was against the public interest. By contrast the TM Directive, which was framed during a period when free trade and unrestricted competition represented the economic orthodoxy, gives proprietors a largely free hand in dealing with their marks. With very few exceptions, it also allows the registration of any sign, including shapes, so long as it is acting as a trade mark, that is, as an indicator of origin, in the market. Some have argued that an increasingly unrestricted trade mark regime will create broad monopolies with little concern for the general public good. Others take the view that it is in the self-interest of proprietors to maintain their marks as indicators of origin, without the prodding of government regulation (Davis, 'European Trade Mark Law and the Enclosure of the Commons' [2002] *Intellectual Property Quarterly* 342).

Interpreting the Trade Marks Act 1994

5.8 The TM Directive is a collection of broad statements of substantive law, but individual Member States have a relatively free procedural hand. In the UK, the courts have taken a purposive approach to interpreting the TMA 1994, assuming that it must be construed in a manner consistent with its EU origins and purposes (*Procter & Gamble's Trade Mark Applications* (1999); *Wagamama Ltd v City Centre Restaurants* (1995)). In this chapter, we will refer both to the provisions of the 1994 TMA and the equivalent provisions of the TM Directive, as is the practice of the UK courts. At times, it may also be necessary to identify the equivalent provisions of the CTM Regulation.

Registration

5.9 In the case of domestic applications, these are made to the Trade Marks Registry (TMR). They include a representation of the mark and a list of the goods or services with which the proprietor intends to use the mark. Goods and services have been classified into classes, periodically updated by WIPO. For example, Class 23 represents yarns and threads for textile use. It is possible to register a mark in respect of goods or services in one or any number of classes, as well as only some of the goods or services within a single class. The filing date of the application is generally that mark's 'priority date'. If the application is successful, the filing date becomes the date of registration, and the rights endowed by registration, such as to pursue infringers, are backdated to the filing date.

5.10 The TMR will examine the mark to determine whether if falls foul of the absolute grounds for the refusal of registration (para **5.18** et seq). It will also examine the mark to see if it conflicts with any marks with an earlier priority date. Until 2007, the TMR would refuse to register a mark which conflicted with an earlier registered mark. However, following the Trade Marks (Relative Grounds) Order 2007 (SI 2007/1976) and the Trade Marks (Amendment) Rules 2007 (SI 2007/2076), the Registry will now simply inform the applicant if there is an earlier conflicting mark. If the applicant were to proceed with the application, the proprietor of the earlier conflicting mark would be notified. It will then be up to the latter to decide if he wants to oppose the application. If the mark passes the examination stage, which now centres on the absolute grounds for refusal of registration, it will be advertised in the *Trade Marks Journal*. At this stage, an opposition may be entered against it by any other party, which seeing the advertisement, believes that it has a conflicting mark. Conflict will be resolved either at TMR level, or in the High Court. If there is no opposition, the trade mark will proceed to registration. Initial registration is for ten years, but may be renewed an indefinite number of times thereafter.

Collective and certification marks

5.11 The proprietor of the mark is likely to be the intended user of the mark, although he may assign or license it. There are two exceptions. A certification mark is held by an association that must not trade in the goods or services itself. The mark indicates that the goods or services of the members of the association are certified to be of a certain quality (TMA 1994, s 50). Examples are the 'Woolmark' or 'Harris Tweed'. The collective mark (s 49 and Sch 1) is also likely to be held by an association. Its purpose is to distinguish the goods and services of its members from those of other undertakings. It may, for instance, be held by an association of tradesmen, such as stationers, a professional body with a common field of activity, or traders from a particular area.

International protection

5.12 Under the Madrid Protocol, to which the UK acceded in 1996, it is possible to obtain protection for a UK trade mark in any of the 29 or so countries which are parties to the Protocol, and the Madrid Agreement from which it derives, by a single application made through the national trade mark office to WIPO for an International Registration (IR). The examination of the mark, and the rules for opposition and infringement will be those of the countries to which the IR extends. If the application fails in one country designated by the applicant, it may nonetheless be registered in any of the others.

The Community Trade Mark

5.13 The CTM was introduced in 1996. It is distinct from a national registration and is a separate unitary mark covering all the countries in the EU. An application is made through the national trade marks registry or direct to the Community Trade Marks Office in Alicante (OHIM). The terms of the CTM are set out in the Regulation. Conditions of registrability and infringement are, in most important respects, the same as those of the TM Directive and, hence, the UK's own trade mark regime. Upon receiving an application, the OHIM looks to see whether the mark fulfils the formal requirements for a trade mark. It also searches to ensure that the mark applied for does not conflict with an earlier registered mark or CTM registration. The OHIM then publishes the mark. The results of the search are purely advisory, and it is up to the owner of the earlier mark or right to mount an opposition. Oppositions are heard by the OHIM Examiners and then by the OHIM Board of Appeal. Appeals from the Board go first to the General Court and may eventually find their way to the Court of Justice. In cases of infringement, a national court is designated to hear cases in the first instance, with appeals going to the Court of Justice. Since its introduction, the CTM has proved popular, and increasingly the Court of Justice has been called in to settle questions of interpretation, in decisions which directly impact upon domestic trade mark law.

The definition of a trade mark

5.14 Section 1(1) TMA 1994 (Art 2 TM Directive) defines a trade mark as 'any sign capable of being represented graphically which is capable of distinguishing the goods or services of one undertaking from those of other undertakings'. To understand this definition, it is useful to break it down into its three constituent parts:

- any sign;
- capable of being represented graphically;
- capable of distinguishing the goods and services of one undertaking from those of others.

Any sign

5.15   The sign is the subject matter of a registered trade mark. For instance, the word 'Nike' or the 'swoosh' with which that company marks its goods are signs. Conversely, a mark consisting 'of a transparent bin or collection chamber forming part of the external surface of the vacuum cleaner' (in any conceivable shape) was held by the Court of Justice to be not a sign but a concept, and as such could not be registered (*Dyson v RTM* (2007)). Any sign may serve as a trade mark, provided it can be represented graphically and does not fall foul of the absolute grounds for refusal of registration, which are looked at below (see para **5.18**). The 1994 Act continues: 'A trade mark may, in particular, consist of words (including personal names), designs, letters, numerals or the shape of goods or their packaging.' This is an open-ended list. Applications have been made to register the shapes of containers (the 'Coca-Cola' bottle), the shapes of goods ('Toblerone' triangular chocolate), slogans, radio jingles and sensory marks such as colours, smells, sounds and even gestures. To some, this open-ended definition of what may constitute the subject matter of a trade mark registration represents the unacceptable appropriation of signs into private ownership which have been in common use in the past. Others argue that traders have, anyway, had a de facto monopoly of a multitude of signs (including shapes) through the common law protection offered by passing off. The 'Jif' lemon is an obvious example (*Reckitt & Colman Products Ltd v Borden Inc* (1990), see para **4.23**).

Capable of being represented graphically

5.16   Marks must be capable of graphic representation, so that the TMR can easily record and search for them, and so that they can be advertised in a two-dimensional form. This may be a low hurdle to overcome for two-dimensional marks. However, the going may be more difficult for less traditional marks, such as smells, colours and shapes, which may have no direct corporeal embodiment. The difficulty of registering a non-corporeal mark was illustrated by the Court of Justice decision in *Sieckmann v Deutsches Patent- und Markenamt* (2002). The applicant sought to register an olfactory mark in Germany. It deposited with its application a description of the smell ('balsamically fruity with a slight hint of cinnamon'), its structural formula and an 'odour sample' in a container. The registration was refused on the ground that the proposed mark could not be represented graphically. On appeal, the national court addressed two questions to the Court of Justice. First, did 'capable of graphic representation' mean only signs that could be reproduced directly in their visible form, or could it also be construed as meaning signs, such as odours or sounds, which could not be perceived visually but could be reproduced indirectly? If the answer was 'yes', the second question was: What would be an acceptable graphical representation of an odour? The Court of Justice held that it was possible to register a sign that was not in itself capable of being represented visually, provided that it could be represented graphically, particularly by means of images, lines or characters, and provided the representation was clear, precise, self-contained, easily accessible, intelligible, durable and objective. On the question of what constituted an adequate graphic representation of an odour, the Court of Justice held that its requirements were not satisfied by a chemical formula or a description, being not sufficiently clear or precise, nor by a deposit, being not sufficiently stable or durable, nor by a combination of the three. Commentators have questioned whether the decision in *Sieckmann* will effectively disallow the registration of any smell mark, despite the Court of Justice's view that such registrations are not debarred in principle, as it is difficult to see how else a smell might be represented. Indeed, since *Sieckmann*, registrations have also been refused for taste marks (*Eli Lilly's CTM Application* (2004)) and the onomatopoeic sound of a cock crowing (*Shield v Joost* (2004)), for failing to meet the *Siekmann* criteria, suggesting that, in general, non-corporeal signs may indeed be difficult to register. By contrast, in *Libertel Groep BV v Benelux-Merkenbureau* (2003), the Court of Justice held that a colour may meet the *Sieckmann* standard for graphic representation, if it is described by using an internationally recognised identification code. In the UK, the TMR will accept marks described by reference to Pantone colour standards.

Capable of distinguishing the goods and services of one undertaking from those of other undertakings

5.17 All signs (except a very few absolutely excluded on public interest grounds (para **5.29** et seq)) are deemed capable in principle of distinguishing the goods or services of a particular trader from those of any other trader. Whether or not a sign will actually succeed in being registered depends upon whether it is capable, in practice, of being distinctive of a particular trader's goods or services, that is, to consumers in the market place (*Koninklijke Philips Electronics NV v Remington Consumer Products Ltd* (2002) (ECJ). For example, two boxes of soap powder, one red displaying the word 'Soap' in white and one green displaying the word 'Soap' in black will, of course, be distinguishable from each other. But s 1(1) will only be satisfied if the designs of these boxes distinguish for the public the goods of one particular trader from any other trader. It is up to the applicant to persuade the TMR or the courts that his sign is capable of functioning as a trade mark. The task will be easier with an entirely invented word (a strong mark) such as 'Google', but harder with one which is essentially descriptive of the product. The categories of signs (and marks) for which it is necessary to prove distinctiveness in practice, before they will be registered, are identified in s 3 of the TMA 1994 (art 3(1)(b)–(d) TM Directive), to which this chapter now turns.

Absolute grounds for refusal of registration

5.18 The basic approach of the TM Directive and the TMA 1994 is that any sign which is de facto operating as a trade mark in the market place, that is, acting as an indicator of origin, can be registered, although there are some signs which, on public interest grounds, should not be registrable at all or should be registrable only in certain limited circumstances. This latter category of marks is identified in s 3 (art 3) which sets out the absolute grounds for refusal of registration. They are absolute because it is the nature of the mark itself which renders it inappropriate for registration, not the mark's relationship with other marks (as in the relative grounds for refusal listed in s 5 TMA (Art 4 TM Directive) (see para **5.35** et seq)). Section 3 covers three categories of marks (and signs):

- signs which do not satisfy the requirements of s 1(1) (art 2) and so cannot be registered (s 3(1)(a)) (art 3(1)(a));

- trade marks which shall not be registered unless, according to the proviso, by the date of application they have 'in fact acquired a distinctive character through use' (the proviso) (s 3(1)(b)–(d)) (art 3(1)(b)–(d));

- trade marks which shall not be registered because registration would be against the public interest (s 3(2)–(6)) (art 3(1)(e)–(g)).

Each of these categories is considered below.

Signs which do not satisfy s 1(1) TMA

5.19 Signs which are not capable of distinguishing the goods or services of one undertaking from those of other undertakings, or which cannot be represented graphically, cannot be registered. The meaning of s 3(1)(a) was addressed in *Philips Electronics NV v Remington Consumer Products* (1998), which eventually found its way to the Court of Justice. The facts were these. Since 1966, Philips had marketed a three-headed rotary shaver with the heads arranged in an equilateral triangle. In 1985, it registered a picture of this face for electric shavers. The design is not now protected by patent. Nonetheless, until the defendant began marketing its own rotary shaver with a similar head design, but with the mark 'Remington' prominently displayed, rotary shavers were unique to Philips. Philips sued Remington for trade mark infringement and Remington claimed the Philips' registration was invalid. The parties agreed that the registration should be treated by the Court as covering the three-dimensional shape of the head and was not just a pictorial representation of it. In the High Court, the mark was held to be invalid because, inter alia, it was not capable of distinguishing the goods of one trader from another. The claimant appealed. The Court of Appeal first considered whether the mark satisfied s 3(1)(a) and held that it did not. In essence, the court accepted that the public generally associated the three-headed razor shape with Philips. However, since Philips had had an effective monopoly of three-headed shavers for many years, this did not mean that the shape was distinctive in a trade mark sense. Philips still had to establish that the shape had features which would distinguish it from those of a competitor who put similar goods on the market. The Court of Appeal went on to say that the shape of an article could not be registered in respect of goods of that shape, unless it contained some addition or 'capricious alteration' which made it capable of distinguishing those goods from the same sort of goods sold by someone else. It would be that addition which made it distinctive, and so capable of registration. In this case, it held that the primary meaning of the trade mark as it stood was a three-headed rotary shaver. There was no distinctive addition to the shape and it failed to fulfil the conditions of s 3(1)(a). The Court of Justice disagreed. According to the Court of Justice, any mark which was understood by the public as a badge of origin was registrable. It followed that the shape of an article for which a sign is registered does not require any capricious embellishment which has no functional purpose, so long as the public understand it to be a badge of origin. Furthermore, it was irrelevant that the proprietor of such a trade mark, in this case the three-headed shaver, was the only supplier of the goods. If, as a result of use, a substantial proportion of the relevant public associated the mark with that trader and no other undertaking, then the mark was registrable.

Marks which must satisfy the proviso

5.20 Signs which cannot satisfy the provisions of TMA 1994, s 1(1) cannot be registered under s 3(1)(a). Some marks may satisfy s 3(1)(a), but still cannot be registered unless they have satisfied the proviso. There are three categories of marks which must satisfy the proviso to be registered. These are:

- marks devoid of distinctive character (s 3(1)(b) (art 3(1)(b));
- descriptive marks (s 3(1)(c) (art 3(1)(c));
- generic or customary marks (s 3(1)(d)) (art 3(1)(d)).

In *Philips*, the Court of Justice held that the public interest behind each of these grounds for refusal was distinct. Each category of mark will now be considered in turn.

Marks devoid of distinctive character

5.21 In *Linde AG's Trade Mark Application* (2003), the Court of Justice held that there was no public interest in registering signs which were not fulfilling their essential function and acting as a badge of origin. There are some marks which may not be prima facie distinctive, for instance, a common surname such as 'Smith'. These marks may nonetheless become associated by the public with a particular product, because of the way they are used in the market place. If they have become distinctive of a particular trader through use, they will have satisfied the proviso and can be registered. In the latter case, they will have become trade marks, in the oft-quoted words of Geoffrey Hobbs QC in *AD2000 Trade Mark* (1997), through 'nurture' not 'nature'. In *Linde*, the Court of Justice explained that, in deciding whether a mark is factually distinctive under the art 3(1)(b) TM Directive, 'regard must be had both to the ordinary use of trade marks as a badge of origin in the sectors concerned and the perception of the relevant public'. There is as yet no clear category of signs which will be registered only with proof of acquired distinctiveness.

5.22 In *Libertel Groep BV v Benelux Merkenbureau* (2003), the Court of Justice found that colours per se might be devoid of distinctive character, but were capable of registration if they had acquired distinctiveness through use. The same was held to be true by the Court of Justice in relation to common names (*Nichols v Registrar of Trade Marks* (2004)). Conversely, in *Linde*, it held that the three-dimensional shape of goods may not be devoid of distinctive character. But the Court of Justice also recognised that, as a practical matter, it may be more difficult to establish factual distinctiveness for such marks, because consumers may expect words or logos to be trade marks, but not shapes. Thus, in *Mag Instrument v OHIM* (2004), concerning an application to register the shape of a torch, the Court of Justice held that only a shape of goods which departs significantly from the norm, might be deemed distinctive without use. Conversely, slogans have been held to be distinctive without evidence of use if they exhibit 'originality' and have 'resonance' for the consumer (*Audi v OHIM* (2010)).

5.23 In judging distinctiveness under s3(1)(b), the mark must be looked at as a whole and not broken down into its constituent parts. In *SAT.1 v OHIM* (2004), the mark at issue was 'SAT.2' for satellite dishes. The General Court held that as 'sat' was short for satellite dishes and '1' was widely used in the trade to identify goods, the mark lacked distinctiveness and could not be registered. However, the Court of Justice held that the General Court was wrong to judge these elements separately. Taken together, they might well be sufficiently distinctive to be registered. Nor should the relevant authority assume that certain categories of signs lack distinctiveness without proper examination. For example, in *OHIM v BORCO*

(2010), the applicant sought to register the single Greek letter 'α' for alcoholic beverages as a CTM. The Court of Justice held that the OHIM should not have withheld registration on the basis that a sign consisting of a single letter could not in principle be distinctive. Instead, it was necessary to look at the particular facts surrounding the application, including the type of goods or services against which the sign is to be registered, the view of the average consumer and the evidence presented by the applicant.

Descriptive marks

5.24 There are some marks which consist exclusively of signs or indications serving to designate the kind, quality, quantity, intended purpose, value, geographical origin, the time of production of the goods or rendering of services, or 'other characteristics of goods or services'. Examples might be 'Jumbo', 'Mini', 'Personal' or 'Best', '24 Hour Service', 'Slim 'n Fit' for a slimming preparation (designating the intended purpose). Such wholly descriptive marks will only be registered if they have satisfied the proviso, by acquiring distinctiveness through use. The public interest underlying this provision is that descriptive signs should be freely available and not be reserved to one undertaking through registration (*Linde AG's Trade Mark Application* (2003)). In *Linde*, the Court of Justice held that trade marks which consist of the three-dimensional shape of goods, such as the shape of a torch for a torch, are marks which consist exclusively of signs or indications which serve to designate the characteristics of the goods. Unless they have acquired distinctiveness, they should not be registered. Obviously, some geographical names are prima facie registrable because they attach to very small areas, or areas having no reputation for particular goods. The example of 'North Pole' for bananas is often cited. Others might be applicable to more than one trader's goods, if used descriptively. These will be registered only on evidence of acquired distinctiveness (*Windsurfing Chiemsee v Boot* (1999)). In *Windsurfing*, the applicant had sought to register the word, 'Chiemsee', the largest lake in Bavaria and an important tourist and sporting attraction, for clothing. The applicant manufactured and sold clothing in the area. The Court of Justice was asked, inter alia, whether signs which consist exclusively of geographical indications may be registered. It held that geographical names were not registrable under art 3(1)(c) TM Directive, if they were currently associated with the relevant category of goods, or if it could be reasonably assumed that they might be so associated in the future. Nonetheless, there was nothing to prevent geographical marks from acquiring sufficient distinctiveness through use, and in assessing whether they had done so no stricter criteria should be applied than to any other type of mark. Other characteristics of goods or services may amount to descriptions common in the trade (such as a red cap or gold cap for whisky). Again the proviso would apply to these examples.

The limits of descriptiveness

5.25   While some marks are obviously descriptive, such as 'Treat' for ice cream toppings, others may be more ambiguously so. The line between marks which are descriptive, and hence should not be registered without proof of distinctiveness, and marks which are 'allusive' of a product's characteristics without being descriptive is not an easy one to draw. The case law emanating from the Court of Justice has aroused considerable controversy. In *Procter & Gamble Co v OHIM* (2001), the applicants sought to register 'Baby-Dry' for nappies. The OHIM refused the application on the grounds that 'Baby-Dry' was a descriptive mark, consisting exclusively of an indication which might serve in trade to designate the intended purpose of the goods. The applicant's appeal eventually reached the Court of Justice, which ruled that art 7(1)(c) of the CTM Regulation (s 3(1)(c) TMA) applies only to marks that are purely descriptive. Conversely, if their descriptive components are presented in such a way that the resultant whole is distinguished from the usual way of designating the goods or their essential characteristics, they will be registrable. If considered from the viewpoint of the average English-speaking consumer, the Court of Justice took the view that the words 'Baby-Dry' would not be the normal way to refer to nappies. While the words in combination might form part of a description of the function of nappies, the words 'Baby-Dry' were also distinctive and could be registered. At the time, 'Baby-Dry' was praised by some as offering greater certainty to trade mark applicants (Griffiths, 'Modernising trade mark law and promoting economic efficiency: an evaluation of the Baby-Dry judgment and its aftermath' [2003] *Intellectual Property Quarterly* 1). Others saw the decision as unacceptably widening the pool of signs which might be monopolised by a single trader through registration (*Re Nichols plc's Trade Mark Application* (2002), per Jacob J). Subsequently, in *OHIM v Wm Wrigley Jr* (2003), the Court of Justice seemed to retreat from the permissive approach taken in 'Baby-Dry' and retrace its steps to *Windsurfing*. This case involved an application to register the word 'Doublemint' for chewing gum as a CTM. The Court of Justice confirmed an initial finding that the mark was descriptive and should not be registered, noting that signs both in current descriptive use and those which might be so used in the future could not be registered without acquired distinctiveness, even though there might be alternative descriptive words available. Since *Wrigley*, the Court of Justice has taken a consistently more cautious approach to registering descriptive signs. In *Campina Melkunie v Benelux* (2004), it held that even a neologism, in this case 'Biomild' for yoghurt, would be held to be descriptive if it was made up of two descriptive words. While in *Koninklijke KPN Nederland NV v Benelux-Merkenbureau* (2004), which concerned an application to register 'Postkantoor', the Dutch word for post office, for goods including stamps, paper and advice, the Court of Justice held that even if a synonym exists for a descriptive word, such a word may not be registered if it is the normal way of referring to the goods.

Generic or customary marks

5.26 Marks which are customary in current language or in bona fide and established practices of trade cannot be registered unless they satisfy the proviso and have acquired distinctiveness through use. This provision covers 'generic' names which may have begun as the mark of a particular proprietor but are now used by the public to describe a general category of goods or services. For example, in *Björnekulla v Procordia Food* (2004), the claimant sought the revocation of the Swedish trade mark 'Bostogurka' used with pickled gherkins because it had become the common name for the product. The proprietor produced evidence to the effect that grocery and catering companies knew is it was a trade mark and hence it had not become generic to the 'trade'. However, the Court of Justice held that the relevant group of consumers for judging whether a trade mark was generic were the end users or consumers of the product. Examples of customary marks given by the TMR include devices of grapes for wines and stars for hotel services.

The relationship between s 3(1)(a) and s 3(1)(b)–(d)

5.27 The court will first look to see whether a mark fulfils the requirements of s 3(1)(b)–(d) and the proviso. If it does, then clearly it has also satisfied the requirements of s 3(1)(a). If it does not satisfy s 3(1)(b)–(d), then the question of whether it is inherently capable of distinguishing is arguably otiose (*Koninklijke Philips Electronics NV v Remington Consumer Products Ltd* (2002) (ECJ)).

Distinctiveness acquired through use

5.28 The test for acquired distinctiveness is the same for all signs, whether or not there is a perceived public interest in allowing other traders to use them (*Windsurfing Chiemsee v Boot* (1999); *Linde AG's Trade Mark Application* (2003)). In *Koninklijke Philips Electronics NV v Remington Consumer Products Ltd* (2002) (ECJ), the Court of Justice held it was for the national court to make such an assessment on the basis of specific and reliable data. Such data might include the market share held by the mark; the amount invested in promoting the mark; the proportion of the relevant class of persons who, because of the mark, identify the goods as originating from a particular undertaking; and statements from chambers of commerce and industry or other trade and professional associations (see also *Windsurfing*). Furthermore, it was necessary for a significant proportion of the average consumers of the goods or services in question to see the marks as distinctive. In *Lloyds Schuhfabrik Meyer & Co v Klijsen Handel BV* (1999), the average consumer was deemed to be reasonably well informed, reasonably observant and

shape were functional, then other non-functional elements were irrelevant. In sum, the essential characteristics of the Lego brick were functional and its shape was invalidly registered (see also *Knonklijke Philips N.V. v Remington Consumer Products* (2006) CA).

Contrary to public policy

5.32 Marks which are contrary to public policy or to accepted principles of morality, such as marks likely to be deemed religiously offensive, racist, sexist or obscene are prohibited. The TMA 1938 had a similar prohibition, under which 'Hallelujah' was denied registration in 1976 (*Hallelujah Trade Mark* (1976)). Clearly, standards will change. In applying this section, the TMR will generally use its own judgment, tempered by any relevant evidence. French Connection Ltd successfully registered 'FCUK' as a trade mark, although the mark has not necessarily found favour with members of the judiciary (*French Connection Ltd v Sutton* (2000)). In *Ghazilian's Trade Mark Application* (2001), the mark 'Little Penis', for clothing, was denied registration on the basis that a 'right thinking member of the public would conclude that this trade mark would cause greater offence than mere distaste to a significant section of the public'. The mark 'www.standupify-ouhatemanu.com' for clothing was also denied registration, as it was 'liable to function as a badge of antagonism' and, hence, to increase the incidence of football violence or other offensive behaviour (*CDW Graphic Design's Trade Mark Application* (2003)).

Other prohibited marks

5.33 Deceptive marks are prohibited (s 3(3)(b) TMA) (art 3(1)(g) TM Directive). The standard necessary for deception is that there is 'the existence of actual deceit or a sufficiently serious risk that the consumer will be deceived' (*Consorzio per la tutela del formaggio Gorganzola* (1999) CJEU). It was held by the Court of Justice in *Elizabeth Florence Emanuel v Continental Shelf* (2006), that it was not deceptive for a company to register the name of 'Elizabeth Emanuel' for clothes, even though it no longer employed the fashion designer of that name, who had started the original business but had sold it on. According to the Court of Justice, the mark continued to fulfill its essential function as an indicator of source.

Registrations in bad faith

5.34 Section 3(6) TMA (art 3(1)(f) TM Directive) prohibits registration of a trade mark if, or to the extent that, the application is made in bad faith. The definition of 'bad faith' has generally been viewed as a narrow one, which will involve 'dishonesty' or standards which fall short 'of acceptable commercial behaviour observed by reasonable and experienced men in the area being examined' (*Gromax Plasticulture Ltd v Don & Low Nonwovens Ltd* (1998), per Lindsay J; also *TRILLIUM*, First Cancellation Division, OHIM (28 March 2000, unreported). Typically, there may be a finding of bad faith where the applicant is not the owner of the mark (*Mary Wilson Enterprises' Trade Mark* (2003)) or where he has no intention of using the mark. However, the fact that a proprietor does not intend to use his mark against all the goods for which it is registered does not necessarily lead to finding of bad faith, if this is acceptable commercial practice in a particular trade sector, such as, for example, pharmaceuticals (*Knoll AG's Trade Mark* (2002)). Bad faith was considered by the Court of Justice in *Chocoladefabriken Lindt v Franz Hauswilth GmbH* (2009). Hauswilth had sold chocolate bunnies in Austria and Germany since the 1930s and Lindt had also sold chocolate bunnies in Austria since the 1950s. In 2000, Lindt registered the shape of chocolate bunnies as a CTM and then sued Hauswilth for trade mark infringement. The defendant counter-claimed that the registration had been made in bad faith (under art 5(1)(b) of the CTM Regulation). The Court of Justice looked at the meaning of bad faith in this context. It held that in order to determine whether an applicant was acting in bad faith, the national court had to make an overall assessment taking into account all the relevant circumstances. In this case, a finding of bad faith might depend, inter alia, upon whether, at the time of filing, the applicant knew or ought to have known that a third party was using, in at least one Member State, an identical or similar sign which was likely to cause confusion and the applicant intended to prevent the third party from continuing to use such a sign.

Relative grounds for refusal of registration

5.35 The relative grounds for refusal of registration are set out in s 5 TMA (art 4 TM Directive). They are termed 'relative' since the mark will be refused registration, not because of any quality intrinsic to itself, but because it conflicts with an earlier trade mark or right. Earlier marks, identified in s 6 (art 4(2)), may be UK marks, CTMs, marks registered under the Madrid Protocol and 'well-known' trade marks entitled to protection under art 6*bis* of the Paris Convention (see para **5.70**). The relative grounds for refusal of registration are the same grounds which form the basis for infringement proceedings under s 10 (art 5), where, of course, the issue is also whether a later sign conflicts with an earlier trade mark (*Raleigh International Trade Mark* (2001) (see para **5.59** et seq)).

Grounds for conflict

5.36 The four general situations in which marks may conflict for the purposes of opposing a trade mark registration (or founding an infringement action) are looked at below. They are:

- identical marks on identical goods and services (s 5(1)) (art 4(1)(a));

- identical marks on similar goods and services, with the proviso that there exists a likelihood of confusion on the part of the public, which includes the likelihood of association with the earlier mark (s 5(2)(a)) (art 4(1)(b));

- similar marks on similar or identical goods and services, and the above proviso applies (s 5(2)(b)) (art 4(1)(b));

- identical or similar marks on goods and services which are similar or dissimilar, with the proviso that the use of the later mark without due cause would take unfair advantage of, or be detrimental to, the distinctive character of the earlier mark (s 5(3)) (art 4(3)).

Identical marks on identical goods and services

5.37 A mark which is identical to an earlier registered mark and used in relation to the same goods and services may not be registered. The Court of Justice has held that a sign is identical with a trade mark where it reproduces, without any modification or addition, all the elements constituting the trade mark or where, viewed as a whole, it contains differences so insignificant that they may go unnoticed by the average consumer (*SA Société LTJ Diffusion v SA Sadas* (2003); see para **5.28** for the definition of the average consumer). In *Reed Executive v Reed Business Information* (2004), the claimant alleged that the defendants had infringed its trade mark, 'Reed'. In fact, the defendant had used 'Reed' as part of the composites 'Reed Elsevier' and 'Reed Business Information'. In the Court of Appeal, Jacob LJ held that the additional words would not go unnoticed by the average consumer. The marks were similar but not identical.

Identical marks on similar goods and services and similar marks on similar or identical goods and services

5.38 In these circumstances, conflict between a later mark and an earlier mark is not inevitable. It will arise only if the proviso applies and there exists a likelihood of confusion on the part of the public, which includes the likelihood of association with an earlier mark. Following the implementation of the Directive, the meaning of this section, and in particular the proviso, provoked considerable controversy, since how it was interpreted would have an important bearing on the extent to which the EU trade mark regime recognised the concept of 'dilution'. In the early case of *British Sugar plc v James Robertson & Sons Ltd* (1996), Jacob J suggested that a discrete three-stage approach should be taken to applying this section. First, ask whether the marks are the same or similar. Next, ask whether the goods are the same or similar. Finally, ask whether the proviso applies and whether there is a likelihood of confusion, including a likelihood of association between the two marks. If the answer to all three questions is positive, then there will be conflict. However, subsequent decisions by the Court of Justice made it clear that, rather than applying a staged test, it is necessary to take a 'global approach' to interpreting this section. In other words, the answer to any of the three questions posed by Jacob J may depend upon how the other two have themselves been answered. What this means and the consequences for protecting marks from dilution are examined in the following paragraphs, beginning with the meaning of the proviso.

The proviso: (i) the early years

5.39   The wording of s 5(2)(a)–(b) was new to TMA 1994, and came directly from art 4(1)(b) of the TM Directive. It was generally accepted that 'likelihood of confusion' in the proviso meant the likelihood that the public would be confused as to the origin of the marks. However, some EU Member States, especially the Benelux countries, argued that the addition of the key words, 'including a likelihood of association', to the proviso extended the protection given to trade marks beyond their function as indicators of origin to include protection for their commercial value, or reputation, which might be diluted by a simple association with another mark even when the public was not confused as to origin. *Such an approach had long been* recognised in Benelux law, and was reflected in the case of *Claeryn/Klarein* (1975). Claeryn was a well-known alcoholic drink and Klarein a toilet cleaner. There was no argument that the public would believe the products originated from the same source. They would not. What the drinks maker argued was that, if the 'Klarein' mark continued to be used, the public would associate the two products, and that the reputation of the 'Claeryn' mark and, therefore, its value, would suffer. The Benelux court accepted that there was a likelihood of association, although not confusion as to source, and the drinks maker won its case. Conversely, the UK courts believed the proviso should be interpreted narrowly. In *Wagamama Ltd v City Centre Restaurants* (1995), Laddie J held that 'likelihood of association' meant only that marks 'are associated in the sense that one is an extension of the other'. In other words, a 'likelihood of association' was contained within the concept of likelihood of confusion rather than constituting an additional ground for finding infringement. It fell to the Court of Justice to decide whether the broad Benelux or the narrow UK interpretation of 'likelihood of association' would prevail.

The proviso: (ii) *Sabel* and beyond

5.40 The issue was decided by the Court of Justice in *Sabel BV v Puma AG* (1997). Puma was the registered proprietor of two German trade marks comprising bounding puma and leaping puma devices, registered in respect of jewellery and leather goods. Puma opposed the registration of Sabel's sign of a bounding chee-tah device with the name 'Sabel', also for jewellery. The German Supreme Court decided that the marks were not sufficiently similar to give rise to a likelihood of confusion as to origin, but that the similarity of the 'semantic' content of the marks, that is, the bounding felines, might give rise to a likelihood of association. Would this be sufficient grounds for Puma to oppose registration of the 'Sabel' mark? The Court of Justice held that it would not. It ruled that a likelihood of association was merely one element of a likelihood of confusion as to origin, not a separate ground for opposition. The Court of Justice then went on to consider how the likelihood of confusion should be assessed. It said that it must be appre-ciated 'globally', taking into account various factors, including:

- the recognition of the trade mark on the market;
- the association which can be made between the registered mark and the sign;
- the degree of similarity between the mark and the sign and the goods and the services.

5.41 Did *Sabel BV v Puma AG* (1997) endorse the UK approach to the proviso? It appeared to do so, since it said that the likelihood of association helped to define the scope of the likelihood of confusion, but it was not a separate factor in find-ing conflict. This perspective was given further support by the decision in *Marca Mode CV v Adidas AG* (2000), which concerned Adidas's three stripes logo. The Court of Justice held that, even where a trade mark has a particularly distinctive character, the reputation of that mark does not give grounds for presuming the existence of a likelihood of confusion simply because there exists a likelihood of association if a similar or identical sign is used on identical or similar goods. Nonetheless, those who argued for an anti-dilution approach to the interpreta-tion of the proviso were also able to take some comfort from the *Sabel* decision, since the Court of Justice had also held that whether there was a likelihood of confusion might be influenced by the 'reputation' of the mark in question.

The global approach and assessing the similarity of marks

5.42 According to Sabel, in applying the global approach, it is necessary to ask three questions: are the marks confusingly similar; are the goods confusingly similar;

and finally is the proviso satisfied. However, we have also seen from *Sabel* that the answer to any one of these questions might depend upon the answer to each of the others. We will now go on to look at the criteria for assessing whether marks are confusingly similar before considering the same question in relation to goods and services. In *Sabel*, the Court of Justice looked at the similarity between the two marks. It held:

> The global appreciation of the visual, aural or conceptual similarity of the marks in question, must be based on the overall impression given by the marks, bearing in mind, in particular, their distinctive and dominant component... The average consumer normally perceives a mark as a whole and does not proceed to analyse its various details.
>
> In that perspective, the more distinctive the earlier mark, the greater will be the likelihood of confusion. It is therefore not impossible that the conceptual similarity resulting from the fact that two marks use images with analogous semantic content may give rise to a likelihood of confusion where the earlier mark has a particularly distinctive character, either per se or because of the reputation it enjoys with the public.

In the event, the Court of Justice held that neither of the marks was particularly distinctive, and their use did not give rise to a likelihood of confusion.

5.43 In *Lloyds Schuhfabrik*, the Court of Justice also considered the test for similar marks. A German company distributed shoes under the mark 'Lloyd'. A Dutch company marketed shoes under the mark 'Loints' and sold them in Germany. Among the questions for the Court of Justice was whether the aural similarity between the marks was sufficient to find a likelihood of confusion. The Court of Justice ruled that a mere aural similarity was sufficient to create a likelihood of confusion. In reaching its judgment, the Court of Justice said that, in order to assess the degree of similarity between the marks concerned, it was up to the national courts to determine the degree of visual, aural or conceptual similarity between them and, where appropriate, to evaluate the importance to be attached to these elements, taking into account the category of goods or services in question and the circumstances in which they are marketed. Since *Sieckmann v Deutsches Patent- und Markenamt* (2002), it is, of course, necessary to add smells to the list of possible similarities. It was further noted, by the Court of Justice in *Lloyds* that, in assessing the likelihood of confusion, account should be taken of the fact that the average consumer will rarely have a chance to make a direct comparison between the two marks and that his level of attention is likely to vary according to the category of the goods or services in question.

The global approach and assessing the level of distinctiveness

5.44   We have seen that in assessing the likelihood of confusion between two marks, the distinctiveness of the earlier mark is one factor to be taken into account. In *Lloyds*, the Court of Justice held that, in determining the distinctive character of a mark and, accordingly, in assessing whether it is highly distinctive, it is necessary to make 'a global assessment' of its capacity to identify the goods or services for which it has been registered as coming from a particular undertaking (and, hence, its capacity to distinguish). It went on to say that it is appropriate to use a quantitative assessment of the degree of public recognition attained by a mark to determine whether it has a strong, distinctive character. More recently, in *Picasso v OHIM* (2006), DaimlerChrysler sought to register the mark 'Picaro' for motor vehicles as a CTM. Its application was opposed by the estate of the artist, Pablo Picasso, which had a CTM for 'Picasso' also for motor vehicles. It was also alleged that the 'Picaro' mark would infringe the 'Picasso' mark. Both the OHIM and the General Court found that there was no conflict between the two marks. The proprietors of the 'Picasso' mark appealed to the Court of Justice and one basis of their appeal was that the distinctiveness of the 'Picasso' mark compensated for any lesser degree of objective similarity between it and the 'Picaro' mark. The Court of Justice agreed with the General Court in finding that the sign 'Picasso' was devoid of any highly distinctive character for motor vehicles. On the contrary, it believed that on seeing the sign 'Picasso', the relevant public would inevitably view it as a reference to the painter and, given Picasso's fame, 'that particularly rich conceptual reference is such as greatly to reduce the resonance with which . . . the sign is endowed as a mark' for motor vehicles. Recently, in *Calvin Klein Trademarks Trust v OHIM, Zafra Marroquineros SL* (2011), the Court of Justice held that, even applying the global approach, where there was no similarity between the two marks, then the fact that the earlier mark had a considerable reputation was irrelevant. It could not lead to a finding that the marks were confusingly similar when objectively they were not.

The global approach and assessing the similarity of the goods (or services)

5.45   Thus far, this chapter has considered the criteria for deciding whether marks are similar. The next question to ask is whether the goods (or services) are sufficiently similar in the context of the global approach to assessing confusion. This question was addressed by the Court of Justice in *Canon Kabushiki Kaisha v Metro-Goldwyn-Mayer Inc* (1998). MGM applied to register 'Cannon' for video cassettes, production, distribution and projection of films for cinema and television. Their application was opposed by Canon, which had registered the mark 'Canon' for cameras, projectors, television and recording equipment. The question put to the Court of Justice was whether, when determining whether the similarity of the goods and services covered by the two marks at issue is sufficient to give rise to a likelihood of confusion, not only the objective nature of the goods and services at issue, but also the distinctive character of the earlier mark, in particular its reputation, must be taken into account. The Court of Justice held that they should be. Following *Canon*, the test for determining whether goods and services are confusingly similar was summarised in *Sunrider Corp v OHIM* (2006). According to the Court of Justice, the Court will look at the relevant features of the relationship between the goods, 'in particular, their nature, their intended purpose, their methods of use and whether they are in competition with each other or complementary'. The Court will also consider the marks to which they attach, in particular how similar they are, whether the earlier mark is particularly distinctive or whether it has a reputation. A lesser degree of similarity between the goods might be compensated for if the marks are identical or the earlier mark has a reputation or is particularly distinctive (see also *British Sugar plc v James Robertson & Sons Ltd* (1996)).

The global approach and the likelihood of confusion

5.46 As we have seen, under the global approach, there are three elements in finding conflict–similarity of marks, similarity of goods (or services) and the likelihood of confusion–which are, in a sense, mutually dependent. In *Canon Kabushiki Kaisha v Metro-Goldwyn-Mayer Inc* (1998), the Court of Justice summarised the approach to a finding of the likelihood of confusion. It said:

> A global assessment of the likelihood of confusion implies some interdependence between the relevant factors, and in particular a similarity between the trade marks and between these goods and services. Accordingly, a lesser degree of similarity between these goods and services may be offset by a greater degree of similarity between the marks and vice versa. It follows that . . . registration of a trade mark may have to be refused, despite a lesser degree of similarity between the goods or services covered, where the marks are very similar and the earlier mark, in particular its reputation, is highly distinctive.

The global approach applied

5.47 The global approach was applied in *Och-Ziff Management Europe Ltd v Och Capital LLP* (2010). *Och-Ziff* involved a claim for infringement under art 9(1)(b)

CTM Regulation (equivalent to s10(2) TMA), but the principles for finding conflict are the same as those that would apply under s 5(2). The claimant was part of a leading asset management group, with a number of CTMs, including the mark 'Och' in relation to financial services. It objected, inter alia, to the use by the defendant, an independent investment house, of the sign, 'Och Capital'. Mr. Justice Arnold looked first at whether the mark and sign were identical or similar. Applying *Reed Executive Plc v Reed Business Information Ltd* (2004), he concluded that the addition of the word 'Capital' to the defendant's sign would not go unnoticed by the average consumer. He thus proceeded on the assumption that the mark and sign were similar and the services identical. Next Arnold J identified the average consumer for the services in question. He accepted that there would be two groups of consumers. The first would be financial services professionals, who would be knowledgeable and highly attentive. The second group would be ordinary customers, with some knowledge of the mark, who would be moderately attentive. Turning then to the question of whether the marks were confusingly similar, It was accepted by both sides that the 'Och' mark was not only inherently distinctive but it had also acquired a reputation in the field. Furthermore, comparing their visual, aural and conceptual similarities, the only difference between the mark and the sign was the word 'capital' in the latter. Because 'capital' was a non-distinctive and even a descriptive word in relation to financial services, Arnold J concluded that both sets of average consumers would be confused. Interestingly, in this case Arnold J held that confusion was most likely to arise in the viewing of the defendant's advertisements for its services rather than at the actual point of sale. Arnold J opined that such 'initial interest confusion' was an accepted part of EU trade mark law, and was sufficient for a finding of a likelihood of confusion (for initial interest confusion in passing off see para **4.30**).

Marks with a reputation on similar or dissimilar goods

5.48 Section 5(3) TMA) (art 4(4)(a) TM Directive) states that a mark will not be registered if it is identical or similar to an earlier mark, if the earlier mark has a reputation in the UK (or a CTM in the EU) and the proviso applies, that is, that the use of the later mark without due cause would take unfair advantage of, or be detrimental to, the distinctive character of the earlier mark. Originally, s 5(3) applied only to situations where the goods were dissimilar. However, in *Zino Davidoff v Gofkid* (2003), the Court of Justice held that a mark with a reputation should receive the same protection in cases where the goods are similar–and the proviso applies–as it receives where the goods are dissimilar. The 1994 Act was amended accordingly. To find conflict under s 5(3), there is no need for a likelihood of confusion as to source. Rather, according to the

Court of Justice in *Adidas-Salomon v Fitnessworld* (2003), 'it is sufficient for the degree of similarity between the mark with a reputation and the sign to have the effect that the relevant section of the public establishes a link between the sign and the mark'.

What is a reputation?

5.49 The Court of Justice considered the criteria for assessing whether a mark has a reputation for the purposes of art 5(2) TM Directive (which is the intringement provision equivalent to art 4(4)(a)) in *General Motors (GM) v Yplon SA* (1999). Yplon had registered 'Chevy' for cleaning products in Benelux, and GM wanted to restrain use of the mark on the grounds that it diluted the reputation of its own trade mark 'Chevy' for cars, and damaged its advertising function. Yplon responded that GM had not shown that its mark had a reputation in the Benelux countries. The Court of Justice was asked by the national court for the proper construction of 'repute of the trade mark'. The Court of Justice made it clear that art 5(2) was intended to apply only when the public had sufficient knowledge of the earlier registered mark so that, when confronted with the later mark, it might make an association between the two even if they were used for different products or services. It then went on to list a number of factors relevant to assessing whether the earlier mark has a reputation. First, the relevant public with whom the mark must have acquired a reputation is the public 'concerned with the trade mark'. The relevant public might, depending upon the product, be either the general public or a more specialised public, for instance, traders in a specific sector. The necessary degree of knowledge is then reached when the earlier mark is known by a significant part of the relevant public. It is up to the national court to decide if it has been reached by taking into account all the relevant facts, including the trade mark's market share, the intensity, geographical extent and duration of its use, and the size of the investment made in promoting it. To have a reputation, a mark does not have to be known throughout a Member State, as long as it is known in a 'substantial' part of it.

Applying the proviso

5.50 To find conflict under s 5(3) (art 4(4)(a) TM Directive), the proviso must also apply, so that the use of the later mark without due cause would take unfair advantage of, or be detrimental to, the distinctive character or reputation of the earlier mark. In *Adidas-Salomon AG v Fitnessworld Trading Ltd* (2003), AG Jacobs analysed the three types of harm covered by the proviso. According to the Advocate General, the concept of taking unfair advantage of the distinctive character or repute of the mark includes instances where there is exploitation (or free-riding) on the coattails of a famous mark, or an attempt to trade on its reputation. Detriment to the distinctive character of the mark encapsulates the concepts of dilution, which is often referred to as 'blurring'. Dilution or blurring means that the mark is no longer capable of arousing an immediate association with the goods for which it is registered or used. The concept of detriment, often referred to as 'tarnishment', describes the situation where the goods for which the infringing sign is used appeals to the public's senses in such a way that the mark's power of attraction is affected. *Claeryn/Klarein* (1975) is a case in point.

Applying the proviso: the case law

5.51 The interpretation of the proviso was considered by the Court of Justice in two recent cases, *L'Oreal v Bellure* (2009), which was an infringement action, and the slightly earlier case of *Intel Corporation Inc v CPM United Kingdom Ltd* (2008), in which the claimant sought a declaration of invalidity of the defendant's mark (for invalidity see para **5.100** et seq). Taken together, these two judgments have helped to set the parameters of the protection which the law will accord to the extrinsic qualities of famous marks in circumstances where there is no customer confusion.

Detrimental to the distinctive character and repute of the mark

5.52 In *Intel v CPM* (2008), the claimant's mark, 'Intel', had a 'huge' reputation for computers and computer-linked products. CPM had a registered trade mark, 'Intelmark', for marketing and telemarketing. Intel sought a declaration of invalidity arguing that CPM's mark would be detrimental to the distinctiveness of its own. In particular, Intel argued, following the decision in *Adidas-Salomon AG v Fitnessworld Trading Ltd* (2004), that for a finding of detriment to distinctive character, although the relevant public must make a 'link' between the two marks, that 'link' could constitute any kind of mental association, even a mere bringing to mind. In the Court of Appeal (*Intel Corp Ltd v CPM United Kingdom Ltd* (2007)), Jacob LJ had accepted that 'Intel' was an invented word in that it had no other meaning beyond its identification with the products of Intel Corp, that it was unique in that it had not been used by any other trader in relation to other goods or services and that it had a 'huge reputation' in the UK for computers and related products. Jacob LJ also accepted that the marks were similar and that the goods were dissimilar. Further, he assumed that the use of the 'Intelmark' by CPM did not suggest to the relevant public that there was a trade connection with Intel Corp. Jacob LJ then asked a number of questions of the Court of Justice. In particular, were the circumstances of this case sufficient for the necessary link to come into play? If not, what factors would allow a national court to find such a link? And, finally, what is required to find detriment to the distinctive character of the mark with a reputation? According to the Court of Justice, whether there was a relevant 'link' must be assessed globally taking into account all relevant factors. The fact that the average consumer calls the earlier mark to mind is tantamount to there being such a link. However, the fact that the earlier mark has a 'huge' reputation, the goods and services at issue are dissimilar or substantially so and that the earlier mark is unique does not necessarily imply that such a link exists. Second, the question of whether use of the later mark takes unfair advantage of or is detrimental to the distinctive character or repute of the earlier mark must also be assessed globally, taking into account all the relevant factors. These would include the factors already set out, as well as the fact that the average consumer calls the earlier mark to mind. But, as is the case with the relevant 'link', the mere presence of these factors is not sufficient to establish detriment. Finally, proof that use of the later mark will be detrimental to the distinctive character of the earlier mark necessitates evidence of a change in the economic behaviour of the average consumer of the goods and services for which it is registered or at the very least a serious likelihood that such a change will occur in the future.

Takes unfair advantage

5.53 The meaning of unfair advantage was then considered by the Court of Justice in *L'Oreal v Bellure*. The claimants were producers and marketers of expensive perfumes. In the UK, they were the proprietors of a number of well-known trade marks, which were registered for, inter alia, perfumes. These marks covered both the names and the packaging of the perfumes. The defendants sold imitations of up-market perfumes in the UK. Some of their perfumes were packaged in bottles which were similar to those of the claimants. Furthermore, as one of their marketing strategies, the defendants gave their retailers comparison lists which indicated by use of the claimants' word and figurative marks, which of their own perfumes corresponded to those of the claimants. The claimants accused the defendants of infringing their marks under all three of the causes of action set out in Art 5(2) (equivalent to Art 4(4) in relation to registration). In the Court of Appeal, Jacob LJ did not find that the packaging used by the defendants was sufficiently similar to that of the claimants' packaging so that the public would be confused as to the origin of the defendants' goods. Nor were the claimants' marks likely to be blurred or tarnished. He made a similar finding in relation to the use of the claimants' word and figurative marks on the comparison lists. The outstanding question for the Court of Justice was thus whether the use of similar packaging by the defendants and the use of the claimants' word and figurative marks on the comparison lists took unfair advantage of the claimants' marks. Lord Justice Jacob asked the following question of the Court of Justice. Where a trader uses a sign which is similar to a registered mark with a reputation, but is not confusingly similar to it, in such a way that the role of the registered mark as a badge of origin is not impaired or put at risk, there is no blurring or tarnishment and the proprietor's sales and advertising investment are not impaired, but the trader gets a commercial advantage from the use of his sign because of its similarity to the registered mark, does that use amount to the taking of 'an unfair advantage' of the reputation of the registered mark?

L'Oreal v Bellure: the judgment

5.54 The Court of Justice first set out what it understood to be the meaning of taking unfair advantage of the distinctive character or repute of the mark with a reputation. It noted:

> *It covers, in particular, cases where, by reason of a transfer of the image of the mark or of the characteristics which it projects to the goods identified by the identical or similar sign, there is clear exploitation...of the mark with a reputation.*

The Court then set out the circumstances in which unfair advantage might be proved. It stated that it is necessary to undertake a 'global assessment' of the circumstances, taking into account all relevant factors. These might include the strength of the original mark's reputation and how distinctive it is, the degree of similarity between the marks and the proximity of the goods or services covered by both marks. In making this assessment, the more immediately and strongly the mark is brought to mind by use of the later sign, the greater the likelihood that the latter will take unfair advantage of the distinctive character or the repute of the earlier mark. The Court also suggested that a finding of unfair advantage might be influenced by whether the defendant's actions were intentional. In summary, the Court of Justice's answer to the question posed by Jacob LJ was the following:

> *...the taking of unfair advantage of the distinctive character or the repute of a mark, within the meaning of that provision, does not require that there be a likelihood of confusion or a likelihood of detriment to the distinctive character or the repute of the mark or, more generally, to its proprietor. The advantage arising from the use by a third party of a sign similar to a mark with a reputation is an advantage taken unfairly by that third party of the distinctive character or the repute of the mark where that party seeks by that*

use to ride on the coat-tails of the mark with a reputation in order to benefit from the power of attraction, the reputation and the prestige of that mark and to exploit, without paying any financial compensation, the marketing effort expended by the proprietor of the mark in order to create and maintain the mark's image.

L'Oreal v Bellure: the controversy

5.55 The decision of the Court of Justice in *L'Oreal v Bellure* caused considerable controversy. For some, it rightly conferred protection on those extrinsic qualities of a trade mark, such as their advertising function, which a proprietor might have spent many years and a great deal of money nurturing. But for others, the decision gave too much power to powerful brand owners which might be deployed to inhibit legitimate competition. One of the most trenchant critics of the Court of Justice's decision was Jacob LJ himself. Before putting his question to the Court of Justice, he had already made plain what he thought its answer should be. He noted:

Clearly activities which actually harm a trade mark or its reputation ought to be caught by trade mark law. And there may be other activities which can properly be called 'unfair'...But where there is no harm, present or prospective, caused to the mark, its distinctive character or to the mark owner or his business, present or reasonably prospective, I see no reason to say that a use is 'unfair'.

In other words, he did not view an advantage taken as unfair if it did no damage to the earlier mark. As we have seen, the Court of Justice came to an opposite conclusion. Subsequently, when the case returned to the Court of Appeal for judgment, Jacob LJ accepted that he had been left with no choice but to find Bellure liable for trade mark infringement. But he also made amply clear his own belief that such an outcome was unfortunate. He took the view that trade mark law should not prevent traders making honest statements about their products where those products were themselves lawful, as indeed Bellure's products were. To find otherwise, he believed would inhibit free speech, including the right of consumers to be told the truth about products. It would also inhibit free competition, because the Court of Justice's approach would lead to the suppression of information which enabled consumers to make informed and efficient choices. Generally he viewed the Court of Justice's judgment as too protective of trade marks, in effect implying that any use of a mark with a reputation for the purposes of comparison, if it gave an advantage to the user, would be infringing: indeed, more perniciously (in his view), that any 'free riding' should be assumed to be unfair. The question remains open as to whether the *L'Oreal v Bellure* decision will represent the outer limits of the legal protection to be afforded to the extrinsic qualities of trade marks under the TM Directive (Gangjee and Burrell, 'Because you're worth it: L'Oreal and the prohibition on free riding' [2010] *Modern Law Review* 282).

Without due cause

5.56 There is surprisingly little case law which explicitly considers the meaning of this phrase in the proviso to s 5(3). In the early case, *Premier Brands v Typhoon* (2000), Neuberger J held that 'due cause' would mean that the user of the mark could not honestly be asked to desist by the proprietor of the mark from its use. More recently, in *L'Oreal v Bellure* (2007), Jacob LJ held that the onus of establishing 'due cause' lies with the defendant. In this case, he held that use of the claimants' marks in the comparison table was necessary since 'realistically' the defendants would not be able to sell a replica fragrance, which is a lawful product, without such a list. However, this was not true of the shape of the packaging which was, according to the defendants, intended to 'wink' at the original.

Conflicts with earlier rights

5.57 A mark will not be registered which conflicts with an unregistered mark, which would be protected under the law of passing off (s 5(4)(a)) (art 4(4)(b)). Proprietors of other earlier rights, particularly those given by virtue of the law of copyright, design right or registered designs, are also protected from the registration of a later mark, which would infringe those rights (s 5(4)(b)) (art 4(4)(c)). An example might be an application for a shape trade mark, for example, a bottle, which infringes a registered design, or a jingle, which would infringe a copyright. These will not be registered. In *Anne Frank Trade Mark* (1998), the foundation which owned Anne Frank's literary estate tried unsuccessfully to have the trade mark 'Anne Frank' held by the Anne Frank House revoked, because it claimed to have the copyright in her signature. It was defeated because it was held, inter alia, that there is no copyright in a signature.

Consent/honest concurrent use

5.58 All the grounds for refusal in s 5 may be overcome if the proprietor of the earlier mark or right gives his consent to registration of the later mark (s 5(5)) (art 4(5)). If consent is given, the Registrar has no discretion (as under the TMA 1938) to refuse registration of the later mark, even if there will be confusion between the two marks. This is another indication of the deregulatory nature of the TMA 1994. The Registrar shall also accept an application for registration even though it conflicts with an earlier trade mark or an earlier right, if the applicant can show that he has made honest concurrent use of the trade mark for which registration is sought (s 7) and there is no opposition from the proprietor of the earlier right (*Road Tech Systems Ltd v Unison Software (UK) Ltd* (1996)). The definition of what constitutes honest concurrent use lies in previous case law, as there is no similar provision in the TM Directive (s 7(3)). Factors to be taken into account are: the extent of use, the degree of confusion likely to ensue, the honesty of the concurrent use, whether any instances of confusion are proved and the relative inconvenience caused to the public if both marks are registered (*Club Europe Trade Mark* (1999); *Budějovický Budvar NP v Anheuser-Busch Inc* (2009)).

Infringement

5.59 The proprietor of a registered trade mark has exclusive rights in the trade mark which are infringed by its use in the UK without his consent (s 9) (art 5(1)). The acts amounting to infringement are set out in s 10 (art 5). The right to commence infringement proceedings arises once the trade mark has been registered. But infringement itself (and so the starting date for calculating damages) dates from the date of registration, which, under s 40(3) (art 5(1)), is defined as the date of the filing of the application for registration. Although s 9 mentions only the rights of the proprietor, under certain conditions assignees and licensees can also bring infringement proceedings.

The grounds for infringement

5.60 The four main grounds for infringement are set out in s 10(1)–(3) (art 5(1)–(2)). They are the same as the relative grounds for refusal of registration (see para **5.35** et seq). They are:

- use of an identical sign in relation to the identical goods and services for which the trade mark is registered (s 10(1)) (art 5(1)(a));

- use of an identical sign in relation to goods and services similar to those for which the trade mark is registered, with the proviso that there is a likelihood of confusion on the part of the public, including the likelihood of association (s 10(2)(a)) (art 5(1)(b));

- use of a similar sign in relation to goods and services identical or similar to those for which the mark is registered, and the proviso applies (s 10(2)(b)) (art 5(1)(b));

- use of an identical sign in relation to similar or dissimilar goods and services where the mark has a reputation in the UK, with the proviso that the use of the sign, being without due cause, takes unfair advantage of, or is detrimental to, the distinctive character or repute of the mark (s 10(3)) (art 5(2)).

What constitutes infringing use?

5.61 To infringe, the sign must be used in the course of trade, which includes any business or profession (s 103) (art 5(3)). Infringing use is generally defined as use of a trade mark, or of a sign, identical with, similar to or likely to be mistaken for a trade mark (s 103(2)). Actual uses of a sign for the purposes of infringement are set out in s 10(4)–(5) (art 5(3)) and include use in advertising (including, of course, radio advertising, where there might be aural confusion: *Lloyds Schuhfabrik Meyer & Co v Klijsen Handel BV* (2000)), exposing goods for sale under the sign or affixing the infringing sign to goods and packaging. In *Arsenal Football Club plc v Reed* (2002), the Court of Justice defined use in the course of trade as use which 'takes place in the context of commercial activity with a view to economic advantage and not as a private matter'. It does not include all use which may bring commercial benefit to the user. To take an example given by AG Ruiz-Jarabo Colomer in *Arsenal v Reed* (2002), it does not include the use made by Andy Warhol of the Campbell soup mark in his paintings, even though the paintings themselves are extremely valuable. In *Google France Sarl v Louis Vuitton Malletier SA* (2010), the Court of Justice held that the provision by Google of keywords, which were registered trade marks, to advertisers was not use by Google of these trade marks in the course of trade, but use by the advertisers was. While in *Interflora Inc v Marks & Spencer plc* (2011), the Court of Justice held that such use was use in relation to the goods and services of the advertiser even if it did not appear in the advertisement triggered by the keyword. But an online marketplace, such as eBay, uses a trade mark for the purposes of art 5 TM Directive when it appears in offers for sale displayed on its site (*L'Oreal SA v eBay International AG* (2011) (see para **5.87** et seq) (Marsoof, 'Keywords advertising: issues of trade mark infringement' [2010] *Journal of International Commercial Law and Technology* 240)).

Non-trade mark use

5.62 The question of non-trade mark use in relation to infringement has been a matter of some controversy. In *Philips Electronics BV v Remington Consumer Products*

(1999), the Court of Appeal held that a finding of trade mark infringement did not call for the later sign to be used in a trade mark sense. The Court of Appeal pointed out instead that s 11 of the TMA 1994 (art 6 TM Directive) listed a number of exclusions which would almost certainly provide a defence against infringement for a sign which was not used as an indicator of origin. The question as to whether trade mark use was needed to find infringement was directed to the Court of Justice by the High Court in *Arsenal Football Club plc v Reed* (2001).

Non-trade mark use and infringement

5.63 Arsenal Football Club (AFC) (the 'Gunners') was associated with two logos–one a crest and one a cannon–and had also registered the words 'Arsenal' and 'Gunners' as trade marks. AFC earned considerable income through licensing its marks for use on clothing and other goods. Reed sold identical products outside AFC's stadium, featuring both the devices and word marks. He also displayed signs stating that his products were not official AFC merchandise. AFC sued Reed for passing off and trade mark infringement under s 10(1). Its claim for passing off failed (see para **4.33**). In the High Court, Laddie J took the view that when Reed had placed the devices and words on his products, he had not been using the marks in a trade mark sense, that is, as an indicator of origin. Instead, Reed had intended, and purchasers had perceived, the signs on his products as a badge of support, loyalty or affiliation to the club. Laddie J referred the questions of whether such use was non-trade mark use and, if so, whether nonetheless it was infringing, to the Court of Justice. The Court held that the rights of a proprietor to prevent a third party from using his mark extended to any situation where such use was liable to affect its essential function as a guarantor of origin. Thus, any use which damages the origin function of the mark will be infringing whether or not it is trade mark use. The Court of Justice then looked at the facts of this particular case. It found that the marks, as they were used by Reed, created the impression that there was a material link in the course of trade between his products and those of AFC. This impression was not affected by Reed's sign because, although his direct customers might not be confused, if the goods were taken away from the stall, others might be. Furthermore, there was no guarantee that the goods sold by Reed under the marks had been manufactured or supplied under the control of a single undertaking. In fact, they did not come from AFC. As a result, the use of the marks by Reed, whether or not they were perceived by the public as a badge of loyalty or affiliation, would jeopardise their essential function, and AFC could prevent their use. It was infringing use. When the case returned to the High Court, Laddie J did not follow the Court of Justice's conclusion that Reed had infringed. Instead, he held that the Court had exceeded its jurisdiction by ruling on matters of fact as well as law. He held that as the public did not view the marks on Reed's goods as indicators of origin, his use of the Arsenal marks could not affect their origin function and was non-infringing. The claimant appealed. Finally, the Court of Appeal overturned Laddie J's judgment and found for the claimant. It concluded, like the Court of Justice, that Reed's use of the claimant's trade marks would affect their origin function, not least because, on seeing Reed's goods, consumers would draw the inference that the marks were an indication of origin and that the goods had come from AFC. This was infringing use.

Infringing use after *Arsenal v Reed*

5.64 There was some disagreement between commentators after the Court of Justice's decision in *Arsenal v Reed* as to whether only trade mark use by a third party of a registered mark was infringing use. Confusion was heightened following the House of Lords judgment in *R v Johnstone* (2003). In this case Johnstone sold bootleg CDs, carrying the names of the artists, including Bon Jovi and the Rolling Stones, which were registered trade marks. Lord Nicholls held that use of a trade mark as an indicator of origin was 'an essential prerequisite to infringement', although, Johnstone was held to have a defence to infringement of descriptive use (see para **5.74**). However, it is submitted that the Court Justice judgment in *Arsenal v Reed* (2003) does not support this conclusion and that the later Court of Justice decision in *Adam Opel AG v Autec AG* (2007) confirms this view. Opel, which manufactures the Opel Astra, has a registered trade mark for, inter alia, motor vehicles and toys. Autec makes scale models of cars, and used the Opel trade mark on the radiator grille of a model Astra. Opel alleged trade mark infringement. Autec responded that its use of the Opel mark was not trade mark use, as the public would know that scale models of cars, which carried the car's logo, did not originate from the car maker. The Court of Justice, referring back to *Arsenal v Reed* (2003), re-iterated that infringing use of a registered trade mark is use which affects the essential functions of a mark, in particular its use as a badge of origin. If the average consumer for toy cars would not assume that the Opel mark on the scale model was a badge of origin, but instead indicated that this was a scale model of an Opel car, then the origin function of the Opel mark, as a mark registered for toys, would not be affected. It would not be infringing use. When the case returned to the German Courts, Autec was held not to have infringed the Opel mark, inter alia, because the use on the model car would not affect the origin function or indeed any other functions of the mark (*Adam Opel GmbH v Autec* (I ZR 88/08) (2010)).

The advertising functions of a trade mark and trade mark use

5.65 In *Arsenal Football Club v Reed* (2003), the Court of Justice held that non-trade mark use of a sign may be infringing if it affects the origin function of a registered mark. The question then arises as to whether non-trade mark use may be infringing if it affects other functions of a registered trade mark, apart from its function as a badge of origin. In *Opel v Autec* (2007), the Court of Justice referred to trade mark functions in the plural. What these functions encompass was elucidated in *L'Oreal v Bellure* (2009), where the Court of Justice held that they include:

> ...not only the essential function of the trade mark, which is to guarantee to consumers the origin of the goods or services, but also its other functions, in particular that of guaranteeing the quality of the goods or services in question and those of communication, investment or advertising.

In other words, non-trade mark use of a sign identical or similar to a registered mark may be infringing if it affects any of these functions of the mark. Given the extended protection increasingly afforded to the extrinsic qualities of trade marks with a reputation in other areas of trade mark law, such an inclusive approach by the Court of Justice to the issue of non-trade mark use is scarcely surprising (see also *Interflora v Marks & Spencer* (2011)).

Finding infringement

5.66 The main circumstances in which infringement arises are looked at below. A more detailed discussion of these circumstances is to be found above in the discussion of the relative grounds for refusal of registration under s 5, where the same grounds for conflict apply (see para **5.35** et seq). It should be remembered that infringement can be found on the basis of 'initial interest' confusion (see para **5.47**).

Identical marks on identical goods

5.67 A sign is identical with a trade mark where it reproduces, without any modification or addition, all the elements constituting the trade mark or where, viewed as whole, it contains differences so insignificant that they may go unnoticed by the average consumer (*SA Société LTJ Diffusion v SA Sadas* (2003)) (see para **5.37**). *Arsenal Football Club plc v Reed* (2001) is an example of an infringement action under s 10(1) (see para **5.65**).

Identical or similar marks on identical or similar goods

5.68 The criteria for the comparison of marks and of goods and services in order to establish similarity are set out in the discussion above of s 5(2)(a)–(b) under the relative grounds for refusal of registration (see para **5.35**). It is, of course, necessary for the proviso to apply, so that there must be a likelihood of confusion on the part of the public, including the likelihood of association, for there to be infringement. The courts will apply the global approach to determining whether there is infringement. When assessing the likelihood of confusion in an infringement action, it is important to look at the context in which the mark is being used (*O2 Holdings v Hutchinson* (2006)). The question of whether the average consumer is likely to be confused between a mark and a sign may differ if the assessment is being made at the point of registration when the two are being compared side-by-side as opposed to during an infringement action when both the mark and the sign are being used. In *Picasso v OHIM* (2006), *the Court of Justice* suggested that the average consumer may be more easily confused in an infringement action, where he would have seen two cars bearing the names Picasso and Picaro respectively on the road, than if that same consumer was actually deciding which of the two cars to buy (see also *Och-Ziff Management Europe Ltd. v Och Capital LLP* (2010)).

Marks with a reputation on similar or dissimilar goods

5.69 The basic criteria for finding infringement under s 10(3) (art 5(2)) are set out above in the discussion of conflicting marks under s 5(3) (art 4(4)(a)) (see para **5.48** et seq). It is necessary to show that the proviso applies and that the use of the sign, being without due cause, takes unfair advantage of, or is detrimental to, the distinctive character of the earlier mark.

Well-known marks

5.70 Section 56, which implements art 6*bis* of the Paris Convention, gives limited protection to well-known marks which are not registered in the UK. It allows the proprietor to obtain an injunction against the use in the UK of an identical or similar trade mark in relation to identical or similar goods or services where use is likely to cause confusion. He may also prevent registration of a later conflicting mark, or seek to have it declared invalid. But he does not have the right to claim damages, nor can he act against the use of his mark on dissimilar goods. Under s 56, there is no need for the proprietor to carry on business or have any goodwill in the UK to obtain injunctive relief, as would be the case if an action was brought under passing off (*Anheuser-Busch Inc v Budějovický Budvar* (1984) (see para **4.13**)). It is also worth noting that TRIPS goes further and extends the protection given under art 6*bis* to goods or services which are not similar to those in respect of which the mark is registered, provided that use of the mark would 'indicate a connection between these goods or services and the owner of the registered trade mark and provided that the interests of the owner of the registered trade mark are likely to be damaged by such use'. A well-known mark is not defined in the TMA 1994, but presumably will have to command a very high degree of consumer recognition, greater than that for marks with a reputation, a view confirmed by the Advocate General in *General Motors (GM) v Yplon SA* (2000). In *Philips Electronics NV v Remington Consumer Products* (1998), the claimant claimed to have protection under s 56 as an alternative to trade mark protection. Jacob J observed that, since s 56 is intended to give the trade mark owner equivalent protection to that which he would have under passing off if he had the requisite goodwill in the UK, then to succeed under s 56 he must be able to show confusion or deception in 'a passing-off sense'.

Limits on the protection afforded by registration

5.71 Section 11 of the TMA 1994 (art 6 TM Directive) sets out five defences to trade mark infringement. It is also possible for a third party to make use of a registered trade mark in the course of comparative advertising without infringing the mark (see para **5.78** et seq). Taken together, these provisions set the limits to the monopoly afforded by trade mark registration.

Defence 1: overlapping registrations

5.72 A trade mark is not infringed where another registered trade mark is used in relation to the goods or services for which the latter is registered (s 11(1)). Both marks are validly on the register and both are entitled to protection. However, it is open to either proprietor to seek to have his opponent's registration declared invalid (*Intel v CPM* (2008) is an example of such an action).

Defence 2: use of own name

5.73 A trade mark is not infringed by the use by a person of his own name and address, provided the use is in accordance with honest practices in industrial or commercial matters (s 11(2); art 6(1)(a)). This exception will apply only if the whole business name is used (*Origins Natural Resources Inc v Origin Clothing Ltd* (1995)). According to Jacob LJ in *Reed Executive plc v Reed Business Information Ltd* (2004), the own name defence applies to company names. Furthermore, it would apply even if such use were trade mark use and were to cause some confusion (as per the Court of Justice, *Gerolsteiner Brunnen v Putsch* (2004)). In *Celine Sarl v Celine SA* (2007), the Court of Justice held that in assessing honest use in relation to the own-name defence, account should be taken both of the extent to which such use is understood by a significant section of the relevant public as indicating a link between the third party's goods and services and the trade mark proprietor and the extent to which the third party should be aware that such a link exists. Another factor to take into account is whether the trade mark enjoys a reputation in the Member State in which it is registered from which the third party might profit.

Defence 3: descriptive use

5.74 A trade mark is not infringed by the use of indications concerning the kind, quality, quantity, intended purpose, value, geographical origin, the time of the production of goods or of rendering of services, or other characteristics of goods or services, provided the use is in accordance with honest practices in industrial or commercial matters (s 11(2)(b)) (art 6(1)(b)). The protection offered by s 11(2) (b) is particularly important since, in theory, it is possible under the TMA 1994 to register any descriptive sign, provided it has acquired sufficient distinctiveness through use. As a result, but for the protection afforded by this section, increasing numbers of common descriptive words would be effectively off-limits to other traders.

5.75 Following the Court of Justice judgment in *Arsenal Football Club plc v Reed* (2002) and later judgments (see para **5.65**), it is now necessary to ask whether the use by the defendant, even if descriptive, affects the functions of the claimant's mark. If so, it will be infringing use. An example of non-infringing descriptive use, which is often cited by the courts, including by the Court of Justice in *Arsenal*, is to be found in the case of *Hölterhoff v Freiesleben* (2002). F was the proprietor of two trade marks, registered in Germany, 'Spirit Sun' and 'Context Cut' for diamonds and precious stones for processing as jewellery. These stones were distinguished by particular cuts. H dealt in precious stones, which he cut himself or purchased from other dealers. In the course of business negotiations, H offered for sale stones which he described by reference to the 'Spirit Sun' and 'Context Cut' names. The jeweller ordered two stones 'in the Spirit Sun cut' from H. There was no reference to the registered marks on the delivery notes or invoices, which simply referred to the stones as 'rhodolites'. The Court of Justice was asked whether there was infringement under art 5(1)(a) and (b) of the TM Directive where the defendant used the registered signs only to describe a particular characteristic of the goods he was offering for sale, but also made it clear that the goods had originated from himself. The Court of Justice held this was not infringing use, but descriptive use. H had made it clear that he had produced the rhodolites and simply described their cut by reference to F's trade marks. The situation can be distinguished from that in *Arsenal*, because here the marks were used only as a description and not in the context of actual sales to customers. As such, they could not affect the origin function of the registered marks.

Defence 4: intended purpose

5.76   It is not an infringement to use the trade mark where it is necessary to indicate the intended purpose of the product or service (in particular, as accessories or spare parts), provided the use is in accordance with honest practices in industrial or commercial matters (s 11(2)(c); art 6(1)(c)). A trader who supplies spare parts for, or makes repairs to, a particular branded product may make this clear to the public. But he must be careful. He may say, for example, 'This film is suitable for a Kodak camera' (to cite an example given by the Court of Appeal in *Philips Electronics BV v Remington Consumer Products* (1999)), but not 'We supply Kodak film', if the film he supplies is not produced by Kodak. The Court of Justice examined this defence in two key cases, *BMW v Deenik* (1999) and *Gillette Co v LA-Laboratories Ltd Oy* (2005). In the former, the Court of Justice held, inter alia, that a proprietor is not entitled to prevent a third party from using the registered mark for the purpose of informing the public that he carries out the repair and maintenance of goods covered by the trade mark and put on the market with the proprietor's consent. Nor can he be prohibited from informing the public that he is a specialist in the sale, repair or maintenance of such goods. But this protection is lost if, in either case, the mark is used in such a way as to create an impression that there is a commercial connection between the two undertakings and, in particular, that the seller's business is affiliated to the trade mark proprietor's distribution network, or that there is a special relationship between the two (see also, *Volvo v Heritage (Leicester) Ltd* (2000)). In *Gillette Co v LA-Laboratories Ltd Oy* (2005), the claimant marketed razors, including replaceable blades, under the mark 'Gillette' and 'Sensor' in Finland. The defendant also sold razors and replaceable blades, under the mark 'Parason Flexor'. The defendant affixed stickers to the packaging of its blades stating, 'all Parason Flexor and Gillette Sensor handles are compatible with this blade'. Gillette argued that this was infringing use, inter alia, because the defendant could state that its blades were compatible with other razors, without the necessity of using the Gillette marks. The Court of Justice held that use by a third party of the registered mark was necessary, and hence non-infringing, where in practice such use would be the only means of providing the public with 'comprehensible and complete' information as to the purpose of the product. It also held that it was not honest use, for the purposes of art 6(1)(c), if use by a third party affected the value of the trade mark by free riding on or denigrating its reputation.

Defence 5: local signs

5.77 A registered trade mark is not infringed by the use in the course of trade in a particular locality of an earlier right which applies only in that locality (s 11(3)) (art 6(2)). Examples of what might be protected are a pub sign or a local service.

Comparative advertising

5.78 Until the TMA 1994, it was not possible for an advertiser to compare his product with that of a competitor, by reference to the competitor's registered trade mark. The 1994 Act allowed comparative advertising. This was a UK government decision, so the wording of the relevant provision (s 10(6)) was not taken from the TM Directive. Since the passage of the TMA 1994, the EU has enacted the Directive on Comparative Advertising (EC) 97/55 (CAD), which amends Directive (EEC) 84/450 on Misleading Advertising to include comparative advertising. CAD was implemented in the UK by the Control of Misleading Advertising (Amendment) Regulations 2000. A number of early cases concerning comparative advertising were dealt with by the UK courts under s10(6) TMA. Generally, the courts tended to interpret it liberally. Thus in *British Airways plc v Ryanair Ltd* (2001), Jacob J confirmed that the primary objective of s 10(6) is to permit comparative advertising; that so long as the use of the competitor's mark is honest, there is nothing wrong in telling the public of the relative merits of competing goods or services, using the registered mark to identify them; that the test for honesty is objective, that is, would a reasonable reader be likely to say, upon being given the full facts, that the advertisement is not honest bearing in mind what the public would expect of an advertisement for the goods or services at issue; and that the public may expect hyperbole in advertising.

Comparative advertising and the Comparative Advertising Directive

5.79 However, following the Court of Appeal and the subsequent Court of Justice decisions in *O2 Ltd v Hutchison 3G UK Ltd* ((2006) CA; (2008) Court of Justice), the courts now look to the relationship between the TM Directive and CAD when considering the issue of comparative advertising rather than to s10(6). Article 4 (previously art 3a(1)) of CAD) essentially says that comparative advertising is permitted when it is not misleading; when it is non-infringing; and when it is not concerned with advertising imitation or replica goods. In *O2*, the claimant had registered trade marks both for 'O2' and for bubbles used in relation to, inter alia, mobile phone services. The defendant, H3G, was also a mobile phone provider.

H3G started an advertising campaign which compared its services to those of O2, using as a reference the 'O2' mark and also bubbles which were similar but not the same as O2's registered mark. The claimant conceded that the advertisement was not misleading, that there could be no objection to the use of its 'O2' mark, but that the use of a mark similar to its bubble mark was infringing under art 5(1)(b). In the High Court, Mr Justice Pumfrey held that the advertisement was infringing. However, he found that the defendant had complied with art 3a(1) of CAD and that there was a defence of descriptive use. When the case reached the CA, Jacob LJ addressed a number of questions to the Court of Justice. Its answers set out the parameters for addressing comparative advertising under the TM Directive and CAD. The Court of Justice first held that the proprietor of a registered trade mark is not entitled to prevent the use of an identical or similar mark by a third party which satisfies the conditions of art 3(1)(a) (now art 4) of CAD. Under the TM Directive, the trade mark proprietor is only entitled to object to the use of the mark by a third party if it gives rise to a likelihood of confusion.

5.80 It should be noted that the *O2* case involved similar marks on identical goods. It is submitted that the question of the approach to be taken where the mark and goods are identical or the comparative advertisement takes unfair advantage of the registered mark is not fully settled. The latter circumstance was however addressed in *L'Oreal v Bellure* (2009) where the defendants used the claimants' marks in a comparison list (see para **5.53**). In this case, the Court of Justice held that art 4 of CAD should be interpreted to mean that where an advertiser in a comparative advertisement states explicitly or implicitly that his product is an imitation of a product bearing a well-known trade mark, the advantage gained by him must be considered unfair and hence not a legitimate exercise in comparative advertising. The Court of Justice in *L'Oreal* also set out its general view of the approach to be taken to comparative advertising. It emphasised that the conditions set out in art 3a(1) of CAD should be interpreted in the sense most favourable to comparative advertising, while at the same time ensuring that comparative advertising is not used anti-competitively and unfairly or in a manner which affects the interests of the consumer (see also *Lidl SNC v Vierzon Distribution SA* (2010)).

Trade mark infringement and the internet

5.81 The rise of the internet has also posed new problems for trade mark proprietors, as it has for copyright holders. Most obviously, given that trade mark rights are territorial, it may be difficult for a proprietor to take action against an infringing sign if it is used on a website originating from a territory where his mark's protection does not extend. Here, we will look at two particular issues which have exercised the courts in recent years. The first relates to internet domain names.

The second concerns the liability of websites which may display trade marks, although they do not directly sell the goods and services which attach to them, in particular search engines and auction sites.

Trade marks and internet domain names

5.82 In *British Telecommunications plc v One in a Million Ltd* (1998), the claimant succeeded in a s 10(3) infringement action, as well as in an action for passing off (see para **4.35** on passing off). The defendants had registered a number of domain names without the owners' consent, including bt.org, marksandspencer.co.uk, etc. There were no websites attached to them. The defendants admitted that they had no intention of using the marks, and intended to sell them. The Court of Appeal held that, since the domain names were registered to take advantage of the distinctive character and reputation of the marks, this was unfair and detrimental and s 10(3) infringement was made out. Despite cases such as this, it is more often the case that internet domain name disputes will be settled at the international level, and appropriately so. WIPO, through its Arbitration and Mediation Centre, ICANN (the Internet Corporation for Assigned Names and Numbers), a non-profit organisation responsible for internet allocation, and Nominet UK have established 'uniform-domain-name-dispute-resolution' policies. Their aim is to arbitrate domain name disputes.

Trade marks and search engines I: *Louis Vuitton v Google*

5.83 When an individual performs a search for words using Google, the result will display sites which correspond to those words, in decreasing order of relevance, and which are the 'natural' results of the search. However, Google also offers a paid referencing service. Called 'AdWords', this service allows a trader to reserve so-called 'keywords' and if an internet user searches for that word, an advertising link is displayed to the trader's site, under the heading, 'sponsored links'. The sponsored link, which also shows a short commercial message, is displayed either beside or above the natural results. Each time a user clicks onto the sponsored link, the trader pays a fee to Google. In *Google France Sarl v Louis Vuitton* (2010), Louis Vuitton, the luxury leather goods company, had a number of CTMs and national registrations for 'Louis Vuitton' and 'LV'. It became aware that when internet users entered its trade marks into Google's search engine, this triggered the display of sponsored links to sites, some offering its products and others offering imitation versions of them. Indeed, Google gave its advertisers the opportunity not only to select keywords corresponding to Louis Vuitton's trade marks, but also those same keywords together with expressions such as 'imitation' and 'copy'. Louis Vuitton and the other claimants alleged both Google and the advertisers had infringed their trade marks. The French Cour de Cassation, while finding for the claimants, addressed a number of questions to the Court of Justice. For our purposes, the most pertinent were: i. could a search engine provider such as Google be liable for trade mark infringement for selling registered trade marks to advertisers to use as keywords in advertisements with links to sites offering goods or services identical with those for which that mark is registered; ii. will the advertiser be liable for infringement if it uses without authorisation a registered trade mark as a keyword, which triggers the display of a link to a site operated by that advertiser and which offers for sale identical or similar goods or services?

Louis Vuitton v Google: the judgment

5.84   As to whether Google could be held to have infringed by selling trade marks to advertisers for use as keywords in advertisements, the Court of Justice identified as a key question whether Google was using the trade marks in the course of trade (art 5(1)(a) TM Directive). It held that it was not. Although Google operated 'in the course of trade', when it offered its AdWords service, it was in fact only Google's clients who were making use of the signs as part of their commercial communications. Google may have allowed them to do so, but it was not itself making the necessary use of the sign needed for a finding of infringement. Turning to the question of whether advertisers were liable for infringement by purchasing trade marks as keywords, the Court of Justice held that they might be. According to the Court of Justice,[the proprietor of a trade mark is entitled to prohibit an advertiser from advertising, on the basis of a keyword identical with that mark, which that advertiser has, without his consent, selected in connection with an internet referencing service, goods or services identical with those for which that mark is registered. This is so where that advertisement does not enable an average internet user, or enables that user only with difficulty, to ascertain whether the goods or services referred to therein originate from the proprietor of the trade mark or an undertaking economically connected to it or, on the contrary, originate from a third party.]

Trade marks and search engines II: *Interflora v Marks & Spencer*

5.85   *Louis Vuitton v Google* confirmed that use of a registered trade mark by an advertiser might be infringing use. In *Interflora*, the Court of Justice looked more closely at when such use would be infringing both under art 5(1)(a) and art 5(2) TMD (s 10(1) and s 10(3) TMA). Interflora operates a worldwide flower delivery service. Orders for flowers may be placed on Interflora's websites, and the delivery is made by a florist closest to the delivery site. The address of its main website is www.interflora.com. The site redirects customers to country-specific websites such as www.interflora.co.uk. 'Interflora' is a registered UK trade mark and a CTM and it was accepted by both parties that it has a reputation. M&S, a main retailer in the UK, allows customers to order the delivery of flowers through its own website, www.marksandspencer.com, and is in commercial competition with Interflora. M&S selected Interflora and other variants as keywords. As a result if Interflora is entered into the Google search engine, an M&S advertisement appears on the sponsored links, advertising its flower delivery service. Interflora sued for trade mark infringement and the High Court addressed the following questions to the Court of Justice. First, if a trader selects a trade mark as a key word but the sponsored link does not include the sign or a similar sign (as the M&S site did not), does this constitute use within the meaning of Art 5(1)(a). Second, is such use 'in relation to' goods or services identical to those for which the trade mark is registered even if the sign does not appear in the competitor's advert. And as a result, does such use constitute infringement under both Art 5(1)(a) and Art 5(2). Further, would there be a different answer if the presentation of the sponsored link led some members of the public mistakenly to believe the competitor is a member of the trade mark proprietor's commercial network or if the search engine operator does not permit trade mark proprietors to block the selection of signs identical to their trade marks as keywords by other parties, as is the case with Google?

Interflora v Marks & Spencer: the judgment

5.86 We have seen that the Court of Justice held that such use by a competitor is use in the course of trade and it is use in relation to its goods and services (see para 5.61). As to whether it is infringing use under art 5(1)(a), the Court of Justice held that to be infringing it is necessary to show that use of the sign will affect one of the functions of the registered trade mark: its origin function, its advertising function or its investment function. The Court of Justice suggested that the origin function will be adversely affected if the advertisement does not enable reasonably well-informed and reasonably observant internet users, or enables them, only with difficulty, to ascertain whether the goods or services referred to by the advertisement originate from the proprietor of the trade mark or an undertaking economically connected to it or on the contrary originate from a third party. Moreover, the fact that an advertiser cannot object to the use of his mark as a keyword, confirms that it is used without his consent. In this case, the fact that Interflora operated through a number of independent retailers might make it more likely that the average consumer would assume M&S is linked with Interflora's trading network. While the advertising function of the registered mark would not necessarily be affected by its use as a keyword by a competitor, the investment which a proprietor has put into the mark to attract and maintain custom may be jeopardised. Turning to Art 5(2), the Court of Justice held that merely by choosing a keyword identical to a registered trade mark does not necessarily dilute the reputation of the latter. However, there may be dilution if, for example, use of the keyword contributes to turning the trade mark into a generic term. Similarly, while it is not possible to assume there will be unfair advantage taken by use of a keyword similar or identical to a mark with a reputation. It is likely a large number of consumers using the key word will see the competitor's advertisement and if they then choose to purchase the products or service the competitor, it will get a real advantage for which the proprietor is not paid. This may amount to unfair advantage if the mark is used without due cause and is particularly likely to occur if the goods are imitations of the goods of the proprietor.

Trade marks and auction sites: *L'Oreal v eBay*

5.87   L'Oreal, which as well as its UK trade marks also has a number of CTMs, supplies only to authorised distributors who contract not to sell its products on. eBay operates an electronic marketplace which lists goods for sale by individuals who have registered with the site, created a seller's account and who pay eBay a percentage fee on sales. The site then allows prospective buyers to bid for these goods, either by auction or at a fixed price. It is possible to set up online shops on eBay sites which list all the items offered by a seller at any one time. eBay may help sellers to set up these online shops and it advertises some of the products sold on its site through search engines like Google, using its AdWord service. Among other things, sellers agree with eBay not to sell counterfeit items and not to infringe trade marks. In *L'Oreal v eBay* (2011), the claimant brought an action against eBay and some individual sellers in the UK for trade mark infringement. It alleged that some of the goods bearing its marks were counterfeit, some were not intended for sale in the UK and some were sold without packaging. Although there was little question that the sellers had infringed L'Oreal's trade marks in various ways, Arnold J put a number of questions to the Court of Justice. Some of the questions addressed concerns relating to the repackaging and reselling of L'Oreal's products by the sellers (see para **5.119** below on exhaustion of rights). Here we will be concerned with questions specifically addressing eBay's liability in relation to trade mark infringement. These included the following. Did eBay make 'use' of L'Oreal's marks within the meaning of art 5(1)(a) TM Directive (s 10(1) TMA), when they appeared on the sponsored links, as a result of its registering these marks as keywords with Google? Is it infringing use in relation to the infringing goods, if by clicking on the link, it takes users to third party websites offering such goods for sale? Finally, where the services of an intermediary such as eBay are used by a third party to infringe registered trade marks, does the EU Enforcement Directive require Member States to ensure that the proprietor of the marks can obtain an injunction against that intermediary to prevent further infringements?

L'Oreal v eBay: the judgment

5.88 In answer the Court of Justice held that the operator of an online marketplace, such as eBay, does not 'use' signs identical with or similar to trade marks which appear in offers for sale displayed on its site in the sense identified by art 5(1)(a) TM Directive. However, the Court of Justice held that the proprietor of a CTM is entitled to prevent an online marketplace operator from advertising, on the basis of a keyword which is identical to his trade mark and which has been selected in an internet referencing service by that operator, goods bearing that trade mark which are offered for sale on the marketplace, where the advertising does not enable reasonably well-informed and reasonably observant internet users, or enables them only with difficulty, to ascertain whether or not the goods concerned originate from the proprietor of the trade mark. Finally, under art 11 of the EU Enforcement Directive, Member States must ensure that their national courts can issue an injunction against an operator of an online marketplace obliging it to take measures to end the infringement of trade marks by its users and to prevent further infringement.

Google and eBay: liability under the E-Commerce Directive

5.89 In the course of its judgments in both *Louis Vuitton v Google* and *L'Oreal v eBay*, the Court of Justice also considered the defendants' liability, under the E-Commerce Directive, for hosting data which, in both cases, included infringing trade marks. According to art 14(1) of the Directive an operator might escape liability if it has not played an active role which would allow it to have knowledge or control over the relevant data. In *Louis Vuitton v Google*, the Court of Justice held that art 14(1) should be interpreted to mean that an internet referencing service provider could be held liable for the data it had stored at the request of an advertiser if, having obtained knowledge of the unlawful nature of that data or of the advertiser's activities, it had failed to act expeditiously to remove or to disable access to the data concerned. In the *eBay* case, as we have seen, eBay did in fact provide assistance to sellers to optimise their chance of a sale. In addition, the Court of Justice also held that even if eBay had not played an active role, it might not be exempt from liability if it was aware of facts or circumstances which a diligent economic operator should have been, such as that the offers for sale were illegal because it failed to act expeditiously to remove or disable access to the information. It would be up to the national court to decide if either an internet search engine or an online marketplace provider would be so liable given the specific facts of the case.

Losing the mark

5.90 Trade mark registration endows on a proprietor an indeterminate monopoly in the sign which is the subject matter of the mark. But there are various ways in which a trade mark monopoly may be lost, either voluntarily or involuntarily. In the former case, a proprietor of a trade mark may surrender his mark voluntarily (s 45). A proprietor may also lose his mark involuntarily, either by having it revoked or through a finding of invalidity. Each of these is examined below.

Revocation

5.91 A trade mark which has been validly registered may, for a number of reasons, be taken off the register (s 46 TMA) (art 12 TM Directive)). There are three general grounds for revocation:

- non-use (s 46(1)(a)–(b)) (art 10(1);
- the mark has become generic (s 46(1)(c)) (art 12(2)(a));
- the mark has become deceptive (s 46(1)(d) (art 12(2)(b)).

Non-use

5.92 Non-use of the trade mark for a period of five years since registration or use which has been suspended for an uninterrupted period of five years may lead to the trade mark being revoked. Use must be by the proprietor or with his consent, so that use can be by a licensee or, perhaps, by a subsidiary company. There must be genuine use in the UK in relation to the goods or services for which the mark is registered, when there are no proper reasons for non-use. If a registered proprietor claims that there has been use made of his mark, the onus of showing use rests with him (s 100) (*Philosophy Inc v Ferretti Studio Srl* (2002)). The two most common reasons for non-use are that the proprietor does not use the mark as it has been registered or, alternatively, that he has registered the mark for a range of goods or services for which it has not been used.

Use of a different mark

5.93 A proprietor is afforded a defence to non-use of his registered mark, if he can show that he has used a different mark which incorporates its distinctive elements (s 46(2)) (art 10(2)). In *Bud and Budweiser Budbräu Trade Marks* (2002), the makers of the American Budweiser beer, Anheuser-Busch, sought to have the 'Budweiser Budbräu' mark, registered by their Czech rivals, revoked for non-use. The Czech company had used the mark 'Budweiser Budbräu' in block capitals in a circular device depicting a castle and shield, but not in the stylised form in which it was registered. In this case, the distinctive character of the mark was held to be the combination of words, the specific fonts used, the contrast between them, and their size and placement in relation to each other. Use of the words in block capitals was not use of the distinctive elements of the mark. It could be revoked for non-use.

Non-use on the goods for which the mark is registered

5.94 A proprietor may have registered the mark for a wide range of goods and services, but may use the mark only in relation to some. This may lead to the mark being revoked for some or all of the goods registered (see, for example, *Minerva Trade Mark* (2000)). In *Thomson Holidays Ltd v Norwegian Cruise Lines Ltd* (2002), the Court of Appeal held, inter alia, that in order to determine whether there is non-use by a proprietor of the mark against some of the goods and services for which it is registered, the court's task was to arrive at a fair specification of the goods or services, having regard to the use made of the mark. It was appropriate to adopt the mantle of the reasonably informed consumer of the products. The court should then inform itself of the nature of the trade and decide how the notional consumer would describe such use. In other words, would the average consumer view the use made by the mark as relating to all or to only some of the goods and services for which it was registered (see also *Galileo International Technology, LLC v European Union (formerly European Community* (2011)).

Genuine use

5.95 In *Ansul BV v Ajax Brandbeveiliging BV* (2003), the Court of Justice held that 'genuine use' means that a trade mark is used to guarantee the origin of the goods for which it is registered in order to create or preserve an outlet for the goods. Genuine use does not include token use for the sole purpose of preserving the registration. In assessing genuine use, the court must look at all the facts and circumstances relevant to assessing whether the commercial exploitation of the mark is real. These would include whether the mark's use is justified in the economic sector concerned to maintain or create a market share for the goods protected by the mark, the nature of the goods or services at issue, the character-istics of the market, and the scale and frequency of use. In *Laboratoires Goemer v La Mer Technology* (2005), the claimant was a French company selling products under the UK mark 'Laboratoire de la Mer', which had been registered in 1989. It appointed a small company as its agent in the UK. This company had placed five repeat orders with the claimant, although none of the goods had reached the public. However, there was evidence that before the agent ceased trading in 1997, it had made preparations to sell the products. The defendant, La Mer Technology, argued that these activities did not amount to genuine use of the claimant's mark and sought to have it revoked. In the Court of Appeal, Mummery LJ, follow-ing the principles set out by the Court of Justice in *Ansul*, held that the decision as to whether there had been genuine use should be based on objective factors, most notably whether the goods bearing the mark had been placed on the market even if they did not reach end consumers. Furthermore, use could be modest. The claimant's mark was not invalid for non-use. More recently in *The Sunrider Corp v OHIM* (2006), the Court of Justice held that there is no fixed, quantitative threshold, for example a *de minimis* level, which the court uses to determine if there has been genuine use. The only question is whether such use serves a real, commercial purpose.

Proper reasons

5.96   A challenge for non-use can be overcome if there are 'proper' reasons. In *Invermont Trade Mark* (1997), 'proper' was defined as 'apt, acceptable, reasonable, justifiable in all the circumstances'. It is meant to cover, not normal situations or routine difficulties in the trade, but abnormal situations, 'or perhaps some temporary but serious disruption affecting the proprietor's business'. In *Invermont*, the pro-prietor had registered 'Invermont' for alcoholic beverages, and argued that non-use was due to the lengthy and complicated process of launching a new brand onto the market. The Registrar held that this was not a proper reason, since such delays and difficulties were normal to the trade as a whole. Similarly, in *Cabanas Habana Trade Mark* (2000), the proprietor of this mark for cigars failed to con-vince the TMR that the US embargo on Cuban products constituted a proper reason for non-use of its mark. The embargo had been in force for 33 years and had become a normal condition of trade.

Generic marks

5.97   A mark may be revoked on the grounds that, in consequence of the activity or *inactivity* of the proprietor, it has become the common name in the trade for a product or service for which it is registered. In *Levi Strauss & Co v Casucci SpA* (2006), Levi Strauss had a registered trade mark for the stitching design on the pocket of its jeans. It brought an infringement action against Casucci in the Brussels Commercial Court, arguing that the defendant used confusingly similar stitching on its own jeans. Casucci retorted that the claimant's mark had become common to jeans due to its inaction. The Brussels court held that the mark had become generic, but not through any (in)action of the claimant. It then addressed a number of questions to the Court of Justice. First, when an action for infringement is brought, should the court judge infringement on the basis of the distinctiveness of the mark when the sign was first used or at the time of the action? The Court of Justice answered that a finding of infringement will be based on the distinctiveness of the mark when the sign was first used not when the action was brought. To decide otherwise would be to penalise the proprietor, since the loss of distinctiveness of his mark might be due to the actions of the infringer. However, the Court was also asked what would be the situation if by the time of the action, the mark had become generic through the inaction of the proprietor. In this case, the Court of Justice held that the action for infringement would fail, since the registered mark could be revoked under these circumstances and it would be unfair to ask the user of the allegedly infringing mark to cease its use. Obviously, it is crucial for proprietors actively to police the use of their marks by, for instance, ensuring that licensees use them correctly, pursuing infringers and ensuring that if a word mark is applied to their goods it is perceived as a trade mark. This may be done by presenting the mark in a fanciful way, so that it is not taken to be the name of the product itself.

Deceptive marks

5.98 A trade mark may be revoked because, as a consequence of the use made by the proprietor, or with his consent, in relation to the goods or services for which it is registered, it is liable to deceive the public, particularly (but not exclusively) as to the nature, quality or geographical origin of the goods and services). We have looked at the deceptive marks in our discussion of the absolute grounds for refusal of registration (see para 5.33).

Consequences of revocation

5.99 If a trade mark is revoked, it is taken off the register and the mark ceases to have protection from that date, unless the Registrar believes the grounds for revocation existed at an earlier date. Its erstwhile proprietor will not be liable for infringement of an identical or similar mark during the period his mark was registered. The grounds for revocation go to the heart of the trade mark as a monopoly right.

They recognise that a proprietor must justify his monopoly through his activities in the market place. If the proprietor misuses the mark, either through action or inaction, he loses his right to a monopoly in it. In effect, the proprietor's property, his right to exclusive use of the mark, will be confiscated.

Invalidity

5.100 There are three grounds for a finding that a trade mark has been invalidly registered (s 47 TMA) (arts 3(2) & 4(4) TM Directive). They are:

- breach of absolute grounds for refusal of registration (s 47(1)) (art 3(2));
- there is an earlier registered mark (s47(2)) (art 4);
- bad faith (s 47(4)) (art 3(2)(d)).

Each of these is examined below.

Breach of absolute grounds for refusal of registration

5.101 A mark will be declared invalid if it was registered in breach of the absolute grounds for refusal of registration (see para **5.18** et seq), unless in the case of the grounds set out in s 3(1)(b)–(d) it has, after registration, acquired a distinctive character through use (s 47(1)) (art 3(3)). It is worthwhile looking at a hypothetical example of this provision. 'Fizzy' is registered as a mark for a new brand of carbonated water by X. Y, who has been accused of infringing the 'Fizzy' trade mark by marketing a mineral water under the unregistered mark 'Phizzy', seeks to have 'Fizzy' declared invalid on the grounds that the mark is devoid of distinctive character, is descriptive and is a sign which has become customary in current language. On the face of it, Y will probably succeed. But X, after registering 'Fizzy', had mounted a nationwide advertising campaign, involving the entire Tottenham Hotspur football team and the singer Adele. In the year following registration, 'Fizzy' had become *the* water to drink, and the public will only be satisfied if they are sold 'Fizzy' fizzy water. 'Fizzy' may have succeeded in acquiring, subsequent to registration, a distinctive character in relation to the goods which will save it from a finding of invalidity.

Applying s 47(1) (art 3(1))

5.102 The better view, following the Court of Justice decision in *Koninklijke Philips Electronics NV v Remington Consumer Products Ltd* (2003), is first to see whether a mark falls foul of s 3(1)(b)–(d) but has, since registration, gone on to satisfy the proviso, rather than to ask whether the mark is incapable of distinguishing under s 3(1)(a). This was the approach taken in *British Sugar plc v James Robertson & Sons Ltd* (1996). The defendant, Robertson, attacked the validity of the mark 'Treat' on all four grounds of s 3(1), including s 3(1)(a) that it was not a sign capable of distinguishing as defined in s 1(1). The court first looked at whether 'Treat' was devoid of distinctive character under s 3(1)(b), following the logic that if it was not devoid of distinctive character it must satisfy s 3(1)(a). Jacob J found that, at the time of registration, 'Treat' was not sufficiently distinctive to merit registration, despite the fact that it had been used for five years prior to registration. (As has been suggested above (para **5.28**), evidence of use is not necessarily the same as evidence of distinctiveness.) Furthermore, the word 'treat' was a laudatory word and common in the trade. The onus then shifted onto British Sugar to show that 'Treat' had acquired the requisite distinctive character subsequent to registration to stay on the register, and this British Sugar was unable to do. British Sugar did show considerable use–for instance, Treat had 50 per cent of the ice-cream topping sector. Polls indicated public recognition of the product, but it was held this was not the same as a public perception of 'Treat' as a trade mark. For the criteria for assessing distinctiveness, see para **5.28**.

An earlier registered mark

5.103 A registration will be declared invalid if there is an earlier registered mark to which the conditions apply, as set out in s 5(1), (2) or (3) , which describe the relative grounds for refusal of registration (see para **5.35** et seq), or if there is an earlier right in relation to which the conditions set out in s 5(4) are satisfied so that there is a conflict with the later registered mark (s 47(2)) (art 4(4)). The conditions for such conflict have been described above in the discussion of s 5 and also of infringement (s 10) (see para **5.59** et seq).

Bad faith

5.104 If there was bad faith in the registration of the mark, a mark will be declared invalid. What constitutes bad faith was identified in the discussion of the absolute grounds for refusal of registration (see para **5.34**).

Consequences of a finding of invalidity

5.105 If a registration is found to be invalid, the effect is as if the mark had never been registered and, therefore, infringement proceedings can cover the period during which it was invalidly registered. But any past or closed transactions relating to the expunged mark are not affected.

Consent and acquiescence

5.106 A conflict with an earlier mark or right can be overcome if the proprietor of the earlier mark or right consents to the registration (s 47(2) TMA) (art 4(5) TM Directive) (see para **5.58**). Similarly, if the proprietor of a trade mark acquiesces for a period of five years to the use of a later registered trade mark while being aware of such use, he is no longer able to apply to have the later mark declared invalid, unless the later mark was applied for in bad faith (s 48) (art 9(1)). The Court of Justice has recently looked at the meaning of acquiescence under art 9(1). It held that the proprietor of an earlier trade mark cannot be held to have acquiesced when he has long known of the honest use of the later mark if he has been unable to prevent such use. Furthermore, the period of five years begins to run not with the registration of the earlier mark, but rather when the later mark is registered, if the application for registration is made in good faith, and the later mark is used with the knowledge of the proprietor of the earlier trade mark (*Budějovický Budvar v Anheuser-Busch Inc.* (2011)).

Licensing and assignments

5.107 A registered trade mark is a personal property right (s 2(1) and s 22). It is transmissible by assignment, testamentary disposition or by operation of the law in the same way as other personal or moveable property (s 24). It can also be charged. The two most common circumstances in which a trade mark will be used by someone other than its original proprietor are if it has been assigned or licensed.

Assignments

5.108 Assignments must be in writing signed by, or on behalf of, the assignor and, in contrast to the position with unregistered marks, need not include the goodwill attached to the mark (see para **4.14** on passing off). Assignments may be limited to apply to some, but not all, of the goods or services in relation to which the mark is registered or limited so that the assigned trade mark can be used only in a particular locality or in a particular manner (s 24(2)(a)–(b)). As a result, it is entirely possible to have a single trade mark, owned by two different proprietors, being used for similar goods throughout the UK, or on the same goods in different parts of the UK. The TMA 1938 contained provisions which enabled the TMR to reject assignments which rendered the mark deceptive. By contrast, under the deregulatory TMA 1994, such assignments are freely allowed, although marks which become deceptive by virtue of an assignment may be revoked.

Licensing

5.109 Licences, like assignments, may be limited, for instance, to some but not all of the goods or services for which the trade mark is registered or in relation to use in a particular manner or in a particular locality (s 28(1)(a)–(b) TMA; art 8 TM Directive). As a result, there is the same potential for a licensed mark to become deceptive, as there is with limited assignments. The TMA 1938 was the first Act to allow licensing of trade marks, but the registered users regime was hedged with restrictions intended to protect the public from deceptive marks. Now the licensing regime is effectively deregulated, and it is left to the self-interest of the licensor to ensure that his mark does not become deceptive (*Scandecor Development AB v Scandecor Marketing AB* (2001)).

Rights of licensees

5.110 There are two kinds of licence: an exclusive licence, where the licensee uses the mark to the exclusion of all other persons, including the licensor (s 29); and non-exclusive licences (including sub-licences) (s 28). The rights of exclusive licensees are different from those of non-exclusive licensees (see ss 30 and 31). If a licensee steps outside the terms of his licence, he will certainly be in breach of contract, but will he also be infringing the trade mark? Article 8(2) of the TM Directive says he will be, if he contravenes any provisions relating to the duration of the licence, the form of the mark, the scope of the goods and services, the territory or the quality of the goods and services he provides. Use of a mark by a licensee, rather than the proprietor, is sufficient to prevent a mark from being revoked for non-use (s 46).

Character merchandising

5.111 It has been suggested that an action for passing off has traditionally offered the most effective means to protect character merchandising (see para **4.67** on passing off). Certainly, until the TMA 1994, the registered trade mark regime offered little comfort in this area. The TMA 1938 explicitly forbade 'trafficking' in a mark–which meant dealing in the mark as a commodity in its own right–in situations where there would be no trade connection between the proprietor of the mark and the goods or services for which it was registered (a common situation in character merchandising). The fear was that the buying public could not depend upon the mark to be any guarantor either of origin or, indeed, of quality. In recent years, the restrictions on trafficking were widely criticised, particularly by those involved in character merchandising, who were generally denied the protection of trade mark registration for their characters (*Re American Greetings Corpn's Application 'Holly Hobbie'* (1984)). When the government swept away the registered users category in the TMA 1994, thereby allowing trafficking in marks, it justified its action by citing the greater sophistication of the buying public. In other words, today's canny consumers will not necessarily expect that the rights-holder in the character or a famous personality had actually produced the goods on which it appears, but they will assume the merchandiser has a legitimate licence to use the character. This view was endorsed by the courts in the 'Ninja Turtle' passing-off case (*Mirage Studios v Counter-Feat Clothing Co Ltd* (1991) (see para **4.70**)).

Elvis Presley and character merchandising

5.112   Nonetheless, the decision in *Elvis Presley Trade Marks* (1999) (para **4.72**) indicates that the registered trade mark regime still offers only limited comfort to character merchandisers. The applicants (Enterprises), the successors to Elvis Presley's merchandising business, sought to register the marks 'Elvis' and 'Elvis Presley' for toiletries. Opposition came from a Mr Shaw, who had registered the mark 'Elvisly Yours', on the grounds that the applicant's marks would be confusingly similar and that they lacked sufficient distinctiveness for registration. The application was under the TMA 1938, but the High Court and the Court of Appeal made it clear that their judgments would be relevant to the TMA 1994. In his leading judgment in the Court of Appeal, Walker LJ held that the marks lacked the requisite distinctiveness for registration because, by the date of the application, the marks, rather than acting as a badge of origin, had come to be descriptive of the goods to which they attached. The public bought Elvis memorabilia because it carried his name or image–they wanted 'Elvis soap' or 'Elvis perfume' and were indifferent as to its trade source. Or, according to Walker LJ, paraphrasing Laddie J's judgment in the High Court: 'The commemoration of the late Elvis Presley is the product, and the article on which his name or image appears... is little more than a vehicle.' In effect, the marks had become so much a part of the language as to be descriptive of the goods rather than distinctive of their source and it would be wrong to deny other traders an opportunity to use them by allowing them to be registered (see also *Tarzan Trade Mark* (1970)).

5.113   More generally, in *Elvis*, the Court of Appeal rejected the idea that the public will automatically assume that character merchandise comes from a particular source, thus giving a narrow interpretation to *Mirage Studios v Counter-Feat Clothing Co Ltd* (1991) ('Ninja Turtle') (for the position in passing off, see para **4.70** et seq). Following *Elvis*, it will be up to the applicant to prove a trade connection in the minds of the public between the mark and the merchandise in order to secure registration. In recent years, the TMR has refused trade mark applications for 'Diana Princess of Wales', made by her estate (*The Executrices of the Estate of Diana, Princess of Wales' Application* (2001)), and for 'Jane Austen', made by the Jane Austen Memorial Trust (*Jane Austen Trade Mark* (2000)), on the grounds that both marks are devoid of distinctive character (s 3(1)(b)). The outcome of these applications raises the question of whether it is inequitable to deny to famous individuals (or, indeed, their estates) the right to exploit their reputations. In the USA, for example, there is a right of publicity which allows individuals to capitalise on their fame, recognising that it may be the result of careful nurturing and financial investment. Others have argued that fame is, by contrast, a product of popular culture, or at least of an interaction between the individual concerned and the public. If the latter argument is pursued, then it may follow that the associations which adhere to famous individuals belong in the public domain.

5.114   Following *Elvis*, the TMR is in practice most likely to refuse an application for a well-known character or personality only when the intended mark cannot be seen as anything other than descriptive of the subject matter. For example, an application by Sir Alex Ferguson, the manager of Manchester United FC, to register his name for posters was refused on the basis that the mark would be descriptive of the goods (that is a poster of Alex Ferguson) and so would not distinguish posters provided by Alex Ferguson from Alex Ferguson posters provided by other undertakings. In the words of the TMR, the posters would be 'mere image carriers' for the Ferguson name. The TMR was however ready to register the same mark for other goods, such as pre-recorded tapes (see also *Linkin Park LLC's Application* (2006)).

Remedies

5.115   Infringement proceedings cannot begin until the date upon which the trade mark is first registered, although damages for infringement will be recoverable from the mark's priority date. In all legal proceedings relating to a registered trade mark, the registration of a person as proprietor of a trade mark shall be prima facie evidence of the validity of the original registration (s 72). Trade mark actions are brought exclusively in the High Court and now the Patents Court, but it is unusual for a trade mark action to come to full trial. The proprietor's primary concern is typically to prevent further use of an infringing mark as quickly as possible. Interim injunctions are a crucial tool and, if an injunction is obtained, it is frequently the case that the matter is settled with the payment of costs and a token sum for damages by the defendant (who is probably uninterested in continuing to invest in a mark he may be prevented from using in the future). The defendant may, of course, counter-attack by seeking to have the claimant's mark declared invalid or revoked. The injured proprietor should, therefore, always combine an action for infringement with one for passing off. If he loses his registration in the course of the proceedings, he may yet be able to argue that the defendant's use amounts to passing off (*United Biscuits (UK) Ltd v Asda Stores Ltd* (1997) is an example, see para **4.10**). The claimant is entitled to all such relief by way of damages, injunctions and accounts of profits or otherwise as is available in respect of any other property rights (s 14(2)). Specific remedies include an order for the erasure of an infringing sign (s 15) or for the delivery up of goods, materials or articles which bear it (s 16). In the case of CTMs, an injunction granted in one Member State will apply across the EU (*DHL Express France SAS v Chronopost SA* (2011) Court of Justice).

Groundless threats

5.116 Groundless threats to bring infringement proceedings are actionable if they are directed against anyone other than the individual who applies the mark to the goods or packaging, imports the goods or supplies services under the mark (s 21(1)). Other activities, such as the use of a mark in advertising, are not covered by this provision (*Best Buy Co. Inc v Worldwide Sales Corporation Espana S.L.* (2011) CA). In *L'Oreal (UK) Ltd v Johnson & Johnson* (2000), Lightman J defined a threat:

> *…to cover any information that would convey to a reasonable man that some person has trademark rights and intends to enforce them against another. It matters not that the threat may be veiled or covert, conditional or future. Nor does it matter that the threat is made in response to an enquiry from the party threatened…*

Section 21(1) is of purely domestic origin and there are similar provisions against groundless threats in relation to patents and registered designs.

Criminal sanctions

5.117 The criminal provisions are primarily designed to catch those involved in counterfeiting operations, where civil remedies are both inadequate and often difficult to enforce. The prerequisite to finding an offence has been committed is that the defendant must have acted with a view to gain for himself or another, or with intent to cause loss to another, and without the consent of another (s 92). Criminal sanctions apply only to the use of the mark in relation to goods, not services, and only to the use of trade marks that are identical to, or likely to be mistaken for, the registered trade mark (a higher standard of similarity than similar trade marks protected by civil remedies). The goods concerned must be the goods in respect of which the trade mark is registered or, if not, the trade mark must have a reputation in the UK and the use of the sign would take unfair advantage of, or be detrimental to, the distinctive character or repute of the mark (s 92(4)). This is an offence of strict liability, in that there is no need to show that, at the time, the defendant knew that there was a registered trade mark (*Torbay Council v Satnam Singh* (1999)). However, it is a defence for the accused to show that he believed, or that he had reasonable grounds to believe, that the use of the sign in the manner in which it was used or was to be used was not an infringement of the registered trade mark (s 92(5)). It follows that one defence against criminal sanctions would be a recourse to the infringement provisions of the TMA 1994, in order to prove the sign was not infringing. On the other hand, it is not a defence that the quality of the infringing goods was so poor that the public would not be confused into believing they originated from the trade mark proprietor (*R v Boulter (Gary)* (2008))

Trade marks and the EU

5.118 Like patents and other intellectual property rights, trade mark protection may conflict with the prohibitions set out in art 34 TFEU (formerly art 28 EC). National trade mark law (and now the CTM) endows a proprietor with a monopoly right to use his mark in the relevant territory and, again like patent rights, may allow him to keep out the goods of others. For example, if the same mark is owned by company A in Germany and company B in Belgium, where the two enterprises are unrelated, and B seeks to export identical products bearing the mark into Germany, he will need the consent of A to do so (*SA CNL-SUCAL v Hag* (1990)). Trade mark protection has nonetheless been justified by its role as an indicator of origin and quality (see the essential function of the mark and its specific subject matter given in *Bristol-Myers Squibb v Paranova* (1996), at para **5.3**). Thus, art 36 TFEU (previously art 30 EC) recognises that there can be a public interest in the monopoly rights afforded by trade mark protection. However, again like patents, the existence of such a monopoly right must not constitute a means of arbitrary discrimination or disguised restriction on trade between Member States.

Exhaustion of rights in the EEA

5.119 In practice, the territorial monopoly endowed by trade mark protection can be, and indeed has been, effectively used to partition the market and impede the free movement of goods. The Court of Justice has built up a body of case law which has sought to balance the sometimes conflicting imperatives of promoting free competition and protecting the rights of trade mark proprietors. In doing so, it has relied on the principle of 'exhaustion of rights' (which has already been considered in relation to copyright). The present trade mark regime provides for the exhaustion of rights in trade marks if the goods or services to which they attach have been put on the market in the EEA under the trade mark by the proprietor or with his consent (s 12(1) TMA)(art 7(1) TM Directive); for a discussion of consent, see para **5.131** et seq). In the early case of *Centrafarm BV v Winthrop BV* (1975) (see also *Centrafarm BV v Sterling Drug Inc* (1974) in relation to patents, para **6.106**), the American company Sterling Drug had subsidiaries in the UK and the Netherlands (Winthrop BV). Sterling granted both companies a patent licence to produce its drug, 'Negram'. Each was also the registered proprietor of the mark 'Negram' in its respective country. Centrafarm bought Negram in the UK, where, because of government price controls, it was sold more cheaply, and marketed it in the Netherlands. Winthrop BV unsuccessfully sued for trade mark infringement. In reaching its decision, the Court of Justice was concerned to define the specific subject matter of the industrial property right protected by the first part of art 36 TFEU (formerly art 30 EC). It was held to be the guarantee to the proprietor of a trade mark that he has the exclusive right to use the trade mark for the purpose of putting the product into circulation for the first time, and therefore to protect him against competitors wishing to take advantage of the status and reputation of the mark by selling products illegally bearing the mark. In this case, the claimant had already exhausted his rights by putting the goods into circulation for the first time. Further circulation of these goods within the EU could not be prevented on the grounds of trade mark infringement.

Disguised restriction of trade

5.120 The extent to which art 36 TFEU will safeguard the subject matter and essential purpose of trade marks must be considered together with the question of whether the granting of that protection will lead to a disguised restriction of trade. If it does, then protection may be withdrawn. Typically, this question will arise if a proprietor registers different marks for the same product in different Member States. In *Centrafarm BV v American Home Products Corpn* (1978), American Home Products marketed the same drug as 'Serenid' in the UK and as 'Seresta' in the Netherlands. Because of domestic price controls, the UK product was cheaper. Centrafarm bought 'Serenid' in the UK and sold it, re-marked as 'Seresta', in the Netherlands. American Home Products sued for trade mark infringement in the Netherlands and the case went to the Court of Justice. The Court of Justice found that a proprietor of a trade mark which is protected in one Member State is justified, pursuant to art 36 TFEU (formerly art 30 EC), in preventing a product from being marketed by a third party in that Member State, even if previously the product had been lawfully marketed in another Member State under a different mark by the same proprietor. Thus, in principle, it may certainly be lawful for the manufacturer of a product to use different marks in different Member States for the same product. However, if such a practice is designed to partition the market artificially, that would constitute a disguised restriction of trade for the purposes of art 36 TFEU. According to the Court of Justice in *Centrafarm*, the test for whether a proprietor is using trade mark protection as a disguised restriction of trade is a subjective one, that is, what did the trade mark proprietor intend?

Changing the 'condition' of the goods

5.121   Section 12(2) of the TMA 1994 (art 7(2) TM Directive) states that exhaustion of rights within the EEA does not apply where there exist legitimate reasons for the proprietor to oppose further dealings in the goods (in particular, where the condition of the goods has been changed or impaired after they have been put on the market). Section 12(2) thus provides a possible alternative avenue for trade mark proprietors to control the further marketing of their goods. It is one they have been keen to use. It has raised the fundamental question of the extent to which a proprietor can object to the way in which a parallel importer changes the condition of his goods, or uses or applies his mark. This question has given rise to considerable case law, both European and domestic. Much, but not all, of this case law has involved the repackaging or rebranding of pharmaceuticals, typically in order to conform to national regulations or standards (such as, for instance, that labels and instructions are in the appropriate language). The leading case in this regard is *Bristol-Myers Squibb v Paranova* (1996) (for earlier cases, see *Centrafarm BV v American Home Products Corpn* (1978) and *Hoffmann-La Roche & Co AG v Centrafarm mbH* (1978)).

The test of necessity

5.122   In *Bristol-Myers Squibb v Paranova* (1996), the Court of Justice held that repackaging was acceptable, but only if it was 'necessary' in order to market the product in the country of importation. The test of necessity was held to be an objective one. In this case the Court of Justice gave, as an example of necessity, repackaging by a parallel importer if different package sizes are used in different Member States. In *Bristol-Meyers*, the Court of Justice also set out certain obligations that parallel importers have in relation to repackaging, most notably to give the trade mark owner notice of their intentions. Conversely, the Court of Justice noted that poor presentation by the repackager might damage the trade mark's reputation and the trade mark owner may oppose the parallel importation of products in which the repacking is defective, untidy or of poor quality. In the later case of *Pharmacia and Upjohn v Paranova* (2000), the Court of Justice applied the same criterion of 'necessity' to rebranding.

The scope of the 'necessity test'

5.123 What if the parallel importer does not need to repackage or rebrand the goods in order to obtain access to the market? But, nonetheless, he does so in such a way that the origin function of the original mark remains unaffected. Is the mark's proprietor able to oppose their importation? This was the question raised by *Glaxo Group Ltd v Dowelhurst Ltd (No 2)* (2000). This case involved a number of pharmaceutical companies and parallel importers. The products at issue had been marketed under registered trademarks within the EU, and had been purchased by the defendants and imported into the UK. The defendants had repackaged the goods in various ways. For example, some were relabelled, with the original trade mark visible. Others had been repackaged in boxes on which the trade mark had been reproduced. All the repackaged boxes included a leaflet in English with the original trade mark. The claimants sued for trade mark infringement. They argued, following *Pharmacia and Upjohn v Paranova* (2000), that if repackaging of products was permissible only if necessary, then repackaging that was not strictly necessary was infringing, even if it did no harm to the goods or the specific subject matter of the mark.

5.124 The Court of Justice supported the view of the claimants (*Boehringer Ingelheim KG v Swingward Ltd* (2002)). A trade mark proprietor could rely on its trade marks in order to prevent a parallel importer from repackaging pharmaceutical products, unless the exercise of those rights contributed to the artificial partitioning of the market. In other words, it was the very act of repackaging which was prejudicial to the specific subject matter of the mark (that is, its role as a guarantor of origin), in that, by its nature, repackaging entailed a risk of interference with the original condition of the product. It was not necessary to go on to look at its effects. Nonetheless, the Court of Justice also recognised that the simple relabelling of a product, which would not hide the fact that it had originated abroad, could lead a significant proportion of consumers to mistrust its quality. If the effect of consumer resistance to a relabelled product was to deny a parallel importer effective market access, then repackaging of the product might well be necessary. In *Boehringer*, the Court of Justice also held that, if the parallel importer failed to give prior notice to the trade mark proprietor of its intention to repackage the products, then the proprietor was entitled to oppose their remarketing. This was so even if the repackaging was both necessary and did not affect the origin function of the mark. It was up to the national courts to decide whether reasonable notice had been given. The Court of Justice suggested that two weeks might be a reasonable period.

5.125 When the case returned to the Court of Appeal, Jacob LJ interpreted the Court of Justice decision to mean that repackaging or rebranding is not necessary if it affects the condition of the goods or if it damages the reputation of the mark. However, because the Court of Appeal considered the position still to be unclear it asked the Court of Justice to confirm this interpretation and also asked whether the test of necessity was relevant only to repacking or rebranding or whether it extended to the way the repackaged or rebranded product was presented (*Boehringer Ingelheim KG v Swingward Ltd* (2004)). In its judgment (*Boehringer Ingelheim KG v Swingward Ltd* (2007)), the Court of Justice took a stance favourable to the trade mark proprietors. It held, inter alia, that a trade mark owner may legitimately oppose the re-marketing of its product where an external label has been applied unless to do so would contribute to the artificial partitioning of the market or unless the new label does not affect the original condition of the product or damage the reputation of the original trade mark, and notice is given. However, the right of a proprietor to oppose the re-marketing of a product, which has been repackaged or relabelled, because it damages the reputation of the mark is not confined to instances where the repackaging is of poor quality, defective or untidy. It might arise when, for example, the parallel importer prints its own mark in capital letters or fails to affix the original trade mark to the new exterior packaging ('de-branding'). It is up to the national courts to decide in light of the particular circumstances whether the mark's reputation has been damaged. And, it is for the parallel importer to prove not only the existence of the conditions which made such repackaging necessary but also that the repackaging will not affect the original condition of the product or the reputation of the mark (see also, *Wellcome v Paranova* (2009)).

Changing the 'mental' condition of the goods

5.126 In *Bristol-Myers Squibb v Paranova* (1996), the Court of Justice had suggested that trade mark proprietors might object to repackaging if it led to poor presentation and, hence, to damage to the trade mark's reputation. In *Parfums Christian Dior v Evora BV* (1997), the Court of Justice was asked whether legitimate reasons for opposing further dealing in parallel imports extended to use of the brand which would impair or change the 'mental' condition of the goods rather than their physical condition–in this case, the manner in which the reseller advertised the goods. The facts were that Dior France had sought to maintain the high prices paid for its goods and its luxurious image by distributing its perfumes only through exclusive outlets. Evora operated a chain of chemist shops in the Netherlands and sold Dior perfumes obtained through parallel imports. It advertised the perfumes in leaflets which reproduced Dior's marks and also advertised similar goods which were not all of the same quality. The Court of Justice was asked first, whether a reseller can use the marks attached to the goods for advertising purposes. It held that they could. The second question was whether the proprietor could object because the way the reseller uses the mark damages its prestigious image, so that the advertising function (or reputation of the mark) is endangered. Again the Court answered in the affirmative. Finally, it was asked whether such damage constitutes a legitimate reason which would allow the proprietor to oppose the mark's use for further commercialisation. Once again the Court of Justice said that it did. The proprietor could oppose use of the mark where, given the specific facts of the case, use of the trade mark to advertise the goods damaged its reputation, for example, in an advertising leaflet which puts the mark in a context which seriously detracts from its image. In *Zino Davidoff SA v A & G Imports Ltd* (1999), which involved the parallel import of luxury cosmetics from outside the EEA, the High Court gave a narrow interpretation of the *Dior* guidelines. Laddie J accepted that legitimate reasons for a proprietor to object to further commercialisation of his goods encompassed impairment to both their 'physical' and 'mental' condition, but such damage must be substantial. Nor did it mean anything that might undermine the mark's luxury image (such as selling the goods at a lower price). In this case, obliteration of the batch codes (marked on the goods) by the defendant was not sufficient. More recently, in *Copad SA v Christian Dior* (2009), the Court of Justice held that a trade mark proprietor can prevent a licensee selling its goods in such a way that it contravenes a provision in the license agreement if the result is to damage the allure or prestigious image of such goods, for example through sales to discount stores. It follows that an agreement which allows a third party to distribute goods with the consent of the trade mark proprietor is not absolute and unconditional. The trade mark proprietor may prevent further marketing of the goods if it were to damage their 'mental' condition.

Parallel imports from outside the EEA

5.127 The terms of the TMA 1994 (following the TM Directive) ensure that, except in exceptional circumstances, a trade mark proprietor cannot prevent the parallel importation of goods bearing his mark into one state from another in the EEA, where those goods have been put on the market in the EEA by him or with his consent (see para **5.119** et seq). But are the trade mark proprietor's rights similarly exhausted if goods are first put on the market by him or with his consent outside the EEA and subsequently brought into the EEA by a parallel importer? This question has generated heated debate in the EU, which has been fuelled by the practice of retailers selling branded goods acquired on what is known as the 'grey market'. Grey market goods are principally products made by a trade mark owner or a licensee and marketed in countries outside the EEA, which are then re-imported or imported for the first time into the EEA and sold at reduced prices. Price reductions are often possible because the goods are sold at different prices outside the EEA, perhaps because of currency fluctuations, to get rid of out-of-date stock or because they are of a different (perhaps inferior) quality. In the UK, large supermarket chains have been at the forefront of acquiring these grey market goods. In turn, brand-holders, such as Calvin Klein and Levis, have objected to the sale of their goods at reduced prices in unauthorised outlets, claiming that as a consequence the image or reputation of their marks is impaired. At the time of the implementation of the TM Directive, the UK appeared to recognise international exhaustion so long as the public was not deceived as to the quality or source of the goods (*Revlon Inc v Cripps & Lee Ltd* (1979); *Colgate Palmolive Ltd v Markwell Finance Ltd* (1990)). Shortly after the Directive's implementation, the question of whether it had introduced international exhaustion was referred to the Court of Justice.

The decision in *Silhouette*

5.128   In *Silhouette v Hartlauer mbH* (1998), Silhouette, an Austrian company, manufactured high-priced fashion spectacles distributed under its Silhouette mark. In 1995, it sold outdated spectacle frames to a Bulgarian company, which, Silhouette claimed, was instructed to sell the frames only in certain countries outside the EEA. Hartlauer, also based in Austria, had a chain of outlets for cut-priced goods which were not supplied by Silhouette, which preferred more upmarket retailers. Hartlauer acquired the spectacles. The question for the Court of Justice was whether art 7(1) should be interpreted to mean that the trade mark entitles a proprietor to prohibit a third party from using the mark for goods which have been put on the market under that mark outside the EEA. The Court of Justice concluded that the TM Directive neither introduced international exhaustion, nor did it allow individual Member States to adopt international exhaustion or not. In particular, the Court relied on the fact that the TM Directive was intended to approximate laws between Member States in order to promote the free market of goods. Allowing Member States to decide on whether to adopt international exhaustion individually would have erected trade barriers between them.

5.129   The decision in *Silhouette v Hartlauer mbH* (1998) was confirmed in *Sebago Inc v GB Unic SA* (1999), which involved the parallel importation of shoes into Benelux from El Salvador without Sebago's consent. It is possible to distinguish *Sebago* from *Silhouette* because, in the latter, the imported glasses were out of date, whereas in *Sebago* identical shoes to the parallel imports were still on sale in the Benelux countries. The Court of Justice was asked, in essence, whether there was consent within the meaning of art 7(1) where the trade mark proprietor had consented to the marketing in the EEA of goods which were similar or identical to those in respect of which exhaustion was claimed, or whether consent must relate to each individual item of product in respect of which exhaustion was claimed. The Court of Justice held the latter, explicitly reaffirming its decision in *Silhouette* that art 7(1) covered exhaustion in the EEA only.

The debate

5.130 Reaction to the decision in *Silhouette v Hartlauer mbH* (1998) was predictably mixed. It was welcomed by brand owners seeking to maintain control over the marketing of their goods and, hence, the value of their brands' reputations, as well as by those EEA countries where manufacturers might lose out from the importation of cheaper goods from outside the EEA. Those in favour of international exhaustion, however, suggested that it benefitted consumers with lower prices and, in an era of free trade, prevented the erection of tariff and trade barriers by indirect means. From a legal perspective, critics of *Silhouette* also argued that it is the trade mark's basic purpose which should determine whether there is international exhaustion. The essential function of the trade mark is as a badge of origin. However, *Silhouette* allowed a proprietor to object to any unauthorised dealings with his mark even though it continued to fulfill its essential function (Bonadio, 'Parallel imports in a global market: should a generalized international exhaustion be the next step?' [2011] *European Intellectual Property Review* 153).

The question of consent

5.131 After *Silhouette*, the debate shifted from whether or not the Directive had introduced international exhaustion to what constitutes 'consent' to resale. Inevitably, the question returned to the Court of Justice, in the joined cases of *Zino Davidoff SA v A & G Imports Ltd; Levi Strauss & Co v Tesco Stores Ltd* (2001). Essentially, the Court of Justice was asked whether under art 7(1) TM Directive (s 12(1) TMA), the trade mark owner's consent to the marketing of its goods within the EEA, which had previously been placed on the market outside the EEA, had to be express or whether it could be implied. Second, was it relevant that the importer was unaware of the owner's objections or that the foreign vendor had imposed no contractual reservations on resale? The Court of Justice held that the proprietor's consent to the resale of its goods within the EEA which had been put on the market outside with his consent may be implied, depending upon the circumstances of the original placement. However, it emphasised that, in order to infer consent, a national court must be persuaded that the proprietor unequivocally renounced his right to oppose such resale. In particular, the Court of Justice held that consent could not be inferred from the fact that the proprietor did not tell subsequent purchasers of the goods outside the EEA of his opposition to resale within. Nor could it be inferred, even if the goods carried no warning of a prohibition against resale inside the EEA. It could also not be inferred from the fact that the proprietor sold the goods without imposing any contractual prohibition on resale. Finally, for those wishing to prove consent, the Court of Justice held that it is irrelevant that the importer of the goods was unaware that the proprietor objected to their sale in the EEA, or that authorised dealers in the goods did not impose contractual restrictions on purchasers alerting them to the proprietor's opposition, even if they were aware of them. The Court of Justice's approach to consent was welcomed by brand owners. Certainly, following *Zino Davidoff SA v A & G Imports Ltd* (1999), it will prove extremely difficult to persuade a national court that the brand owner has impliedly renounced his opposition to the sale of his goods in the EEA. When *Levi Strauss v Tesco Stores Ltd* (2003) returned to the High Court, it was held that only express consent to subsequent marketing of the jeans in the UK would suffice. Subsequently, in *Van Doren + Q v Lifestyle Sports + Sportswear* (2003), the Court of Justice marginally eased the position of parallel importers by holding that where the need for the parallel importer to prove consent leads to a real risk of partitioning the market, the burden will shift to the trade mark proprietor to establish that the goods at issue were first placed on the market by him or with his consent outside the EEA. If he can do so, then the burden will shift back to the parallel importer to prove that he had subsequently consented to their resale in the EEA.

Consent within the EEA

5.132   Recently in *Makro Zelfbedieningsgroothandel CV v Diesel SPA* (2009), the Court of Justice held that the principles relating to consent which had applied to parallel imports from outside the EEA were equally applicable to cases where the goods at issue had been first marketed and were being sold within the EEA (see para 119 et seq). According to the Court of Justice, art 7(1) should be interpreted to mean that the consent of the proprietor of a trade mark to the marketing of goods bearing that mark carried out directly in the EEA by a third party who has no economic link to that proprietor may be implied. Such consent may be inferred from the facts and circumstances prior to, simultaneous with or subsequent to the placing of the goods on the market in the EEA. However, to find implied consent, the national court must take the view that the proprietor had unequivocally renounced his exclusive rights.

Resale on the internet and art 7

5.133 We have already noted that the international reach of the internet can present particular problems for trade mark proprietors, in particular when the internet is being used to resell the their goods or services (see para **5.81** et seq). In *L'Oreal v eBay* (2011) the Court of Justice was asked whether goods which are advertised for sale, which have not been put on the market in the EEA by the proprietor or with his consent, will be caught by the provisions of art 7, if the offer for sale is merely targeted at consumers within the territory where the trade mark has protection. Or, alternatively, must the proprietor show that the offer for sale necessarily entails actually putting the goods on the market in that territory. According to the Court, mere targeting would be sufficient and this would arise when the offer for sale or an advertisement displayed on an auction site is accessible to consumers in that territory. The recent case *Portakabin Ltd v Primakabin BV* (2010) also looked at the application of art 7 to goods which are resold on the internet, in this case at the manner in which they are advertised. The Court of Justice was asked whether a proprietor could oppose the resale of his goods which have been placed on the market either by him or with his consent when the seller advertises on the internet using a keyword. The Court of Justice held that the proprietor could not oppose such an action unless there are legitimate reasons as defined in art 7(2). These might include the fact that the advertisement gives the impression that the reseller and the trade mark proprietor are economically linked or that the advertisement is seriously detrimental to the reputation of the mark. It is for the national court to assess whether there are legitimate reasons for such opposition, but the Court specifically noted that neither of these conditions would be fulfilled if the seller is simply adding words to the trade mark to indicate that they are being resold, for example, 'used' or 'second hand'. However, if in the advertisement, the reseller has removed the original trade mark and has relabelled the goods, then art 7(2) might apply. Finally, if a specialist seller of second-hand goods carrying the trade mark of the proprietor sells other second-hand goods which might damage the 'mental' image of the mark, because they may be of poor quality, then that would be a legitimate reason to oppose their sale.

Trade mark protection and competition law in the EU

5.134 Articles 101 and 102 TFEU (formerly articles 81 and 82 of the Treaty of Rome) are designed to protect and promote fair competition. These principles may also conflict with registered trade mark protection, particularly in the context of licences which may restrict the use of the mark between and within Member States.

A market-sharing agreement which prevents other traders from competing in a particular market may well fall foul of art 101. Such a situation might arise if a proprietor who has a trade mark registered in different Member States grants an exclusive licence in one country, for example, with the restriction that the licensee does not attempt to market the product abroad. Similarly, in *Davide Campari-Milano SpA* (1978), the Commission held that an exclusive trade mark licence which restricted the right of the licensor to license other users within the same territory was, in principle, a restriction of competition likely to affect Member States and, therefore, was a breach of what is now art 101 TFEU. However, the Commission will also look at the effects of such a licence. If it decides the licence is actually beneficial to competition with other brands, as it did in the *Campari* case, it might grant it an individual exemption under art 101 TFEU. Exclusive trade mark licences might also ride on the back of block exemptions granted to certain technology transfers and distribution and purchasing agreements, so long as the trade mark licence is ancillary to the technology transfer.

The relationship between the TM Directive, arts 34, 36 and art 101 TFEU

5.135 In *Oracle America, Inc (Formerly Sun Microsystems, Inc) v M-Tech Data Ltd* (2010), Oracle, a computer manufacturer, sued the defendants for trade mark infringement, alleging that they had sold second-hand components which had not been put on the market in the EEA either by itself or with its consent. In the High Court, the defendants were found liable for trade mark infringement and appealed. There is a substantial market in second-hand computer hardware in the EEA. The market is generally carried on outside authorised networks of computer manufacturers and as such, according to Arden LJ, in the Court of Appeal, helped to ensure that the market for such hardware was competitive. Much of the market is in relation to components which have first been placed on the markets by or with the consent of the original manufacturers. However, Oracle does not publish the information which would enable resellers to ascertain whether this is the case. This is a deliberate policy of Oracle which, together with its practice of pursuing independent dealers who sell components not first imported into the EEA, deters the latter from trading in these components. It was argued by the defendants that Oracle's activities, in this regard, were contrary to arts 28 and 30 EC (now arts 34 and 36 TFEU). In addition, Oracle's distributors and resellers must agree to obtain Oracle products from its supply network whenever possible. The result is that the independent network selling Oracle components has disappeared. The defendants argued that this was detrimental to competition and led to an artificial partitioning of the relevant market. Indeed it allowed Oracle to control the market. As such, Oracle's activities were contrary to Art 81

EC (now art 101 TFEU). In response to the defence's contention that there can be no trade mark infringement where the aim of the proprietor is to partition the market, Oracle replied that trade mark infringement is exclusively governed by art 5 and 7 TM Directive. According to the claimant, art 7 strikes a balance between the public interest and the rights of the proprietor and hence sets the limits in EU law on the protection of the internal market in relation to trade marks. The judge disagreed. Arden LJ took the view that arts 5 (on infringement) and art 7 (on exhaustion) must be interpreted by reference to arts 28 and 30 EC and as a result Oracle's right to sue the defendant might indeed be affected. The practices alleged arguably had more to do with restricting imports, with the object of preventing price competition within the EEA and thereby protecting Oracle's profit margins, than with the proper exercise of the right to control the first marketing of Oracle equipment within the EEA. Turning to competition law, Oracle accepted, for the purpose of the appeal, that its agreement with its distributors was contrary to art 81 (art 101 TFEU), but maintained that there was not a sufficient connection between that and its trade mark rights. Again LJ Arden disagreed. The Court of Justice had not held that art 81 could not be used in trade mark cases., The allegation that the agreements with distributors and resellers formed part of an overall scheme for excluding secondary traders from the market might be a legitimate defence which should be considered by the High Court. However, she went on to note that since the issues raised by the case involved questions of economic policy that were likely to affect the European Union as a whole, a reference to the Court of Justice might be warranted. We have seen that the same point might be made about trade mark law more generally.

SELF-TEST QUESTIONS

1   David Simone, the world-famous footballer who plays for Neasden Wanderers, learns that his cousin Frank Simone is planning to sell 'Simone' football shirts. Frank is also planning to publish a fan magazine called Neasden Football and an exposé of the club, a book entitled The Wanderers: The Naked Truth. David has applied to register 'Simone' as a trade mark for cosmetics and footwear, including football boots. Neasden Wanderers have two registered marks, one consisting of the word 'Neasden' printed inside a football, which they use on their programmes. The second is the word 'Wanderers'. Both are registered, inter alia, for printed matter. Advise David and Neasden Wanderers on trade marks generally in relation to Frank's business plans.

2   Andrea has designed a hat, with a distinctive bell shape, which is both decorative and an excellent design for protecting the head from high winds. She plans to make it out of cheap plastic, and she has named it 'Bell Armour'. There is a

French fashion house which produces a world-famous perfume, 'Belle Amour'. What trade mark protection can Andrea obtain for her hat?

3 To what extent are the advertising functions of trade marks protected against dilution and the taking of unfair advantage?

FURTHER READING

Bonadio, E, 'Parallel imports in a global market: should a generalized international exhaustion be the next step?' [2011] *European Intellectual Property Review* 153.

Davis, J, 'European Trade Mark Law and the Enclosure of the Commons' [2002] *Intellectual Property Quarterly* 342.

Dinwoodie, G and Janis, M, *Trade Mark Law and Theory: a Handbook of Contemporary Research* (Edward Elgar, 2008).

Gangjee, D, and Burrell, R, 'Because you're worth it: L'Oreal and the prohibition on free riding' [2010] *Modern Law Review* 282.

Griffiths, A, 'Modernising Trade Mark Law and Promoting Economic Efficiency: An Evaluation of the Baby-Dry Judgment and its Aftermath' [2003] *Intellectual Property Quarterly* 1.

— 'The Trademark Monopoly: An Analysis of the Core Zone of Absolute Protection under Art 5(1)(a)' [2007] *Intellectual Property Quarterly* 312.

Horton, A, 'The implications of L'Oreal v Bellure–a retrospective and a looking forward: the essential functions of a trade mark and when is an advantage unfair?' [2011] *European Intellectual Property Review* 550.

Kerly's Law of Trade Marks and Trade Names (15th edn, Sweet & Maxwell, 2011).

Marsoof, A, 'Keywords advertising: issues of trade mark infringement' [2010] *Journal of International Commercial Law and Technology* 240.

Simon Fhima, I, 'Dilution by blurring–a conceptual roadmap' [2010] *Intellectual Property Quarterly* 44.

6

Patents

SUMMARY

- The Patents Act 1977 and patent law: its development and justifications
- Routes to international protection
- Obtaining a patent
- A patentable invention: excluded inventions, novelty, the inventive step, and industrial applicability
- The need for sufficiency
- Infringement and defences
- Losing the patent and enforcement
- Patents in the international context

Introduction: Patents Act 1977 and patent law

6.1 The patents system in the UK is governed by the Patents Act 1977 (PA 1977). There are also a number of relevant provisions in the Copyright, Designs and Patents Act 1988 (CDPA 1988). The PA 1977, which succeeded the Patents Act 1949 (PA 1949), was intended to harmonise UK law with that of the European Patent Convention (EPC), the Community Patent Convention (CPC) and the Patent Co-operation Treaty (PCT). At the end of 2007, the Patents Act 2004 (PA 2004) (by the Regularity Reform (Patents) Order 2004 (SI 2004/2357)) introduced a number of amendments to the PA 1977. Most of these relate to procedural rules in order to make them compatible with the PCT and the subsequent amendments which have been made to that treaty, most importantly, the Patent Law Treaty 2000. There are however two substantive amendments to the PA 1977 which relate to patents for medical treatment which are looked at below (see para 6.32). The PA 1977 is organised into three parts. Part I sets out the domestic law relating to substantive matters such as patentability, infringement and registration of patents. Part II covers international matters, principally the EPC and the CPC. Part III contains a number of general provisions relating to the working of the PA 1977 and like matters.

Development and justifications

6.2 At its simplest, a patent may be thought of as a monopoly right to the use of an invention. The first patent for a new invention is thought to be Aconicio's Patent, for a grinding machine, granted by the Crown in 1565. From being within the power of the Crown to grant at its discretion, the patent was declared a creature of the common law by the Statute of Monopolies 1628. However, as an increasing number of Acts dealing with patents were passed in the nineteenth and twentieth centuries, it effectively became a creature of statute. The longevity of the patent suggests its critical importance to the economic concerns of governments. It also means that the justifications for, and the relative utility of, the patent regime have varied depending upon the political and economic climate in which it has operated.

6.3 There are three broad justifications which are today most often canvassed for the existence of a patents system. The first is based on justice for the inventor, since it rewards him for the labour which has gone into his invention by preventing others, who have made no similar investment, from 'free riding' on it. Some have questioned the cogency of this justification, since justice would presumably require any number of inventors of the same invention to be granted equal patent protection as long as their inventions were independent of each other (as is the case with copyright protection). In fact, patent protection is granted only to the first to file a patent application. Furthermore, if patent protection were designed largely to ensure the inventor received his just reward, then the relatively short period of protection which patents provide would be difficult to justify when compared with that granted by copyright or trade mark registration. The second and third justifications may be said to have more to do with the broader economic aims of the patent system: to encourage (investment in) innovation, and, through the publication of patent applications, to disseminate information on the basis of which others may further innovate or compete. In the latter case, the patent system is said to gain its justification through an exchange by which the inventor is given a limited monopoly to exploit his invention in return for making its workings public: information which, without patent protection, he might be tempted to conceal. The fundamental importance of the patent as a disseminator of information may be seen in the courts' insistence that a valid patent application must contain an 'enabling disclosure', which enables the reader to reproduce the invention which is its subject (*Asahi Kasei Kogyo Application* (1991), per Lord Oliver).

6.4 The question of whether patents are also necessary to encourage investment in innovation has been hotly debated and the evidence is unclear. Over the last century, companies have dedicated increasing resources to research and development by specialists. Today, this policy is most visible in the biotechnology industry, but it has also characterised the development of other 'cutting edge' technologies in the past. Patents may be justified as encouraging expensive and speculative research by companies, in the knowledge that they alone will reap the initial rewards, and hence recoup their investment, if it is successful. However, it is the exceptional invention, such as the anti-impotence drug Viagra, which brings exceptional rewards. It is possible that these rewards would in any event have been earned by the invention's being first on the market, even without the benefit of patent protection.

6.5 It has been suggested that there may be a fourth justification for the patent system. It can be an important instrument of competition policy. It is probably true that most technological advances occur incrementally, and few such advances involve a real 'inventive step' (a necessary criterion for patenting) which carries it beyond the existing know-how. Nonetheless, the European Patent Office (EPO) has chosen to grant broad protection to patents which have been characterised less by a clear inventive step than by the fact that their development involved major financial investment and resulted in a breakthrough in a highly competitive international field, biotechnology. An example is the EPO's decision in *Genentech 1/Polypeptide Expression* (1989), which presents an interesting contrast with the more cautious and narrow approach taken by the House of Lords in *Biogen Inc v Medeva plc* (1997) (see para **6.55**). By giving broad patent protection to technological advances in Europe, the EPO can be seen to be promoting the competitiveness of European industries against their international rivals, most notably in the USA, where similarly broad patent protection is available (McInerney, 'Biotechnology: *Biogen v Medeva* in the House of Lords' [1998] *European Intellectual Property Review* 14).

Routes to international protection

6.6 The protection given by a patent is generally territorial. It is limited to the country in which it was granted. However, it is possible to obtain patent protection in more than one country through a single application. The Patent Co-operation Treaty (PCT), under the aegis of WIPO, provides a route by which an application can be made through a 'receiving office' (the UK Intellectual Property Office is one, as is the European Patent Office (EPO)) for patent protection in any of the contracting states. The appropriate bodies of each of the states named by the applicant decide, on the basis of their national patent law, whether to grant the patent (which is a national patent). A second route is through an application for a European Patent to the Munich-based EPO, which was established by the European Patent Convention (EPC). In contrast to the procedure under the PCT, the EPO makes its own decisions, on the basis of substantive law set out in the EPC, as to whether to grant a patent application. If approved by the EPO, a European Patent (EP) would in the past be granted for each of the contracting states designated by the applicant. Under the amendments brought in by the PA 2004, an application for an EP will be deemed to have designated all the contracting states. An EP has the same status as a national patent. Thus, an EP (UK) is treated as if it has been granted under the PA 1977, and questions of infringement and invalidity are decided by the domestic courts. The long-debated Community Patent (CP), which has yet to be introduced, is intended to be a single unitary patent for the EC (much like the Community Trade Mark). The Paris Convention (to which the UK adheres) ensures that nationals of one member state will have the same level of patent protection in any other member state which the latter grants to its own nationals. In addition, as a signatory to TRIPS, the UK has made some alterations to its national patent law to meet the minimum requirements laid down in the Agreement (Patents and Trade Marks (World Trade Organization)) Regulations 1999 (SI 1999/1899). The changes relate primarily to the granting of compulsory licences (see para **6.97**).

UK patent law and the EPC

6.7 Specific sections of the PA 1977, primarily those dealing with patentability, infringement and validity, 'are so framed as to have, as nearly as practicable, the same effects in the UK as the corresponding provisions of the EPC, the CPC and the PCT' (s 130(7)). The UK courts have frequently followed EPC decisions or have sought to interpret the PA 1977 so that the same meanings are given as to equivalent provisions in other EPO countries or by the EPO. Nonetheless, there remain important areas where UK and EPO interpretations of the relevant law are at odds (see, for example, para **6.20** et seq on excluded categories). In part, this is because the EPO is not concerned with questions of infringement or invalidity, although, unlike in the UK, it is possible to oppose the grant of a patent by the EPO. Nor is it possible to appeal from the UK Intellectual Property Office or national courts to the Board of Appeal of the EPO, just as the latter's decisions are not open to appeal in the national courts. It is arguable that full harmonisation between domestic patent regimes and the EPC has been delayed by this absence of any final court of appeal concerning itself with the interpretation of the relevant law in all jurisdictions. Indeed, a plan for a central court, the European and Community Patents Court, which had been proposed by a number of EU Member States as part of a unified patent regime, covering both European patents and the proposed Community patent, was recently blocked by the Court of Justice. The Court of Justice held that it was not compatible with the EU Treaty, since such a court would not come under its final jurisdiction (Opinion 1/09 dated 8 March 2011).

Obtaining a patent

6.8 Any person may apply for a patent (s 7(1)), but the broad principle is that a grant will be made only to the inventor (or joint inventors) (PA 1977, s 7(2)(a)). There are exceptions. The inventor may transfer his rights to an invention by specific agreement, such as by assignment. The right to the grant of a patent may also pass to others through the operation of the law, most notably in the case of employee inventions. Finally, under s 7(4), unless the contrary is established, the person who makes the application for a patent is taken to be the person who is entitled to the patent under s 7(2).

Employee inventions

6.9 An employer may be entitled to ownership of an invention in two circumstances. First, if it was made by the employee in the course of his normal duties or in the course of other duties specifically assigned to him *and* the circumstances were such that an invention 'might reasonably be expected to result' from carrying out those duties (for example, the employee has been hired specifically to undertake research and development) (PA 1977, s 39(1)). Second, he may be entitled to the invention if the employee had a special obligation to further his employer's interests and the invention was made in the course of his duties (s 39(2)). An invention not made in any of the above circumstances belongs to the inventor, as in *Harris' Patent* (1985), where the employee's invention could not reasonably have been expected to result from his duties in sales and service, and his status in the company was not sufficiently responsible to place him under any special obligation to his employer.

Compensation for employee-inventors

6.10 An employee-inventor may be compensated if he can show that the invention or the patent or a combination of the two has been of 'outstanding benefit' to his employer (s 40). The amount of compensation shall be such as to award the employee 'a fair share (having regard to all the circumstances) of the benefit which the employer has derived, or may reasonably be expected to derive' from the invention and/or the patent (s41). Previous to the Patents Act 2004, the benefit and subsequent compensation related only to the patent, not to the invention. To date, *Kelly v GE Healthcare Ltd* (2009) has been one of the few successful applications under ss 40–41, not least because of the 'vagueness' of the wording of this provision (as per Floyd J). *Kelly v GE Healthcare* was decided under the old rules, however it is submitted that its principles remain sound. In *Kelly*, Floyd J held that to be outstanding the benefit to an employer has to be more than 'substantial' or 'significant'. It has to be 'out of the ordinary' or 'something special'. As to what constitutes a 'fair share of the benefit', Floyd J looked at the nature of the employees' duties, and balanced their contribution to the patent against that of their employer, as well as the advantages both they and the employer derived from it. It has been suggested that the decision in *Kelly* will not open the floodgates to further claims, not least because those who bring such claims might prejudice their future career prospects. In this instance, at the time of the action, Kelly had retired and Chiu, his co-inventor, no longer worked for the defendant (Howell, 'Compensation at last for employee inventors: Kelly v GE Healthcare Ltd' [2010] *Journal of Business Law* 41; see also, *Shanks v Unilever Plc* [2010] CA).

Entitlement 1: *Markem v Zipher*

6.11   Even though individual B applies for a patent, individual A might believe that he rather than B is rightfully entitled to the patent as sole inventor or to a share in it as a joint inventor with B. It is possible for A to challenge the granting of the patent to B, so long as he does so before the actual grant (s 8). The Court of Appeal addressed this issue in *Markem v Zipher* (2005) which concerned ex-employees of a company, who sought to patent an invention which they had begun to investigate while they were still employed by the claimant. The Court of Appeal held that it was not enough for A to assert that he was entitled to the patent, for which B applied, by virtue of s 7 (ie that he was the inventor or joint inventor). Rather, A had to show that B was not entitled to apply for the patent either at all or alone. In order to do so, according to the Court of Appeal, A must invoke some other rule of law (apart from s 7) to establish his entitlement to the patent or a share of it. In this case, Markem failed to prove its entitlement because, inter alia, it did not succeed in establishing that its former employees were in breach of confidence (see also *University of Southampton's Applications* (2006), CA).

Entitlement 2: *Markem v Zipher* overruled

6.12   Subsequently, the House of Lords held that the Court of Appeal's reasoning in *Markem v Zipher* was wrong. In *Yeda Research and Development Co Ltd v Rhone-Poulenc Rorer International Holdings Inc* (2007), the facts were similar. Scientists at the Weizmann Institute of Science in Israel had been working on a new chemical treatment for cancer. The scientists wrote up their experiment in an academic paper. Before publication, they sent it to a scientist who worked at Weizmann, but was presently on leave working for the defendant. The defendant secured European patents, based on this research. Subsequently, the claimant, which was the assignee of rights of the inventors at Weizmann, applied to be named as sole inventor on the European patent. Section 37 of the PA 1977 allows the Comptroller of Patents to make such a ruling. In its initial application, Yeda had not specified any breaches of the law, which following *Markem* were necessary for the patent to be transferred. Indeed, when the case was heard in the High Court and the Court of Appeal, its attempt to amend its application to allege breach of confidence by the defendants was overruled. The House of Lords addressed the question, inter alia, of whether it was indeed necessary for the claimant to prove that the defendant had acquired the patent by breach of some other rule of law. They held that it was not necessary to do so. Instead, s 7(2) and (3) were exhaustive. The first step in any dispute over entitlement was to decide who was the inventor(s), in other words, 'who came up with the inventive concept'. The effect of s 7(4) of the PA 1977 was that any other party who seeks to be named as a joint inventor must prove that he contributed to the claimed invention. Similarly, any person who claims to be the sole inventor must prove that the person wrongly named as inventor did not in fact contribute to the inventive concept. Fortunately, although the House of Lords held the reasoning in *Markem v Zipher* to be wrong, it found that the decision was correct. The invention at issue in that case had been devised by the claimant's ex-employees while they were working for the defendant.

The application

6.13 Patent applications are now filed at the UK Intellectual Property Office. A complete application includes an application form, the fee, the specification, which is made up of a description of the invention and the claim(s), plus any drawings, and an abstract (PA 1977, s 14). The specification must disclose the invention clearly and completely enough to be performed by a person skilled in the art (s 14(3)). The description tells a person skilled in the art how to work the invention. The claim(s), which delimit the extent of the monopoly being claimed through the application, must be clear and concise, be supported by the description and relate to one invention or a group of inventions which are so linked as to form a single inventive concept (s 14(5)). Generally, the patent will have a first broad claim, Claim 1, and then a number of subsidiary claims. It is possible to amend the claims in certain limited circumstances, once the application has been filed. An application must cover only one invention but it is possible to 'divide' the application if it covers more than one (s 14(6)). If the specification and/or the claim fail to fulfill the standards set down by the PA 1977, the application may be rejected for insufficiency. Whether or not an application will fail for insufficiency depends upon the application of the relevant legal rules and case law. The substantive conditions necessary for a finding of insufficiency will be considered below when the validity of patents is examined (see para **6.70**).

The priority date (PA 1977, s 5)

6.14 The date at which an application is filed is its 'priority date'. The priority date provides the cut-off point for determining what is included in the 'state of the art' (see para **6.34**), against which the novelty of the claimed patent is measured (PA 1977, s 2(2)). If an application is filed after the priority date of an earlier application for the same invention, the later application will fail. The priority date of an earlier application filed in countries covered by the EPC, PCT and the Paris Convention will be the priority date for a UK application, provided the latter is made within certain specified time limits. An early priority date may also be obtained by filing a skeleton application at the UK Intellectual Property Office, which need meet only minimum conditions, most notably by including a description, but not the claim(s) or the abstract (s 15). The earlier priority date, obtained by a skeleton application, will hold good only for material in the later full application which was also disclosed in the earlier description (*Asahi Kasei Kogyo Application* (1991)). Furthermore, the skeleton application, like all patent applications, must contain an 'enabling disclosure', that is, sufficient information to enable a skilled person to work the invention (*Asahi*; see para **6.37** on what constitutes an enabling disclosure). If the full application is then filed inside a specified time period, its priority date will be that of the first informal filing. Because it takes time to prepare a successful patent application, the earliest inventor may want to ensure that his patent claim is not defeated simply because a later inventor submits an application more quickly. The skeleton application allows him to secure an early priority date, even though he may still be unsure about the full implications of his invention.

Preliminary examination and publication

6.15 Within a specified period (now 12 months) following the filing of either the full application or the earlier application establishing priority, the applicant must request a preliminary examination and a limited search by the UK Intellectual Property Office. The preliminary examination determines whether the application complies with the formal requirements of the PA 1977 and whether it covers only a single invention. Within a specified period (18 months) from either the filing of the application or an earlier priority date, the application is published.

Once the application has been made available to the public, it becomes part of the 'prior art'. This means, for instance, that if this application is subsequently withdrawn and the *same* applicant re-submits it or a closely related one, the later application will fail because it has been anticipated by (its own) prior art. The publication date is the date to which subsequent claims for infringement will be backdated. As amended by the PA 2004 all patents applied for under the EPC will automatically represent a document which might constitute prior art under s 2(3) of the PA 1977.

Substantive examination and acceptance

6.16 The applicant must request the substantive examination within a specified period (now six months) from publication. It is during the second examination that the examiner will decide whether the invention meets the substantive requirements for patentability (see para **6.18** et seq). A patent may then be granted, or the examiner may raise objections. If the latter, the applicant has an opportunity to put his case to the examiner, either through correspondence or at a hearing, and also to make some limited amendments, for instance, by limiting his claims so they avoid overlapping with prior art. If the applicant is finally unable to meet the objections within a specified period (now four-and-a-half years from the priority date or date of filing) or 12 months from the first substantive examination report, the application will fail.

Length of grant

6.17 Patents are granted for four years in the first instance and are renewable for up to 20 years. Certain patents for pharmaceutical products or processes may gain up to five years' additional protection through the EU's supplementary protection certificate (SPC) procedure. These SPCs (granted by national patent offices) recognise that many pharmaceuticals must undergo a prolonged period of government testing after the patent grant and before being placed on the market, cutting into the full 20 years of patent protection. According to the Court of Justice, the SPC's object is to encourage research in the pharmaceutical field by offering this additional protection (*Farmitalia Carlo Erba SRL's SPC Application* (1999)).

Patentability

6.18 Patent protection is given, not to all inventions, but only to patentable inventions. As Lord Hoffmann noted in *Biogen Inc v Medeva plc* (1997), the PA 1977 does not define an 'invention', supposedly because the parties to the EPC could not agree on one. Instead, it sets outs the necessary characteristics of a 'patentable' invention (s 1(1)), and identifies excluded categories for which a patent will not be granted either because they are not considered to be 'inventions' for the purpose of s 1(2) or because, despite being 'inventions', a patent should not be granted on public interest grounds (s 1(3)). A patentable invention may be either a product or a process or a 'product by process'. The latter, identified in art 64(2) of the EPC, is a claim to a product which is defined by how it is produced, often because there is no alternative way of describing it (Decision T150/82 *International Flavors & Fragrances/Claim categories* (1984)). In *Kirin-Amgen Inc v Transkaryotic Therapies Inc* (2005), the House of Lords held that to be patentable, a product by process patent must involve a new product.

A patentable invention

6.19 The Act identifies four attributes of a patentable invention. They are:

- it must be new (it must not have been anticipated);
- it must involve an inventive step (it must not be obvious);
- it must be capable of industrial application;
- it must not fall within any of the categories excluded by s 1(2) and (3).

However, it is important to remember that, even if an inventor believes his invention is a patentable invention, because it has all the positive characteristics listed above and does not fall into any of the excluded categories, he may still fail to obtain a patent because of some insufficiency in the application itself. The four attributes of patentability are looked at below, beginning with the excluded categories.

Patentable inventions 1: the excluded categories

6.20 The PA 1977 sets out four broad categories which 'among other things' are not considered inventions to the extent that the patent relates to that thing 'as such' (s 1(2)(a)–(d)). (The implementation of the PA 2004 has added a fifth category, that is methods of medical treatment (see below, para **6.32**).) Recently, the Court of Appeal has, in two cases relating to computer programs and business methods, enunciated a four-stage test for identifying whether a patent claim falls within an excluded category (*Aerotel Ltd v Telco Holdings Ltd/Macrossan's Patent Application* (2006)). The excluded categories are considered in turn below and then the test is considered (paras **6.25** et seq).

Discoveries, scientific theories or mathematical methods (s 1(2)(a))

6.21   Discoveries and ideas are not patentable, but discoveries or ideas which have a technical aspect or make a technical contribution are (*Fujitsu's Application* (1997)). It is the practical application of a discovery which leads to patentability, even if that practical application is inherent in the discovery or is obvious once the discovery has been made (*Genentech's Patent* (1989)). In *Genentech*, the discovery was the gene sequence of t-PA, a protein which might be used as an anti-coagulant. The patent failed, inter alia, because it did not set out, sufficiently, claims for the practical application of the discovery or was too speculative as to what those applications might be (for an opposite result, see *Human Genome Sciences v Eli Lilly (2011)*, para **6.64**). Natural laws, for instance, Einstein's theory of relativity, are not patentable. Or, as was put in one famous judicial example by Lindley LJ: 'An invention is not the same as a discovery. When Volta discovered the effect of electric current from the battery on a frog's leg he made a great discovery, but no patentable invention' (*Lane Fox v Kensington and Knightsbridge Electric Lighting Co* (1892)). However, if an inventor employs a natural effect, such as an electric current, as part of a new method to produce a new product, he could patent the method.

6.22   The dividing line between a discovery and a patentable invention is highly contentious, no more so than in the field of biogenetics, as the intense debate over the Directive on the Legal Protection of Biological Inventions (EC) 98/44; incorporated into UK law by the Patents Regulations 2000 (SI 2000/2037 in July 2000) illustrated. Much of the debate focused on the question of whether a gene sequence is a discovery or an invention. The Directive states that genes and gene sequences, as they exist in nature, are not patentable because they are discoveries, but goes on, in art 22: 'biological material [such as genes] which is isolated from its natural environment or processed by means of a technical process may be the subject of an invention even if it already occurred in nature', provided a use can be ascribed to it. Processes used to isolate genes and gene sequences and therapies involving, for example, delivery of these genes to the body were already patentable inventions before the Directive. The UK Intellectual Property Office has stated that the Directive neither changed UK patent law nor led to anything being patentable in the UK which was not already patentable (see, for example, *Biogen Inc v Medeva plc* (1997); *Chiron Corpn v Murex Diagnostics Ltd* (1996)). For those who argue against the patenting of genes, a major concern has been that academic and non-profit organisations, which cannot muster the resources of private companies, will be deprived of the opportunity freely to undertake genetic research and to employ its results, for instance, in the area of diagnostic tests for genetic diseases. Others have answered that, because genetic research is so expensive, those who invest in such research must be able to count on some monetary return from their investment through at least a limited monopoly, otherwise such research would not be undertaken and the public would not benefit from its results. Another telling argument in favour of the Directive was that the USA already granted patents in this area, and the failure of the EC to follow suit would damage the competitiveness of its biotechnology industry. The implications of the Directive's approach to the patenting of gene sequences has been particularly intense because of the output of the Human Genome Project, which had as its object the identification of the DNA sequences of the entire human genome. Interestingly, the UK Prime Minister and the US President, responding to these concerns in 2000, issued a joint statement endorsing the idea that raw fundamental data on the human genome, including the human DNA sequence and its variations, 'should be made freely available to scientists everywhere'. Cynics might note that beyond this statement of best practice, the law of patents as it now stands both in the UK and the USA was left unaltered.

Literary, dramatic, musical or artistic works or any other aesthetic creations (s 1(2)(b))

6.23 These are, of course, protected by other means, most notably through the provisions of the Copyright, Designs and Patents Act 1988. Original computer programs which are excluded from patent protection will be protected by copyright (see para **2.95**).

Schemes, rules or methods for performing mental acts, playing a game or doing business, or a program for a computer (s 1(2)(c)) and the presentation of information (s 1(2)(d))

6.24 These are not patentable. Generally, a 'mere idea' is not patentable, but a method of putting a principle or an idea into effect might be. An early example of a rejected application was for a method of lessening the noise on a jet engine, which the court viewed merely as a flight plan and 'as much outside the operation of any of the useful arts as would be a trainer's direction to a jockey in his control of a racehorse' (*Rolls-Royce Application* (1963)). It has been suggested that a computer program might, itself, qualify as a method of performing a mental act (even if the human mind could not do the act on its own (*Fujitsu's Application* (1997))). The criteria employed by the courts for excluding mental acts, business methods and computer programs are closely intertwined and must be considered together. The wider disparity is between the criteria developed by the EPO (which recognises similar exclusions under art 52 of the EPC) and the UK courts.

Excluded subject matter and the technical contribution test

6.25 In the early cases both at the EPO and before the UK courts, the test for patentability was to ask whether the invention as claimed involved 'a technical contribution' or had a 'technical effect'. In *Vicom/Computer-related inventions* (1987), heard before the Technical Board of Appeal at the EPO, the claimed invention involved the processing of real images by a computer program, but the technical contribution was claimed to be the generation of an enhanced picture. The application was approved. In this case, the means for implementing the invention had been through a computer program, but the invention was held not to be a computer program 'as such'. Instead, it was a technical process, with the computer set up to operate in accordance with a specified program for controlling or carrying out a technical process. Similarly, the UK courts would not refuse to patent an invention merely because it was implemented in the form of a computer program, if the 'novel effect' went beyond the computing process or the operation of the computer itself (*Gale's Application* (1991)). Thus, the courts rejected applications where the invention claimed was for computer hardware, but the essential novelty lay in the software it embodied (*Merrill Lynch's Application* (1989)). The recording of a series of instructions for calculating square roots on a ROM was held not to be a patentable invention, since it did not contain a technical contribution; the ROM was merely the vehicle for carrying the instruction (*Gale's Application*). In *Fujitsu's Application* (1997), the claim was for a method and an apparatus for modelling a synthetic crystal structure through the manipulation of a computer program, where previously this had been done by hand modelling. The technical contribution claimed by the patentee was either the processing of images of real objects or, alternatively, the provision of a labour-saving tool. It was held that a method for the production of images of real objects did not on its own provide a technical contribution. It was also held that, although the program did, indeed, avoid the labour and error which came from hand modelling, this was not a technical contribution, since avoidance of labour and error was precisely the sort of advantage expected from a computer program.

The EPO and the 'any hardware approach'

6.26　More recently, the EPO set out a different test for judging whether a claim is excluded under art 52. This is the 'any hardware approach,' developed in three cases: *Pensions Benefit Systems Partnership* (PBS) (2000), *HITACHI/Auction Method* (2004) and *MICROSOFT/Data transfer* (2006). In *PBS*, claim 1 was for a method of controlling a pension benefits system through the input of information on employees and their benefits using data processing and cost computing means. Claim 5 was for an apparatus for controlling the system. The Examining Division of the EPO rejected the application as being a method of doing business, without any technical character. The applicant appealed. The Enlarged Board of Appeal (EBA) rejected the appeal, but it took different approaches to claim 1 and to claim 5. In relation to the method claim (claim 1), the EBA found that processing and producing the relevant information were typical steps in a method of doing business. Using technical means for a non-technical purpose did not confer any technical character on the invention. However, in assessing the apparatus claim (claim 5), the EBA diverged from previous EPO case law, such as *Vicom*, which had looked for a 'technical contribution'. The EBA distinguished claim 1 from claim 5, holding that the latter was a claim for the apparatus to perform a business method and that, as a 'physical entity', it was not excluded by art 52. The EBA took this 'any hardware' approach because it judged the technical contribution approach to be akin to asking whether the claimed invention involved an inventive step rather than more properly asking whether it should be excluded under art 52. In *PBS*, the EBA nonetheless rejected the apparatus claim because it lacked an inventive step. In the later case of *Hitachi*, the TBA went further and applied the 'any hardware approach' to business methods themselves, and not merely to the apparatus which put them into effect.

The UK courts after PBS: the Aerotel test

6.27 The Court of Appeal had an opportunity to consider whether to adopt the 'any hardware approach' in *Aerotel Ltd v Telco Holdings Ltd/Macrossan's Patent Application* (2006). The *Aerotel* appeal was against the revocation of its patent for a method of making telephone calls from any telephone through the use of a special code and for apparatus for storing and transmitting the code. In the High Court, the Aerotel patent had been considered a method for doing business. The *Macrossan* appeal was against the rejection of its application to patent a method for producing documents to form a company, by means of a user sitting at his computer answering a series of questions posed by a remote server. The Patents Court held that this was both a method of performing a mental act and also that it was a computer program as such. In his judgment, Jacob LJ noted first that the excluded categories formed a disparate group with no common reason for their exclusion. He therefore rejected the 'any hardware approach' which was based on the assumption that the excluded categories were united by being too abstract or intangible to be patentable. In the case of computer programs, he took the view that this would mean defining the exclusion very narrowly. A better view was that the EPC had meant to exclude computer programs, even in a practical or operable form, not just as abstract entities. It followed from this that the correct approach was to continue using the 'technical effect' or 'technical contribution' test which had been developed by the UK courts in cases such as *Merrill Lynch* and *Fujitsu*. Jacob LJ then proposed a four-step test which would embody the technical contribution approach and would be appropriate for all categories of subject matter identified in s 1(2) of the PA 1977. The steps were as follows:

- properly construe the claim;
- identify the actual contribution;

- ask whether it falls solely within the excluded subject matter (or alternatively, ask whether the contribution thus identified consists of excluded subject matter as such);

- check whether the actual or alleged contribution is actually technical in nature.

Applied to the facts of *Aerotel*, the Court of Appeal found that the claim was, inter alia, for a new system including a physical device and was clearly technical in nature. It was not excluded as a method of doing business. However, Macrossan's application failed both because it was a business method and a computer program as such, since there was no technical contribution involved merely in running the computer program. The *Aerotel* approach as it related to excluded categories, and to business methods and computer programs in particular, was subsequently roundly criticised by the Enlarged Board of Appeal in *Duns Licensing Associates L.P.* (2007). The EBA suggested that the UK court had failed to realise that excluded matter might actually contribute to the solution of a technical problem and hence the overall invention would be patentable as having a technical character. However, in the later case of *Symbian v Comptroller General of Patents* (2008), the Court of Appeal endorsed the *Aerotel* approach (Salmon, 'Patenting Computer Software and Business Methods in the UK' [2007] *Tottels Communications Law* 18).

Business methods and computer software: policy considerations

6.28 In *Aerotel*, Jacob LJ held that the four-step test was applicable to all non-patentable subject matter. Furthermore, he noted that the technical contribution test was wider than the 'any hardware' test, and hence likely to exclude more applications. Jacob LJ acknowledged that this approach carried with it policy implications not least because other jurisdictions, most notably the USA, have been far readier to allow patents for business methods and computer software. Thus, in *State Street Bank & Trust v Signature Financial Group* (1998), the software in question embodied a method for determining the apportioned value of pooled mutual funds. It was held by the US Court of Appeals for the Federal Circuit that mathematical algorithms, provided they were reduced to a practical application, and business methods might be patentable provided they were useful, novel, non-obvious, based on a written description which enabled an individual skilled in the art to make and use the invention, and provided the patent set forth the best mode contemplated by the inventor for carrying it out. Following *State Street*, the US Patent Office has shown a general willingness to allow the patenting of software and business methods. By contrast, a proposed EU Directive on the patentability of computer-related inventions was rejected by the European Parliament in 2005. Its supporters had claimed that the Directive was not a proposal to patent software as such, but would be limited in its effect to genuine inventions. However, critics argued that such an initiative would inevitably lead to the patenting of software, with the result that software would increase in cost and there would be less consumer choice. It is certainly the case, as was noted by Jacob LJ in *Aerotel*, that innovation in software design both in the USA and elsewhere has proceeded 'at immense speed' without the benefit of patent protection, while the introduction of computer software patents in the USA had led to a considerable increase in litigation. These developments led Jacob LJ to conclude that, 'if the encouragement of patenting and patent litigation as industries in themselves' was the purpose of the patent system then the case for a narrow test for the excluded categories was made out. 'But not otherwise.' Finally, art 27(1) of TRIPS does not, in principle, exclude the patenting of computer programs which are also protectable by copyright. However, in its decision in *IBM Application* (1999), the EBA made it clear that, since TRIPS is not directly binding on the EPO, it would continue to rely on the EPC to determine the law in this area.

Inventions which encourage offensive, immoral or anti-social behaviour are not patentable (s 1(3)(a))

6.29 These may have all the attributes of a patentable invention, but will be excluded on other grounds, as being not conducive to public order and morality. An invention will not necessarily come within this prohibition only because it is illegal (s 1(4)). For instance, the EC Directive on Biological Inventions and the UK Regulations state that the following are not patentable on the basis that their commercial exploitation would be contrary to public order and morality:

- processes for cloning human beings;
- processes for modifying the germ line genetic identity of human beings;
- uses of human embryos for commercial purposes;
- processes for modifying the genetic identity of animals which are likely to cause them suffering without any substantial benefit to man or animal, and also animals resulting from such processes.

This list is not exhaustive. According to the Directive, all processes which 'offend against human dignity' are also excluded from patentability (38th Recital to the Directive; *Netherlands v European Parliament* (2002)). A prominent example of the moral issues involved in this exclusion was the attempt to secure an EP for a transgenic animal, the 'Harvard onco-mouse', which, as a result of germ cell manipulation, contained human cancer-causing genes (*HARVARD/Onco-mouse* (1990)). The onco-mouse was granted a patent in the USA. The EPO also granted a patent. In the process, the EPO considered the 'public order' objection. It concluded that the suffering of the animal and possible environmental risks should be weighed against the usefulness of the invention to mankind; in this case the EPO concluded the latter outweighed the former. This 'balancing' test has now been written into the EC Directive on Biological Inventions and the Implementing Regulations (see para **6.22**). The *Onco-mouse* decision was then revisited by the EPO (*Harvard/Transgenic Animal* (2005)). In this case, the EPO amended the balancing test, and suggested it should first be asked whether the use of animal testing was allowed in Member States, because if that were the case then it would be wrong not to allow a patent for the results of that testing. This approach would appear to differ from Directive's approach which suggests that the balancing test should precede the question of patentability. The grant of a patent to the onco-mouse has been heavily criticised, not least on the grounds that causing animal suffering can never be justified, even if it may also produce other positive by-products.

6.30 Inevitably, such decisions by the Court of Justice are controversial. None more so, than the recent case of *Oliver Brustle v Greenpeace eV* (2011). The environmental group sought the annulment of a German patent held by Mr Brüstle. The patent concerned neural precursor cells, processes for their production from embryonic stem cells and their use for the treatment of neural defects. The patent claimed that the transplantation of brain cells into the nervous system is a promising method of treatment for a number of neurological diseases, in particular the treatment of Parkinson's disease. The patent specified that embryonic stem cells offer new prospects for the production of these neural precursor cells. The patent therefore sought to make it possible to use embryonic stem cells to produce the necessary precursor cells. In Germany, the patent was declared invalid in so far as it covered precursor cells obtained from human embryonic stem cells. Brüstle appealed. Broadly put, the question for the Court of Justice was whether the patent, in so far as it concerned precursor cells obtained from embryonic stem cells, was excluded from patentability under the Directive. First the court held that a human ovum once it is fertilised must be regarded as a human embryo, but so too must an unfertilized ovum because it may be capable, once fertilized, of developing into a human being. Secondly, the Court held that the concept of 'uses of human embryos for industrial or commercial purposes' within the meaning of the Directive also covers the use of human embryos for purposes of scientific research, where the results are patented. Thirdly, the Court held that an invention is unpatentable even though its purpose is not the use of human embryos, if it concerns a product whose production necessitates the prior destruction of human embryos or a process which requires a base material obtained by destruction of human embryos. The fact that destruction may occur at a stage long before the implementation of the invention, as was the case here, was irrelevant. It is important to note that the Court did not, nor was it able to, outlaw research using embryonic stem cells but rather it was denying the patentability of the results of such research: a distinction which was largely overlooked by the popular press in reporting the case.

Any variety of animal or plant or any essentially biological process for the production of animals or plants not being a microbiological process or the product of such a process (s 1(3)(b))

6.31 These are excluded inventions. Living material may be patented, provided it is not produced by a biological process. For instance, microbiological processes and their products, such as viruses, may be patented. This exclusion has been interpreted narrowly by the EPO. In the case of the onco-mouse, the EPO held that the application claimed an animal, not an animal variety, referring as it did to 'a transgenic non-human mammalian animal', and so did not fall under the exclusion. The *Onco-mouse* case also presents an example of an animal which was not produced biologically. The process by which the onco-mouse was produced was accomplished, not through natural means, but through the insertion of the onco-gene into the animal. The Directive and the UK Implementing Regulations also make it clear that products and processes involving gene sequences are patentable, if they are divorced, by means of an inventive process involving a new technical solution, from how they exist in nature (see para **6.21**). Plant varieties are protected, in the UK, by the Plant Varieties and Seeds Act 1964, as amended by the Plant Varieties Act 1983 and generally by the International Convention for the Protection of New Varieties of Plants. In the context of the patenting of plants, the 'variety' exclusion has also been given a narrow interpretation by the EPO since the exclusion exists merely to take into account other intellectual property rights for the protection of plant varieties provided by the contracting states (for example, *CIBA-GEIGY/Propagating material* (1984); Llewelyn, 'The Patentability of Biological Material: Continuing Contradiction and Confusion' [2000] *European Intellectual Property Review* 191)).

The method of treatment exclusion

6.32 Methods of treatment cannot be patented. Until the implementation of the PA 2004, these could not be patented because they were deemed to lack industrial applicability (s 4(1)). Following the implementation of the PA 2004, methods of medical treatment are not patentable not because they are not industrially applicable but in the interests of public health (s 4A(1)). Methods of treatment include treatment of a human or animal body by surgery or therapy, and of diagnosis practised on the human or animal body (s 4(2)). The treatment exclusion covers both product and process claims, and methods of testing. Generally, this exception reflects a concern not to allow the patent system to constrain the freedom of doctors in how they treat patients, rather than from any intention to proscribe the patenting of pharmaceuticals (*John Wyeth & Brother's Application/Schering's Application* (1985)). It applies to animal as well as human treatment. It does not cover an invention of any substance, or composition (or apparatus) which is used in the treatment (s 4(3), amended by the PA 2004 as s 4A(2)). Therapy has been interpreted to mean any medical treatment of a disease, whether preventative or curative (*Unilever Ltd (Davis's) Application* (1983)). Relevant EPO decisions have interpreted the exception narrowly (*EISAI/Second medical indication* (1985)). Thus, in *Medi-Physics* (2010), the EBA held that an imaging method which would be employed for diagnostic purposes during surgery did not fall within the exclusion even though the data would be immediately used by the surgeon during the same operation. On the other hand, in that same decision, the EBA held that to fall within the exclusion, the treatment did not necessarily have to have a life or death effect (see also, *Bristol-Myers Squibb Co v Baker Norton Pharmaceuticals Inc* (1999) CA).

Patentable inventions 2: novelty (PA 1977, s 2)

6.33 An invention is novel if it does not form part of the state of the art (s 2(1)). An invention which already forms part of the state of the art is said to have been 'anticipated'. If an invention has been anticipated, it is not a patentable invention.

The state of the art

6.34 This comprises all matter (whether a product, process or any information relating to either) which has been made available to the public, whether in the UK or elsewhere, before the priority date of the invention. Information is made available not just by written or oral description, but 'by use or in any other way' (s 2(2)). 'Elsewhere' in s 2(2) means matter made available worldwide. The state of the art includes matter contained in applications for patents which, although published after the invention in question, nonetheless have an earlier priority date (s 2(3)). It is necessary to consider first how novelty, or its absence, is assessed, before going on to look at the circumstances in which a prior invention is considered to have been 'made available to the public'.

Anticipation

6.35 In *General Tire and Rubber Co v Firestone Tyre and Rubber Co* (1972), the Court of Appeal held that to determine whether an invention has been anticipated, the prior publication and the later claim are to be construed as at their 'respective relevant dates' (that is, their dates of publication) by a reader skilled in the art (for the definition of which, see para **6.48**). This means that, when construing the earlier document (or other prior art), the 'reader skilled in the art' will be assumed to be skilled in the art as it was at the time of its publication, and any later technical advances are irrelevant (*Kirin-Amgen Inc v Transkaryotic Therapies Inc* (2001)). Similarly, the later claim will be construed in the light of the state of the art at its own publication date. The construction of the prior art and the later claim is the job of the court, which assumes the role of 'the reader skilled in the art', often with the help of expert witnesses, since it is unlikely to have the relevant expertise itself. The court decides as a matter of fact whether the patentee's claim is new or whether it has been anticipated. According to Lord Bingham in the leading case, *Synthon BV v Smithkline Beecham plc* (2005), there are two requirements for anticipation: prior disclosure and enablement. Let us look at each of these in turn.

Disclosure

6.36 In *Synthon*, Lord Bingham held that the disclosure condition is satisfied whenever subject matter described in the prior disclosure is capable of being performed and is such that, if performed, would necessarily result in the patent, or claimed invention, being infringed, whether or not this would be apparent to anyone at the time. Lord Bingham summarised this position by quoting the famous phrase from *General Tire v Firestone Tyre* (1972), 'A signpost however clear, upon the road to the patentee's invention will not suffice. The prior inventor must be clearly shown to have planted his flag at the precise destination before the patentee.' Lord Bingham also made it clear that infringement must not merely be a possible or even likely consequence of performing the invention disclosed by the prior art. If there are two possible outcomes, one infringing and one not, then it is not possible to say that performing the disclosed invention would infringe. In the latter case:

> The flag has not been planted on the patented invention although a person performing the invention disclosed by the prior art may carry it there by accident or (if he is aware of the patented invention) by design. Indeed it may be obvious to do so. But the prior disclosure must be construed as it was understood by the skilled person at the date of disclosure and not in the light of the subsequent patent.

However, if the performance of the invention disclosed by the prior art would not infringe the patent, but nonetheless would make it obvious to a person skilled in the art as to how he might adapt it to infringe the claimed invention, then the latter might be invalid for obviousness but would not be anticipated (for obviousness, see para **6.46** et seq).

Enablement

6.37 In *Synthon*, Lord Bingham defined enablement as follows: 'Enablement means that the ordinary skilled person would have been able to perform the invention which satisfies the requirement of disclosure.' The ordinary skilled person is assumed to have the common general knowledge. The test for enablement is the same as that for the revocation of a patent on the grounds of insufficiency (s 72(1) (c)) (for sufficiency, see para **6.67**). (The person skilled in the art and the common general knowledge are also relevant to obviousness and are discussed at paras **6.48** and **6.50**.)

Disclosure and enablement contrasted

6.38 In *Synthon*, Lord Bingham emphasised the need to keep the concepts of disclosure and enablement distinct when deciding on anticipation. In effect, although the test for anticipation will assume that the person skilled in the art with the common general knowledge might be willing to make experiments to get the invention to work, such experiments are pertinent to the requirement of enablement not to disclosure. This is because, as we have seen, disclosure entails planting a flag exactly on the invention. Furthermore, in the case of disclosure, the person skilled in the art is deemed to be trying to understand what the description of the invention means. However, once the meaning is clear, then the common general knowledge of the addressee is no longer relevant. In the case of enablement, on the other hand, the question is not what the addressee thinks the invention means, but rather whether he would be able to work the invention from the disclosure in light of the common general knowledge.

Synthon: *the facts*

6.39 The case involved an application by Synthon for the revocation of SmithKline Beecham's (SB) patent under s 2(3) of the PA. In 1997, Synthon applied for an EP. Its application involved Paroxetine, a compound used to treat depression. Initially this compound was marketed in the form of hydochloride hemihydrate salt. However, in 1997, both parties to the proceedings discovered that a different paroxetine salt, paroxetine methanesulfonate (PMS) had properties which made it more suitable for pharmaceutical use. Sython's invention was to provide a compound which had better solubility and stability than the salt previously used. The specification of its application set out, by reference to a formula, a class of such compounds, including PMS. It went further and identified a preferred group within the class which were particularly soluble and illustrated this class with an example. Example 1 described how to make PMS in crystalline form. After Synthon had filed its application but before it was published, SB filed a document giving it a priority date for a UK patent, which was subsequently granted.

This patent confined itself to a particular form of crystalline PMS, paroxetine methansulfonate. The characteristics of the PMS identified in the SB patent application would have led a person skilled in the art to think that it was a different polymorph (a polymorph being a collection of molecules which may arrange itself in different crystalline forms) to that identified by Synthon because, for example, it displayed a different infra-red (IR) spectrum. However, the specification of the SB application made it clear that the inventive step was the discovery of the sulfonate salt of paroxetine as an alternative to the hydrochloride salt. The SB specification went on to suggest various methods of isolating the salt, including in crystalline form. All these methods were described as conventional and not involving an inventive step. Synthon commenced proceedings to have the SB patent revoked on the grounds that the crystalline form of PMS described in claim 1 of SB's patent was not new. In particular, Synthon claimed that the SB patent was anticipated by its own patent application.

Synthon: *the judgments*

6.40 To succeed in its application, as explained by Lord Bingham, Synthon had to satisfy a court on two counts: first that its application disclosed the invention in claim 1 of the SB patent (disclosure); second, that an ordinary skilled man would be able to perform the disclosed invention by using the disclosed matter and common general knowledge (enablement). In the High Court, Synthon claimed its application disclosed the existence of PMS in crystalline form, although perhaps not the same crystalline form as claimed in SB's patent. Before trial, Synthon engaged experts to use the method described in its patent application to produce PMS in crystalline form (enablement). They succeeded only after skilled manipulation not described in the Synthon application. Furthermore, the PMS produced did not have the same IR spectrum predicted by Synthon, but rather that described in the SB patent. As a result, at trial, Synthon adjusted its arguments. It claimed that the IR spectrum described in its application was the result of a mistaken reading by its own laboratory. Furthermore, Synthon argued that the evidence obtained by its experts (including the IR reading) showed that PMS was actually monomorphic so that any PMS crystal would have the same characteristics as that described in the SB patent. Jacob J agreed. The disclosure of a crystalline form of PMS meant it would be in the form described by the SB patent, even if someone, who set out to make the PMS described by Synthon, would assume he was making something different. As regards enablement, Synthon conceded that the method described in its application did not crystallise PMS because it specified an unsuitable solvent, ethanol, which inhibited crystallisation. However, Synthon argued that the ordinary skilled man, when not confined to using a particular solvent, would through trial and error succeed in crystallising PMS. In support of this argument, Synthon relied, inter alia, on SB's own specification which described the process of crystallisation as conventional and possible with a number of solvents in a number of different ways. Once more, Jacob J agreed. He found that the ordinary skilled man on reading Synthon's application would be able to overcome any problems presented by the unsuitable solvent and crystallise PMS in a reasonable time. These crystals would inevitably be the same as those described in SB's patent. He concluded that Synthon's application did contain an enabling disclosure. SB's patent was therefore invalid for anticipation and should be revoked. SB appealed.

6.41 The Court of Appeal reversed the High Court decision. Synthon then appealed to the House of Lords, which in turn found for the appellant. Lord Bingham found that Aldous LJ in the Court of Appeal had wrongly 'intermingled' disclosure and enablement. For example, referring to claim 1 of Synthon's application, Aldous LJ had noted that the ordinary skilled man would not expect to produce PMS in crystalline form by carrying out its teaching, and therefore the application did not anticipate the SB patent. However, Aldous LJ also noted, that since there was only one form of crystalline PMS, the addressee would inevitably produce it in any event. Lord Bingham found that Aldous LJ's reasoning confused disclosure and enablement because it appeared to posit that the disclosure must enable the invention. In fact, the two are distinct. Thus, Lord Bingham held that Synthon's application did disclose the invention. Turning to enablement, Aldous LJ had held that Synthon's application 'did not contain clear and unmistakable directions to make the claimed form of PMS', and that an ordinary skilled man would not have been able to produce PMS as claimed without making 'obvious modifications'. It was true, as Lord Bingham acknowledged, that the Synthon application appeared to claim a different form of PMS because of the different IR readings, for example, but this was a matter of disclosure and not enablement. Conversely, Aldous LJ's reference to 'obvious modifications' was a matter for enablement and not disclosure. In the event, Lord Bingham saw no reason to disturb Jacob J's finding of fact in relation to enablement, which was that an ordinary skilled man would have been able to reproduce the invention. The SB patent was invalid (Sharples and Curley, 'Experimental Novelty: *Synthon v Smith Kline Beecham*' [2006] *European Intellectual Property Review* 308).

Anticipation by prior use

6.42 In *Synthon*, the SB patent was anticipated by a prior patent application. A product which embodies an invention may already be in public use. Does this constitute an enabling disclosure for the purposes of anticipation? Since the passage of the PA 1977, the answer has turned upon whether it is possible, by means of analysis (such as 'reverse engineering'), to uncover the invention embodied in that product. If the product can be analysed or examined to disclose the later claimed invention and to enable its performance, prior use may invalidate a patent (*Merrell Dow Pharmaceuticals Inc v Norton & Co Ltd* (1996)). In *Merrell Dow*, the claimant held a patent for a method of making the drug terfenadine, an anti-histamine. It then patented a second compound, metabolite, which was found to be produced in the human body when the terfenadine was taken. The second patent was revoked. The House of Lords found that there was no invalidity for prior use, since the patients were ingesting the terfenadine, not the metabolite. Nonetheless, the second patent was still invalid, in that the first patent already disclosed the later invention and provided a method for performing it (that is by the ingestion of terfenadine), even if it was not known about at the time. Further, it is enough for a finding of anticipation that a product, which has been sold prior to patenting, can be analysed to establish its composition by any purchaser, without establishing that it had been done (*WL Gore v Kimal Scientific Products Ltd* (1988)).

Made available to the public

6.43 'Made available to the public' has been understood to have the same meaning as 'published' in the Patents Act 1949 (*PLG Research Ltd v Ardon International Ltd* (1993)). However, unlike under the PA 1949, information disclosed secretly is not a disclosure for the purposes of the PA 1977 since it is not made available to the public. To constitute prior art, the information given must have been communicated to any member of the public 'who was free in law and equity to use it as he pleased' (*Humpherson v Syer* (1887), per Bowen LJ). According to Purchas LJ in *Genentech's Patent* (1989) the public is the 'community of research workers skilled in the art in general'. An invention is not made available to the public if the disclosure is by someone under a duty of confidentiality, for instance, by a researcher to a fellow employee while both are under a duty of confidentiality to their employer. Indeed, the PA 1977 makes specific provision to protect the novelty of an invention in certain situations when disclosure has been obtained unlawfully or in breach of confidence (s 2(4)). So, in *Pall Corpn v Commercial Hydraulics* (1990), sending out examples of filter cartridges under confidence to recipients who knew that they were experimental and secret was not making available to the public. Nor is it made available to the public if it is merely known to one or two individual research workers pursuing their own experiments in private (*Genentech*, per Purchas LJ). In *Bristol-Myers Squibb (BMS) Co v Baker Norton Pharmaceuticals Inc* (1999), the invention was made available to the public through a lecture by the Director of Research and Development of BMS to an audience of 500 at a 'major symposium' in Amsterdam before the priority date of the patent. The patent concerned a drug, Taxol. The drug was used to combat cancer, but was in short supply and, if taken over an extended period of 24 hours, often caused serious side-effects in patients. Through research, BMS 'discovered' that, taken for a three-hour period with different dosages, the drug might still be effective while reducing the incidence of neutropenia, one of its side-effects. This discovery constituted the subject matter of the patent. BMS sued Baker Norton for patent infringement. In response, Baker Norton argued that the patent was invalid, inter alia, because the lecture had made the invention available to the public. The High Court held the patent invalid, BMS appealed and the Court of Appeal came to a similar conclusion. Aldous LJ said that anyone listening to the lecture would realise that Taxol was suitable for trying to treat cancer using a three-hour 'infusion'. It was true that in the lecture the issue of reduced neutropenia was not mentioned. However, the courts agreed that reduced neutropenia was an inevitable result of the three-hour dose, and that the public could, using the information from the lecture, carry out the three-hour infusion without the need for any information from the patent, thus inevitably finding that a reduced amount of neutropenia had occurred. It followed that the lecture contained clear and unmistakable directions to carry out such a three-hour infusion and the result would inevitably be that which was claimed. The patent was invalid for lack of novelty (see also the EPO decision *American Cyanamid/Melamine derivatives* (1999) with which this decision is consistent).

Available through use

6.44 An invention may be made available to the public through a published document or even a lecture. Use of an invention has also been held to fulfil the requirements of disclosure to the public. An invention relating to the heads of ballpoint pens was held to have been anticipated by the circulation of a 'few' ballpoint pens embodying this invention (*Fomento Industrial SA v Mentmore Manufacturing Co Ltd* (1956); see also *Humpherson v Syer* (1887)). In another case, use was public and therefore anticipatory because a boy had used a sailboard (embodying the claimed invention) in a public park (*Windsurfing International Inc v Tabur Marine Ltd* (1985)).

The medical exception (s 2(6))

6.45 A substance or composition which already forms part of the state of the art may still be novel if the claimed invention is for its first use in a method of human or animal medical treatment. The question of whether second medical uses are patentable is looked at below, under industrial applicability (see para **6.63**).

Patentable inventions 3: the inventive step (PA 1977, s 3)

6.46 In order to decide whether an invention is a patentable invention, it must be novel. If the invention is novel, next it is necessary to consider whether it required any inventive step. An invention shall be taken to involve an inventive step, if the invention is not obvious to a person skilled in the art, having regard to any matter which forms part of the state of the art (at the priority date of the invention) (s 3)–what constitutes the state of the art is defined in s 2(2) (see para **6.34**). Just as a claim which lacks novelty is said to be anticipated, so a claim which lacks an inventive step is said to be obvious. It has been suggested that, while it is comparatively easy to decide whether a claim falls strictly within the wording of an earlier disclosure and so has been anticipated, the question of whether the same invention is obvious because of its proximity to the existing field of knowledge is a more difficult one because of the elusive nature of the inventive step. Indeed, the inventive step may represent 'a very small advance' (*Killick v Pye* (1958), per Omerod J).

The test for obviousness

6.47 The test for obviousness most likely to be followed by the courts was set out by Oliver LJ in *Windsurfing International Inc v Tabur Marine Ltd* (1985). It is a four-stage test, later restated in a slightly different order in *Pozzoli SpA v BDMO SA* (2007). As restated in *Pozzoli*, the steps are:

- (a) identify the notional 'person skilled in the art', and
  (b) identify the relevant common general knowledge of the person;

- identify the inventive concept of the claim in question or if that cannot readily be done, construe it;

- identify what, if any, differences exist between the matter cited as forming part of the 'state of the art' and the inventive concept of the claim or the claim as construed;

- viewed without any knowledge of the alleged invention as claimed, do those differences constitute steps which would have been obvious to the person skilled in the art or do they require any degree of invention?

The person skilled in the art

6.48 The person skilled in the art is relevant to a finding both of obviousness and anticipation (see paras **6.47** and **6.35**). He is assumed to be the notional addressee of the patent. Descriptions of him abound in patent law. According to Buckley LJ in *Valensi v British Radio Corporation* (1972), as cited with approval by Lord Bingham in *Synthon*,

> he is not a person of exceptional skill and knowledge, that is he is not expected to exercise any invention nor any prolonged research, inquiry or experiment. He must, however, be prepared to display a reasonable degree of skill and common knowledge of the art in making trials and to correct obvious errors in the specification if a means of correcting them can readily be found.

He is neither a 'mechanical genius', nor is he a 'mechanical idiot' (*Gillette Safety Razor Co v Anglo-American Trading Co Ltd* (1913), per Lord Moulton). There can be more than one addressee. The directions for the invention may need to be carried out through the co-operation of a number of individuals with diverse skills. For instance, where the field of the patent is one of advanced technology, such as genetic engineering, the notional addressee may not be a single person but a team whose combined knowledge would allow them to carry out the instructions contained in the patent (*Genentech's Patent* (1989), per Mustill LJ).

6.49   In *Richardson-Vick's Patent* (1997), the proprietor had obtained a patent for a new cough mixture which mixed a well-known NSAID, ibuprofen, with three well-known decongestants. This combination had no synergistic effect, but was still more effective than previous combinations of other NSAIDs and decongestants. The proprietor accepted that it would have been obvious to the notional skilled man to consider this combination, but he would have rejected it because it would not have gained drug regulatory approval. The proprietor claimed that the notional skilled man in the case of a pharmaceutical company would have been a team which included an expert on drug regulatory affairs and he would have advised that the combination was not obvious to try because it would not have got approval. The Court of Appeal was asked whether the skilled addressee comprised a team which included a person who was an expert on drug regulatory affairs. Aldous LJ held that it did not. A person skilled in the art of obtaining regulatory approval was not a person skilled in the art of producing new combination drugs. To be part of a team, he must be someone who is directly involved in the product described in the patent. Thus, in *Convatec Ltd v Smith & Nephew Healthcare* (2011) which concerned wound dressings, the skilled person was identified as: i) a scientist with experience in developing wound dressings (who may or may not have a PhD); ii) a chemist with knowledge of cellulose chemistry; and iii) a clinician who could provide guidance on the products, if asked. The court suggested that the skilled person might be a single individual with all of this knowledge, or a group of two to three people, each of whom had some of this knowledge. However, it is also the case that an invention may involve an inventive step precisely because it puts together individuals (or teams) with expertise in two different arts, in circumstances where it would not be obvious to do so. The team skilled in the art in these cases would not be assumed to have the combined knowledge taught by the invention (*Schlumberger Holdings Limited v Electromagnetic Geoservices* (2010))

Common general knowledge

6.50   The obviousness of an invention is measured against what will be obvious to a person skilled in the art: the same notional individual who is central to the test for anticipation (see para **6.35**). He is deemed to have the common knowledge in the field to which the invention relates. This has come to be called the 'common general knowledge' of the art. There is some divergence of views as to the relationship between common general knowledge and the state of the art against which the novelty of an invention is measured and which comprises, more or less, all the relevant knowledge which is in the public domain. There is authority to the effect that the notional addressee is 'deemed to have read all the publicly available documents, in whatever jurisdiction or language. But he is also deemed never to think laterally' (Arden LJ in *Dyson Appliances Ltd v Hoover Ltd* (2000); see also *Pfizer Ltd's Patent* (2001)). However, the better view appears to be that common general knowledge should not be confused with the 'state of the art' (*Sabaf SpA v Meneghetti SpA* (2002)). The notional skilled man (both for the purposes of judging anticipation and obviousness) is not assumed to know everything which comprises the state of the art, some of which may, of course, be extremely esoteric. In assessing what is common general knowledge, the court will look at the sources from which the skilled man may have acquired his information. If he works for a large company, he may have ready access to advanced information technology which facilitates the retrieval and circulation of information. In fact, the ordinary skilled man is not assumed to be the employee of a large company or to have such advantages and it is assumed that he may not be aware of such information until it is accepted generally and put into practice (*Beloit Technologies Inc v Valmet Paper Machinery Inc* (1997)). Evidence may be adduced in court as to what is the common general knowledge. But evidence that a fact is known or even well known to a particular witness, who may of course have been chosen precisely because he is an expert in the field, does not establish that it is part of the common general knowledge for the notional skilled man (*Beloit*). Nor will a fact form part of the common general knowledge simply because it is recorded in a document. Earlier patent specifications, for instance, normally do not form part of the common general knowledge (*General Tire and Rubber Co v Firestone Tyre and Rubber Co* (1972)), unlike anticipation, where a previously published patent application will form part of the state of the art (see para **6.35** et seq)). Disclosures in scientific publications may do so. However, it is not necessarily the case. Even if a scientific paper is widely read or widely circulated, it will only become general knowledge if the disclosure contained in it is accepted generally by those engaged in the art to which it relates. In other words, if it becomes part of their common stock of knowledge relating to the art (*British Acoustic Films Ltd v Nettlefold Productions* (1935), per Luxmore J).

Applying Windsurfing/Pozzoli

6.51 In *Windsurfing*, the invention claimed was a sailboard with an unstayed spar connected through a universal joint and a sail attached along one edge to the spar and held taut between a pair of curved booms mounted on the spar at one end and jointed together at the other (what is known as a Bermuda rig with a wishbone spar). The advantage of this combination was that the free sail could be used to steer and could also be easily jettisoned in case of trouble. The defendants claimed that the invention was obvious in view of prior use by C and because of the existence of a prior publication by D. C had, as a 12-year-old boy, built a sailboard which he had used in public over two summers. This had a sail held between straight booms, but they were flexible enough to assume a curved shape on use. D had written an article, 'Sailboarding: Exciting New Water Sport', describing the same basic concept as the patent, but the sailboard was fitted with a square-rigged sail. The question was whether the claimant's patent involved an inventive step beyond the sail arrangements employed by C and described by D. The Court of Appeal held that the inventive concept was the free sail. Anyone familiar with sailing would have known, as part of his common general knowledge, the difference between square sails and Bermuda rigs and the disadvantages as regards manoeuvrability presented by the former, and would also have been familiar with twin booms, curved in shape, known as 'wishbone booms'. The skilled man must be assumed to appreciate and understand the free sail concept taught by D and to consider, in the light of his knowledge and experience, whether and how it would work. He would know the disadvantages from which the kite rig, suggested by D, would suffer and therefore be led to the claimant's solution. Similarly, the step from the replacement of the primitive straight boom of C's craft to the wishbone boom of the patent would be an obvious one to take for the notional skilled man with common general knowledge. The claimant's patent was, therefore, invalid for obviousness.

An objective approach

6.52 The *Windsurfing/Pozzoli* test is an objective one. It asks not what is in the mind of the actual inventor, but whether the step would be obvious to the notional person skilled in the art having regard to any matter which forms part of the state of the art. According to Jacob LJ in *Actavis UK Ltd v Novartis AG* (2010), the first three questions 'orientate' the court, so that it may then ask the fourth statutory question. In answering the fourth question, it is open to the court to consider a number of subsidiary questions which have been formulated in the case law. In other words, in answering the fourth question, it is possible to take a multifactorial approach (see also *Generics (UK) Ltd v Daiichi Pharmaceutical Co Ltd* (2008)). The most important of these factors are considered below.

Was the inventive step obvious to try?

6.53 This is the most widely canvassed test for answering the fourth *Windsurfing/Pozzoli* question. The leading case where the inventive step was held obvious to try is *Johns-Manville's Patent* (1967). In this case, the claimed invention was the addition of polyacrylamide, a flocculating agent, during the process of filtration of asbestos cement slurry, in the manufacture of shaped asbestos cement articles. The idea that flocculating agents might aid filtration was well known, but until the invention of polyacrylamide none had been effective. A research worker for the alleged infringer had himself tried using polyacrylamide as a flocculating agent, but had abandoned his experiments when he had found the result was the formation of a thicker skin for asbestos cement, which had its own disadvantages. Later on, returning to the problem, he discovered that a simple technical adjustment to the equipment would overcome this problem. The Court of Appeal held that the invention would have been obvious to the 'notional' man skilled in the art, even though, for the research worker in this case, his 'glimpse of the obvious was spasmodic'. The appellants could not rely on the research worker's failure to complete the initial experiment as evidence of an inventive step, since they had not included the necessary technical adjustment in their original claim. Conversely, even if it had been included, since the adjustment was obvious once the thicker skin resulted, the claim would have been invalid for obviousness. More recently, in *Merck Sharp & Dohme Corp v Teva UK Ltd* (2011), the Court of Appeal noted that the test for obviousness would not be undermined simply because it might take the notional skilled man considerable time to complete the routine tests which would lead to the invention.

6.54 An opposite result to *Johns-Manville* was reached in *Saint-Gobain PAM SA v Fusion Provida Ltd; Electrosteel Castings Ltd* (2005), in which the obvious to try test was further clarified. The claimant, Saint-Gobain manufactured underground pipes. The defendants were alleged to have infringed the claimant's European patent, which had a priority date of February 1993, and the defendants in turn claimed that the patent was obvious having regard to a disclosure in a paper (called Johnsson), published in December 1992. The relevant claim in the patent consisted of using a Zn/Al alloy in place of Zn as an anti-corrosive coating for buried pipe. Johnsson was entitled, 'Corrosion resistant coating of Al, Zn and their alloys. Results of 11 years' exposure to soil.' In the High Court, the patent was held to be valid and infringed. The defendants appealed arguing that, on the basis of Johnsson, the claimed invention would be 'obvious to try'. In the Court of Appeal, Jacob LJ employed the *Windsurfing* test for obviousness. The inventive concept was held to be black pipe but made with Al/Zn alloy instead of Zn. The person skilled in the art was identified as an 'unimaginative person (or team) in the research department of a company in the underground pipe manufacturing trade, who would have considerable knowledge of the problems of corrosion suffered by buried pipework'. It would be assumed that part of his background knowledge would be, inter alia, that buried pipe should be resistant to corrosion over long periods; that 'black pipe' had been in use for many years as a successful corrosion resistant iron piping for buried use and was made from three layers, one of which was Zn; that mixtures of Zn and Al (as an alloy) were well-known for general use in corrosion protection and had been used for years above ground but not for buried pipes. But he would not know whether such an alloy would also form a protective corrosion skin or would do so as well as Zn alone. The difference between the prior art and the alleged invention was the use of Al/Zn instead of Zn alone. The case then turned upon the fourth *Windsurfing* question: whether the use of Al/Zn for buried pipe would have been an obvious step. In the High Court, the step was held to be non-obvious, despite the fact that this was a case of a simple substitution of one known protective layer for another, as suggested by Johnsson. The court's finding was based on 'historical considerations', ie that despite the common general knowledge, no one hitherto had tried to make this simple substitution. One basis of the claimant's appeal was that it was the Johnsson paper which now made the invention obvious to try, not the earlier knowledge. In the Court of Appeal, Jacob LJ held that Johnsson did not, in fact, affect the earlier common general knowledge because although it suggested that galvanic corrosion might be slowed by using Zn/Al it did not make it clear whether this would be the case for buried pipes, which were generally thought to be protected by white rust. Furthermore, a 'buried pipe man' (that is a person skilled in the art) would want a minimum of 50 years' life, and as a result the paper would not self-evidently be part of his common general knowledge. As a result, Johnsson did not make the use of the Zn/Al alloy obvious to try. In making his judgment, Jacob LJ distinguished the situation in *Johns-Manville*. In that case, the court had decided that the invention was obvious to try because 'the person vested in the art would assess the likelihood of success as sufficient to warrant actual trial'. In the present case, the idea of using Zn/Al was not obvious because it was not something that was self-evident to the unimaginative man skilled in the art. Jacob LJ concluded:

> *Mere possible inclusion of something within a research programme on the basis of which you will find out more and something might turn up is not enough. If it were otherwise there would be few inventions that were patentable. The only research which would be worthwhile (because of the prospect of protection) would be into areas totally devoid of prospect. The 'obvious to try test' really only works where it is more-or-less self-evident that what is being tested ought to work.*

In *Conor Medsystems Incorporated v Angiotech Pharmaceuticals Inc* (2008), the House of Lords endorsed Jacob LJ's approach to the obvious to try test, holding that 'the notion of something being obvious to try was useful only in a case in which there was a fair expectation of success'.

The 'worthwhile to try' test in **Biogen**

6.55 An application of the 'worthwhile to try' test occurred in *Biogen Inc v Medeva plc* (1997). The claimant's claim was for a product, a recombinant DNA molecule made by rDNA techniques and expressed to produce a polypeptide displaying HBV antigen specificity in certain circumstances. The priority date for the invention was 1979. The manner in which the antigen was produced was by expressing random pieces of DNA, in a hit-and-miss way, rather than by identifying the antigen as part of a complete sequence of HBV DNA, which would first have to be described. In fact, it was described by another scientist in 1979 before Biogen's priority date and Medeva used the sequence, after the priority date, to produce the antigen. The question before the House of Lords was whether Biogen's hit-and-miss approach involved an inventive step. Biogen argued that the inventive step consisted in doing something a skilled person might not have thought worth doing. The Court of Appeal, following the decision in *Genentech's Patent* (1989), had earlier held that there was no inventive step. There had merely been a business decision to pursue an identified goal by known means. The court offered the analogy of putting a bet on a horse, hoping it would come in first. This was not an inventive step. Meanwhile in Europe, where simultaneous opposition hearings were proceeding, the Technical Board of Appeal of the EPO found there was an inventive step based, in particular, on the fact that many others were also seeking to reach the same invention. The House of Lords took a third view. It said that anything inventive done for the first time was the result of adding a new idea to the existing stock of knowledge. If it was the idea of using established techniques to do something which no one had previously thought of doing, the inventive idea would be doing the new thing. If it was finding a way of doing something which people had wanted to do but could not think how, the inventive idea would be the way of achieving the goal. If many people might have had a general idea of how they might achieve a goal but did not know how to solve a particular problem which stood in their way, and someone devised a way of solving the problem, the inventive step would be that solution, but not the goal itself or the general method of achieving it. The House of Lords declined to overturn the trial judge's decision that there had been an inventive step. It found that the trial judge had made a reasonable evaluation on the facts. If the inventive step in this case was looked at as the idea of *trying* (author's emphasis) to express unsequenced eukaryotic DNA in a prokaryotic host, then it was reasonable for the judge to conclude this was not obvious (see also *Actavis v Novartis* (2010)).

Self-evident extension of prior art

6.56 This would be obvious. In *Hallen Co v Brabantia UK Ltd* (1991), the claimants had a patent for a 'self-pulling corkscrew' coated with a non-stick polymer, 'PTFE', which they claimed not only eased the penetration of the corkscrew but also, less predictably, helped with the removal of the cork. The same polymer had already been used with 'twin-lever' corkscrews to facilitate penetration. The Court of Appeal found that it was an obvious extension of the prior art to coat the self-pulling corkscrew or any other type of corkscrew with polymer once it had been shown to be useful on one type of corkscrew. Could the patent be saved by the surprising effect the polymer had on removal? The court accepted that it was not obvious that the polymer would have this additional effect. Although this was 'a golden bonus', it held that it was common ground that an added benefit, however great, will not found a valid patent if the claimed innovation is obvious for another purpose. An opposite result was reached in the earlier EPO case of *Bayer AG (Baatz's) Application* (1981). The application concerned a carbonless copying paper. On the paper's surface was a dye contained in micro-capsules. An earlier published German specification revealed that the walls of the capsules could be made of a particular class of chemicals, polyureas. The claimed invention was said to lie in the selection of diisocyanates, a sub-group of this class. The Examining Division at the EPO said that the selection was obvious. On appeal, the applicant produced comparative tests showing an advantage of the selection to be that the paper did not lose its copying capacity so readily. The application was held to involve an inventive step.

A successful step

6.57 The courts have used evidence of commercial success as an indication that there may be an inventive step. For instance, commercial success might suggest there has been a long-standing need for the successful product that others have tried but failed to supply. But commercial success is not to be used as primary evidence that there is an inventive step (*Mölnlycke AB v Procter & Gamble Co Ltd* (1992)). Commercial success may be due to other factors such as the way the product is marketed. According to Jacob LJ in *Angiotech Pharmaceuticals v Conor Medsystems Inc* (2007), 'the usefulness of commercial success as a tool in deciding a question of obviousness generally depends upon being able to isolate what it is that has contributed to success–so it normally has application only to simple inventions'. An example is the case of *Haberman v Jackel International Ltd* (1999), where the inventive concept was the use of a simple slit valve to prevent leakage from a training cup for babies. Laddie J found that the invention had been cheap, simple and effective, and also a commercial success. The inventive step had been one that many people in the trade would have taken during the past decade if they had come up with it. It was not obvious. In *Dyson Appliances Ltd v Hoover Ltd* (2001), the Court of Appeal accepted that the failure by the vacuum cleaner industry to consider a technical development, in part for commercial reasons, might have some indirect relevance to the issue of obviousness. In this case, the claimant's invention turned upon the use of cyclone units to purify dirt-laden air from a vacuum cleaner, replacing the usual method of collecting the dirt in bags. The vacuum cleaner industry, however, was, according to Sedley LJ, 'functionally deaf and blind to any technology which did not involve a replaceable bag. The fact that the handicap was entirely economically determined made it if anything more entrenched.' He concluded

> that it was entirely in accordance with what we know of innovation that this commercial mindset will have played a part in setting the notional skilled addressee's mental horizon, making a true inventor of the individual who was able to lift his eyes above the horizon and see a bag-free machine.

The fact that a particular line of research is adopted for commercial, rather than purely scientific, reasons does not mean that there is no inventive step. As Lord Hoffmann realistically observed in *Biogen Inc v Medeva plc* (1997), 'Most patents were the result of research programmes undertaken on the basis of hard-headed cost-benefit analysis.'

Hindsight

6.58 Sometimes an invention seems obvious in hindsight. It may be easy to retrace the steps leading from the invention to the prior art, and to show that, since each step was a simple one, there was no inventive step. This is particularly the case where the problem solved is obvious or the technology involved is not particularly complex. Often the court will be tempted to use hindsight when answering the fourth *Windsurfing* question as to whether the step from the prior art to the invention was obvious. In this case, the court may find the step obvious because the destination, that is, the invention, is already known. However, such ex post facto reasoning should be avoided (*Panduit Corpn v Band-It Co Ltd* (2002)). It is common ground that obviousness in hindsight will not lead to a finding of invalidity (*Beloit Technologies Inc v Valmet Paper Machinery Inc* (1997); *Fichera v Flogates Ltd* (1984)).

The EPO problem/solution approach (PSA) to obviousness

6.59 The approach to assessing obviousness in the UK courts differs from the problem/solution approach adopted by the EPO. The PSA has three stages:

- determine the 'closest prior art';
- establish the 'objective technical problem' to be solved;
- consider whether or not the claimed invention, starting from the closest prior art and the objective technical problem, would have been obvious to the skilled person.

It has been suggested that the third step here is more or less equivalent to the fourth step in *Windsurfing/Pozzoli*. But it has also been suggested that there may be a number of problems with the PSA, which do not arise with the *Windsurfing/ Pozzoli* test. For example, the 'objective technical problem' may not be the same problem which the patentee has set out to solve. It may be 'reformulated' by the court to match the claimed solution. However, in so doing the court may be guilty of hindsight or, indeed, of assuming there has been an inventive solution to a problem, although the problem itself might be illusory (for an example, see *Actavis v Novartis* (2010), para **6.60** below). Alternatively, the inventive step might actually lie in identifying the problem to be solved, although once identified the solution itself might be obvious, as was the case in *Haberman v Jackel International* (see para **6.57**). Employing the PSA test in *Haberman*, there would almost certainly be a finding of obviousness, but not necessarily employing the *Windsurfing/Pozzoli* test. However, there may also be times when the PSA is a useful approach to take. Such was the case in *Actavis v Novartis*.

The PSA applied

6.60 In *Actavis v Novartis*, the Court of Appeal applied both the PSA and the *Windsurfing/Pozzoli* tests for obviousness in reaching the conclusion that the invention at issue was an obvious one. A patent was granted to the defendant, Novartis, in 1996, for a sustained release formulation of the drug 'fluvastatin'. In 1996 both fluvastatin and the benefits of sustained-release formulations were well known. However, fluvastatin is highly water-soluble and this might have been expected to pose a problem for creating a sustained, slow-release formulation. It was this problem that the patentee sought to overcome. There were three accepted methods for creating slow-release formulations. In the event, the patentee 'discovered' that it was possible to make a slow-release fluvastatin, despite its solubility, using any of these three accepted methods. The claimant sought to have the patent revoked for, inter alia, obviousness. Among the arguments put by the defendant was that even if the idea of a slow-release formulation of fluvastatin would occur to the person skilled in the art and he realised it *could* be done it would only be obvious if he *would* implement the idea. Jacob LJ disagreed, noting that there may be various reasons why a person skilled in the art does not implement an obvious idea, for example commercial considerations, but this did not make it any the less obvious. Jacob LJ went on to hold that once the obstacle put forward to making a sustained formulation of fluvastatin was shown to be illusory then the formulation was indeed obvious. Applying *Pozzoli*, 'the only difference between the prior art and the claim is the idea of making a sustained release formulation. For that there was a technical motivation and no difficulty, real or apparent.' Jacob LJ then applied the PSA and reached the same conclusion. The objective problem was to produce a sustained-release fluvastatin. And the solution was obvious since any of the standard methods for reaching such a formulation would clearly work. He refused to reformulate the problem, as suggested by the defendant, as one of looking for better medical effects, since the patentee had not initially seen this to be the problem. What had been sought had simply been a sustained-release formulation of fluvastatin which would work. The fact that the skilled person (or in this case, a team) might not think it worthwhile to pursue this obvious course did not make it any less obvious.

The new use of old things

6.61 This is another area where English case law appears to diverge from the view taken by the EPO. English authorities hold that the new use of a known thing, where there is no additional ingenuity, is not a patentable invention. Conversely, an invention involving the new use of a known thing is patentable, if the new use overcomes practical difficulties which the patentee was the first to identify (*Parks-Cramer Co v Thornton & Sons Ltd* (1966); *Gadd and Mason v Manchester Corpn* (1892)). By contrast, in the EPO case concerning a new use of an old thing, *BASF/Triazole derivatives* (1989), the claim was for compounds for controlling fungi and the patent application contained teaching as to how to carry this out so as to achieve the desired effect. It was held by the Enlarged Board of Appeal (EBA):

> *With respect to a claim to a new use of a known compound, such new use may reflect a newly discovered technical effect described in the patent. The attaining of such a technical effect should then be considered as a functional technical feature of the claim (for example, the achievement in a particular context of that technical effect). If that technical feature has not been previously made available to the public by any of the means as set out in the EPC Act 54(2), then the claimed invention is novel, even though such technical effect may have inherently taken place in the course of carrying out what has previously been made available to the public.*

The later EPO case, *MOBIL/Friction-reducing additive* (1990) confirmed that it was possible to patent an invention which involved the new use of a known thing. The claim was for the use of a friction-reducing additive in a lubricating oil. This same additive was already known to be rust-reducing. No new means were employed to produce the lubricating effect. The question was whether the claim lacked novelty. The EBA, following *BASF/Triazole derivatives* (1989), found that, if the friction-reducing effect had not previously been made available to the public, the claimed invention was novel, even though it may inherently have taken place in the course of carrying out the rust-reducing effect (see also 'Second medical use' at para 6.66). The EBA acknowledged that this finding might contradict national patent law. However, neither the House of Lords in *Merrell Dow Pharmaceuticals Inc v Norton & Co Ltd* (1996) nor the Court of Appeal in *Bristol-Myers Squibb Co v Baker Norton Pharmaceuticals Inc* (1999) concluded that the *MOBIL* decision had been wrongly decided. By contrast, it has been suggested that the EPO has been taking a narrower approach to what may be patented as a new use (see, for example, *ROBERTET/Deodorant compositions* (1999)).

Collocations

6.62 If the invention simply combines two integers so that each performs its normal function, it is not patentable. However, if the two integers work together to produce a new or improved result then the invention may be patentable (*British Celanese Ltd v Courtaulds Ltd* (1935), per Lord Tomlin). This has sometimes been called 'the law of collocation' (*Sabaf SpA v Meneghitti SpA* (2004) HL, per Lord Nicholls). Similarly, the EPO Guidelines for Substantive Examination suggest that an invention must be considered as a whole. Thus, where the invention consists of a combination of features, which taken by themselves may be obvious, but which produce a synergistic effect greater than the sum of their individual technical effects, it may be patentable. Conversely, where the invention is merely 'an aggregation or juxtaposition of features' and not a true combination, it is enough to show that the individual features are obvious for the invention to fail for obviousness. In *Merrell Dow Pharmaceuticals Inc v Norton & Co Ltd* (1996), the combination of ibuprofen with a decongestant was not an inventive step, even though the product was a more effective drug, because each ingredient was performing its usual and known function. More recently, in *Sabaf SpA v Meneghetti SpA* (2004), HL, the claimant's patent related to burners for gas hobs. In particular, the patent addressed the fact that current burners were too tall to be used for hobs, causing problems for the mixing of oxygen and gas. The defendant argued that at the heart of the claimant's patent was a mere collocation of two known concepts, that is, a radial mixing passage and the drawing in of air from above the hob unit, which the claimant had simply combined to produce the desired effect. It was therefore invalid for obviousness. The High Court agreed. The decision was then reversed in the Court of Appeal and the claimant appealed to the House of Lords. The House of Lords upheld the decision of the trial judge. According to Lord Nicholls, while, for the purposes of examination, two or more inventions which are linked so as to form a single inventive concept might be considered as one invention (PA 1977, s 14(6)), equally one should not consider as a whole what are, in fact, two separate inventions. Lord Nicholls found that Laddie J had correctly applied these principles to the facts in finding the claimed invention obvious. The radial mixing passage and the drawing of air did not interact, and taken separately neither involved an inventive step.

Patentable inventions 4: industrial applicability (PA 1977, s 4)

6.63 The third attribute of a patentable invention is industrial applicability. An invention shall be taken to be of industrial application if it can be made or used in any kind of industry, including agriculture (PA 1977, s 4(1); see also arts 2 and 57 of the EPC).

6.64 *Human Genome Sciences Inc (HGS) v Eli Lilly* (2011) presents an interesting example of how s 4(1) might be applied, not least because it relates to the important biotechnology industry and demonstrates some of the particular problems which might arise in the patenting of gene sequences. The patent at issue had been granted to HGS in 2005. Eli Lilly challenged the patent on the grounds that it was obvious, insufficient and lacked industrial applicability. The appeal to the Supreme Court focused on the question of industrial applicability. The patent described the encoding nucleotide, the amino acid sequence and certain antibodies of a novel human protein, Neutrokine-α. HGS claimed the protein was expected to have valuable therapeutic functions based on the fact that Neutrokine-α is a member of the TNF ligand family, and listed a very large number it and its antibodies *might* have (emphasis added). Information contained in the patent, in particular, the polynucleotide sequence encoding, was obtained through research using 'bioinformatics', that is through computing rather than 'wet lab' research. In other words, there was no experimental evidence to support HMG's contentions about the possible therapeutic functions of its invention. In the High Court, Kitchin J had held that the patent contained extravagant and sometimes contradictory claims, and that the skilled person would conclude that the patent did not identify an industrial application, except speculatively. The Court of Appeal subsequently endorsed his judgment and HGS appealed. In the Supreme Court, Lord Neuberger first noted that s 4(1) PA on industrial applicability should be interpreted in line with the EPO's interpretation of art 57 EPC. He then rehearsed the various Technical Board of Appeal's judgments at the EPO which have looked at industrial applicability in relation to biotechnological inventions and in particular at the case involving the same protagonists and the same patent which had been heard before the Board. Significantly, unlike in the UK, the Board had found the patent had industrial applicability and was valid. Lord Neuberger concluded not that the UK courts had misapplied the facts to reach their contrary conclusion, but rather they had failed to follow the principles developed by the EPO. Lord Neuberger then set out these general principles to be applied to biological inventions. First, the patent must disclose a practical application and some profitable use for the claimed substance, so that the ensuing monopoly can be expected to lead to some commercial benefit. Second, the invention's use in industrial practice must be derivable directly from the description, coupled with common general knowledge. Third, a merely speculative use will not suffice. And, fourth, the patent and common general knowledge must enable the skilled person to reproduce or exploit the claimed invention without undue burden. He then set out a number of narrower principles relating particularly to this class of invention including, for example, that the patent, when taken with common general knowledge, must demonstrate a real as opposed to a purely theoretical possibility of exploitation and that the absence of any experimental or wet lab evidence of activity of the claimed protein is not fatal. A plausible or reasonably credible claimed use, or an 'educated guess', can suffice. Based on these criteria, Lord Neuberger held that the invention did not lack industrial applicability

First medical use

6.65 When discussing anticipation, it was noted that the first medical use of a known product was patentable (PA 1977, s 2(6)) (see para **6.32**). If the product is state of the art, the first medical use can be new if that use does not form the state of the art. Following the implementation of the PA 2004, new s 4A(3) will have the same effect, so that such an invention is considered novel where the substance or composition is first used in a method or treatment or diagnosis.

Second medical use

6.66 What if the substance already has a known medical use and a second novel use is uncovered? Unless it is a claim for a method of treatment, it can, in principle, be patented. Section 4A(4), PA 2004, states that patent protection may be obtained for the second or subsequent use of a substance or composition in a method of treatment or diagnosis, by framing the claim as 'substance X for use in treatment of disease Y'. Until 2010, a claim for a second medical use could also be made using the so-called 'Swiss style' claim, which was approved by the EPO in *EISAI/Second medical indication* (1985) and was subsequently confirmed by the UK courts in *John Wyeth & Brother's Application/Schering's Application* (1985). An example of a 'Swiss style' claim was at issue in *Monsanto Co v Merck & Co Inc* (2000) which concerned patents relating to non-steroidal anti-inflammatory drugs (NSAIDs). The 'Swiss style' claim was framed as follows: 'Use of a compound of claim 1 for preparing a medicament for treating inflammation or an inflammation associated disorder', where claim 1 was an earlier patent claim. Crucially, the claim is for the 'preparation' of the substance rather than its new use in a method of treatment. However, a decision by the EBA in *Abbott Respiratory* (2010) held that applicants may no longer use the Swiss-type claim for second medical use inventions. The EBA reasoned that the Swiss-type claim lacked clarity because although it defines a method of manufacturing a medicament, the invention itself does not relate to the method of production but rather to its intended use. A practice notice issued by the UK Intellectual Property Office in 2010 states that it will no longer accept patent applications for a second medical use which are framed as Swiss-type claims.

Sufficiency (Patents Act 1977, s 14)

6.67 A patentable invention must be novel, involve an inventive step, have industrial applicability and not fall into any of the excluded categories. These are external criteria against which the patentability of an invention will be judged. But a patent application may fail or a patent be revoked, not because of any objective shortcomings of the invention which form the subject matter of the patent. Instead, there may be shortcomings in the way the specification is drafted which will defeat the application or lead to the later revocation of a patent. The patent may fail for insufficiency. In effect, whether an invention is a patentable invention turns, not simply upon the nature of the invention, but also upon how it is described. Compare this with registered trade marks, where the subject matter of registration is clear and the question is simply whether the mark meets the external criteria set out by the Trade Marks Act 1994 for registration.

The need for an enabling disclosure (PA 1977, s 14(3))

6.68 The specification for an application must disclose the invention in a manner which is clear enough and complete enough for the invention to be performed by a person skilled in the art (PA 1977, s 14(3)). In other words, the application must contain an enabling disclosure (*Biogen Inc v Medeva plc* (1997); *Asahi Kasei Kogyo Application* (1991)). This is the same enabling disclosure which is necessary to fix a patent's priority date (see para **6.14**) and which was described by Lord Bingham, in *Synthon*, in relation to anticipation (see para **6.36**). The courts have made it clear that the need for an enabling disclosure is not simply a formal requirement (such as the need to include an abstract in the application), but a substantive one which goes to the heart of the patent regime (*Biogen*). The limited monopoly granted by a patent can be justified only if, when it expires, the specification provides sufficient information to enable the invention to be exploited more generally.

6.69 The importance of the enabling disclosure is also crucial because, for a patent to be valid, the claim or claims must be supported by the description (s 14(5)(c)). A description of an invention will not 'support' the claims for the purpose of s 14(5) (c) unless it contains sufficient material to enable the specification to constitute the enabling disclosure required to satisfy s 14(3) (*Asahi Kasei Kogyo Application* (1991) applied in *Biogen Inc v Medeva plc* (1997)). This had been the approach of the TBA at the EPO in *Genentech 1/Polypeptide Expression* (1989), which was quoted with approval by Lord Hoffmann in *Biogen*. The TBA said:

> Furthermore, Article 84 EPC also requires that the claims must be supported by
> the description, in other words, it is the definition of the invention in the claims
> that needs support. In the Board's judgment, this requirement reflects the gen-
> eral legal principle that the extent of the patent monopoly, as defined by the
> claims, should correspond to the technical contribution to the art in order to be
> justified.

It is for this reason that failure to satisfy s 14(5)(c) not only leads to a patent
application being rejected for insufficiency, but also constitutes later grounds for
revocation under s 72(1)(c) (*Biogen*).

Assessing sufficiency

6.70 Essentially, a man skilled in the art must be able to perform the claimed invention across the full width of the claims and not just a single embodiment (*Biogen
Inc v Medeva plc* (1997)). In most respects and on most occasions, the person
skilled in the art is the same individual who appears in the tests for anticipation
and obviousness. He is prepared 'to display a reasonable degree of skill and a
common knowledge of the art in making trials or to correct obvious errors in
the specification if a means of correcting them can be readily found'. If correc-
tion of such errors involves prolonged study or an inventive step, then there is
insufficiency (*Valensi v British Radio Corpn Ltd* (1972); *Chiron Corpn v Murex
Diagnostics Ltd* (1996)). Furthermore, in attempting to perform the invention, the
skilled person is 'deemed to be seeking success rather than failure' (*Kirin-Amgen
Inc v Transkaryotic Therapies Inc* (2002), per Aldous LJ). If a team is involved,
then it should be credited with sufficient time and the best available equipment
to carry out the work (*Genentech's Patent* (1989)). The performance required is
not the production of a commercial product, but rather of a workable prototype
(*Chiron*, per Morritt LJ). However, there is no enabling disclosure if the instructions lead a second notional addressee to arrive at different results to the first,
some of which are within and some of which are outside the claimed invention
(*Chiron*; *Synthon*). Subsequently, in *Schlumberger v Electromagnetic Geoservices*
(2010), Jacob LJ suggested that the person skilled in the art may not always be
the same for the purposes of inventiveness and sufficiency. As we have seen, the
inventive step in a patent may lie in putting together a team with different sorts
of expertise (see para **6.48**). The inventive step, in such a case, would not be obvious to a team skilled in the art, since it would be assumed that without the benefit of hindsight, the team would not have been put together and their expertise
combined in the first place. By contrast, in the case of sufficiency, the person
(or indeed the team) skilled in the art would have the patent to tell them how to
perform the invention and what the claimed monopoly is. In other words, they

would have the benefit of hindsight. The Supreme Court has now been asked to consider the decision in *Schlumberger*.

The claim/specification balance

6.71 The breadth of the claim must not exceed the technical contribution to the art embodied in the invention (*Exxon/Fuel oils* (1994) EPO). In *Biogen Inc v Medeva plc* (1997), Lord Hoffmann, following the TBA's decision in *Genentech 1/ Polypeptide Expression* (1989), said that:

> ... the specification must enable the invention to be performed to the full extent of the monopoly claimed. If the invention discloses a principle capable of general application, the claims may be in correspondingly general terms. The patentee need not show that he has proved its application in every individual instance. On the other hand, if the claims include a number of discrete methods or products the patentee must enable the invention to be performed in respect of each of them.

The technical contribution of the claim in *Biogen* was to show that recombinant techniques could be used to make HBV antigens in a prokaryotic host cell. But this did not, according to Lord Hoffmann, justify a claim to a monopoly of any recombinant method of making the antigens. The claim was too broad. It did not establish any new principle that *must* (author's emphasis) be followed to achieve the same results. Other means could be used to reach the same result, which owed nothing to the invention. The patent was invalid for insufficiency (*Biogen*).

Insufficiency post-*Biogen*

6.72 Previous to *Biogen*, it had been assumed that a patent contained an enabling disclosure if a single embodiment of the invention could be performed. However, since *Biogen*, the position is that the specification must allow the invention to be performed across the full width of its claims. This was confirmed by the House of Lords in *Kirin-Amgen Inc v Hoechst Marion Roussel Ltd (TKT)* (2005) (see para **6.80** et seq). However, the decision by the House of Lords in *Generics (UK) Ltd v H Lundbeck A/S* (2009) suggests that the application of *Biogen*-insufficiency is limited to product-by-process claims and not to product claims, more generally. In *Generics v Lundbeck*, the product in question was the (+) enantiomer of citalopram. Citalopram is an organic compound which acts as an anti-depressant and is a racemate made up of negative and positive molecules. Until the patent in suit, it was not known how to separate these and hence what were their respective contributions to the anti-depressant quality of citalopram. The patentee,

Lundbeck, devised a novel means of separating them and, as a result, discovered that it was the (+) enantiomer which had the antidepressant effect while the (-) enantiomer had an inhibiting effect. This discovery allowed the patentee to market a much more effective anti-depressant made up of the former. Claim 1 of the patent was a product claim for the enantiomer, claim 3 was for a pharmaceutical compound of the enantiomer and claim 6 was for a method of preparing the compound. In the High Court, claims 1 and 3 were held to be invalid for insufficiency because although the claim was for the enantiomer made by any method, the specification disclosed only two ways of making it. The finding of insufficiency was overturned by the Court of Appeal, and the House of Lords upheld this decision. In particular it was noted, by Lord Neuberger, that while *Biogen* concerned a product-by-process claim (or indeed 'a product identified in part by how it was made and in part by what it did–almost a process-by-product-by-process claim'), the patent in question here was for a product claim. Furthermore, it was for a single product whereas in *Biogen* the claim covered a class of products. In other words, the technical contribution here was the product itself and the specification supported the claim because it enabled the product to be made. The Court acknowledged that by finding one method of making a product sufficient, the patentee could obtain a monopoly on that product, but this was true of all product claims. The decision in *Generics v Lundbeck* has been criticised for allowing a patentee to acquire a broad monopoly over a useful product, where the real inventiveness might reside solely in how it was produced (Leung, 'Generics (UK) Ltd v H Lundeck A/S: In search of optimal patent protection: Biogen insufficiency and the chequered history of product claims' [2010] *European Intellectual Property Review* 165.)

Infringement

6.73 The Patents Act 1977 sets out those acts which will infringe a patent if they are done without the patentee's consent (s 60(1)). These will be considered below. However, an act will only be infringing if it falls within the scope of the patent's claims. To determine whether an act is an infringing act, the court must first determine the extent of the monopoly claimed by the patent. How does the court construe the claim for the purposes of finding infringement?

The 'fence post' approach

6.74 This was the traditional approach to construction taken by the UK courts. The 'fence post' approach takes the literal wording of the claim as marking off the boundaries of the monopoly. In the famous words of Lord Russell: 'What is not claimed is disclaimed' (*EMI v Lissen* (1938)). Alongside this literal approach, the courts developed the somewhat less narrow 'pith and marrow doctrine', which ignored immaterial deviations by the alleged infringer from the exact wording of the claim. For example, if the alleged infringer substituted one non-essential 'integer' of a claim with a 'mechanical equivalent', that is, one that made no essential difference, there would still be infringement if all the essential 'integers' were reproduced. In *Rodi and Wienenberger AG v Henry Showell Ltd* (1968), which concerned an expandable watch strap, the 'integer' substituted by the alleged infringer was a c-shaped bow for a u-shaped bow in the strap's links. The court held the u-shape to be an essential feature of the invention and there was no infringement.

The purposive approach

6.75 The break with the strict 'fence post' approach came with the decision by Lord Diplock in *Catnic Ltd v Hill & Smith Ltd* (1980). In *Catnic*, Lord Diplock took what has come to be known as a 'purposive' approach when construing the claim in question. Using this approach, the court is less concerned with the literal meaning of the claim, and more with the intention behind its wording (although intention should be judged objectively). Lord Diplock put it thus:

> A patent specification should be given a purposive construction rather than a purely literal one derived from applying to it the kind of meticulous verbal analysis in which lawyers are all too often tempted by their training to indulge. The question in each case is: whether persons with practical knowledge and experience of the kind of work in which the invention was intended to be used, would understand that strict compliance with a particular descriptive word or phrase appearing in a claim was intended by the patentee to be an essential requirement of the invention so that any variant would fall outside the monopoly claimed, even though it could have no material effect upon the way the invention worked.

In *Catnic*, the claim was for a load-bearing lintel with a back plate extending vertically. The alleged infringer had slightly inclined the back plate from the vertical position. The question was whether a builder familiar with ordinary building operations would understand the claim to have excluded back plates which were not strictly vertical. Giving the claim a purposive construction, Lord Diplock concluded that 'it would be obvious to him that the patentee did not intend to make exact verticality in the positioning of the back plate an essential feature of the invention claimed.' On this construction, the patent was infringed.

The *Improver* test

6.76 *Catnic Ltd v Hill & Smith Ltd* (1982) concerned infringement of a patent granted under the PA 1949. The judgment was followed by Hoffmann J in *Improver Corpn v Remington Consumer Products Ltd* (1990). In his judgment, he set out the *Catnic* test for infringement in a systematic way. When deciding whether a feature, embodied in an alleged infringement which falls outside the primary, literal or a contextual meaning of a descriptive word or phrase in the claim (a variant) is nonetheless within its language as properly interpreted, the court should ask the following three questions:

- Does the variant have a material effect upon the way the invention works? If yes, the variant is outside the claim (and there is no infringement). If no:

- Would this (that is, that the variant had no material effect) have been obvious at the date of publication of the patent to a reader skilled in the art? If no, then the variant is outside the claim (and there is no infringement). If yes:

- Would the reader skilled in the art nevertheless have understood from the language of the claim that the patentee intended that strict compliance with the primary meaning was an essential requirement of the invention? If yes, then the variant is outside the claim (and there is no infringement).

Conversely, if the answer to question three is a negative, then it is possible to conclude that the patentee was not intending that word or phrase to have a literal meaning, but rather to denote a class of things which included the literal meaning and the variant. In this case there would be infringement.

Applying the *Improver* test

6.77 In *Improver Corpn v Remington Consumer Products Ltd* (1990), the claim was for an electric hair remover, the 'Epilady', with a helical spring which caught the hairs. The defendants used a slitted rubber rod in its place. The claim included an 'equivalence' clause which stated 'that all variations which come within the meaning and range of equivalency of the claims are therefore intended to be embraced therein'. The question for the court was whether the claim should be construed widely enough to include the defendant's variant. The court found that the defendant's variant did not have a material effect upon the way the invention worked (question 1 of the test) and that this would have been obvious to a skilled reader (question 2). It found that the 'helical coil' should not be given a wide general meaning, and that a skilled man would not understand it to have had one (question 3). There was no infringement, since the equivalence clause did not change the outcome.

Statutory provisions

6.78 Under the PA 1977, the extent of an invention is taken to be that specified in the claim (s 125(1)). The construction of a patent claim must be in accordance with the Protocol on the Interpretation of art 69 of the EPC (s 125(3)). The Protocol states that art 69 (of which s 125(1) is the equivalent) should be interpreted to mean that the extent of protection occupies the middle ground between the two extremes of a strictly literal meaning of the wording of the claim or seeing the claim only as a guideline. It reads:

> *Article 69 should not be interpreted in the sense that the extent of the protection conferred by a European Patent is to be understood as that defined by the strict, literal meaning of the wording used in the claim, the description and the drawings being employed only for the purpose of resolving an ambiguity found in the claims. Neither should it be interpreted in the sense that the claims serve only as a guideline and that the actual protection conferred may extend to what, from a consideration of the description and drawings by a person skilled in the art, the patentee has contemplated. On the contrary, it is to be interpreted as defining a position between these two extremes which combines a fair protection for the patentee with a reasonable degree of certainty for third parties.*

In *Wheatley v Drillsafe Ltd* (2001), Aldous LJ re-named the *Improver* questions, the 'Protocol questions'.

The doctrine of equivalents

6.79 Despite the UK view that the three-stage test developed in *Improver Corpn v Remington Consumer Products Ltd* (1990) coincides with the Protocol, other signatories to the EPC have not taken a similar approach to the construction of claims. For example, in actions between Improver and Remington in Germany and Holland, on similar facts to those in *Improver*, the courts reached an opposite conclusion to that of the House of Lords. They found infringement by asking only the first two Protocol questions, which they answered in the same way as Hoffmann J, but by not asking the third. The European approach may be described as a doctrine of equivalents: the function of the elliptical coil and the slitted rod were the same, and so the defendant's variant fell within the claim. The Protocol questions were recently re-examined by the House of Lords in *Kirin-Amgen v TKT* (2004).

Kirin-Amgen and infringement

6.80 *Kirin-Amgen* concerned the production of erythropoietin (EPO), a protein that regulates the production of red blood cells, and so is particularly useful in the treatment of anaemia. Amgen invented a method of sequencing the EPO gene, for which it obtained a European (UK) patent in 1984. The method set out in its patent involved isolating and cloning the DNA sequence encoding EPO and introducing it into a 'host' cell. As a result of the introduction of the DNA sequence, the 'host' cell would be stimulated to produce the EPO. Crucially, in the Amgen process for producing EPO, the DNA was *exogenous* to the cell into which it was introduced. By contrast, the defendant, TKT, employed a process of gene activation to produce EPO. Using the *endogenous* DNA sequence which is present in human cells, TKT inserted a 'promoter' sequence into the cell in order to stimulate the production of EPO. Amgen sued TKT for patent infringement. There were three claims which were relevant to the issue of infringement. Claim 1 was to a DNA sequence for securing expression of EPO in a 'host cell'. Claim 19 was to EPO which was the expression of an exogenous DNA sequence with a higher molecular weight than EPO isolated from urinary sources. Claim 26 was to EPO which was the product of the expression of DNA according to claim 1. In the High Court, claim 19 was held invalid for insufficiency and claim 26 was found to have been infringed. The Court of Appeal held that both claims 19 and 26 were valid and that neither had been infringed. Both TKT and Kirin-Amgen appealed to the House of Lords.

6.81 In addressing infringement, Lord Hoffmann began by reviewing the English courts' approach to patent construction. According to Lord Hoffmann, the object of the EPC Protocol is 'to combine a fair protection for the patentee with a reasonable degree of certainty for third parties'. The '*Catnic* principle of construction', which involves a purposive construction of the patent, accords with the Protocol, as 'it is intended to give the patentee the full extent, but not more than the full extent, of the monopoly which a reasonable person skilled in the art, reading the claims in context, would think he was intending to claim'. The question then arises whether any uncertainty as to the patentee's intentions can be alleviated by the structured approach to construction offered by the three Protocol questions. Lord Hoffmann's view was that while the *Catnic* principle is the 'bedrock' of patent construction, the Protocol questions are not always appropriate to use. He noted that they are not legal rules but rather guidelines which may help to decide what a skilled man would understand the patentee to mean. In Lord Hoffmann's view, the present case exposed the limits of the applicability of the Protocol questions. In the High Court, the judge had taken evidence as to what a man skilled in the art would understand the *Kirin-Amgen* claim to mean. He concluded that the person skilled in the art would not regard the endogenous expression of EPO as falling within claim 1 and therefore it would not infringe claim 26. At this point, according to Lord Hoffmann, TKT might have rightly concluded that they had not infringed the Kirin-Amgen patent. However, the judge, taking the view that thus far his construction had been literal rather than purposive, then moved on to the Protocol questions. This had wrongly led him to conclude that TKT had in fact infringed.

6.82 In Lord Hoffmann's view, the Protocol questions, which involve asking whether the patentee had actually intended strict compliance with the conventional meaning of words or phrases in the claim, might be appropriate when applied to figures or measurements and the like, as was the case in *Catnic*. However, in the present case no one had suggested that an exogenous DNA sequence coding for DNA could have a wider meaning which included an endogenous coding. Instead, the relevant question was whether a person skilled in the art would understand the invention as operating at a level of generality which made it irrelevant whether the DNA which codes for EPO was exogenous or not. Here the answer would depend entirely upon what the invention was. In other words, Lord Hoffmann concluded that there was only one compulsory question to be asked in determining the extent of protection conferred by a patent. This question was set by art 69 and its Protocol. It was: What would a person skilled in the art have understood the patentee to have used the language of the claim to mean? The Protocol questions were merely a guide to answering that question. There was certainly no point in applying the Protocol questions when the anterior questions had already been answered, as was the case here. In the present case, Lord Hoffmann agreed with the Court of Appeal which had held that an invention should normally be taken to have been claimed at the same level of generality as that at which it was defined in the claims. A person skilled in the art would be unlikely to understand a specification to be claiming an invention at a higher level of generality than that chosen by the patentee. At trial, the judge had held that claim 26 was infringed, because, after applying the Protocol questions, he had concluded that the claim was for the discovery of a sequence of EPO. The expression of this sequence was possible using both exogenous or endogenous means and this would have been obvious to the skilled person. Lord Hoffmann preferred the Court of Appeal definition of the invention as being not the gene sequence itself but its method of expression. A person skilled in the art would not have understood the claim as sufficiently general to include gene activation through endogenous means, but rather that it was limited to the expression of the gene sequence through an exogenous sequence coded for EPO. It followed that TKT had not infringed and Amgen lost its appeal on infringement (Rich and James, 'Patents: Claim Construction' [2005] *European Intellectual Property Review* N42).

The *Kirin-Amgen* approach to infringement summarised

6.83 Following *Kirin-Amgen*, the only compulsory question to ask in construing a claim is: What would a person skilled in the art have understood the patentee to have used the language of the claim to mean? However, the Protocol questions may still have some relevance. They are most likely to be useful in cases involving 'old technology', where the wording of the claim might involve conventional words and phrases, such as for instance figures or other measurements. In these cases, the wording of the claim might allow for some degree of approximation which the Protocol questions are designed to address. In cases involving 'new technology', however, the Protocol questions would not be helpful not least because there may be no obvious answer to the second Protocol question. Recently, in *Ancon Ltd v ACS Stainless Steel Fixings* (2009), Jacob LJ suggested that, following *Kirin-Amgen*, while it is still necessary to take a purposive approach to construing a claim, it is also important to remember that one must be concerned with the meaning of the language used, so that 'if the patentee has included what is obviously a deliberate limitation in his claims, it must have a meaning'. In other words, the court will continue to steer a middle course between literalism and viewing the claim as a 'mere guideline'.

Infringing acts

6.84 A person infringes a patent for an invention if, but only if, while the patent is in force, he does any of the infringing acts in the UK in relation to the invention without the consent of the proprietor (PA 1977, s 60(1)). There are two types of infringement: primary and contributory. Whether the infringement falls into one category or the other depends upon the acts in question.

Primary infringement

6.85 Acts which constitute primary infringement are divided between those done in relation to product and those done in relation to process inventions. Where the invention is a product, the infringing acts are making, disposing of, offering to dispose of, using or importing, or keeping the product, whether for disposal or otherwise (s 60(1)(a)). Keeping a product in the capacity of a 'mere warehouseman' is not an infringing act (*Smith, Kline & French Laboratories Ltd v Harbottle (Mercantile) Ltd* (1979)). Where the invention is a process, the infringing acts are using or offering the process for use in the UK, where the person knows, or where it is obvious to a reasonable person in the circumstances, that its use without the consent of the proprietor would be an infringement; disposing of, offering to dispose of, using or importing any product obtained directly by means of the process; or keeping any such product whether for disposal or otherwise (s 60(1)(b)–(c)).

Contributory infringement

6.86 A person (other than the proprietor of the patent) also infringes a patent for an invention if, while the patent is in force and without the consent of the proprietor, he supplies or offers to supply in the UK a person other than a licensee or other person entitled to work the invention with any of the means, relating to an essential element of the invention, for putting the invention into effect when he knows or it is obvious to a reasonable person in the circumstances, that those means are suitable for putting, and are intended to put, the invention into effect in the UK (s 60(2)).

Defences (PA 1977, s 60(5)(a)–(f))

6.87 An act that would constitute an infringement of a patent will not do so if it falls within a limited number of exemptions set out by the PA 1977. The most noteworthy are private and non-commercial use of the invention (s 60(5)(a)) and use for experimental purposes (s 60(5)(b)). Experiment, in this context, carries its ordinary English meaning. In *Smith, Kline & French Laboratories Ltd v Evans Medical Ltd* (1989), Aldous J held that 'if an act is to fall within sub-s (5)(b) it must be done for purposes relating to the subject matter of the invention found in the claims alleged to be infringed'. The exemption does not cover experiments which are carried out for commercial purposes which do not relate to the subject matter of the invention. However, in *Monsanto Co v Stauffer Chemical Co* (1985), the Court of Appeal recognised that the two might overlap. In *Monsanto*, the act carried out was field trials of a herbicide in order to obtain clearance from a regulatory body. This was held to be outside the exemption. But Dillon LJ also noted that the purposes for which tests or trials are carried out 'may in some cases be mixed and may in some cases be difficult to discern'. This broad approach was followed in the German case, *Klinische Versuche (Clinical Trials)* (1998). In this case, the German court held that research may have a commercial orientation, but it was exempted as long as it related to the subject matter of the invention. For instance, the court noted that in cases which related to genetic engineering, such as in *Klinische Versuche*, it was highly likely that the experimentation would be based on commercial considerations because of the high cost of undertaking such research, but this did not necessarily mean it would fall outside the exemption. More recently, in *Auchinloss v Agricultural & Veterinary Supplies Ltd* (1999), the Court of Appeal held, following the approach in *Monsanto*, that trials which had been undertaken, using the patented composition, to obtain official approval for the product from MAFF did not fall within the exemption, because they were not undertaken to discover something unknown or to test a hypothesis relating to the invention. Prescriptions made up by pharmacists are also exempted (s 60(5)(c)). Finally, if a person has used the invention before its priority date, he may continue to do so, provided that use is in good faith (for example, not as the result of a breach of confidence) (s 64).

Repair

6.88 Are repairs to a patented article exempted from the infringement provisions of the PA 1977? This was the issue before the Court of Appeal in *United Wire Ltd v Screen Repair Services (Scotland)* (2000). The early case of *Dunlop Pneumatic Tyre Co v Neal* (1899) had recognised that the mere repair of a patented article did not amount to infringement. In *British Leyland Motor Corpn Ltd v Armstrong Patents Co Ltd* (1986), according to Lord Templeman:

> *A patent for an invention is only infringed…where the invention is a product, by a person who 'makes' or 'uses' the product without the consent of the proprietor of the patent. Where therefore a patented product is sold for use with the consent of the proprietor, repair of the patented product will not constitute an infringement; repair amounting to reconstruction will constitute the manufacture of a new and infringing article.*

Later, in *Canon Kabushiki Kaisha v Green Cartridge Co (Hong Kong) Ltd* (1997), Lord Hoffmann observed that:

> *Because repair is by definition something which does not amount to the manufacture of the patented article, it is not an infringement of the monopoly conferred by the patent. It cannot therefore be an infringing act and needs no special licence to make it lawful.*

In *United Wire*, the repair was to screens used in sifting or filtering machines used in oil exploration. The patents related to the filter meshes and their interaction and the frames to which they attached. The filters had a short life, but the frames were routinely sent to the defendants for 'repair'. Repair involved supplying new meshes at the correct tension. Following *British Leyland* and *Canon*, the Court of Appeal held that genuine repair did not infringe the patent. Nonetheless, although a patentee exhausted his patent rights on sale, allowing the owner to make repairs, this did not mean that the owner also had a licence to perform any of the infringing acts. Acts prohibited by s 60 were infringing acts whether or not they could be categorised as repairs. What constituted a repair was an objective question. In this case, the defendants were making a product of the invention. They had infringed the patents. (Both *British Leyland* and *Canon* are considered in greater detail at paras **7.2** and **7.3** in relation to industrial design.)

6.89 The question of what constituted repair was recently revisited by the Court of Appeal in *Schütz (UK) Ltd v Werit UK Ltd* (2011). The claimant, Werit, was the exclusive licensee under a European Patent (UK) that related to intermediate bulk containers (IBCs), which consisted of an outer protective cage and a removable plastic inner bottle capable of holding 1,000 litres of material. The bottle had to fit 'snugly' into the cage so it would not rattle around in transit. In fact, the cage had a longer shelf life than the bottle, which might be damaged for a number of reasons. Indeed, in the life of the cage, the bottle might need to be replaced up to five times, either by 'rebottling', which meant the new bottle came from the original manufacturer or by 'cross bottling', where the bottles came from a different source. In this case, Werit supplied replacement bottles to a company, Delta, which repaired and reconditioned the cages and installed Werit's bottles. One question for the court was whether Delta, and by extension Werit, infringed the claimant's patent under s 60(1) when it put Werit's bottles into the cages. Both sides agreed that the House of Lords decision in *United Wire* was determinative of the case. In the High Court, the judge held, following *United Wire*, that to determine whether there was infringement rather than mere repair, it was necessary to apply the 'whole inventive concept' test. In this case, it was the cage which embodied the whole of the inventive concept of the claim. Hence, he reasoned, merely putting a new bottle into a cage was not 'making' the patented article. Lord Justice Jacob disagreed. Rather, applying *United Wire*, the test was whether in the course of repair the defendant was in fact 'making' the product, and as a consequence infringing the patent. That is, the right to repair is a residual right, forming part of the right to do whatever does not amount to making the product. Jacob LJ concluded that Delta, when it fitted Werit bottles into Schütz cages, was making IBCs which fell within the patent and were doing so without the licence of Schütz. He also noted about Delta that the fact that 'they themselves on their own website say they are "re-manufacturing" says it all'.

Losing the patent: revocation (Patents Act 1977, s 72)

6.90 A patent may be surrendered (PA 1977, s 29). It may also be revoked. There are four grounds for revocation. The first is that it is not a patentable invention (s 72(1)(a)). It follows that a patent may be revoked on the grounds of anticipation, or obviousness, or because the invention is not capable of industrial application, or because it fits one of the excluded categories, including, following the implementation of the PA 2004, methods of medical treatment (s 4A). Second, a patent may be revoked on grounds of insufficiency if the specification does not disclose the invention in a manner clearly enough and completely enough for the invention to be performed by a person skilled in the art (s 72(1)(c)). This ground is identical to that which would lead to an application being rejected for insufficiency (s 14(3)). In addition, since sufficiency calls for an enabling disclosure, and since a description will only support a claim if it has an enabling disclosure, then a patent may be revoked if the description does not support the claim (*Biogen Inc v Medeva plc* (1997); this is also a ground for the application to be rejected: see para **6.13**). When considering whether a patent should be revoked, sufficiency will be judged at the date the patent application was filed and not later, to avoid an insufficient application becoming sufficient because of subsequent developments in the state of the art (*Biogen*; *Kirin-Amgen Inc v Transkaryotic Therapies Inc* (2002) CA). Third, a patent may be revoked for non-entitlement (s 72(1)(b)): entitlement to a patent has been considered at para **6.8**. Finally, a patent may be revoked because it has been amended impermissibly. For instance, an amendment that leads to the matter disclosed on the specification extending beyond disclosure on the application can lead to revocation (s 72(1)(d)). Nor, following the grant, are amendments allowed which extend the protection conferred by the patent (s 72(1)(e)), although such amendments are, in certain circumstances, allowed before the grant (*Palmaz's European Patents* (1999); see also, *Yeda v Rhone-Poulenc Rorer* (2006)). In addition, the PA 2004 introduces some procedural changes in relation to revocation of a European Patent.

Revocation proceedings

6.91 Applications to revoke a patent can be made to the UK Intellectual Property Office or to the courts at any time during the life of a patent. In fact, an application to revoke a patent is most likely to be made as a counterclaim to an allegation of infringement (together with the defence that the patent is invalid). Anyone can petition for a patent to be revoked, unless it is on the grounds of non-entitlement, where only the person who has the right to the patent can apply. Applications for the revocation of an EP(UK) are brought in the UK courts. It is worth remembering that, unlike the EPO, there is no opposition procedure in the UK. As a result, an EP may be the subject of opposition proceedings at the EPO and an application for revocation in the UK simultaneously. Until recently, the UK courts had refused to stay revocation proceedings in these circumstances, in part because the inordinate amount of time it took to complete opposition proceedings in the EPO (as long as six to eight years) might have inflicted injustice on the UK applicant (*Beloit Technologies Inc v Valmet Paper Machinery Inc* (1997)). In *Biogen Inc v Medeva plc* (1997), this led to a situation where the Court of Appeal found the patent invalid for obviousness, while the EPO found the invention to have involved an inventive step (although the Court of Appeal's decision was subsequently reversed by the House of Lords: see para **6.55**). However, in

Kimberly-Clark Worldwide Inc v Procter & Gamble Ltd (1999), Aldous LJ observed that 'the preferred option' when there are opposition proceedings before the EPO is to stay the UK proceedings, provided such a stay does not cause injustice.

Patents as property

6.92 A patent or a patent application is personal property. Patents, patent applications or any rights in them may be bequeathed, mortgaged, assigned or licensed (s 30). There are two types of licences: voluntary licences and compulsory licences. Voluntary licences may or may not be exclusive licences.

Assignments

6.93 These must be in writing (ss 30, 68). It is possible to assign some rights in a patent, but not others: for instance, the right to use the product for one purpose but not another, so-called 'field-of-use' provisions, such as to use the patented product as a chemical but not as a medicine, or the right to exploit the patent only within a particular locality. Assignments do not have to be registered. However, failure to register may affect the assignee's rights in infringement proceedings. Registration also protects the patentee against a bona fide purchaser without notice (ss 33, 68).

Exclusive licences

6.94 These need not be in writing. Like assignments, they need not be registered, but failure to register may affect infringement proceedings (ss 33, 68). Again, like assignments, they may be for 'any right' under the patent, but not necessarily for all. The exclusive licensee has the same rights as the proprietor of the patent to bring infringement proceedings and to collect damages (s 67).

Void licence provisions

6.95 The PA 1977 prohibited certain conditions from being included in licensing agreements. These related to certain 'tie-in' and non-competition clauses, and were set out in s 44. Such prohibitions were designed to limit the ability of a patentee to extend his monopoly beyond that given by the patent itself, or to impose onerous conditions on a less powerful licensee. They illustrated the perceived need to balance the advantages of patent protection against a commitment to free competition which continues to underpin EU and UK economic policy. The Competition

Act 1998 (CA 1998) repealed ss 44 and 45 of the PA 1977. The intention of the CA 1998 is to bring domestic legislation into line with EU competition law. Chapter 1 of the CA 1998 echoes the prohibition in art 101 TFEU (formerly art 81 EC), so that agreements which may affect trade within the UK are prohibited. Chapter 2 prohibits conduct amounting to abuse of a dominant position in the UK (art 102 TFEU, formerly art 82 EC). In judging whether an agreement falls within the prohibitions set out in Chapter 1, European case law will be followed. There are exemptions from Chapter 1 prohibitions, however, and these include certain patent agreements which might fall within EU block exemption regulations. These are looked at below (see para **6.109**) when EU competition law is considered. By contrast, the CA 1998 also identifies contractual terms which will be seen as anti-competitive or an abuse of a dominant position (s 18(2)(a)), and may apply to patent licences, for example, terms which impose obligations on the licensee which are not connected to the subject matter of the patent.

Licences of right (PA 1977, s 46)

6.96 A patentee may voluntarily make his patent available for licensing to anyone who applies. These are called 'licences of right', and the fact that they are available will be endorsed on the register. Obviously, these licences will not be exclusive. The terms of licences of right may be agreed between the parties or, in default of agreement, by the Comptroller. An endorsement may be useful for a small inventor who lacks the resources to exploit his own invention.

Compulsory licences

6.97 Under certain circumstances, the licence of right endorsement may be compulsory. The Comptroller (or the courts) may compel a patentee to license his invention to a specific licensee or to make a licence of right endorsement. The power to issue compulsory licences stems from a fundamental belief, underpinning the patent system, that it is in the public interest for patented inventions to be worked, a reason specifically referred to in the PA 1977. When deciding whether to grant a compulsory licence the Comptroller must take into account a variety of circumstances, which are set out in the PA 1977, and which include the nature of the invention, measures already taken by the patentee to exploit it and the ability of any future licensee to do so (s 50(2)(a)–(c)). Any person may apply for a compulsory licence, but very few applications are made, suggesting that these provisions serve more as an expression of principle than any pressing utilitarian purpose. There are five grounds under which a compulsory licence will be granted. These refer generally to a failure to work the patented invention in the UK or to grant a licence on reasonable terms (s 48(3)(a)–(e)). These grounds are narrowed to three for a WTO proprietor (s 48(5) as amended) who is defined as being a national of, or domiciled in, a country which is a member of WTO or who has a place of business there. A key difference is that a WTO proprietor may avoid being penalised for not working his invention in the UK if, instead, it was imported into the UK market. Compulsory licences cannot be applied for until three years after the patent has been granted.

Crown use (PA 1977, ss 55–59)

6.98 The Crown (that is, any government department or any person authorised by a government department) has wide powers to exploit a patented invention, without the permission of the proprietor. The purposes for which a patented invention may be exploited include defence, use by the National Health Service and use by the Atomic Energy Commission. The patentee will be compensated by an amount either agreed with the government department or fixed by the courts. In one case, Crown use of a patent was allowed for building a blast-resistant police station in Northern Ireland (*Henry Bros (Magherafelt) Ltd v Ministry of Defence and Northern Ireland Office* (1999)).

Enforcing a patent

6.99 Patent actions may be brought either in the Patents Court, which is part of the Chancery Division of the High Court, or the Patents County Court, or the UK Intellectual Property Office. In the latter instance, the case will be heard by a specialist Hearing Officer, although the remedies available to the UK IPO are limited (s 61(3)). It is commonly the case that an action for infringement of a patent will provoke both a defence that the patent is invalid, as well as a counter-claim for its revocation. As a result, an infringement action may be complicated and expensive to pursue. This reality has been commonly held to undermine the extent to which patents really provide a useful protection for inventors who do not have the backing of corporate funds.

The Patents Court

6.100 The specific rules to be followed in patent actions differ from those of other civil actions in the High Court. However, as with other cases of intellectual property infringement, the primary aim of the claimant will be to stop the infringement as quickly as possible through the use of a pre-trial (interim) injunction. Once such an injunction is obtained, this may bring an end to the matter.

The Patents County Court

6.101 This was introduced by the CDPA 1988 and it opened for business in 1990 (ss 287–292). Its purpose was to provide a less costly and speedier forum for patent actions than the High Court, and so to give an opportunity for a wider range of patent-holders, beyond those with very deep pockets, to bring patent actions. Parties at the Patents County Court may be represented by patent agents, as well as by solicitors and barristers. The procedure was also been streamlined to make it both quicker and simpler than in the Patents Court. In order to serve as a true alternative to the Patents Court, the normal county court limitations as to damages did not apply. As in the Patents Court, there are specific procedural rules in the Patents County Court which reflect its specialist nature. In its first decade or so, it proved to be a popular forum. Nonetheless, even here, costs could be substantial, as much as £250,000 for a two-day trial. A review of Civil Litigation Costs by Lord Jackson suggested a number of reforms of the Patents County Court which came into effect in 2010. These include a limit to the length of trials of one or two days and to recoverable costs of £50,000 for determining liability and £25,000 for an enquiry as to damages or an account of profits.

Remedies

6.102 The successful claimant is normally entitled to an injunction restraining the defendant from further infringement, together with an inquiry as to damages or an account of profits, an order for delivery up or destruction of the infringing articles, and a declaration from the defendant that the patent is valid and has been infringed by him (s 61). Damages may be calculated from the date on which the application was published, provided the court or the Comptroller concludes it was reasonable to expect, on the basis of the application, that a patent would be granted.

Innocent infringement

6.103 If the infringer can establish that he was not aware of the patent, or had no reasonable grounds for supposing it existed when he committed the infringing act(s), he may avoid liability for damages (s 62(1)). This provision emphasises the importance of marking the patented object with both the word 'patent' or 'patented' and the number of the patent (the word alone is insufficient, under the section, to prove awareness).

Groundless threats (PA 1977, s 70)

6.104 Groundless threats are prohibited unless they are made against the manufacturer, the importer or the user of the patented invention. A primary purpose of this provision is to prevent the patentee from intimidating the customers of the alleged infringer, when he has no real intention of bringing an action against the latter for infringement. Any aggrieved person may bring an action against the person making the threats. A defence would be to prove that the patent had, in fact, been infringed. It is not considered a groundless threat simply to notify anyone (including, for example, the customer) that a patent exists.

Patents and the EU

6.105   It is a fundamental concern of the EU to ensure the free circulation of goods. Article 34 TFEU (previously 28 EC) prohibits 'quantitative restrictions on imports and all measures having equivalent effect' between Member States. Like other intellectual property rights, patent protection may conflict with this prohibition. National patent law endows a proprietor with a monopoly right to his patent invention in the relevant territory, and may allow him to keep out others' goods which embody his invention. The existence of patent protection, as with other intellectual property, can nonetheless be justified by public interest considerations which balance, in importance, the benefits of free trade. Thus, art 36 TFEU (previously art 30 EC) recognises that there can be a public interest in the monopoly rights afforded by intellectual property protection, and that prohibitions or restrictions on imports or exports are justified on grounds of the protection of industrial or commercial property, including intellectual property. However, such prohibitions or restrictions must not constitute a means of arbitrary discrimination or disguised restriction on trade between Member States. The Court of Justice has built up a body of case law which has sought to balance the sometimes conflicting imperatives of promoting free competition and protecting the rights of proprietors of intellectual property. In doing so, it has enunciated the principle of 'exhaustion of rights'. Earlier chapters have considered exhaustion of rights in relation to copyright and trade marks. The principle of exhaustion is now examined in relation to patents both inside and outside the EU.

The exhaustion of rights

6.106   The principle of 'exhaustion of rights' in relation to patents was established by the Court of Justice in *Centrafarm BV v Sterling Drug Inc* (1974). Sterling owned patents relating to an anti-infection drug, Negram, in both the UK and the Netherlands. Centrafarm acquired supplies of Negram which had been put on the market in the UK and exported them into the Netherlands, where they could be sold at a higher price. In common parlance, Centrafarm was the 'parallel importer' of the drugs. Sterling sued for patent infringement in the Netherlands. In its judgment, the Court of Justice held that derogation from art 30 EC (now art 36 TFEU) concerning the free movement of goods was allowed only to safeguard those rights which constitute the specific subject matter of the property. In the case of patents, the specific subject matter protected by the patent is:

> …the guarantee that the patentee, to reward the creative effort of the inventor, has the exclusive right to use an invention with a view to manufacturing industrial products and putting them into circulation for the first time, either directly or by the grant of licences to third parties, as well as the right to oppose infringements.

However, it went on to hold that a derogation from the free movement of goods is not justified where the product has been put on the market in 'a legal manner' by the patentee or with his consent, in the Member State from which it has been imported. To decide otherwise would be to 'partition off national markets' and thereby restrict trade between Member States in a situation where no such restraint is necessary to safeguard the specific subject matter of the patent.

6.107 Exhaustion of rights and parallel imports were examined once again by the Court of Justice in *Merck & Co Inc v Stephar BV* (1981). The difference in this case was that the product in question, a drug for use against hypertension, had originally been put on the market by Merck in a Member State, Italy, where it was not patented. It had then been bought up by the parallel importer, Stephar, and sold in the Netherlands, where it was. Merck sued for patent infringement in the Netherlands. The Court of Justice confirmed its judgment in *Centrafarm BV v Sterling Drug Inc* (1974). It said that the substance of a patent is essentially the exclusive right to first placing of the product on the market. This enables the inventor to obtain a reward for his creative effort, 'without however, guaranteeing that he will obtain such a reward in all circumstances'. It was up to the patentee to decide the conditions under which he would market his product. If he decided to market it in a Member State where there was no patent protection, then he must take the economic consequences, including the possibility that it will be imported into other Member States.

The importance of consent

6.108 Key to the decisions in *Centrafarm* and *Merck v Stephar* is the matter of consent. In both cases the patentee had consented to the first sale of his goods in a Member State (*Pharmon BV v Hoechst AG* (1985)). In the ECJ case of *Merck & Co Inc v*

Primecrown Ltd (1996), the Court of Justice was asked to reconsider its decision in *Merck v Stephar*. Once again the case involved drugs which were placed on the market by Merck in Member States, Spain and Portugal, where there was no patent protection. They were then bought by Primecrown, which marketed them in the UK where they were more expensive. Merck alleged infringement of its patents in the UK. The Court of Justice approved the reasoning in *Merck v Stephar*. It was a case of 'proprietor beware'. If a proprietor chose to market a product in a Member State where it was unpatentable, he had to accept the consequences of that choice. Nor was the rule in *Merck v Stephar* affected by the fact that the authorities in the exporting Member State had fixed the sale price of the product in question, as is often the case with pharmaceuticals. Although price controls might, in some circumstances, distort competition between Member States, it did not justify a derogation from the principle of the free movement of goods. An exception would be where the patentee was under a genuine legal obligation to market his product in the Member State or it was marketed under a compulsory licence (*Pharmon*). In these cases, he would not have consented to first sale of the patented goods and his rights would not be exhausted.

Patent rights and competition law in the EU

6.109 Since patents endow the proprietor with a monopoly right, the question arises as to whether the ownership of a patent or dealings with it may be anti-competitive. In *Parke, Davis & Co v Probel* (1968), it was held that the exercise and existence of patent rights per se do not infringe arts 81 and 82 EC (now arts 101 and 102 TFEU). They are not an abuse of a dominant position in relation to art 82 (art 102 TFEU). Nor is the refusal to license the patent on reasonable terms an abuse of a dominant position, unless such refusal involves abusive conduct, for example, the arbitrary refusal to supply spare parts or the fixing of prices for spare parts at an unfair level, 'provided that such conduct is liable to affect trade between member states' (*Volvo AB v Veng (UK) Ltd* (1989), a case actually involving registered design). In the UK case, *Pitney Bowes Inc v Francotyp-Postalia GmbH* (1990), Hoffmann J said that bringing or threatening patent proceedings did not constitute an abuse of a dominant position, nor did strengthening a dominant position necessarily involve abusing it. In this case, a 'cross licence' between the patentee and another would not abuse art 82 (art 102 TFEU) unless it was, itself, procured through abuse of the dominant position. The decision in *Pitney Bowes* allowed for the possibility that, in the right circumstances, art 82 (art 102 TFEU) might be raised as a defence against patent infringement.

The 'Euro' defence

6.110 In the case of *Intel Corpn v VIA Technologies Inc* (2002), the defendant raised precisely this defence, which has been termed the 'Euro' defence. The claimant designed and made microprocessors (CPUs) and 'chipsets' for personal computers. Intel claimed that the defendant had infringed two of its patents in relation to these products. In the past, Intel had licensed VIA to produce and market the patented products. It was now offering VIA a revised licence which would obviate the need, as Intel saw it, to continue with the patent action. In its defence, VIA denied that it had infringed the patents and challenged their validity. It also claimed that bringing the proceedings was an abuse by Intel of the exercise of its intellectual property rights, in that the terms of the revised licence were contrary to EC Treaty, arts 81 and 82 (arts 101 and 102 TFEU) (assuming Intel had a dominant position in the relevant market). In particular, the defendant's claims related to two terms of the revised contract. The first dictated that VIA could only apply the licensed technology to chipsets compatible with Intel's Pentium 4 CPUs and not to any later versions. The second was that, while VIA was licensed to use only Intel's patents which related to chipsets compatible with its Pentium 4, a cross-licence granted Intel unrestricted use of all VIA's CPU and chipset technology. At first instance, the proceedings were divided between the patent action and the competition issues. The claimant applied for and was granted summary judgment in relation to the Euro defences, on the basis that they had no real prospect of success. The defendant appealed. The Court of Appeal overturned the decision of the High Court. It also addressed the question of whether it is a defence to an action for infringement of a patent that its enforcement would enable the owner of the patent to act in breach of arts 81 and 82 (art 101 and 102 TFEU). It held that it was. In particular, the Court of Appeal held that if the willingness to grant licences, but only on terms which involved breaches of art 81, was part of the abusive conduct about which the complaint was made, then those facts could be relied on both for the purposes of the defence under art 82 and a free-standing defence under art 81 (for this point, the Court of Appeal relied on *British Leyland Motor Corpn v T I Silencers* (1981), which related to copyright). The Court of Appeal went further to hold that, even if VIA's defence under art 81 was insufficient to avoid liability for patent infringement, it might yet allow VIA to avoid the remedies of an injunction, delivery up or an account of profits. Instead, if some of the terms of the licence were invalid, then the proper remedy might be to order VIA to pay compensation to Intel rather than to prevent it from using the technology at all (Hickman, 'Patents: Competition Law–A Defence to Patent Infringement Claims' [2003] *European Intellectual Property Review* N114).

Patents and EU block exemptions

6.111 Article 101 TFEU (formerly art 81 EC) prohibits agreements which have as their object or effect the prevention, restriction or distortion of competition within the common market. It is easy to see how exclusive patent licences might fall within this prohibition. Nonetheless, it is also the case that the monopoly afforded by patents offers countervailing benefits such as an encouragement to research and development. In the light of this dichotomy, the EU has developed a system by which certain agreements may be exempted from the prohibitions set out in art 101, either individually or as a block under art 101(3). In particular, the EU's block exemption regulations confer an automatic exemption on agreements relating to, inter alia, patents and 'know how' under the Technology Transfer Regulation (Commission Regulation (EC) 772/2004)), provided they fall within its terms. The aim of the Technology Transfer Regulation is to meet the two requirements of ensuring effective competition and providing adequate legal security for undertakings. As a result of the Regulation a patent licensing agreement which might be void under art 101(1) will be acceptable if it falls within the terms of the block exemption. The exemption applies differently to agreements between competing and non-competing undertakings. Furthermore, it will apply only if the market share of non-competing parties does not exceed 30 per cent or, in the case of competing parties, 20 per cent.

Patents and the rest of the world

6.112 The question arises as to whether patent rights are similarly exhausted if the relevant products are put on the market outside the EU and are imported into the UK without the patentee's consent. The answer to this question has reflected more general rules of contract law. The leading case is *Betts v Willmott* (1871). The principle enunciated in *Betts v Willmott* is that, where a patentee sells his goods abroad without reservation or condition, he cannot then prevent the importation of those same goods into the UK. According to Lord Hatherley:

> When a man purchases an article he expects to have control of it and there must be some clear and explicit agreement to the contrary to justify the vendor in saying that he has not given the purchaser his licence to sell the article or to use it wherever he pleases as against himself.

In *National Phonograph Co of Australia Ltd v Menck* (1911), the Privy Council held, following *Betts v Willmott*, that 'a sale having occurred, the presumption is that the full right of ownership was meant to be vested in the purchaser'. However, it was also the case that 'the owner's rights in a patented chattel will be limited if there is brought home to him the knowledge of conditions imposed by the patentee or those representing the patentee, upon him at the time of sale'. According to the Court of Appeal in *Gillette Industries Ltd v Bernstein* (1941), it was essential that any restriction must have been brought home to the defendant at the time of sale. In *Roussel SA v Hockley International Ltd* (1996), Jacob J added the further caveat that, to avoid exhaustion of his rights, notice of any limitations on a licence of a patented article must be 'brought to the attention of every person down the chain'. *Roussel* involved the sale of insecticide in the UK which the defendant had obtained in China. The insecticide had been sold by the French patentee to a Chinese company, and the patentee claimed that the insecticide had been sold subject to the restriction that it was to be used only in China and not exported. The claimant relied, inter alia, on the fact that the drums bearing the insecticide had been marked with the information, 'Re-export forbidden'. The defendant replied that the drums it obtained through intermediaries carried no such notices and that the insecticide was advertised worldwide by various third parties without restrictions, so a purchaser would not know of the restriction. Jacob J found that the claimant had failed to establish that it had brought home to the Chinese company that there should be no re-export. As a consequence, the defendant was free to sell the insecticide in the UK without infringing the claimant's patent rights. In particular, Jacob J stated:

> It is the law that where the patentee supplies his product and at the time of the supply informs the person supplied (normally via the contract) that there are limitations as to what may be done with the product supplied then, provided those terms are brought home first to the person originally supplied and second, to subsequent dealers in the product, no licence to carry out or do any act outside the terms of the licence runs with the goods. If no limited licence is imposed on them at the time of the first supply no amount of notice thereafter either to the original supplyee…or persons who derive title from him can turn the general licence into a limited licence.

The decision in *Roussel* has been criticised, not least for imposing an impossible evidential burden on the patentee (Wilkinson, 'Breaking the Chain: Parallel Imports and the Missing Link' [1997] *European Intellectual Property Review* 319). Interestingly, on the issue of international exhaustion and consent to resale in relation to trade marked goods, the Court of Justice has taken a view which is far more favourable to the trade mark proprietor (see para **5.131**).

SELF-TEST QUESTIONS

1   Axel Ltd has a patent for a fuel derivative, X, which is used to run central heating systems. Axel's Chief Marketing Officer, Ms Y, has noticed that X is also excellent for cleaning motor engine parts. She plans to announce this during a speech she is giving at an exclusive luncheon for Axel's most prized customers very soon, since Axel is sure that the use of X for cleaning has enormous commercial potential. For instance, it seems that a Mr W, in Milton Keynes, has been using X to clean his own central-heating boiler for some time. Also Axel has discovered that its great rival, Brim Ltd, has been producing X and burning it as part of a testing programme to see whether it passes environmental standards. Advise Axel on whether it can patent X for use as a cleaning product and whether Brim Ltd or Mr W is infringing the company's present patent for X.

2   The purposive approach to patent construction is certainly the most likely to produce a patent system which both fulfils its basic functions and satisfies the interests of those who use it. Do you agree?

3   Discuss the problems raised by (a) the patenting of gene sequences, and (b) computer software.

FURTHER READING

Batteson, A and Karet, I, 'Lundbeck v Generics: "Biogen insuffiency" explained' [2009] *European Intellectual Property Review* 51.

Brennan, D, 'Biogen sufficiency reconsidered' [2009] *Intellectual Property Quarterly* 476.

Curley, D and Sheraton, H, 'The Lords Rule in *Amgen v TKT*' [2005] *European Intellectual Property Review* 154.

Dutfield, G, 'Who invents life: intelligent designers, blind watchmakers, or genetic engineers?' [2010] *Journal of Intellectual Property Law & Practice* 531.

Hickman, D, 'Patents: Competition Law–A Defence to Patent Infringement Claims' [2003] *European Intellectual Property Review* N114.

Howell, C, 'Compensation at last for employee inventors: Kelly v GE Healthcare Ltd.' [2010] *Journal of Business Law* 41.

Llewelyn, M, 'The Patentability of Biological Material: Continuing Contradiction and Confusion' [2000] *European Intellectual Property Review* 191.

McInerney, A, 'Biotechnology: *Biogen v Medeva* in the House of Lords' [1998] *European Intellectual Property Review* 14.

Pila, J, 'Software patents, separation of powers and failed syllogisms: a cornucopia for the Enlarged Board of Appeal and the European Patent Office' [2011] *Cambridge Law Journal* 203.

Rich, A and James, W, 'Patents: Claim Construction' [2005] *European Intellectual Property Review* N42.

Sharples, A and Curley, D, 'Experimental Novelty: *Synthon v Smith Kline Beecham*' [2006] *European Intellectual Property Review* 308.

Terrell on the Law of Patents (17th edn, Sweet & Maxwell, 2010).

7 Industrial design

SUMMARY

- Development and context of the present industrial design regime
- The 1988 reforms and the EU Directive
- The relationship between industrial design and copyright
- Exclusions from protection
- The creation, ownership and duration of design rights
- Infringement
- Registered designs
- Exclusions from protection
- Infringement
- Ownership
- Industrial designs in their international context

Development and context

7.1 By the time of the passage of the Copyright, Designs and Patents Act 1988 (CDPA 1988), it was generally accepted that there were some troubling anomalies in the law relating to industrial design. In particular, the Copyright Act 1956 gave the same copyright protection to design documents from which functional, mass-produced articles were produced as it gave to artistic works, that is, for the life of the author plus 50 years. In addition, a three-dimensional object made from the drawing acquired similar copyright protection. Curiously, if the articles had 'eye appeal' and the design was capable of being registered under the Registered Design Act 1949 (RDA 1949), it would be protected for only 15 years. Obviously, the industrial design regime lacked logic. But by the 1980s, the considerable copyright protection given to functional, mass-produced articles was also viewed by many to have other unfavourable consequences. Not least of these was the monopoly it gave to manufacturers of industrial articles over the production of spare parts, and their consequent ability to control markets and prices. In the 1980s, as ideas of free trade became more prevalent, this de facto monopoly granted to manufacturers was widely criticised. For instance, in 1985, the Monopolies and Mergers Commission criticised the Ford Motor Company for its policy of monopolising the sales of its car replacement panels, through the use of copyright protection of their design.

7.2 The decision of the House of Lords in *British Leyland Motor Corpn Ltd v Armstrong Patents Co Ltd* (1986) also reflected this prevailing view. In *British Leyland*, the question to be answered was whether artistic copyright in the design drawings of functional, mass-produced articles, in this case for motor spare parts, was infringed by their three-dimensional reproduction. The House of Lords, in a majority decision, held that it was. However, the House of Lords also went on to hold that the right of a car owner to purchase spare parts at a reasonable price should take precedence over the protection endowed by copyright. It based its decision on a concept which it borrowed from land law–that a person may not derogate from his grant. In other words, a car owner must be allowed to acquire on the open market the spare parts necessary to make his car go. There can be little argument that the decision in *British Leyland* was driven by public policy concerns, as the House of Lords sought to side-step what had come to be seen as the increasingly indefensible monopoly of car manufacturers over the supply of spare parts.

British Leyland criticised

7.3 While the decision in *British Leyland Motor Corpn Ltd v Armstrong Patents Co Ltd* (1986) arguably reflected the tenor of its time, 14 years later its creative approach was criticised and its implications limited by the Privy Council in *Canon Kabushiki Kaisha v Green Cartridge Co (Hong Kong) Ltd* (1997). In this case, the claimant manufactured printers and photocopiers, containing replaceable cartridges known as Customer Replacement Units (CRUs). These needed to be replaced when the toner ran out. The defendant first began refilling and refurbishing the CRUs, but eventually moved on to manufacturing its own cartridges. The claimant sued, inter alia, for copyright infringement. In its judgment, the Privy Council was asked to consider the scope of the 'spare parts exception' which had been formulated by the House of Lords in *British Leyland*. Lord Hoffmann was critical of *British Leyland*. He stated that the judgment 'cannot be regarded as truly founded upon any principle of the law of contract or property'. Instead, he saw it as 'a clear expression of public policy'. He went on to suggest that it was both 'a strong thing' but also 'constitutionally questionable', for the judiciary to treat public policy as overriding an express statutory right (that is, copyright). Therefore, the courts should be cautious in extending the *British Leyland* exception. The Privy Council went on to hold that the scope of the decision in *British Leyland* was clearly limited to the spare parts necessary for repair rather than for articles such as cartridges as any purchaser would be aware that these would need replacing on a regular basis.

The 1988 reforms

7.4 The reform of the law relating to industrial design reflected both an attempt to eliminate the anomalies in the law which had grown up over time, and also the new ideological commitment to free trade. The CDPA 1988 took away copyright protection from almost all industrial designs. To replace copyright protection, the Act introduced a new right, the unregistered design right. At the same time, it amended the RDA 1949.

The UK design regime and the EU Directive

7.5 The protection afforded to designs in the EU differs between countries. Given that so much production, not least of cars, now takes place across national boundaries, it is scarcely surprising that the EU has sought to harmonise the industrial design regime. The Design Directive (EC) 98/71 was adopted by the EU in 1998 and implemented by the UK in December 2001. The Directive is intended to harmonise national laws relating to the registration of industrial designs. Its overall purpose is to overcome those obstacles to the free movement of goods which may have resulted from there being a different level of protection for registered designs in individual Member States. At the same time and with the same objectives in mind, Council Regulation (EC) 6/2002 on Community Designs introduced, in 2002, a Community registered design and an unregistered design right. The new law on registered designs in the UK is set out in the Registered Designs Act 1949 as amended by the CDPA 1988, the Registered Design Regulations 2001 and the Registered Design Regulations 2003.

The Community registered and unregistered design

7.6 The Community registered design and the Community unregistered design are separate from national rights, and the protection they offer has effect in all Member States. Applications for design registration are made to the Office for Harmonisation of the Internal Market (OHIM) in Alicante, which also deals with the Community Trade Mark (CTM) (see para **5.13**). While the OHIM deals with registration, domestic Community design courts deal with issues of infringement, and counterclaims for invalidity. Protection of the Community registered design is for a maximum of 25 years. In the case of the Community unregistered design, protection will be for three years only and will apply from the date of disclosure of a design to the public within the EU. Disclosure may be by sale, prior marketing or publicity. In most important respects, the substantive law relating to the Community design is the same as that set out in the Design Directive. The same is true of the law relating to Community registered and unregistered designs. However, a Community registered design will be a monopoly right, which protects against both copying and independent creation. A Community unregistered design will be protected only against copying. The motivation behind the introduction of both a registered and unregistered Community design is that the latter will give immediate protection to designs during the 12-month window which is allowed for the registration of Community designs. The Community unregistered design will also offer protection for designs for which, because of their short 'shelf-life', the time and expense involved in registration would not be worthwhile. Since its introduction, the Community registered design has proved both popular and versatile as to what it will protect, ranging from furniture to graphic symbols, logos and websites (which are deemed 'products' for the purposes of registration). Although an attempt to simplify the regime for protecting designs across Europe, it might be argued that the Design Directive has had the opposite effect. As a result of the Directive, there are now five ways in which a design might be protected in the UK. They are the following:

- as a Community registered design
- as a UK registered design
- as a Community unregistered design
- as a UK unregistered design
- by copyright.

This chapter will first examine the relationship between copyright and industrial designs. It will then look at the UK unregistered design right and at the law relating to registered designs.

The relationship between design right and copyright 1: CDPA 1988, s 51

7.7   Under the CDPA 1988, it is not an infringement of copyright in a design document or model recording or embodying a design for anything other than an artistic work or a typeface to make an article to the design, or to copy an article made to the design. Note, however, that it will continue to be an infringement of copyright to copy the design document itself. Clearly, the intention of this section is to prevent artistic copyright from stifling the market in spare parts, as it had done prior to the CDPA 1988. X draws a design for a useful new door hinge. Y finds the design document and makes door hinges to that design. He has not infringed X's copyright in the design document. If Y had secretly copied the design document in order to make the hinges, he may have infringed X's copyright in the document, provided the document itself displays sufficient originality to attract copyright. Even if the original design document or model embodies an artistic work, it will not be an infringement of copyright to copy the articles made from these if the design document or model was intended for the production of non-artistic works. If X had first drawn his dog, Fido, and then produced a design document from which mass-produced teapots shaped like Fido would be manufactured, it would not infringe X's copyright in the design document if Y also produced the teapots. For the purposes of s 51, a 'design' means any aspect of the shape or configuration *other than* surface decoration. If X had taken a conventionally shaped teapot and imprinted the portrait of Fido on the sides, Y would infringe his copyright by reproducing this portrait on his own teapots. However, as we shall see, protection for the portrait, in this context, would last only 25 years.

7.8 In *Lambretta Clothing Co Ltd v Teddy Smith (UK) Ltd* ((2003) HC; (2004) CA), the claimant designed and produced fashion clothes. In particular, it produced a track-top in a striking combination of colours. The top itself was of a standard design. The design had been recorded in two documents which included, inter alia, instructions as to the colours to be used, and also the fabric. It was successfully marketed in 2002. That same year, the defendants, Teddy Smith and Next plc marketed track-tops in a similar fabric and colour combination. The claimant alleged that the defendants' tops infringed its design right, and also its copyright in the design documents. The defendants argued, relying on CDPA 1988, s 51, that design documents did not record an artistic work, and therefore it was not an infringement of copyright to copy the design of the tops. In the event, the High Court found that no design right subsisted in the tops, as the originality of the design lay in the surface decoration (or colourways). The question then arose as to whether s 51 should be interpreted to mean that, in relation to the design, matters which would not be protected by design right would be protected by copyright. The court held that they should not. Such an interpretation would have the result that a design document would have to be divided between those parts which attracted design right protection and those which attracted copyright, with different legal tests applied to each in an action for infringement. The High Court did not believe that such a result had been intended when s 51 had been drafted.

However, it did find on the facts that Teddy Smith had copied the claimant's tops, while Next plc had not. Both Lambretta and Teddy Smith appealed.

Section 51 as a defence

7.9 The Court of Appeal upheld the High Court's decision in relation to design right (see para **7.22**). As to the s 51 defence, the Court of Appeal held that s 51 does not apply if the design document is itself an artistic work (ie a sculpture). But it disagreed with the claimant's argument that if the design of its tops was not protected by design right, they must be protected by copyright because Parliament in passing the Copyright Act 1988 could not have intended to leave a gap between design right protection and copyright protection. According to Jacob LJ, there would be occasions when a work is neither protected by copyright nor design right. It was wrong to assume that everything worth copying is worth protecting. In this case, there was no doubt that the original drawings of the top's design were 'design documents', but what was copied was only the colourways, which could not physically or conceptually exist apart from shapes of the parts of the articles. However, Jacob LJ noted that if artistic copyright were to be enforced here, it would be enforced in relation to the whole document, but that is not allowed by s 51, which applies only to aspects of the shape or configuration of the article. Accordingly he agreed with the Etherton J in the High Court:

> that such an approach…would appear to give rise…to an impossible task. It would require the court to consider the existence and infringement of copyright in respect of the juxtaposition of the colourways divorced from the shape and configuration of the article in question, even though the shape and configuration of Lambretta's garments provide the borders of the colourways and the means by which the colourways are juxtaposed. In other words, such an interpretation would have the result that a design document would have to be divided between those parts which attracted design right protection and those which attracted copyright, with different legal tests applied to each in an action for infringement (see also BBC Worldwide Ltd v Pally Screen Printing Ltd (1998)).

Section 51 was also considered in *Lucasfilms Ltd v Ainsworth* (2010). As we have seen (para **2.21**), the High Court and the Court of Appeal had agreed that the storm trooper helmets were neither sculptures nor works of artistic craftsmanship and hence had no copyright protection. It followed that the original drawings on which they were based were not artistic works but design documents. As a result, Ainsworth had a defence under s 51 (see also, *Flashing Badge Co Ltd v Groves* (2007)).

The relationship between design right and copyright 2: CDPA 1988, s 52

7.10 Copyright protection, of course, continues to be given to artistic works, including drawings and works of artistic craftsmanship. However, here too the CDPA 1988 introduced changes. Under s 52, if an artistic work is exploited by producing it industrially, the protection afforded to the industrially produced article is reduced to 25 years after the first marketing of the article. Reproduced industrially means making 50 or more articles to the design. After 25 years, Y (see para **7.7**) would be free to copy Fido's portrait onto his own teapots. However, if he reproduced the original Fido portrait to sell in his gallery, he would infringe copyright in the original drawing, which lasts the full 70 years plus the life of the author. In *Lambretta v Teddy Smith*, Jacob LJ noted that in an outcome where Teddy Smith were found to have infringed Lambretta's copyright in the colourways, the 'bizarre oddity' would arise that the claimant would have had 25 years of protection for an article which was not sufficiently original to qualify as a design right. In *Lucasfilms*, Ainsworth was also able to rely on s 52 as a defence because of the period of time that the claimants had been making and selling the helmets before he began to exploit his own reproductions.

Design right

7.11 The design right regime has been described as embodying 'a modified copyright approach'. Like copyright, the right arises automatically, and there is no need for the design to be registered to obtain protection. Also like copyright, design right does not confer a 'monopoly right' in the way that a patent or a registered design does (see para **7.34**). Instead, again like copyright, a design right gives its holder more limited protection against copying. Unlike copyright, however, design right protection lasts for a far more limited term and the protection given against copying is also more restricted. The design right regime has been criticised by some for weighting the balance too far in favour of a free market in functional designs, particularly in relation to spare parts, rather than towards protecting the investment of those who produce such designs. For instance, the length of design right protection (see para **7.28**) has been criticised as being too short. It is certainly shorter than that accorded to registered designs, which had traditionally emphasised eye appeal rather than the functionality of a design. But it has been suggested that a functional design should be no less worthy of protection, since it may well involve the same, if not more investment of resources and skill in its creation than a design with eye appeal. Furthermore, under the new regime there is no longer a requirement for a registered design to have 'eye appeal'. As a result, the contrasting periods of protection afforded to design right and registered designs might appear even more anomalous (Bainbridge, 'Why the Design Right is Failing Innovators Opinion' [1999] *European Intellectual Property Review* 423). In *Lucasfilms Ltd v Ainsworth* (2011), the Supreme Court considered the balance between the protection given to copyright, registered design and unregistered designs. It saw a legislative purpose in protecting three-dimensional objects in 'a graduated way'. Thus artistic works, such as sculptures have the fullest protection. Then come works with 'eye appeal', protected as registered designs. Finally, purely functional objects protected by unregistered design right have a more modest level of protection. It concluded that, 'There are good policy reasons for the differences in the period of protection,' although it did not adumbrate on what these reasons were.

The definition of a design

7.12 Design right is a property right which subsists in an original design (CDPA 1988, s 213(1)). Before going on to look at what constitutes originality for the purposes of design right, it is first necessary to consider the definition of a design. A general definition is set out in s 213(2) and states: 'a design means the design of any aspect of the shape or configuration (whether internal or external) of the whole or part of an article'. These may be functional elements of design or configuration. They may also be elements which are aesthetically pleasing. However, it is important to note that design right will not subsist in surface decoration, which is the province of registered design (s 213(3)(c)). The definition of 'design' is a broad one. It can include the shape or configuration of individual parts of an article, but it may also cover the article as a whole. To give an example, provided by Laddie J in *Ocular Sciences Ltd v Aspect Vision Care Ltd* (1997): 'If the right is said to reside in the design of a teapot, this can mean that it resides in the design of the whole pot, or in a part such as the spout, the handle or the lid, or, indeed, part of the lid.'

The relationship between the design and the 'article'

7.13 It follows from the example given by Laddie J that the term 'article' may likewise mean: individual parts, a combination of parts, or the parts made up into a whole. According to Mummery LJ in *Farmers Build Ltd v Carier Bulk Materials Handling Ltd* (1999), these are all '"articles" with a shape or configuration' (for the facts, see para **7.19**). The 'article' need not be one which is intended for, or is even capable of being, reproduced by an industrial process, as with the old registered design. According to Jacob LJ, in *Dyson v Qualtex* (2006), the definition of a design is 'very wide', meaning that a single article might embody a multitude of designs. Jacob LJ also noted in *A Fulton Ltd v Totes Isotoner (UK) Ltd* (2003), that the use of the word 'aspect' in the definition of a design is meant to convey that it is discernible or recognisable. However, the design, or even the article in which it is embodied, will not necessarily be visible to the naked eye. The design may be an aspect of shape and configuration of a larger article, such as a strainer inside a teapot. Or a design may only be identifiable through the use of specialist equipment. In *Ocular Sciences Ltd v Aspect Vision Care Ltd* (1997), which involved the relative dimensions of a contact lens, these dimensions were too small to be seen by the naked eye.

Originality and design right

7.14 Design right subsists if the design is 'original'. According to the CDPA 1988, a design is not original, 'if it is commonplace in the design field in question at the time of its creation' (s 213(4)). *C & H Engineering v Klucznik & Sons Ltd* (1992) was the first reported decision to consider what was meant by 'original' in this context. The case involved the design of a pig fender, which is a pen outside of a pigpen low enough for a sow to step over, but too high for her piglets. A customer suggested to the claimant, who manufactured pig fenders, that the fender be redesigned to avoid the sow injuring her teats when stepping over it. The claimant subsequently placed a bar along the top of the fender. In the event, the High Court was unable to conclude who had originated this idea. Nonetheless, Aldous J did consider the question of originality. He held that 'original' had the same meaning in design right as it did in relation to copyright in original literary, dramatic, musical and artistic works. As in copyright, an original design is one that has not been copied, but is 'the independent work of the creator'.

7.15 In *Farmers Build Ltd v Carier Bulk Materials Handling Ltd* (1999), the Court of Appeal endorsed the definition of originality given in *C & H Engineering v Klucznik & Sons Ltd* (1992) and summarised the position under the CDPA 1988. Mummery LJ identified two elements to an original design for the purposes of design right protection. First, it must have been originated by the designer in the sense that it is not simply a copy by him of a previous design made by someone else. Second, where it has not been slavishly copied from another design, it must in some respect be different from other designs, so that it can be fairly and reasonably described as 'not commonplace' (for the meaning of which, see para **7.17** et seq). Mummery LJ also appeared to suggest, in *Farmers Build*, that originality meant that 'sufficient, time, labour and skill' had been expended in originating the design as would be necessary to attract copyright protection. In *Guild v Eskander Ltd* (2002), the Court of Appeal warned that in assessing originality it was necessary to guard against taking 'a piecemeal' approach. The question was whether all, not just any one, of the elements of a design gave rise to the requisite quality of originality. It was, however, acknowledged that some consideration of individual features was unavoidable.

The relationship between originality and the commonplace in design

7.16 A design is not original if it is 'commonplace' in the design field in question at the time of its creation (s 213(4)). This means that the same design may be original in the copyright sense, that is, it was 'originated' by the designer and was not copied, but can still fail to attract design right protection because the design is commonplace (*Farmers Build Ltd v Carier Bulk Materials Handling Ltd* (1999)). If it is commonplace, then it is not 'original' for the purposes of design right.

When is a design commonplace?

7.17 This question was considered in detail by the Court of Appeal in *Farmers Build Ltd v Carier Bulk Materials Handling Ltd* (1999). (The specific facts of the case and the subsequent judgment are set out at para **7.19** et seq.) The Court of Appeal took the view that 'commonplace' in design right should be interpreted narrowly. Its approach was shaped by its recognition that design right generally afforded narrower protection than copyright, and that it was directed at offering protection to functional articles. By contrast, an opposite approach would risk many designs of functional articles being found to be commonplace simply because they were well known. The Court of Appeal also held that whether a design is commonplace is an objective fact. It is a question for the court to decide, based upon the evidence before it.

7.18 A design which is not commonplace will be one which is not found in other articles in the same field. Conversely, the closer the similarity of designs to each other, the more likely the design is to be commonplace, especially if there is no evidence of copying. Thus, if a number of independent designers produce similar design solutions to the same design problem, the court is entitled to infer that there is only one way of designing the article in question and that the design may be described as commonplace (*Farmers Build*). Commonplace is not, however, the same as 'well known'. It is possible for a commonplace article to embody aspects of shape and configuration which are not commonplace. In other words, the nature or character of the 'commonplace' article, such as a fork, should not be confused with aspects of shape and configuration of the article which might not be commonplace at all, for instance, the design of the handle of said fork. In *Farmers Build*, the Court of Appeal also endorsed Laddie J's view in *Ocular Sciences Ltd v Aspect Vision Care Ltd* (1997) that even if some features of a design are commonplace, the design which combines them may not be.

The *Farmers Build* case

7.19 The Court of Appeal's definition of commonplace was applied in *Farmers Build Ltd v Carier Bulk Materials Handling Ltd* (1999), which concerned the design of a slurry separator, a machine which separates manure into solid and liquid parts for use as fertiliser. The claimant owned the intellectual property rights in a slurry separator, the 'Target', which the defendants had designed for the claimant in 1991. The design for the Target had improved upon designs for two earlier separators. In 1992, the defendants started manufacturing and selling their own separator, the 'Rotoscreen', which looked different from the Target, but was almost identical inside. The claimant claimed that the Rotoscreen infringed its design rights in various component parts of the Target, both individually and in combination with other parts and with the insides of the machine as a whole. The defendants argued that the design of the Target was not original, but commonplace in the design field in question at the time of its creation. At first instance, the judge held, inter alia, that design right subsisted in the Target as a whole, and in a number of its component parts; the defendants appealed. Among their counter-arguments was a claim that the hopper (a chamber within the slurry) had long existed as a part of agricultural machinery in general and that its design variants were strictly limited. They also argued that the Target as a whole was commonplace, because it was simply a recombination of parts of two earlier machines, which improved its functionality. In reply, the claimant claimed that the design of the Target was original, being significantly better than the earlier machines, that a new machine could be made out of 'trite' ingredients and, in any event, that the relevant field to judge the 'commonplaceness' of the Target was not agricultural implements generally, but slurry separators in particular.

7.20 In its judgment, the Court of Appeal held that, while a hopper is a commonplace article, the design of this particular hopper was not commonplace. It then looked at various other parts of the Target, some of which it decided embodied original designs, some of which did not. Finally, it concluded that the design of the Target, as a whole, was not commonplace. There were no other machines like the Target in the field of slurry separators. While design right did not subsist in each and every part of the Target machine, it did subsist in the overall shape and configuration of the combination of parts which it made up. In effect, the Court of Appeal agreed with the claimant's argument that a combination of 'trite' or commonplace designs can result in aspects of shape or configuration which are not commonplace.

The design field in question

7.21 A design is commonplace if it is commonplace in the design field in question. It is, therefore, necessary to identify the design field within which its originality should be judged. In *Farmers Build Ltd*, the defendants argued that the relevant field was that of agricultural implements. The Court of Appeal disagreed. The relevant field was that of slurry separators and not agricultural machinery generally or other engineering fields. In *Scholes Windows Ltd v Magnet Ltd* (2001), the Court of Appeal held that 'the design field in question' was to be understood in its ordinary and natural meaning, bearing in mind that its purpose was to withhold protection from designs which were commonplace. The 'outer bounds' of the field would be a matter of fact and degree, taking into account the circumstances of the particular case. In this case, the High Court had included, for comparison with the window design at issue, a design which had been produced many years ago, although it was still to be seen on windows. The Court of Appeal held that this was the correct approach. There was nothing to exclude old designs from inclusion in the design field in question, particularly if they could still be seen by designers or interested members of the public. More recently, in *Fulton Co Ltd v Totes Isotoner (UK) Ltd* (2003), it was held by Fysh J that, in deciding whether a design was commonplace, the proper comparison was with designs which were available in the UK at the time the design was created. Such a narrow field reflected the territorial nature of the design right and the fact that, given its 'junior nature', it would be impractical to subject a design right to a universal comparison, as is the case with patents, for example. In *Lambretta v Teddy Smith* (2004), Jacob LJ endorsed the definition of commonplace in *Farmers Build*. He noted that what really mattered was which prior designs the experts were able to identify and how much those were shown to embody the current thinking of designers in the field, at the time of the creation of the designs. He added that were a very good design to become popular, this would not make it commonplace. An apt example might be the Apple iPhone. However, a variant of the popular design which is only different from the original in a commonplace manner would not attract unregistered design right.

Exclusions from protection (CDPA 1988, s 213(3))

7.22 There are four exclusions to design right protection. The 'must fit' exception and the 'must match' exceptions are sometimes called the 'interface exclusions', and were designed to avoid creating the same impasse over the supply of spare parts which had dogged the old design regime (discussed at para **7.2**). Design right will also not subsist in a method or principle of construction (s 213(3)(a)). This third exception has a rather different purpose. It may be construed as an attempt to avoid protecting an idea in the copyright sense, although, under certain circumstances, methods or principles of construction might be patentable. In the case of *Landor and Hawa International Ltd v Azure Designs Ltd* (2006), the Court of Appeal held that this exclusion is not intended to preclude protection for a design simply because it is functional. If there are other ways of achieving the same function through a different design, then the original design may attract an unregistered design right. This is in marked contrast to registered trade marks, where signs which consist exclusively of the shape of goods necessary to obtain a technical result will not be registered, even if there are other means of achieving the same result (see para 5.30). The disparity between these two principles may be in part explained by the fact that design right gives only a limited period of protection whereas a trade mark can be protected for an indefinite period so long as it remains distinctive. The fact that a particular principle of construction might have to be used in order to create an article with a particular shape does not mean there is no design right in the shape itself. However, competitors may use the same principle of construction to create a competing design, so long as that design does not have the same shape as the design at issue (*Fulton Co Ltd v Grant Barnett & Co Ltd* (2001); see also *Baby Dan AS v Brevi Srl* (1999)). Finally, design right will not subsist in surface decoration (s 213(3)(c)). This was one of the issues rehearsed by the Court of Appeal in *Lambretta v Teddy Smith* (2004). In that case, the claimant argued that the stripes on its tops were not surface decoration as they were dyed right through the material. Jacob LJ disagreed. He noted that this exclusion should cover circumstances both where the surface was covered by a thin layer or where the decoration permeated the article. He cited with approval the judgment in *Mark Wilkinson Furniture Ltd v Woodcraft Designs (Radcliffe) Ltd* (1997) which concluded that not only essentially two-dimensional decoration lying on the surface of the article was excluded as surface decoration, but also the decorative features of the surface itself, such as the 'cornice' and 'cockbeading' on kitchen cabinets (see para 7.31).

The 'must fit' exclusion (CDPA 1988, s 213(3)(b)(i))

7.23 Design right does not subsist in a feature of shape or configuration which enables the article to be connected to, or placed in, around or against, another article so that either article may perform its function. Conversely, a design for an article which is to be placed in, around or against another article but does not affect the function of either, such as a case for a folding umbrella, is not excluded from design right protection (*Fulton Co Ltd v Grant Barnett & Co Ltd* (2001)). It has been suggested that, to fall within this exclusion, a design need not be the only design which can achieve the proper interface. There may be a number of designs which will allow the articles to be fitted together, but on the basis of this exception, each of these designs would be excluded. In *Dyson v Qualtex* (2006), the case concerned spare parts for Dyson vacuum cleaners. The parts at issue were known in the trade as 'pattern' parts, that is replicas of the original parts. As was pointed out, by Jacob LJ, the original equipment manufacturers (OEMs) would have an interest in controlling the market for spare parts, and hence stopping the sale of pattern parts by a third party. Conversely, the spare part manufacturer would have an interest in making the parts look as close as possible to the originals, as it might be assumed that the consumer would have more confidence in a part which is identical to the broken one. In the High Court, the claimant argued that 14 spare parts had been copied. However, the Court of Appeal looked at only six parts which covered all the issues in the case, and which were themselves reduced to the particular features of the parts which each side believed illustrated their argument. Dyson succeeded in the High Court and the defendant appealed. The Court of Appeal upheld the decision of the High Court. In relation to the 'must fit' exception, Jacob LJ held that it would apply both to parts which are not touching and also to parts without which the system would not work. If it were otherwise, then none of the working parts of an article would be covered by design right. (See also *Ocular Sciences Ltd v Aspect Vision Care Ltd* (1997) and *Baby Dan AS v Brevi Srl* (1999).)

The 'must match' exclusion (CDPA 1988, s 213(3)(b)(ii))

7.24 Design right does not subsist in features of shape or configuration of an article which are dependent upon the appearance of another article of which the article is intended by the designer to form an integral part. As with the 'must fit' exception, the 'must match' exclusion is clearly designed to address the question of when spare parts should be excluded from protection. In this case, the concern is with the appearance of an article which depends upon the original article for its design. Thus, the design of the body panel of a car which is an integral part of the overall design of the car, and the appearance of a new door would be dependent upon the original design, and hence be covered by the exclusion. Conversely, the exclusion is generally held not to apply to car components such as wing mirrors, whose design can be changed without compromising the integrity of the overall design of the car (*Ford Motor Co Ltd's Design Applications* (1993) looked at the identical provision in the context of the old law of registered designs). The 'must match' exception was considered by Jacob LJ in *Dyson v Qualtex* (2006). Jacob LJ held that if substitutions can be made without radically affecting the appearance of the article, then as a practical matter there was freedom of design for the spare part, and there was no dependency. It was not enough to argue that the consumer 'preferred' an exact copy. He concluded that the extent to which a design of a spare part was 'dependent' upon the design of the original article was a value judgment for the judge. (See also *Mark Wilkinson Furniture Ltd v Woodcraft Designs (Radcliffe) Ltd* (1997).) In the case of components for a conservatory roof, Laddie J held that the fact that certain features of their design helped to achieve a 'consistent theme' for the conservatory as a whole did not mean that they were 'dependent upon the appearance of another article'. Indeed, the fact that these particular features were of 'little visual impact' meant that they were less likely to be dependent upon similar features on other articles, and vice versa (*Ultraframe UK Ltd v Fielding* (2003)).

The limits of the 'must fit' and 'must match' exclusions

7.25 It has been suggested that a key motivation behind the introduction of the design right had been to free up the market in spare parts. The inclusion of 'must fit' and 'must match' exceptions to design right protection is obviously crucial to achieving this aim. However, it is equally true that the scope of these exclusions represents a retreat from the broad principles enunciated in *British Leyland Motor Corpn Ltd v Armstrong Patents Co Ltd* (1986). In *British Leyland*, the House of Lords essentially withdrew all protection from the reproduction of spare parts, by holding that copyright could not be used to prevent the manufacture or sale of parts for industrial items (see para **7.2**). In *Dyson v Qualtex* (2006), Jacob LJ held that it was not possible to adopt a purposive approach to interpreting the 'must fit' and 'must match' exclusions. He believed that these exceptions 'did not give a carte blanche to pattern spares. Those who wish to make spares during the period of design right must design their own spares and cannot just copy every detail of the OEMs part.' It has been argued that this approach favours the interests of OEMs over the interests of the maker of spare parts (Smith and Burke, 'Design Rights: Original Manufacturers Maintain Control of Unregistered Design Rights' [2006] *European Intellectual Property Review* N110).

Creation of design right

7.26 The designer is the person who creates the design (CDPA 1988, s 214(1)). The designer need not be the same individual as the one who records the design. In the case of a computer-generated design, the designer is the individual who makes the arrangements necessary for the creation of the design (s 214(2)). A design right will not subsist unless and until the design has been recorded in a design document, or an article has been made to that design (s 213(6)). A design document can range from a drawing to data stored in a computer.

Ownership of design rights

7.27 The designer is the first owner of a design right, provided the design was not produced pursuant to a commission or in the course of employment. In the latter two cases the design will belong to the commissioner and the employer, respectively (s 215). In certain circumstances, the design may be owned by the person who first markets the design. Furthermore, for design right to subsist, the design must be a qualifying design (ss 217–220). Qualification is by reference to the nationality or country of residence of the designer, commissioner or employer, by reference to the country in which the article was made or first marketed, or, in some circumstances, by reference to the nationality or habitual residence of the person who first markets the article. In general, the qualifying nationalities and countries are those which give reciprocal protection to UK designs.

Duration of design right

7.28 The term of unregistered design right protection is either 15 years from when first recorded or, if the design is marketed within the first five years, 10 years from when it was first made available for sale (s 216). During the final five years of the 10-year period of protection (that is, from the date of first marketing), licences of right may be granted for unregistered designs (s 237). They are obtained through an application to the Patent Office. The Comptroller will settle the terms of the licence if they cannot be agreed directly between the parties. Once granted, the original owner of the design right cannot prevent the licensee from exploiting the right, but the licensee must pay a royalty for its use. It is possible for a single design right to be subject to any number of licences. If a defendant infringes a design right during its final five years, it is possible for him to give an undertaking to enter into a licence to avoid injunctive relief and minimise damages.

Infringement

7.29 Design right, like copyright, will only protect against copying. In *Farmers Build v Carier Bulk Materials Handling Ltd* (1999), it was suggested that it is possible for two individuals to have design right in the same design, as long as each produced it independently (and as long as the design is not commonplace). This contrasts with the law relating to both patents and registered design, where a proprietor has a right against all competitors, even those who originated the subject matter independently.

Primary infringement (CDPA 1988, s 226)

7.30 The owner of the design right has the exclusive right to reproduce the design for commercial purposes by making articles to the design or by making a design document recording the design for the purpose of enabling such articles to be made. Design right is infringed by the making of articles exactly or substantially to that design. Furthermore, as was noted by Birss J in *Albert Packaging Ltd v Nampak Cartons & Healthcare Ltd* (2011), since design right can subsist in part of an article, then it may be infringed by the copying of that part, rather than the whole article in which the part is incorporated. Whether the allegedly infringing design is exactly or substantially the same as the original design is determined through the eyes of the person to whom the design is directed (*C & H Engineering v Klucznik & Sons Ltd* (1992)). In *Baby Dan AS v Brevi Srl* (1999), where the designs at issue were for parts of child safety barriers, the relevant persons included those 'interested in the design of such gates'. If the difference between the original design and earlier designs is a small one, then infringement will be found only if the difference between the infringing design and the original design is even smaller (*Ocular Sciences Ltd v Aspect Vision Care Ltd* (1997)). In *Ocular Sciences*, the designs at issue differed from each other only 'in fine dimensional details'. In fact, a member of the public would not be able to gauge the differences through visual inspection. It was held that, in such circumstances, if the dimensions which supported the claimant's claim to the existence of design right were particularly detailed and specific, then there would be infringement if the defendant's designs were extremely close. Design right is infringed by a person who does, or authorises another to do, anything which is the exclusive right of the design right owner without the relevant permission (s 226(3)). Therefore, authorising copying is an infringement (*C & H Engineering*).

Proving infringement

7.31 To prove infringement, the claimant must show that the defendant has copied his design. There will be no infringement if the defendant arrived at the design independently (see para **7.29**). Copying may be direct or indirect (s 226(4)). In *Mark Wilkinson Furniture Ltd v Woodcraft Designs (Radcliffe) Ltd* (1998), Parker J stated that, to prove infringement, the 'same general principles' apply as apply to copyright (citing *Francis, Day and Hunter Ltd v Bron* (1963), see para **2.46** on copyright). There has to be a sufficient objective similarity (excluding surface decoration) between the two articles or a substantial part thereof. There also has to be a causal connection. However, later cases have not supported Parker J's view in relation to 'a substantial part'. In *C & H Engineering v Klucznik & Sons Ltd* (1992), the test for infringement was whether the two designs were 'not substantially different'–a test taken from the old registered design regime. If they were not, there would be infringement. According to Aldous J in *C & H Engineering* (at 428):

> Section 226 appears to require the owner of a design right to establish that
> copying has taken place before infringement can be proved; that is similar to

copyright. However the test of infringement is different. Under s 16 copyright will be infringed if the work, or a substantial part of the work, is copied. Under s 266 there will only be infringement if the design is copied so as to produce articles exactly or substantially to that design. Thereafter the court must decide whether copying took place and, if so, whether the alleged infringing article is made exactly to the design or substantially to that design. Whether or not the alleged infringing article is made substantially to the plaintiff's design must be an objective test to be decided through the eyes of the person to whom the design is directed.

In *C & H Engineering*, the court compared the objects as a whole. Because the allegedly infringing copy had sloping side walls which the original did not, the judge found there was no infringement, as the designs were substantially different. In fact, it is generally the case that an object might consist of a number of different aspects of shape or configuration, each of which might be subject to a separate design right, and, therefore, each of which may be infringed. Aldous J's approach to copying in *C & H Engineering* was affirmed by the Court of Appeal in *L Woolley Jewellers v A & A Jewellery* (2002).

Secondary infringement (CDPA 1988, ss 227–228)

7.32 Design right is infringed by a person who, without the licence of the design right owner, imports into the UK for commercial purposes, or has in his possession for commercial purposes, or sells, lets for hire, or offers or exposes for sale or hire, in the course of a business, an article which is, and which he knows or has reason to believe is, an infringing article (s 227). An article is infringing if its making to that design was an infringement of design right in the article (s 228). Further, it is also an infringing article if it has been, or is proposed to be, imported into the UK, and its making to that design in the UK would have been an infringement of design right in the design.

UK design right and community design right compared

7.33 To gain protection as a Community unregistered design right, the design must be first made available or disclosed in the EU. The definition of 'design', 'product', 'novelty' and 'individual character' are the same as those for the Community registered design, as are the exceptions to protection (see para **7.53**). There are two key differences between the UK design right and the Community unregistered design. The first is that the latter is protected for only three years from the date at which the design was first made available or disclosed within the EU. The second is that while the UK design right protects only three-dimensional shapes, the Community unregistered design will also protect two-dimensional designs.

Registered designs

7.34 The law governing registered designs has been radically transformed by the implementation of the Design Directive (EC) 98/71 in 2001. Before 2001, the law relating to registered designs was governed by the Registered Design Act 1949, as amended by the CDPA 1998. The relevant law is now the RDA 1949, as amended by the CDPA 1988, the Registered Design Regulations 2001 and the Registered Design Regulations 2003. As a result, much of the case law which had accumulated before 2001 in relation to registered designs will no longer be authoritative. Instead, UK Design Examiners and judges will look to the Court of Justice to see how it interprets the Community Design Directive and Regulations (*Dyson Ltd v Vax Ltd* (2010)).

Contrast with other rights

7.35 Before the implementation of the Design Directive and Regulations, a registered design had to have 'eye appeal'. It thus contrasted with unregistered design right, which will not protect aspects of surface decoration, and with copyright, which protects original works, without requiring them to be visually pleasing. Under the new law, a registrable design need not have 'eye appeal'. However, it has been suggested that registration will still be primarily concerned with the 'look and feel' of a design, in particular its surface decoration, rather than its functionality (see para **7.46**). Like a patent, a registered design is a monopoly right. This means that to prove infringement of a registered design there is no need to show copying, as is the case for infringement of copyright or design right. Unlike copyright or design right, but like patents, it is necessary to go through the registration procedure to obtain protection for the design. Furthermore, again unlike copyright or design right, it is possible to act against infringers only when registration has been granted, although damages will be backdated to the date of application. As a result, registration may often be a cumbersome way of protecting designs whose commercial appeal depends upon immediate and passing fashion (such as some wallpaper or textile designs). Certainly, designs with a relatively short shelf-life may not need the full 25 years or even the initial five years of protection offered. As a result, it has often been the case that the cost of the registration might be disproportionate to the gains. However, following the implementation of the Directive, the author of a design is now offered a one-year window before his design loses its novelty and cannot be registered (see para **7.39**). This period will allow him to 'test the market', to determine whether or not the cost of registration is worthwhile.

Registrable designs (RDA 1949, s 1(2))

7.36 A design is defined as the 'appearance of the whole or part of a product resulting from the features of, in particular, the lines, contours, colours, shapes, texture or materials of the product or its ornamentation' (s 1(2)). Under the amended Registered Design Act 1949, the definition of a design is wider than before. In particular, there is no longer any requirement for a registrable design to have eye appeal or, in the words Design Directive (EC) 98/71, 'aesthetic quality' (Recital 14).

The definition of a 'product' (RDA 1949, s 1(3))

7.37 A 'product' is defined in s 1(3) as:

> *any industrial or handicraft item other than a computer program; and in particular includes packaging, get-up, graphic symbols, typographic type faces and parts intended to be assembled into a complex product.*

It is noteworthy that a registrable design does not now have to be applied to a product by an industrial process. In addition, it is no longer necessary, as before the RDA 1949 was amended, to register the design in respect of a specific article or group of articles. Protection is afforded to any product into which the design is incorporated. It has been suggested that, following this definition, it may now be possible to protect the 'get up' of a supermarket product as a registered design as a means of protection against 'lookalike' products (see para **4.57** for passing off). A 'complex product' means a 'product which is composed of at least two replaceable component parts permitting disassembly and reassembly'. The Registered Design Regulations 2001 have defined a 'complex product' as having 'at least two parts'. However, in practice, the Patents Office will understand a complex product to mean a product with 'multiple components', which are costly, long-lasting and complex, that is, a motor car or a computer, but not a 'tea pot'.

Requirements for registration (RDA 1949, s 1B)

7.38 A design will be protected by a right in a registered design to the extent that the design is new and has individual character (s 1B(1)). Each of these will be considered in turn.

Novelty

7.39 A design is new if no identical design or no design whose features differ only in immaterial details has been made available to the public before the relevant date (s 1B(2)). The relevant date is defined in s 1B(7). Most commonly it will be the date on which the application for the registration of the design was made or is treated as having been made (an exception would be if a design has been substantially modified since an application was first made). A design will have been made available to the public before the relevant date if it has, inter alia, been published (whether following registration or otherwise), exhibited or used in trade (s 1B(5)(a)). If the design is registered, it may, of course, be subsequently challenged on the wider grounds set out in s 1B(5)(a). There are also circumstances in which, although the design has in effect been made public, it will not be treated as having been made available to the public for the purposes of s 1B(2). These are set out in s 1B(5). The most important exception is, perhaps, s 1B(2)(d), which states that a design will not be treated as having been made available to the public if the disclosure is made by the designer or his successor in title in the 12 months immediately preceding the relevant date. In effect, this exception allows the designer to test the market for his design before deciding whether or not to expend the time and money involved in seeking its registration. However, its novelty would be undermined if, during that period, an identical but independently created design is made available to the public. Other exceptions include situations where the design is made available to the public in breach of an express or implied obligation of confidence (s 1B(5)(b)), or where the design could not reasonably have been known before the relevant date in the normal course of business to persons carrying on business in the EEA and specialising in the sector concerned (s 1B(5)(a)). From 2006, it is also possible to register multiple designs with a single application.

Individual character

7.40 A design will have individual character if the overall impression it produces on the informed user differs from the overall impression produced on such a user by any design which has been made available to the public before the relevant date (s 1B(3)). Furthermore, in judging individual character, it is necessary to take into account the relative 'design freedom' which exists for the relevant design (as per Jacob LJ in *Procter & Gamble v Reckitt Benckiser* (2007) which concerned a European registered design). Where there is little room for manoeuvre in terms of product design, then small differences between an earlier design and a later design may be telling.

The informed user and design freedom

7.41 In *PepsiCo Inc* (2011), the designs at issue related to small, collectable children's toys which are often distributed as free gifts inside the packaging of other products and are known as 'pogs'. PepsiCo had filed an application for a Community registered design at the OHIM. Priority was based on a Spanish design which had been filed in 2003, for goods including promotional items for games. In 2004, Grupo Promer asked for a declaration of invalidity on the basis that it had a prior registered design for 'metal plates for games'. The Cancellation Division upheld its application and declared the design registered by PepsiCo to be invalid. PepsiCo successfully appealed against this decision before the Board of Appeal, which confirmed the validity of its registered design. Promer appealed to the General Court. The General Court held that the differences between the designs at issue were insufficient to produce a different overall impression on the informed user. In particular, it confirmed that the concept of 'conflict' between designs, for the purposes of art 25 of the Regulation (s11ZA RDA, grounds for invalidity), implies that the designs produce the same overall impression on the informed user. It also confirmed that, for the purposes of ascertaining the designer's degree of freedom, reference should be made, not to the entire category of promotional items, but to the particular category of 'pogs' with the result that the actual freedom of the designer is somewhat constrained. According to the General Court, however, even within the restricted confines of the creative scope available to the designer for developing new designs for 'pogs', it would have been possible for the design registered by PepsiCo to achieve a greater degree of distinctiveness as compared with the design registered by Promer. In conclusion, the General Court held the differences between the designs at issue to be insufficient to produce a different overall impression on the informed user and accordingly annulled the decision of the Board of Appeal. PepsiCo could not register its design and appealed to the Court of Justice. It based its appeal, inter alia, on whether the General Court had correctly identified the informed user.

7.42 In its appeal, PepsiCo argued that the General Court had applied incorrect criteria when denying that the designs at issue conveyed a different overall impression on the informed user. It contended that the informed user is not the same as the average consumer in trade mark law, who is reasonably well informed and reasonably observant and circumspect. Nor is the informed user solely the end-user of the goods at issue. PepsiCo also argued that the informed user must be assumed to be in a position to compare the goods side-by-side and could not rely on 'imperfect recollection' as in trade mark law. If these criteria had been adopted by the General Court, PepsiCo suggested that the informed user would have easily distinguished the two designs because of 'significant' differences between them: two additional concentric circles visible on the surface of its own design and the curved shape of its design compared to Grupo's flat design. Further, PepsiCo submitted that the informed user would not only focus on the most visible surfaces or easily perceived elements of the design, but would consider the design as a whole and in detail, comparing it to earlier designs and taking account of the designer's freedom. The OHIM argued, in addition, that any comparison would be based on a direct comparison of the designs. The Court of Justice denied PepsiCo's appeal and endorsed the findings of the General Court. It held that the concept of the informed user lies somewhere between the average consumer of trade mark law and the 'sectoral' expert with detailed technical expertise. In other words, the informed user should be understood to be not a user with average attention, but a particularly observant one either because of his personal experience or his extensive knowledge of the sector in question. In this case, the informed user might be a child from five to ten years old or a marketing manager in a company which makes goods promoted by 'pogs'. Further, although the informed user when possible will make a direct comparison between the designs at issue, there may be times when such a comparison is impractical or uncommon in the sector concerned. In sum, the informed user is not the average consumer of trade mark law, but he is also not an expert or specialist capable of observing in detail the minimal differences between the designs. The Court concluded:

> the qualifier 'informed' suggests that, without being a designer or a technical expert, the user knows the various designs which exist in the sector concerned, possesses a certain degree of knowledge with regard to the features which those designs normally include, and, as a result of his interest in the products concerned, shows a relatively high degree of attention when he uses them.

Prior art and registered designs

7.43 In *Green Lane Products v PMS International Group* (2008), the Court of Appeal was specifically asked to consider how the Design Regulation views 'prior art' and, in particular, when a design would have been made available to the public and hence lack the novelty which is required both for registration and infringement (art 7 Regulations) (s1B(1)& (2), s7A RDA). Green Lane made and sold spiky plastic balls for use in tumble driers to soften fabric and reduce drying time. There were blue ones with square nodes and pink ones with rounded nodes. Green Lane registered the design of its balls as Community registered designs. PMS had marketed spiky plastic balls in the EU since 2002. They were sold as massage balls, not as laundry balls but in 2006 PMS decided to sell its balls for other purposes too, including as laundry balls. Green Lane argued that PMS would infringe its Community registered designs, if they continued to sell their products for anything other than use as a massage ball. PMS counterclaimed arguing that Green Lane's Community registered designs were invalid by reason of its own prior sale of the massage balls. An important aspect of Green Lane's argument was that a prior design is not taken to be made available to the public, even if in reality it was, where its use in trade could not reasonably have become known in the normal course of business to the circles specialising in the sector concerned. According to Green Lane, the 'sector concerned' meant the sector for which the design was registered (in this case laundry balls) and not the sector of the alleged prior art (massage balls). Thus, as identified by Jacob LJ, the exact question being asked by the parties was whether when judging the novelty of a registered design, one looks only at the class of goods for which it is registered, as argued by Green Lane. Or, alternatively, does one look at the class of goods of the allegedly infringing party. Or does one, as in patent law, look at all 'prior' art. Jacob LJ said that in judging whether a design is novel, the same standards apply as is the case in patent law when asking whether an invention has been made available to the public. Thus, it will include all prior use of the design, whatever its intended purpose. Save that, unlike with patents, the prior art will include only designs which have been made available in the EU. It is submitted that Jacob LJ's conclusions in *Green Lane* accord with those of the Advocate General in *PepsiCo* when he opined that for the purpose of conflict between two designs, one should compare the goods as they are used rather than the designs as they are registered.

Component parts (RDA 1949, s 1B(8))

7.44   A design applied to, or incorporated into, a product which constitutes a component part of a complex product (see para **7.37**) shall only be considered new and to have individual character: (a) if once it has been incorporated into the complex product it remains visible during normal use; and (b) to the extent that those visible features of the component part are themselves new and have individual character. It has been suggested that a component part indicates a separate, removable part rather than just the inside surface of a product. Similarly, this section will not apply to a product which is not visible in use, but is not a component part of a product (Designs Practice Notice (DPN) 1/03). For example, consumable items used in complex products (such as staples in a staple gun) are not component parts, whereas the spring assembly inside the staple gun is an example of a true component part. Normal use is defined as use by the end-user, and does not include any maintenance, servicing or repair work in relation to the product (s 1B(8)–(9)). The end-user of a motorcar would mean its owner rather than a service mechanic. It follows that 'visible in normal use' would exclude, for example, engine components which are visible only during the repair of a car. The same might apply to the internal components of computers, such as chips or connectors. Conversely, a motorcycle engine might not be subject to the requirements in s 1B(8) if it is designed to be visible.

Grounds for refusal of registration (RDA 1949, s 1A)

7.45 Anything which does not fulfil the requirements of s 1(2) for a registrable design (s 1A(1)(a)) will be refused registration. A design will also be refused registration if it fails to fulfil the s 1B requirements in that it is not new or lacks individual character (see para **7.40**). A design which, on the relevant date, is neither new nor has individual character when compared to a design which is protected from a date prior to the relevant date by a Community Design Registration, or an application for it, will also be refused registration (s 1(1)–(2)). Finally, a design will be refused registration if it falls within the terms of s 1C(1) and (2), and s 1D. These are looked at below.

Designs dictated by their technical function (RDA 1949, s 1C(1))

7.46 A right in a registered design shall not subsist in features of appearance of a product which are solely dictated by the product's technical function. It has already been noted that registered designs need no longer have 'eye appeal'. Does this section mean that the requirement of 'eye appeal' has essentially been re-introduced by denying protection to functional designs? This question was considered in *Lindner Recyclingtech GmbH v Franssons Verkstäder AB* (2009) by the OHIM Board of Appeal. The Board held that purely functional designs are not registrable. Rather, the Community registered design is concerned with the visual appearance of products. Thus, the Community registered design denies protection to those features of a product's appearance chosen exclusively because they are functional. Instead, according to the Board of Appeal, the intention is to protect those features which are chosen to enhance a product's visual appearance. This is an objective test based on the viewpoint of a 'reasonable observer' who looks at the design and asks himself whether anything other than purely functional considerations could have been relevant when a specific design feature was chosen. The law does not, however, introduce aesthetic judgments into registered design protection, rather it asks that at a minimum there must have been some element of concern with the design's visual appearance.

The 'must fit' exception (RDA 1949, s 1C(2))

7.47 A right in a registered design shall not subsist in features of appearance of a product which must necessarily be reproduced in their exact form or dimension so as to permit the product in which the design is incorporated, or to which it is applied, to be mechanically connected to, or placed in, around or against another product so that either product may perform its function. If a product 'must fit' with another product, there will, of course, be very little design freedom. According to the UK IPO, the Examiner should ask whether there is any part of the design which is not required to be of the appearance it is in order for it to fit the end product. If the answer is 'yes', then the application should proceed. If the answer is 'no', in that the designer could not alter the product and still have it fit the end-product, it cannot be registered. However, the 'must fit' exception does not apply to a design being registered which serves the purpose of allowing multiple assembly or the connection of mutually interchangeable products within a modular system (s 1C(3)). An example of such products would be stackable chairs.

Contrary to public policy or morality (RDA 1949, s 1D)

7.48 Designs contrary to public policy or to accepted principles of morality will not be registered.

Length of protection (RDA 1949, s 8)

7.49 The length of protection is the same as under the old law of registered designs. Registered designs (and Community registered designs) are registered for five years in the first instance. Protection may be extended for four further terms of five years for a total of 25 years.

Ownership of a registered design (RDA 1949, s 2)

7.50 Again, the terms of ownership have not changed. The author (that is, the creator) of a registered design is treated as the original owner. However, if the design is created in pursuance of a commission for money or money's worth, ownership rests with the commissioner. Similarly, if a design is created in the course of employment, ownership rests with the employer.

Applications (RDA 1949, ss 3 and 3A)

7.51 Applications are made to the UK Intellectual Property Office. An application will be examined by a Design Examiner. Section 3A directs that an application may be refused if it does not comply with the formalities, or if it falls within any of the substantive grounds for refusal of registration. Under the Regulatory Reform (Registered Designs) Order 2006 (SI 2006/1974), there will be no substantive examination by the Examiners for novelty or individual character. And the same is true for the Community registered design. There will however be an examination of the design to see if it falls within the exclusions to registration, eg if it is functional or offends against public morality. It follows that a design may be registered but subsequently be vulnerable to a challenge for invalidity (see *PepsiCo Inc*, para **7.41**). Such objections have been facilitated by the publication of new designs. This provides an opportunity for a third party to initiate a challenge if, for example, it sees a registered design which overlaps with its own earlier design.

Rights given by registration (RDA 1949, s 7)

7.52 The registered proprietor has the exclusive right to use the design and any design which does not produce on the informed user a different overall impression (s 7(1)). Use of the design includes making, offering, putting on the market, exporting, or using a product in which the design is incorporated or to which it is applied, or stocking such a product for such purposes (s 7(2)). Use is defined more broadly than under the previous law, which did not include stocking or exporting products which incorporate the design. In determining whether a design produces a different overall impression on the informed user, the degree of freedom of the author in creating the design is to be taken into consideration (s 7(3)) (for design freedom, see para **7.41**).

Infringement and exceptions to infringement (RDA 1949, s 7A)

7.53 A registered design is infringed by a person who, without the consent of the registered proprietor, does anything which by virtue of s 7 is the exclusive right of the registered proprietor. There are a number of exceptions to infringement. Acts which are done privately for non-commercial purposes (s 7A(2)(a)), acts done for experimental purposes (s 7A(2)(b)), and acts of reproduction for teaching purposes (s 7A(2)(b)) are not infringing. Furthermore, s 7A provides explicitly for the exhaustion of the registered design right within the EEA. However, there are no grounds for the proprietor of a registered design to object to the resale of his goods once they are put on the market in the EEA with his consent, if their condition is altered, as is the case with trade marks.

7.54 *Dyson Ltd v Vax Ltd* was an infringement action of a Community registered design. The designs in question were for vacuum cleaners, the Dyson DC02 and the Mach Zen respectively. The question to be asked was whether the Mach Zen produced on the informed user a different overall impression so that it did not infringe the Dyson DC02. According to Jacob LJ in the Court of Appeal what mattered is what the two designs looked like. The Court accepted that the existing corpus of designs for judging individual character or the overall impression on the informed user was 'cylinder cleaners' by and large consisting of sledge or tank types. It was accepted by the defence that Dyson's registered design was a great departure from what had gone before. The Court accepted that the informed user was the one identified by the General Court in *PepsiCo Inc*, who as we have seen was subsequently accepted by the Court of Justice (see para **7.42**). Most particularly, he was not the same as the average consumer in trade mark law. Looking at the degree of design freedom in this case, Jacob LJ explained that this referred to the designer of the registered design and not the allegedly infringing one. The claimant argued that the designer of the DC02 had had a great deal of design freedom as it was a major departure from what went before, and as such its degree of protection was correspondingly wider. Nonetheless, in this case, the Court of Appeal agreed with Arnold J in the High Court that there were substantial differences between the two designs which the informed user would consider significant and there was no infringement. (see also *Procter & Gamble v Reckitt Benckiser* (2007) involving a UK registered design).

The 'spare parts' exception (RDA 1949, s 7A(5))

7.55 It has already been noted that the UK courts and, indeed, successive governments have sought to protect the market in spare parts from being monopolised through the protection afforded to industrial designs. No agreement was reached between Member States as to how the provisions of a harmonised registered design regime might affect the internal market in relation to spare parts (Design Directive (EC) 98/71, Recital 18). In its absence, according to the Directive, Member States are to maintain their existing law in relation to spare parts and registered designs. Furthermore, Member States are able to introduce changes to national law in this area only if they are intended to 'liberalise' the market for spare parts (Recital 14). Section 7A(5) concerns the sale of spare parts incorporating a registered design. It states that the right in a registered design of a component part, which may be used for the purpose of repair of a complex product so as to restore it to its original appearance, is not infringed by use for that purpose of any design protected by registration. In other words, producing a part which incorporates a registered design is not an infringing act if it is intended for the repair of a 'complex product'.

Invalidity (RDA 1949, s 11ZA)

7.56 A design may be declared invalid on any of the grounds for which registration may be refused under s 1A (s 11ZA(1)) (see para **7.45**). A design may also be declared invalid if it incorporates a registered or unregistered trade mark, or a copyright work for which use is unauthorised. These latter two grounds are new to the registered design regime and, although optional under the Directive, have been adopted in the UK.

Industrial designs and the rest of the world

7.57 The protection afforded to unregistered designs from parallel imports from outside the EU is also similar to that afforded by copyright (see para **2.116**). The design right is infringed by a person who, without the licence of the proprietor, imports into the UK for commercial purposes an 'infringing' article (CDPA 1988, s 227). An infringing article is, inter alia, infringing if its making to that design in the UK would have been an infringement in design right in the design (s 228). It is submitted that the situation in relation to registered designs will be the same as that for trade marks. There will be no exhaustion of rights in a registered design if goods embodying that design, which have been placed on the market outside the EEA with the proprietor's consent, are offered for sale by a third party inside the EEA without the proprietor's consent.

SELF-TEST QUESTIONS

1   Keith decides to start a business making spare parts for the best-selling Grasso Lawnmower. He plans to manufacture new blades, which are a particular design feature of the Grasso but which quickly wear out. He also plans to manufacture replacement seats and a rear-view mirror especially designed to fit the Grasso, which allows the user to check that the way behind him is clear, but which Grasso does not supply. The mirror has an attractive engraved grass-like design on its back, and is also cleverly designed so that the concave glass will not cause glare. Grasso is so impressed that it is thinking of making its own mirror. Advise Keith on whether his business risks infringing any of Grasso's rights, and of the best way for him to prevent Grasso from selling a mirror similar to his own.

2   Identify and compare the different protection given to industrial designs by copyright, design right and registered designs.

3   Do you think design law as it stands is overly protective of industrial designs?

FURTHER READING

Bainbridge, D, 'Why the Design Right is Failing Innovators Opinion' [1999] *European Intellectual Property Review* 423.

Connor, I, 'The design trigger: case comment on Procter & Gamble v Reckitt Benckiser' [2007] *European Intellectual Property Review* 293.

Headdon, T, 'Community Design Right Infringement: An Emerging Consensus or a Different Overall Impression' [2007] *European Intellectual Property Review* 33.

Kingsbury, A, 'International harmonization of designs law: the case for diversity' [2010] *European Intellectual Property Review* 382.

Rawkins, J, 'British Leyland Spare Part Defence: *Canon Kabushiki Kaisha v Green Cartridge Company (Hong Kong) Ltd*' [1998] *European Intellectual Property Review* 674.

Russell-Clarke and Howe on Industrial Designs (8th edn, Sweet & Maxwell, 2010).

Saez, V, 'The Unregistered Community Design' [2002] *European Intellectual Property Review* 585.

Smith, J and Burke, S, 'Design Rights: Original Manufacturers Maintain Control of Unregistered Design Rights' [2006] *European Intellectual Property Review* N110.

Index